The YMCA in Late Colonial India

Critical Perspectives in South Asian History

Series Editors
Professor Janaki Nair (Jawaharlal Nehru University, India),
Professor Mrinalini Sinha (University of Michigan, USA),
Dr Shabnum Tejani (School of Oriental and African Studies,
University of London, UK)

Editorial Board
Nira Wickramasinghe (Leiden University, Netherlands), Willem van Schendel (University of Amsterdam, Netherlands), Carole McGranahan (University of Colorado Boulder, USA), J. Devika (Centre for Development Studies, Trivandrum, India), Farina Mir (University of Michigan, USA), Daud Ali (University of Pennsylvania, USA), Samira Sheikh (Vanderbilt University, USA), Nandini Chatterjee (University of Exeter, UK), Sunil Amrith (Harvard University, USA).

Critical Perspectives in South Asian History publishes innovative scholarship on South Asian pasts that will be widely accessible to a broad scholarly audience. Titles in the series interrogate existing themes and periodizations as well as open up new areas of inquiry by welcoming a range of disciplinary and theoretical perspectives within a historical argument. The series focuses on three broad scholarly developments: a growing engagement with the public life of South Asian History, a conceptual shift from South Asia being the 'object' of study to becoming the generator or driving force behind new and distinctive research and a concerted effort to study hitherto obscured regions, peoples, methods and sources that point to a reframing of the current boundaries in South Asian history. This series invites new works that creatively engage with public debates about the past, draw attention to the distinctiveness of different South Asian contexts, integrate South Asia within global histories and draw upon South Asian material. Welcoming South Asian histories from the ancient world to the modern day, this series looks to bring scholarship on South Asia from different parts of the world in closer conversation and showcase the range and variety of new research in the field.

Published:
Forms of the Left in Postcolonial South Asia, Sanjukta Sunderason & Lotte Hoek (eds)
Political Imaginaries in Twentieth-Century India,
Mrinalini Sinha & Manu Goswami (eds)
Workplace Relations in Colonial Bengal, Anna Sailer
The Emergence of Brand-Name Capitalism in Late Colonial India, Douglas E. Haynes

Forthcoming:
Towards a People's History of Pakistan, Asad Ali & Kamran Asdar Ali (eds)

The YMCA in Late Colonial India

*Modernization, Philanthropy and
American Soft Power in South Asia*

Harald Fischer-Tiné

BLOOMSBURY ACADEMIC
LONDON • NEW YORK • OXFORD • NEW DELHI • SYDNEY

BLOOMSBURY ACADEMIC
Bloomsbury Publishing Plc
50 Bedford Square, London, WC1B 3DP, UK
1385 Broadway, New York, NY 10018, USA
29 Earlsfort Terrace, Dublin 2, Ireland

BLOOMSBURY, BLOOMSBURY ACADEMIC and the Diana logo are trademarks of Bloomsbury Publishing Plc

First published in Great Britain 2023
Paperback edition published 2024

Copyright © Harald Fischer-Tiné, 2023

Harald Fischer-Tiné has asserted his right under the Copyright, Designs and Patents Act, 1988, to be identified as Author of this work.

For legal purposes the Acknowledgements on p. x constitute an extension of this copyright page.

Cover design: Terry Woodley
Cover image from the Kautz Family YMCA Archives, located at the University of Minnesota, Minneapolis, USA

All rights reserved. No part of this publication may be reproduced or transmitted in any form or by any means, electronic or mechanical, including photocopying, recording, or any information storage or retrieval system, without prior permission in writing from the publishers.

Bloomsbury Publishing Plc does not have any control over, or responsibility for, any third-party websites referred to or in this book. All internet addresses given in this book were correct at the time of going to press. The author and publisher regret any inconvenience caused if addresses have changed or sites have ceased to exist, but can accept no responsibility for any such changes.

A catalogue record for this book is available from the British Library.

A catalog record for this book is available from the Library of Congress.

ISBN: HB: 978-1-3502-7528-7
PB: 978-1-3502-7527-0
ePDF: 978-1-3502-7529-4
eBook: 978-1-3502-7530-0

Series: Critical Perspectives in South Asian History

Typeset by Newgen KnowledgeWorks Pvt. Ltd., Chennai, India

To find out more about our authors and books visit www.bloomsbury.com and sign up for our newsletters.

Inspiré par le soufi électrique, je dédie ce livre à ceux qui le comprendront mal et à ceux qui ne l'aimeront pas.

Contents

List of Illustrations		viii
Acknowledgements		x
Introduction		1
1	'A mission to modernize': Colonial administrators, nationalists and religious bodies in South Asia (1870s–1930s)	15
2	'Make them pure, fit and brotherly!': The Indian YMCA's welfare work for railwaymen and soldiers (*c*. 1904–1945)	47
3	'Physical ministry': The Indian YMCA's sports and physical education programmes (*c*. 1900–1950)	81
4	'One-fifth of the world's boyhood': American 'boyology' and the Indian YMCA's work with early adolescents (*c*. 1900–1950)	109
5	'The gospel of rural reconstruction': The YMCA's rural development programmes in South Asia (*c*. 1916–1955)	139
Conclusion: Modernization without modernity		165
Notes		173
Bibliography		243
Index		285

Illustrations

1.1	Postcard from 1910, showing the YMCA's headquarters in Madras	35
1.2	Indian student residents at the Madras YMCA Hostel (*c.* 1910s)	37
1.3	Rural secretary Daniel Swamidoss at work in a YMCA agricultural demonstration centre (1919)	40
2.1	A British YMCA poster advertising its newly opened army centres in India (*c.* 1915)	53
2.2	Territorials posing in front of the YMCA headquarters in Madras (November 1914)	55
2.3	Five members of the pioneering first detachment of Indian YMCA secretaries in Rouen, France (1915)	58
2.4	Map showing the Indian YMCA's expanding army work in Mesopotamia in early 1917	60
2.5	YMCA brochure showing an open air film projection for troops in Mesopotamia (1916)	63
2.6	The YMCA hut in Amara (Mesopotamia, 1916)	64
2.7	Dictionary of French words and phrases in Urdu transliteration (1915)	66
2.8	A YMCA centre for 'Terriers' near Bangalore (*c.* 1916)	71
2.9	A YMCA hut for Indian sepoys in Central India (*c.* 1916)	71
2.10	American YMCA secretary Duane Spencer Hatch doing army work at Risalpur, NWFP (1916)	73
3.1	Luther H. Gulick and students of the YMCA Training College (1980)	86
3.2	Promotional poster of the YMCA's International Training College (1932)	89
3.3	Harry Buck with the graduates of the MCPE's class of 1935	96
3.4	Map indicating the region of origin of the MCPE graduates (1937)	98
3.5	Participants of the 'perfect physique competition' organized by the Colombo YMCA (1939)	104
4.1	An Indian YMCA secretary with a high school student (Madras, *c.* 1924)	122
4.2	Box training at the Madras YMCA boys' branch (*c.* 1926)	126
4.3	Teatime at the 'united scout camp' organized by the Lahore YMCA (1922)	129

4.4	An Indian Scout patrol from Patiala posing in front of the British and American Flags in Murree Hills (1929)	130
4.5	British army officers inspect a tent pitching during a scouting contest (1929)	130
4.6	Indian army commander greeting YMCA workers at Boys Town in Madras (1950)	132
4.7	Members of the Madras boys' branch at work during the city cleaning campaign (1938)	133
4.8	Library and reading room of the Calcutta YMCA, boys' branch (1920)	134
5.1	The Martandam Rural Demonstration Centre's logo	147
5.2	Spencer Hatch and some of his Indian fellow workers during working session in Martandam (1927)	148
5.3	Promotional poster for the MGM's documentary *Give Us the Earth* (1947)	159
5.4	Spencer Hatch at the first FAO conference in Quebec (1945)	160
5.5	Spencer Hatch on the front page of the US propaganda magazine *Free World* (1951)	161

Acknowledgements

This book has been in the making for an unduly long time. In fact, the first serious engagement with the topic goes back to the year 2012, when I had the privilege of being a fellow in residence at the Lichtenberg-Kolleg, University of Göttingen. Over the many years, I have benefitted from discussions with the researchers in my team at ETH Zurich and the feedback from many colleagues. I am especially grateful to Amalia Ribi-Forclaz, Andreas Greiner, Bernhard C. Schär, Carey Watt, Carolyn Kerchof, Christoph Dejung, Corinne Pernet, Daniel Speich-Chassé, David Arnold, David Pomfret, Heike Liebau, Joanna Simonow, Jon Weier, Judith Große, Julia Hauser, Kama Maclean, Katrin Bromber, Marc Frey, Mark Frost, Martin Dusinberre, Martina Andermatt, Michael Brunner, Monique Ligtenberg, Nico Slate, Nikolay Kamenov, Paul Hillmer, Paul Kramer, Paula Thanner, Projit B. Mukharji, Pushkar Sohoni, Rahel Gutmann, Robert Kramm, Ryan Bean, Stefan Hübner, Sujeet George and Vinayak Chaturvedi.

Particular gratitude is also due to Vasudha Bhardwaj for polishing my Teutonic English, to Denise Lim for finalizing the index, to Elena Valdameri for providing fast and helpful comments on the final manuscript and to Eliane Schmid for helping a slightly chaotic old school scholar with her digital skills and impeccable sense of order and tidiness. Finally, I also want to thank Maddie Holder from Bloomsbury for her support of this book project.

Introduction

This study aims to shed new light on the early twentieth-century history of South Asia, North America and the world by exploring the trajectories and agendas of one of the oldest and most influential international civil society organizations – the YMCA (also referred to as Y), or Young Men's Christian Association. It does so mainly by looking at the Y's activities in the Indian subcontinent. Inspired by recent reinterpretations of American imperialism and its entanglements with other colonial empires, this book focuses primarily on the multifarious extra-religious activities of North American Y workers in India and their interactions with the local population, representatives of the British colonial state and a host of international actors. Challenging the conventional wisdom that the advance of modernity in British India was mainly related to the agendas of the colonial state and its nationalist opponents, I argue that these Y 'secretaries', as they were called in official parlance, were involved in various undertakings that proved to be key to far-reaching modernizing efforts and important social engineering projects in South Asia. Additionally, *The YMCA in Late Colonial India* suggests that, from the 1940s onwards, the Y's knowledge about the Indian subcontinent, as well as its experiences and networks, had a considerable impact on US foreign policy, diplomacy, as well as educational and development programmes in the region and beyond.

In spite of this double significance, the multifaceted 'secular' work of the YMCA in India and its adjacent countries has thus far been mostly overlooked by scholars. Arguably, this is due to the prevailing fixation on British colonialism and South Asian nationalisms that still structures the bulk of the research on the history of the Indian subcontinent in the nineteenth and early twentieth centuries.

By concentrating primarily on the social work schemes launched by a US-dominated Christian lay organization in the Indian subcontinent and following its protagonists and their impact on other regions of the world when justified, the study also seeks to transcend the limitations of established missionary history, Britain-centred 'imperial history' and a conventional 'area history' approach, all of which tend to have a restricted spatial frame of analysis. In addition to the obvious significance of its findings for scholars of modern South Asian history and the history of US overseas missionary interventions, the book addresses broader issues relating to the persistent role of religion in global modernization processes in general and the emergence and growth of morally tinged American soft power in South Asia during the first half of the twentieth century in particular, thus highlighting an aspect that is often neglected in the burgeoning field of studies on Indo-US interactions during the development decades in the 1950s and 1960s.

Alongside these broader lines of argument, the individual case studies in this monograph trace the translocal trajectories of exchanges and entanglements between actors from several continents. In doing so, they situate themselves at the intersection of several historiographical subfields, including (but not limited to) the history of development, the history of childhood and youth, the global history of sports, the history of Protestant internationalism and, last but not least, the history of the 'United States in the world'.

Rationale of the book

This monograph has grown out of an attempt to synthesize two historiographical meta-projects that I have been pursuing for more than two decades. Firstly, as a scholar who originally trained as a South Asianist and now holds a chair for global history, I have consistently aspired to combine micro- and macro-perspectives, and especially to demonstrate the rich potential of global and transnational approaches to regional histories and 'area studies'. Secondly, ever since I started to work on my PhD thesis in the late 1990s, I have been intrigued by questions of how 'global civil society' emerged in the late nineteenth and early twentieth centuries, how it related to the prevailing imperial world order, and how historical contingencies and cultural specificities played out and affected the ways in which it unfolded in different settings.[1]

These overarching concerns led to the choice of the specific topic of the YMCA in India, and its role in spreading sport and physical culture, organizing youth work and initiating rural development schemes. As a historian specializing in the history of South Asia during the late colonial era, I was increasingly sceptical of the continued pre-eminence of received imperial, national and regional framings in the historiography of the Indian subcontinent. To be sure, over the past two decades, there have been several pleas for 'connected' or 'entangled' histories that might 'globalize' the perspective on South Asian history in the early modern and modern eras, and some concrete studies have even been undertaken.[2] Nonetheless, when it comes to the big themes of historiography such as the history of anticolonial nationalism or modernization under colonial rule, conventional imperial and national perspectives still largely dominate the field, leaving a significant gap in the literature.[3]

My first attempt to overcome these constraints consisted of writing the global biography of a diasporic South Asian revolutionary who wove his anti-imperial networks and cultivated his long-distance nationalism for decades from the European metropoles of London, Paris and Geneva.[4] For my second global take on South Asian history, I wanted to reverse the perspective. In other words, I was looking for a topic that would allow me to focus less on how South Asia(ns) went out into the world, but rather on how the (extra-imperial) world came to South Asia and on the effects this encounter produced. At this juncture, I recalled a moment of bewilderment I had experienced at the beginning of my career as a historian. The year was 1999, and I was struggling to finish my PhD thesis on the history of the conservative wing of the Hindu reform movement Arya Samaj and its educational institutions in northern India. I could hardly believe it when I found a report in an in-house pamphlet published by the reformers in the 1910s, which announced that the die-hard Hindu revivalists in Lahore and other Indian cities had founded Young Men's Associations. The source made it clear that these so-called Arya Kumar Sabhas were modelled on a template provided by some American-run YMCA branches in India.[5] The fact that the existing YMCA outlets were apparently popular with Indian urban youth, primarily because they offered libraries, sports facilities and fitness equipment, increased my cognitive dissonance at the time. Preliminary research reassured me that my 1999 finding did not refer to an isolated phenomenon and that there had indeed been an intense and protracted engagement of the North American YMCA – an institution I had previously associated primarily with a popular 1970s disco funk track – in India and adjacent countries. My curiosity grew when I learned that the Association was apparently involved in areas such as citizenship training and social engineering, widely regarded as cornerstones of modernization and 'nation-building', between the 1890s and the late 1940s, leading to the conception of this monograph.

The questions that I try to answer in this book are many and wide-ranging, and have evolved from my negotiating the cognitive dissonances uncovered by those materials. To what extent, I asked myself, might the application of a transnational perspective brought by studying an unexpected set of historical actors enrich the historiography on late colonial South Asia? How would it change our understanding of seemingly familiar phenomena such as educational reforms, village development schemes or the inculcation of 'public spirit' and civic engagement by means of philanthropic schemes when the narrative shifts away from the usual protagonists – that is, either colonial administrators or Indian nationalists and reformers – and towards a few dozen North American expats working for a Christian lay organization with a global presence? This question is especially compelling as this unique group of historical actors cannot be grouped with imperial reformers and technocrats despite being white and Anglophone. Neither did the American Y secretaries conform to the image of 'regular' Western missionaries. How would our perspective on the issues studied change when we take into consideration the fact that these American do-gooders participated in ambitious modernization and reform schemes in late colonial South Asia? How would our views of 'colonial modernity' change if we also take into account the fact that these actors brought their own preconceived knowledges, methods and practices that sometimes overlapped with but often profoundly differed from those of imperial officials? And finally, how were the knowledges, methods and practices of these American actors tested, adapted and discarded in the challenging new environment that was British India?

The nature of these questions and the insights that they might provide persuaded the global historian in me of the attractiveness of such a project. It is not difficult to see why the YMCA, a universally operating international non-governmental organization (INGO) synonymous with a Christian internationalist agenda, presents an exceptionally fascinating object of study for transnational and global history. Indeed, the history of international organizations and institutions has been one of the most popular topics studied by an earlier generation of global historians.[6] However, many of the numerous studies done⁷ have suffered from a tendency to privilege Western perspectives. In contrast, this book provides an opportunity to tell the story of how an international non-governmental body such as the YMCA expanded across the globe from a non-West-centric angle. In fact, it demonstrates that telling the story of the Y's expansion in South Asia as a one-directional narrative of transference or diffusion going from the Association's headquarters in London, Geneva and New York to far-flung places in Asia would be one-sided, incomplete and rather predictable. Far more nuanced and intriguing is the multilayered approach that this study required, which made the planned research project even more exciting. Instead of following a few cosmopolitan elites on their frequent travels to international conferences and congresses,⁸ one can embed the global civil society in regional history by situating the selected INGO in a concrete, complex and highly heterogeneous space outside the West. Doing so situates the project at the intersection of various South Asian cultures, religions and linguistic regions, while also allowing one to study the impact it had on civil society by British imperialism, competing anticolonial nationalisms and a number of other regional, transregional, and global trends and stimuli.

As the following five chapters demonstrate, such an approach provides a fresh perspective on seemingly well-studied aspects of South Asian history. I contend that *The YMCA in Late Colonial India* offers a particularly novel and differentiated understanding of South Asia in the age of imperial overhaul, indigenous reformism and decolonization. By overcoming the received wisdom that modernization processes in early twentieth-century South Asia gained traction chiefly due to the competing agendas of the colonial state and its nationalist challengers, this study provides a helpful corrective to existing historiographies.⁹ In a nutshell, I argue that this sharply focused case study helps render visible a third space: one occupied by international (and surprisingly often: American) civil society actors that also contributed in significant, if controversial, ways to the shaping of South Asia's modernity.

It is precisely through this focus on North American actors, methods and money that this book can simultaneously complement the important work done by scholars working on expanding the historiographical subfield of 'the United States in the world'.¹⁰ Firstly, it offers a fresh perspective on the historical trajectories of America's late-start imperialism and particularly the building of its 'moral empire', the spread of Christian internationalism and its role in the history of international organizations more broadly.¹¹

Secondly, this case study also provides valuable insights into 'Americanization' processes and the workings of American soft power in South Asia. For instance, it serves to illuminate the origins of US developmentalism as described by scholars such as David Ekbladh, Daniel Immerwahr, Nicole Sackley and others.¹² Historians studying US development and foreign aid initiatives in South Asia, for instance, tend to concentrate their attention almost exclusively on the period between the late 1940s and the 1980s. Their selective, exclusive focus on post–Second World War phenomena downplays and even completely cuts out much of the essential prehistory of the 'development decades' from their narratives. This study, on the other hand, adds much-needed historical depth to the flourishing literature of post-independence development schemes in India.

Thirdly, and on the most general level, the YMCA case study further dismantles the questionable dichotomy between 'the religious' and 'the secular'.[13] Although *The YMCA in Late Colonial India* is not a book about religion per se, but rather about the decidedly this-worldly agenda of a religious organization, it demonstrates that what we think of as 'secular' often does in fact have religious origins and entanglements, and underscores the pervasive influence of Protestant Christianity in modernizing projects even well into the second half of the twentieth century. Arguably, this insight holds particularly true when it comes to US interactions with the global South on the level of politics and civil society.[14]

Modernization or Modernity?

Given that this book is about the YMCA's modernizing mission in South Asia and its intersections with other modernization efforts simultaneously undertaken in the region, it is necessary to briefly clarify how the term 'modernizing' is understood and used in the following pages. As we know, 'modernity' has become a highly controversial term over the past four decades, and there is no broad consensus as to whether there is a single modernity or many modernities, how the term should be defined and even if the concept makes any sense at all.[15] The constraints of space here make it impossible to engage in debates on the meta-level of historiography or the abstract definitions of sociological concepts. However, it is helpful and indeed important for the purpose of this study to distinguish between *modernization* (understood as the structural transformation of the environment mainly through the promotion of technological innovations) on the one hand, and the more ideologically laden term *modernity* on the other. Modernity, in this sense, is associated with an overarching political project advocating egalitarianism, democracy and freedom from social oppression. Indeed, the precise thrust of modernity consists of, in Rana Mitter's words, 'flattening hierarchies'.[16] In an oft-quoted article, Dipesh Chakrabarty has convincingly argued that 'the "libertarian" or emancipatory project' of *modernity* constituted 'a certain kind of European self-reflexivity with regard … to the technological project of modernization'.[17] To be sure, formations of modernity in various contexts have been 'revealed as contradictory and contingent processes of culture and control, as chequered and contested histories of meaning and mastery'.[18] Thus, for example, 'Europe' or even the 'the West' ought not to be assumed to be the sole fountainheads of either modernization or modernity. It has been plausibly argued that there were elements within South Asian and other non-Western societies that indicated 'modernizing' developments well before European influence was felt in a significant way.[19] Yet one cannot deny that the quest for improvement, rationalization and reform reached a new level of intensity during the second half of the nineteenth and the early decades of the twentieth century. It is, therefore, reasonable to inquire into the kind of modernity/modernities that South Asians came into contact with during this period of colonial domination and into the outcomes of such contact.

In another helpful historiographical intervention, the late David Washbrook has reminded us that key elements of the emancipatory project of modernity – notions of individuality, democracy and rationality, for example – were highly problematic in the context of the Raj. Despite the ubiquitous British imperial self-depictions as torchbearers of liberty, democratic principles were obviously difficult to combine with the colonial 'rule of difference',[20] without which British India would not have been '"British" for very long'.[21] In other words, the inherent contradictions and limitations of the colonial type of modernity propagated by the British in the Indian subcontinent themselves stimulated the "native" elites into searching for alternatives. Of the various substitutes that were found, the indigenous proto-modern traditions,[22] the emergent Japanese brand of modernity[23] and, last but not least, the American liberal Protestant variety as offered by the YMCA were considered particularly attractive by South Asians, who were long used to 'processes of highly eclectic [transcultural] borrowing and adaptation'.[24]

There is reason to believe that the shifting geopolitical constellations during the period under survey in this study further reinforced the attractiveness of the American version of modernity. After all, the years between the early 1890s, when American YMCA workers began engaging with South Asia, and the late 1940s, which saw the emergence of the independent nation-states of India, Pakistan and Ceylon, witnessed the meteoric rise of the United States from an aspiring *parvenu* in the realm of Western nations to a military, economic and 'humanitarian superpower'.[25] Indeed, by the mid-1940s, the United States was widely perceived as the most powerful and influential country on the planet. In other words, American liberal modernity apparently worked in raising the profile of the country and increasing its clout, and hence was a worthwhile model for emulating – at least in the view of the educated 'bourgeois' segments of the South Asian population that sympathized with the project of modernity generally.

With these conceptual reflections in mind, we now proceed to have a closer look at the sources and secondary literature on which this study draws.

Note on Sources and Literature

The Covid-19 pandemic that hit the world in early 2020 left few of us untouched, and unfortunately, but not surprisingly, thwarted my plans to collect a final round of materials from the Indian and British archives. That said, this study is nevertheless based on an extensive range of primary sources gathered from a number of repositories in India, the United Kingdom, Switzerland and the United States. A definitive advantage of a global or transnational approach to South Asian history is that it facilitates the use of novel untapped archives. For the first time in my career as a South Asianist, I visited archives in the United States and was positively surprised by the quantity and quality of the material there. Without a doubt, the most fruitful visits were my long stints at the University of Minnesota (UoM) in Minneapolis. The Kautz Family YMCA Archives, located in the library of the UoM, hold incredibly rich resources on the Y's work in South Asia. More than 130 boxes of material in the *International Work* series refer to India, Burma (now Myanmar) and Ceylon (now Sri Lanka).[26] Similar amounts of relevant material are scattered through other series like the *Subject Files* and *Biographical Files*.[27] Written sources aside, the Kautz Family YMCA Archives also has a wealth of visual source materials in the form of photographs, magic lantern slides and films.

The Archives and Special Collections at Springfield College in Massachusetts also yielded copious materials, relevant especially to Chapters 4 and 5.[28] Since graduates of this college were the main actors in the Indian YMCA's Physical and Boys' departments, the institution's collections provided valuable insights into the exchange of knowledge and personnel between Springfield and various branches of the South Asian YMCA. A particularly fascinating genre of 'grey sources' retrieved here were the graduation theses of several Springfield graduates who later became conspicuous in South Asia.[29] The archive also possesses complete sets of rare journals like *Foreign Mail*, a monthly that regularly featured reports on the Y's work in South Asia, and *Vyayam*, a magazine completely devoted to physical culture and sport, published from the YMCA Colleges of Physical Education in Madras (now Chennai) from the 1920s onwards.

Chapter 5 on the YMCA's rural reconstruction programmes benefitted tremendously from a short but fruitful visit to the University of Arizona in Tucson, AZ. The Special Collections section of the university library holds the Duane Spencer Hatch Collection, which consists of the YMCA rural development expert's private papers, letters and book manuscripts as well as fascinating film and audio materials.[30] The private papers and photographs of two other YMCA India veterans (Sherwood Eddy and Waldo H. Heinrichs) were consulted in New Haven, CT, at the Yale University, Divinity School Special Collections.[31] Finally, material from other collections in the United States proved to be helpful, even though they were eventually sparsely used in the book. The Sophia Smith Collection of Women's History at Smith College has copious material on the YWCA in South Asia while some records at the Rockefeller Archive Center in Sleepy Hollow, NY, have files showing that the YMCA's Rural Demonstration Centre in Martandam was financially supported over a considerable period by the Rockefellers' Davison Fund.[32]

In the United Kingdom, the British Library's Asia, Pacific and Africa Collection once again proved to be a very rich repository. The India Office Records contained a number of helpful reports published by the Government of India and several provincial governments as well as a number of relevant files in the *Public* and *Judicial* series. In addition, the *Military Records* series turned out to be crucial for the YMCA's Army Department and war work discussed in Chapter 2.[33] The manuscript section of the India Office Records also contains the copious private papers of one of the leading functionaries of the South Asian YMCA, S. K. Datta.[34] A second research trip to England took me to Birmingham, where I had the opportunity to explore the holdings of the Cadbury Research Library at the University of Birmingham.[35] Here I was able to access records (including visual material) on the YMCA's work in India during the Great War and consult countless in-house magazines and pamphlets from the perspective of the British branch of the organization.

The Archives of the World Alliance of Young Men's Christian Associations, located in Geneva, was another lesser-known repository.[36] The collection on the YMCA's international committee's work in South Asia is much smaller compared to the Kautz Archive in Minneapolis, but nevertheless it yielded some unique and significant sources. Chapter 5 on the YMCA's Boys' Work, in particular, benefitted from these finds. This repository also gave access to an almost complete set (1890–1950) of the Indian YMCA's most important mouthpiece, *The Young Men of India, Burma & Ceylon*.[37]

As indicated earlier, planned visits to the National Archives of India and several provincial archives fell victim to Covid-19 restrictions, because of which I had relatively little material from these repositories when finishing the book manuscript. The few sources I could use were collected during short, preliminary investigations.[38] Apart from the larger state institutions, I also spent some time in the Library and Archives of the United Theological College at Bangalore, as well as in several YMCA institutions in different parts of India.[39] The small research collection at the YMCA in New Delhi was by far the most significant in terms of the quantity of usable sources that could be recovered.[40] At least over the past few decades, a deplorable lack of interest in record preservation has apparently been prevailing in most institutions entertained by the Indian Y. As a result, many records have been destroyed or lost, and my visits to two Y branches in Kolkata, the YMCA College of Physical Education in Chennai and the Martandam Rural Centre in Tamil Nadu, though rewarding for a variety of other reasons, yielded relatively little in terms of sources I could utilize for this book.

This detailed description of the sources and repositories used for this study underlines one of the greatest challenges I had to deal with while writing up this study. It cannot be denied that the material available to me is quite one-sided and asymmetrical in nature. The bulk of the sources on the Indian YMCA were produced by North American European and South Asian members of the Association itself, suggesting that they are likely to be heavily biased. While this bias gives one ample opportunities to examine archives as 'institutions of power',[41] read the material 'along the archival grain' and reconstruct the social epistemologies that guided the YMCA leadership's perception and practice,[42] it also raises a thorny question: How can a study that has to rely mainly on the artefacts of the Association's propaganda and public relations be critical and reliable? This is an important issue, which I have actively endeavoured to address. To a certain extent, consulting sources outside the YMCA bubble – for example, records from the colonial archive, or contemporary reports from Indian, British and American newspapers and periodicals – can correct some of the partialities of the main archive. At the same time, a close reading of the YMCA in-house sources 'against the archival grain', using the techniques refined by the subaltern studies collective and Africanist historians since the 1980s, remains crucial.[43] A historian engaged in such an exercise will almost inevitably be confronted with 'dissonances, silences, and conflicts that indicate alternative voices and versions of events'.[44] Two forms of silence or absence of documentation were particularly conspicuous in this particular case. The first is the cultural arrogance and racist prejudices of Western YMCA functionaries that are almost completely erased from the archival memory, as are any conflicts that might have arisen as a result. Nonetheless, the existence of such attitudes and of the discord they produced are confirmed by a few scattered sources.[45] The second conspicuous erasure is particularly striking. Given the notoriety of the YMCA in North America and several European countries as 'queer haven',[46] one would have expected to find references to 'sex scandals' and sexual transgressions in the context of the homosocial world of the Indian YMCA. The silence in this case, however, is almost impenetrable, and one can only speculate on the issue. Ultimately, however, I believe that it is still possible to write a critical and reliable history of the Indian YMCA that is sensitive to alternative voices and interpretations of events, so long as one remains alert to the pitfalls and limitations resulting from the often fragmentary character and pre-existing biases of the archival materials.

This book has been enriched by a vast body of secondary literature consulted over the many years that it was in the making. Each chapter includes a detailed discussion of titles relevant to its specific focus in its introductory section. For this general introduction, I will merely confine myself to works pertinent to the entire book. In what follows, I shall focus on studies on the history of the YMCA in South Asia and beyond, and very briefly discuss studies on the macro-processes often dubbed 'Americanization' and US 'cultural imperialism'.

While there is copious historical scholarship on Christian missions and their multifaceted agendas in the Indian subcontinent, studies dealing specifically with the YMCA in India are meagre, to say the least. Quite revealingly, the Association does not even figure in the index for Robert Frykenberg's authoritative history of Christianity in India![47] The only full-fledged monographs that deal with the history of the YMCA in the Indian subcontinent are 'in-house' publications that cannot really be considered 'scholarly.' M. D. David's *The YMCA and the Making of Modern India*, published in two volumes in 1991 and 2017 to celebrate the 100th and 125th jubilees of the Indian YMCA, is by far the most comprehensive work available on the institutional history of the Association in the region.[48] David's volumes are based on thorough empirical research in the Y's own archives and have proved very reliable when it comes to facts and dates. However, they adopt a very descriptive approach and lack both critical acumen and theoretical sophistication. David's magnum opus aside, there are a few older in-house histories written by members of the Indian and the American YMCAs that likewise contain a wealth of factual information.[49] In addition to these official histories, there are several autobiographical writings by American YMCA secretaries who worked in South Asia for longer periods.[50]

Some excellent studies that discuss select aspects of YMCA's work in the Indian subcontinent also need to be mentioned. Susan Billington-Harper's biography of Indian Bishop V. S. Azariah stands out among the books that demonstrated the potential of the topic some time ago.[51] Her study is particularly strong in illuminating the complex relationship between Indian nationalism and prominent South Asian members of the Indian YMCA. Nandini Chatterjee's *The Making of Indian Secularism* devotes an interesting chapter to agricultural reform schemes launched by the YMCA in South India that shows similar connections.[52] Australian historian Ian Tyrrell's landmark publication *Reforming the World* and his article in the pioneering edited collection *Spreading Protestant Modernity* (edited by Tyrrell, Stefan Huebner and myself) are more recent works that must be mentioned.[53] These sophisticated studies provide a useful theoretical framework comparable to the one used in this book, even though they study entirely different source bases with no overlap. The same can be said of Karen Phoenix's as yet unpublished PhD thesis (2010) and her 2014 article 'A Social Gospel for India' published in the *Journal of the Gilded Age and Progressive Era*.[54]

Both offer a helpful conceptual reference point, but unlike this book, Phoenix deals exclusively with the YWCA, the Y's female branch.

It should be noted at this point that, for all the conspicuous paucity of critical scholarship on the YMCA in South Asia, high-quality research on the Association's activities in other Asian countries does exist. The history of the YMCA in China, for instance, has inspired a number of excellent studies.[55] Various aspects of the Christian lay organization's interventions in Japan[56] and Korea[57] have also been subject to sophisticated analyses. This book builds on these studies while also engaging with some of their arguments. Finally, given that American and Canadian YMCA secretaries are the main foci of this study, the copious scholarship on the history of the North American Association was tremendously helpful, particularly the studies on various types of social and educational work done in North America by the organization.[58]

The book's larger arguments transcend the regional focus on South Asia and are also relevant to the wider debates on 'Americanization' and 'American cultural imperialism'. I would like to end this brief literature review by pointing to a few of the most important titles from this historiographical subfield. Ever since the 1902 release of British investigative journalist W. T. Stead's visionary book *The Americanization of the World*,[59] much has been written about the global spread of American values, technology, modes of production, consumption habits and popular culture. The better part of this literature has portrayed the growth of American influence during the twentieth century as a unilateral diffusion of a seemingly stable and homogeneous 'national culture' that has not only transformed other parts of the planet but also provoked strong reactions in terms of anti-American sentiment and outright resistance.[60] *The YMCA in Late Colonial India*, however, rather draws on a model recently proposed by French historian Ludovic Tournés. Tournés rightly places more emphasis on both the malleability and inclusivist character of US cultural exports and the agency and transformative power of those at the receiving end of such influences. He suggests that we understand the process of 'Americanization' as less of a simple imitation or rejection of a readymade US template but as its 'rational and selective use, or its profound transformation, which discards the American reference point in order to create new significations'.[61] This insight extends the political scientist Joseph Nye's popular concept of 'soft power'.[62] In a more sober prose, Nye's discussion, too, points to the fact that 'positive attraction' and voluntary acceptance by the target group are crucial elements of soft power, which he defines as 'agenda setting that is regarded as legitimate by the target'.[63] That such agenda-setting power can be ascribed to the YMCA in late colonial India is evident from the fact that several of the Y's core programmes (e.g. physical education or boys' work) and methods (e.g. the use of new visual media) were copied or emulated even by its most outspoken Indian critics from the Hindu nationalist camp. Even though this study does not treat states and governments as the most important historical actors – unlike Nye's work, which is in the context of international relations – the concept of soft power is therefore valuable in describing the phenomena and processes studied in this book. Part of this usefulness stems from the fact that there are considerable overlaps between Nye's notion of 'soft power' and the Gramscian idea of hegemony, a concept that South Asianists have now been using for over three decades.[64] The case study on the various activities of American YMCA workers in early twentieth-century South Asia, introduced in the following section, provides an ideal test for the concept of soft power in this extended sense.

In sum, then, it is safe to say that *The YMCA in Late Colonial India* makes a unique contribution to the field, while engaging with and complementing several existing bodies of research on the global history of the YMCA, US Protestant internationalism and American 'soft power' more broadly.

Spatio-chronological frameworks and chapter previews

The foci of the chapters in this book parallel those of the main departments or divisions in the US-dominated Indian YMCA. Specifically, they reconstruct the activities and agendas of the Y's Army Department, the Physical Department, the Rural Department and the Boys' Department, in order to demonstrate the astonishing extent to which the Association was involved in projects of social engineering and citizenship training. As has been previously explained, this study concentrates solely on the educational, philanthropic/humanitarian and social engineering schemes of the Association, and the YMCA's religious views and programmes per se are not its main concern. Nonetheless, it is very much a book about 'the spiritual in the secular', to quote Patrick Harries' and David Maxwell's phrase.[65] In other words, despite not being the primary focus, religious aspects will be a recurring theme in the individual chapters as the organization's Christian agenda informed almost all aspects of its 'secular' work.

As the book is organized thematically rather than chronologically, a certain nonlinearity in terms of the time frames of the individual chapters could not be completely avoided. Broadly speaking, the period studied begins in the 1890s, when the first YMCA secretaries from America arrived, and ends around 1950. By that latter date, the new postcolonial governments had imposed severe restrictions on the finances and influence of the Association with the result that very few North American secretaries remained in South Asia. Most chapters focus mainly on the three decades between 1905 and 1935, when the organization reached the pinnacle of its influence and visibility and was expanding and diversifying its multifarious activities. Chapters 3, 4 and 5 also briefly shed light on the transitional phase of the late 1940s and 1950s, when YMCA leaders had to reposition themselves within the nation-building endeavours launched by the emerging postcolonial nation states in South Asia as well as stay relevant in the fledgling international development regime of the early Cold War era. Chapter 1 sets the stage for the case studies presented in Chapters 2 to 5 by expanding upon the global and local contexts prior to the arrival of American Y secretaries.

A brief clarification regarding the spatial focus of this study would also be appropriate here. The book is essentially about North American members of the Indian YMCA and their work in India. In some cases, however, it was necessary to follow their movements overseas when they travelled. This is particularly the case in Chapter 2, wherein the caregiving and welfare work of the Indian YMCA for South

Asian and European soldiers serving in Mesopotamia and France during the Great War play a significant role. Similarly, a section in Chapter 5 follows the global career of the Indian YMCA's renowned agricultural expert Duane Spencer Hatch for about fifteen years after his departure from India in the early 1940s. This excursus serves to illustrate that the development knowledge and practices developed by the Association in South Asia had a significant impact in other parts of the world, too. Not only is the mobility of people crucial to my story but also the movement of ideas, ideologies and knowledges; for this reason, some sections examine developments in the United States insofar as they shaped the agendas of the YMCA in India. It would be hardly possible, for example, to grasp the Indian Y's physical education programme (Chapter 3) or the work of its Boys' Division (Chapter 4) without a more precise idea of the quasi-scientific debates that had given birth to these schemes in the United States in the first place.

It needs to be emphasized, however, that this cross-contextualization does not imply a simplistic understanding of the YMCA's work in India as a case of 'cultural imperialism' in the sense of a simple unilinear transfer of American knowledges, programmes and methods to South Asia. Quite the reverse: in keeping with the perspective suggested by Ludovic Tournès, one of the main goals of this book is to look closely at the complex processes of translation, adaptation or 'pidginization' that took place while also accounting for the complete failure of some attempted transfers from the United States to South Asia.

Lastly, it has been necessary to include Burma and Ceylon into the spatial framework of my analysis to some extent. The reason for this is very pragmatic: The Indian YMCA was officially known as 'The Young Men's Christian Association of India, Burma and Ceylon' during most of the period under survey and consequently conducted work in all three countries.[66] Give my micro-historical approach, which follows individual actors and analyses the development of specific institutions, it would have been unnatural to cut off Burma and Ceylon (or for that matter, the princely states of India) simply because these territories did not fall within the imperial boundaries of British India.[67] Indeed, it was very possible for a YMCA secretary to start his career in Madras, serve a few years in Rangoon and retire from Colombo. In order to reconstruct the developments shaping the attitudes and actions of such a man and understand his decisions and personal agendas, it would be necessary to include, if only to a limited extent, his tenures outside India in the analysis.

Now that the overall structure of the study has been established, let us take a closer look at the individual chapters. The main purpose of this introduction has been to elucidate the main arguments of the book and explain how they relate to broader historiographical debates. It also discusses the sources and methods used to examine the individual case studies in the subsequent chapters.

Next, Chapter 1 provides a broad overview of modernizing missions in colonial South Asia. It acts as a bridge between the introduction and the four chapters, which are built on detailed case studies of the Indian YMCA's various fields of action, and is divided into two large parts. The first part situates the case studies in their regional context by describing the explosion of social reform agendas and social engineering projects in South Asia from the mid-nineteenth to the early twentieth century, promoted as they were by the British Raj as well as its various collaborators and opponents. This portion of the chapter provides a concise account of other modernization schemes and philanthropic campaigns, which were driven by the colonial state, Christian missionaries of various denominations and Indian nationalists and indigenous reformers of diverse backgrounds. It establishes a wider backdrop against which the Association's multifarious activities can be fruitfully analysed by shedding light on the competition and the concrete political and social constellations in which the American workers operated. While some of the information provided here might be familiar to South Asianists (who may want to proceed directly to the next section), I consider this contextualization essential for any reader who does not specialize in South Asian Studies so they might make sense of the following chapters.

The second section of Chapter 1 starts with a brief sketch of the trajectories of the global YMCA movement. It then reconstructs the institutional development of the Christian lay organization in the Indian subcontinent and analyses the difficult acculturation processes that accompanied its growth in the region. The narrative pays due attention to the multifarious exchanges that the American YMCA secretaries had with South Asians of various backgrounds as well as the chequered history of the organization's interactions with the British colonial administrators and a variety of international players.

After this exposition of the broader contexts, I flesh out key aspects of the Association's 'secular' social engineering work in South Asia in the next four chapters so as to assess their local and transregional impact. Chapter 2 considers the various facets of the YMCA's philanthropic and humanitarian activities and examines how the provision of such services was consciously used by the organization's North American workers to gain the acceptance and support of the imperial government. The chapter starts with a brief account of the Association's welfare programme for (Eurasian and European) railway workers, which prepared the ground for the Army Department. The bulk of the chapter is devoted to the Indian YMCA's Army Department's 'war emergency work' during the First World War[68] and closely examines the organization's welfare and caregiving programmes. Most importantly, the Association's support of allied war efforts during the First World War massively enhanced the organization's financial resources as well as its popularity among both South Asian elites and colonial authorities. The chapter conducts an extensive analysis of the various facets of the YMCA's army work, which, among other things, was crucial in advancing certain norms of a 'civilized' masculinity among both South Asian and British troops, and also pioneered the extensive deployment of modern media such as film, gramophone records and magic lantern slide shows for the entertainment and education of Western and non-Western servicemen.

As research focusing on Europe, East Asia and Latin America has amply demonstrated, the YMCA was one of the most significant actors in the global transmission of sport and physical education during the first half of the twentieth century. It was not least for this reason that it became a mainstay of America's soft power or 'moral empire'. The YMCA played a similar role in South Asia as well, although this fact has been largely overlooked both by scholars of history working on the region and by historians of global sport. In an attempt to fill this research lacuna, Chapter 3 explores the Indian YMCA's 'physical ministry', as their sport and physical education programme was occasionally referred to in the parlance of the time. It concentrates particularly on the highly influential Madras College of Physical Education established by American YMCA secretary Harry C. Buck in 1920 and shows how the sports and fitness schemes that the Association successfully spread in the Indian subcontinent and adjacent regions were advertised as specifically *American.* The emphasis placed on the allegedly 'progressive', 'liberal' and 'egalitarian' character of the United States in the public eye marked them as clearly distinct from the kind of Westernness associated with the colonial rulers, apparently contributing to their acceptance by the South Asian populace.

Various experiments in formal and informal education were also an important part of the YMCA's agenda in South Asia in the period studied. Using age as a key analytical category and building on recent research on childhood and colonialism, Chapter 4 analyses the activities of the Indian YMCA's Boys' Division, which established itself in all major YMCA branches in India, Burma and Ceylon between 1901 and 1941 in an attempt to reach out to 'one-fifth of the world's boyhood'. The YMCA's boys' work scheme was designed to channel the energy of Indian youth in the direction of 'useful manhood' and reached the peak of its influence during the quarter century preceding independence in 1947. This chapter traces the wider transnational trends that led to the Indian YMCA's increased attention to boys rather than young adults. One such trend, discussed in detail in the chapter, was the development of the medico-sociological American discourse of 'boyology', a specific body of educational and disciplinary knowledge that emerged around the turn of the twentieth century and was designed to solve the so-called boy problem.

The final case study presented in Chapter 5 emphasizes the links between programmes of the Indian YMCA in the late colonial era and the developments after decolonization. It does so by examining 'the gospel of rural reconstruction' that was partly developed and disseminated by North American experts working for the Indian YMCA. The chapter traces the production and global circulation of a rather unique form of agricultural and sociological 'development knowledge'. This new body of knowledge was originally pioneered by Indian YMCA members K. T. Paul and Daniel Swamidoss in the 1910s. During the interwar years, it was further refined, 'scientized' and disseminated to great public acclaim by the American YMCA secretary Duane Spencer Hatch and his team. The chapter first briefly looks at the origins of the YMCA's rural reconstruction efforts in South Asia during the 1910s and 1920s, and then shifts its focus on the American expert Hatch, who came to dominate the field of rural reform in South Asia from the mid-1920s onwards.

The conclusion summarizes the main results of the previous chapters and discusses their relevance for the questions raised in this introduction. It ends with a brief epilogue that takes stock of the further history of the YMCA in South Asia from the mid-1950s to the 1970s, and briefly discusses the multifaceted legacies of the Association's work in the region.

1

'A mission to modernize': Colonial administrators, nationalists and religious bodies in South Asia (1870s–1930s)

American YMCA secretaries became involved in philanthropic activities, reform work and social engineering in South Asia around the turn of the twentieth century, by when the region had already been under the influence of various 'modernizing missions' for some time. Most significant in this respect was the impact of British colonialism, which, in some parts of the subcontinent, dated back to well over a century. However, as in most colonial territories, the impact of foreign rule in South Asia was felt very unevenly. For one thing, British India was not a monolithic entity and the difference between the administrative approaches and practices in its various presidencies and provinces was considerable – not to mention the indirectly ruled princely states that also felt the effects of modernizing missions to varying degrees. The divergences were further amplified during the final decades of the Raj, particularly after the Montagu–Chelmsford Reforms of 1919. The system of diarchy implemented by 'Mont-Ford' strengthened provincial autonomy and transferred authority on subjects such as education, sanitation, local self-government and agriculture as well as industries to the respective legislative assemblies, which were dominated by elected Indian parliamentarians.[1]

Alongside such political and administrative dissimilarities, there also existed a gaping urban–rural divide. The large urban centres, especially seaport and garrison towns, were usually important hubs of colonial power and sites of large-scale intercultural contact, but the rural hinterland was rarely affected by any direct exchanges. Of course, this observation does not imply that the same rural regions were not affected by structural transformations that accompanied colonial rule, especially from the second half of the nineteenth century onwards. The use of the Punjab as a base for military recruitment[2] and the shift of agricultural practices in vast swathes of India to satisfy the empire's hunger for cash crops like opium, tea, cotton, wheat and sugarcane leading to a large-scale commercialization and globalization of sections of Indian agriculture are only two important examples of this phenomenon.[3]

While the winds of colonial change thus were also blowing in the countryside, it was the subcontinental cities that became most closely associated with the technological and economic facets of *modernization* as well as with key aspects of *modernity* as a liberating societal project. These aspects comprised the new forms of social interaction and political mobilization emerging in the last quarter of the nineteenth century. By the 1890s, the urban experience, especially in the flourishing colonial metropoles of Calcutta, Bombay and Madras (now Kolkata, Mumbai and Chennai, respectively),[4] not only included new professional opportunities for emerging middle-class professionals[5] and radically changed consumption habits[6] but also, crucially, provided access to South Asian 'hybrid', and predominantly Western educational institutions.[7] High schools and colleges often were the venues for the shaping of social reform initiatives and political projects. Unsurprisingly, the cities and towns of colonial South Asia also became the most important sites where an effervescent associational culture took root, with the subsequent emergence of new forms of civil society. Much like in the West, however, the push towards modernization in South Asia during the second half of the nineteenth century did not entail a complete secularization or 'disenchantment'. Quite the reverse: spirituality and religious belief systems frequently merged with philanthropic and social reform agendas, and became more visible and public than ever. Thus, towns and cities also turned out to be the most important 'terrains of religious exchange',[8] with intense encounters and debates between representatives of the predominant religious traditions of South Asia (Hinduism, Islam, Sikhism etc.) and Christian missionaries.[9]

The modernizing activities of the YMCA need to be situated against this wider constellation. The case studies that follow have a strong focus on the ideologies, agendas and methods of North American YMCA secretaries working in the Indian subcontinent. They provide the necessary background for the detailed investigations undertaken in the remainder of this book and demonstrate the core activities of the Christian lay organization.

Modernizing missions in late colonial India: Actors and agendas

We now take a closer look at the concrete historical trajectories of the projects related to modernization and modernity on the Indian subcontinent, keeping the introduction's broader discussion of these concepts in mind. While Chapters 2 to 5 will focus on the first four decades of the twentieth century, the emphasis here is on the prehistory and origin of modernizing missions from the nineteenth century to the years preceding the outbreak of the First World War.

The colonial state and modernizing interventions

According to the narrative and self-fashioning of the Raj (or, for that matter, the assessment of revisionist historians of the British Empire[10]), the British colonial state in South Asia was the main driver of change and the most important modernizing agent on the Indian subcontinent during the second half of the nineteenth and the first half of the twentieth centuries. Casting British colonialism as a 'moral, civilised and civilising regime'[11] was a key strategy to create 'basic legitimacy' through persuasion and to win indigenous support for imperial rule. The portrayal of the Raj as an efficient regime that possessed the military capability to quell rebellions, the intention and means to dispense justice to the population it controlled, and the economic and logistical power to deal with food crises was an essential strategy in stabilizing colonial power relations.[12] Such discursive manoeuvres were necessary as the relations between the rulers and the ruled were always precarious, especially given the fact that Europeans constituted a microscopic minority of the subcontinental population. For precisely the same reason, the construction of state authority also possessed a strong performative element, as Sabyasachi Bhattacharya, one of the few historians to attempt a thorough theorizing of the colonial state in South Asia,[13] reminds us. It relied to no small degree on 'a whole series ... of symbolic representations and rituals of imperial power', ranging from the micro-social level of everyday life to ostentatious mass performances such as the Imperial Durbars.[14]

To what extent, however, did the colonial state deliver on its promise to modernize India and provide stability and security in the process? Even some clear-sighted British observers from the 1880s did not subscribe to the lofty civilizing rhetoric, admitting instead that it was obvious that the Raj, far from being a benevolent institution working for the interest of its subjects, was 'essentially an absolute government founded not on consent, but on conquest'.[15] Historical research over the past four decades has further dismantled the simplistic association between colonialism and modernization. In an insightful article published more than two decades ago, David Washbrook famously depicted the British colonial state in India as a Janus-faced structure and showed how it contributed significantly to the 'traditionalization of Indian society' in various ways despite its purportedly liberal modernizing agenda.[16]

As one might expect, the colonial interventions that were widely viewed as most directly related to the broader agenda of 'modernization' were concerned with technological and infrastructural innovations. However, even this seemingly straightforward technocratic modernization agenda was shot through with contradictions, revealing slight tensions within the imperial self-image. The construction of railways and large-scale irrigation works are good examples of the ways in which *modernization* and *traditionalization* went in tandem. For instance, the British resorted to pre-modern methods of labour recruitment and management that were built on rigid hierarchies and repression in order to rapidly expand their cutting-edge railway lines, bridges and tunnels (*c.* 1860–1914).[17] Similarly, the construction of canal networks in the Punjab (*c.* 1890–1930), one of the world's most ambitious engineering projects in its time, came with equally problematic implications. Apart from the unintended ecological consequences, the imperial efforts to populate the newly created canal colonies with 'healthy agricultural communities' drawn from the region reproduced and reinforced existing religious divides and social hierarchies, as these desirable groups consisted exclusively of selected groups of 'yeoman peasants' and categorically excluded other segments of the population.[18]

Closely related to infrastructural improvement was the matter of agricultural production and food security. Large parts of India were ravaged by several devastating food crises and famines during the last third of the nineteenth century in rapid succession (1866, 1876–8, 1896–7, 1899–1900). These crises, in which at least 12 million Indians lost their lives,[19] wrought havoc on the prestige and credibility of the colonial rulers.[20] The fact that the magnitude of the tragedy was attributable in part to the colonial government's reluctant and half-hearted relief measures dealt a severe blow to the Raj's claims to 'basic legitimacy'. The criticism by Indian elites that followed these events triggered fears that the Raj's basic legitimacy might be eroded, leading to concerted efforts to improve agricultural production through various means.[21] One strategy consisted of setting up new institutions for agricultural education and research, a process that started in the 1870s and continued through the interwar period.[22] The attempt to 'scientize' farming and husbandry was accompanied by various schemes of 'rural reconstruction' or 'village uplift', as they were called in official parlance.[23] These programmes, in turn, relied heavily on notions of 'the Indian village' and 'the Indian peasant' constructed by imperial scholars like Henry Sumner Maine (1822–88) and Baden H. Powell (1841–1901) in the late nineteenth century.[24] These conceptualizations were undergirded by the assumption that South Asian societies were primarily rural in nature and villages were not only home to the vast majority of the population but also sites of an 'authentic' India untainted by foreign influences.[25] The village, often conflated with 'the rural' more broadly, was therefore reconfigured by imperial administrators 'as [a] constitutive element of the colonial modern'.[26] Consequently, large-scale experiments in village development were eventually launched during the interwar period by British administrator-scholars,[27] and the issue of rural reform remained vital for the prestige of the Raj in subsequent decades as more than 85 per cent of the Indian population lived in the countryside in the first decades of the twentieth century. As we shall see in Chapter 5, the Indian YMCA became a significant player in this field, partly competing and partly cooperating with the institutions created by the colonial state.

The colonial regime's modernizing efforts that targeted at the country's much smaller urban population also had far-reaching social and, especially, political consequences. One of the most important spheres of state intervention in urban areas was education. The field of education was and is of peculiar interest because, unlike agricultural 'improvement', it transcends the mere technocratic realm of modernization and brings with it the emancipatory promise of modernity. There has, therefore, been a rich and controversial scholarly debate about the exact effects of the educational policies adopted by the Company state and the Raj.[28] A long-established approach within the scholarship posited a straightforward link between access to Western education and the beginnings of nationalist mobilization in South Asia. This assessment was based on an interpretation of the colonial educational system as an all-pervading British imposition and an effective tool of empire that was mostly accepted and only occasionally resisted by the local population.[29] Recent research has criticized this argument as too simplistic,[30] and instead has drawn a more complex picture by highlighting the continued impact of precolonial educational traditions and emphasizing the agency of South Asians in co-constructing the colonial curricula as well as the educational system as a whole.[31] While this change has added some welcome nuance to how we understand the effects of state education, it cannot be denied that educational policies were among the most hotly debated topics throughout the colonial era. Furthermore, educational institutions, and the teachers and students populating them, played key roles in the power contestations of late colonial India.[32] Therefore, acknowledging that the educational institutions in colonial towns and cities were crucial hubs for the influx of and debate on Western ideas and concepts, and that their graduates played a disproportionately significant role in shaping civil society as well as politics, does not necessarily imply subscribing to outdated concepts of 'Westernization'.

The realm of education was also intimately linked to another key element of modernity: the emergence of a public sphere, or rather, a number of coexisting public spheres.[33] The secondary and tertiary educational institutions in British India started to produce a growing number of English speakers after the cautious implementation of educational reforms in the wake of the famous Anglicist–Orientalist controversy of the 1820s and 1830s.[34] Nonetheless, even after the first six universities had been opened in British India between 1857 and 1887, the number of those literate in English remained extremely small. In 1891, the year when American YMCA workers started work in South Asia, a mere 4.6 per cent (or 12.1 million) of the entire Indian population and 8.7 per cent of the male population (totalling a little less than 262 million) could claim any degree of literacy.[35] Only 3.2 per cent of this literate group (i.e. c. 387,000 people out of the entire Indian population) possessed at least a basic proficiency in English.[36] Half a century later, in the 1940s, when the influence of the Indian YMCA had already dwindled significantly, the numbers had changed but not dramatically, as the literacy rate for men and women combined rose to 16.1 per cent.[37]

As a consequence of the low literacy rates, the anglophone public sphere in India, though highly influential, remained relatively small and fragmented.[38] Well into the twentieth century, few newspapers and magazines in English had a circulation that surpassed 1,000 copies. Concurrently, however, vernacular public spheres, complete with newspapers, pamphlets and publishing houses, developed slowly but steadily after Christian missionaries introduced movable type in various South Asian languages.[39] By the turn of the twentieth century, the products of vernacular printing presses had a relatively stable reading audience. The spread of literacy and print culture also generated unintended side effects. While many books and journals catering to the growing urban 'educated' middle classes were consumed for entertainment,[40] the emerging print capitalism was also deployed in support of religious revivalism, patriotic history writing and outright political mobilization from the 1870s onwards.[41] Colonial administrators observed this fact with growing concern. Although the Government of India estimated a newspaper-reading public of around 200,000 for all of India in the early 1870s, this tiny segment seemed threatening enough that censorship was introduced with the Vernacular Press Act of 1878. Additionally, the government established a board of employees with language expertise to comb through the vernacular periodicals for 'seditious' content on a daily basis and produced the fortnightly 'Native Newspaper Reports' from the 1870s through the 1920s.[42]

Finally, there was another arena which had less to do with modernization and more to do with the egalitarian promises of modernity: discourses and practices related to citizenship and civic responsibility. Debates on citizenship were neither initiated by the state nor fully controlled by the colonial authorities; instead, they took shape through the dialogues between several segments of the Indian population and colonial officialdom. As political scientist Niraja Gopal Jayal rightly points out, the concept of 'imperial citizenship' that gained currency among parts of the educated elite in colonial India in the late nineteenth century was a *contradictio in adiecto* as all Indians were equally subjects and not citizens, but 'some subjects were allowed the delusion that they were citizens'.[43] This fundamental tension notwithstanding, educated Indians increasingly claimed citizenship rights in the name of the liberal political tradition on which Britain's colonial empire was putatively built.[44]

Besides its obvious utility as an instrument of 'claim making' and political leverage,[45] the citizenship discourse also had a seemingly less political dimension. It generated debates about the kind of norms, values and behaviours that qualified one to be or become a respected citizen. As we shall presently see, such debates were not confined to the milieu of anglicized (or 'hybrid') functional elites who formed the backbone of the moderate wing of the Indian Congress, but even spilled over into the wider Indian society. There were many regional and communitarian strands within the citizenship debates.[46] The promise of full participation in modernity and its blessings through the rights associated with citizenship inspired a variety of different and sometimes contradictory imaginings of the future citizenry. What is more, it gave rise to unprecedented civic activism and, eventually, 'citizenship training' schemes. This was especially true of the various segments of the Indian population that can be lumped together as the 'middling sorts', regardless of their religious, regional, linguistic or professional affiliation. At least this group, the YMCA leaders were convinced, would welcome their programme of fostering 'constructive citizenship' enthusiastically.

The above discussion makes clear that, though the Raj did provide significant stimuli and despite its self-fashioning,[47] the colonial state and its representatives by no means monopolized or even dominated the various fields related to modernization. Even more ambiguous is their role in arenas concerned with implementing the societal and political visions of modernity. In order to get a more precise idea of the specific constellations, debates and rivalries that the North American YMCA secretaries were confronted with (and soon became a part of), the next section will revisit the fields of education and philanthropy. Since the activities (or absence) of the colonial state in these fields has already been amply discussed in the literature, particular emphasis is placed on the role of local individuals and organizations in these domains as well as international non-state actors trying to carve out niches for themselves in order to complete this picture.

Shaping the future citizen: Nationalists, religious reformers and missionaries in the field of education

As indicated earlier, most scholars nowadays tend to agree that the spread of modern educational institutions and learned societies in British India cannot productively be understood as a unilinear process of imperial imposition. For one thing, Christian missionaries, whose agenda only partially overlapped with the plans of the colonial state,[48] played an important role in setting up the 'modern' educational infrastructure in the Indian subcontinent from the eighteenth century onwards, feeding the growing desire for Western education in certain sections of South Asian society.[49] An increasing number of South Asians from various backgrounds also became active in the process of establishing a modern educational system in many ways over the subsequent decades.[50] From the 1870s through the interwar years, the sphere of education in India became increasingly diverse as two new sets of actors on the scene turned education into a 'contested terrain':[51] Indian nationalists and socio-religious reform organizations.[52]

As Indian patriotism and anticolonial sentiment gathered momentum in the last quarter of the nineteenth century, government- and missionary-run high schools and colleges came increasingly under fire by 'native' critics. Even though religious instruction was not permitted in state-sponsored educational institutions under the official policy of religious neutrality, English-medium schools were often accused of spreading Christian mores and values in indirect, oblique ways.[53] At the same time, they were castigated for offering no moral instruction at all, thus producing a generation of young men who were both culturally alienated and morally corrupted. The following excerpt from a Hindi newspaper article published in North India in 1899 provides a rather typical example:

> The education imparted in the public schools and colleges not only encourages cramming, but makes its recipients lead a sort of artificial life and increases their wants. Its worst feature, however, is that it has a tendency to undermine both religion and morality.[54]

The alienating and 'artificial' character of student life was stressed by many of the emancipatory indigenous elites who joined the Indian National Congress (INC) from 1885 onwards. The Bengali nationalist Bipin Chandra Pal, for instance, lamented the moral disruption allegedly caused by exposure to the soulless 'Western knowledge' imparted in colonial educational institutions. In a pamphlet published in 1907, he confessed that for him and others of his generation, English education had 'divorced our mind, our heart, our spirit, our character and our manhood from our national life'.[55] His position was quite typical of the many champions of 'national education' who gained prominence with the first anticolonial mass protests of the Swadeshi movement from 1905 to 1908,[56] and later influenced the educational programmes of the INC between the 1920s and 1940s.[57] In the eyes of many Indian critics, this perceived loss of both cultural anchoring and 'manhood' was reinforced by the exclusive focus on book learning and the complete lack of physical education that characterized colonial primary schools and high schools.[58] The criticisms of colonial schools were also directed at their physical conditions, as problems of chronic overcrowding, bad ventilation and poor lighting prevailed in many secondary and tertiary educational institutions.[59] This issue featured regularly on the 'snagging lists' of Indian critics of formal education under the Raj.

These dismal opinions led to a surge of indigenous educational institutions that, on the one hand, conveyed the 'useful' Western knowledge regarded as indispensable for the development of the country, but on the other hand also provided moral instruction based on local religious traditions. The hybrid character of these institutions became visible in names like Muhammadan Anglo-Oriental College in Aligarh, founded by the charismatic Muslim leader Sayyid Ahmad Khan (1817–98), and the Dayananda Anglo-Vedic (DAV) College, opened by the Hindu reformist organization Arya Samaj in Lahore (1877). This trend could be observed in all major religious communities, as Sikhs started the Khalsa College in Amritsar, and the orthodox Hindus who considered the Arya Samaj institutions as too radically reform-oriented, inaugurated the Banaras Hindu University in 1916.[60]

As shall be explored in greater detail in Chapter 4, the general debate over the right type of education often became more specific tussles about shaping children (particularly boys) and adolescents into strong, moral and productive citizens of the future. As the 'bookish' nature of secondary and tertiary education with its emphasis on rote learning was severely under attack, informal methods of education and leisure practices became increasingly important from the turn of the twentieth century onwards. As with educational institutions, imperial and missionary youth organizations such as the Boys' Brigades, the Boy Scouts and the YMCA itself, all of which advocated the improvement of health and 'character building' through outdoor games, camping and exercises, soon had counterparts set up by various Indian organizations.[61] By the 1910s, there were many culturally specific organizations targeting the young, including an Arya Kumar Sabha or Young Men's Arya Association founded by the Arya Samaj, two independent Young Men's Sikh Associations, a Young Men's Muslim Association, a Young Men's Parsee Association, a Young Men's Buddhist Association (which was tremendously influential in Burma and Ceylon)[62] and even a Jain Young Men's Association.[63] Particularly visible was the Young Men's Hindu Association, which was founded in 1910 by H. P. Deshpande 'to promote moral education among Hindu young men and train them in public usefulness'.[64] All in all, the two-volume *Directory of Social Work in India*, published in the mid-1920s, lists more than a dozen different 'Young Men's Associations' in addition to the Christian original.[65] Most of these replica youth organizations, as well as a host of other bodies, offered scouting and camping excursions as well as sport and fitness programmes. These activities were to a large extent inspired by the YMCA's schemes, which we will explore in Chapters 3 and 4, but tended to be presented as their culturally authentic South Asian alternatives, purportedly rooted in the organic traditions and indigenous practices.[66]

Several aspects of these broader developments were particularly important for the YMCA workers entering the field of youth work and informal education for 'natives' in the last decade of the nineteenth century and would shape their approach to a considerable extent. For one, many Indian individuals and communities showed a strong and sustained interest in 'modern' types of knowledge, and particularly in the educational offerings and leisure programmes from the West. Second, educational institutions and schemes of 'informal education' were vastly important as meeting grounds for future elites who would lead the country in the decades to come; they thus became sites that could shape their worldviews and characters. That being said, it is also clear that there were strong reservations and prejudices against the supposedly 'denationalizing' and (physically as well as morally) 'degrading' influence of the Western systems. Both state and missionary institutions therefore had to cope with constant criticism as well as growing competition from indigenous schools, colleges, universities and youth organizations that emulated Western models without their

Christian or imperial superstructure. These considerations meant that a high degree of cultural sensitivity was necessary on the part of the YMCA to win the acceptance of a very demanding and critical Indian public. Finally, YMCA workers entering the densely populated and highly contested terrain of formal and informal education had to cautiously identify the right kind of niche for themselves so as to reach a significant number of people. As we shall see in the following chapters, an essential precondition for the success of the modernizing crusades launched by the YMCA was an awareness of this complex sociopolitical constellation and the chances and pitfalls that resulted from it.

Fostering civil society: Non-state actors between social service, philanthropy and humanitarianism

Besides education in the broadest sense, there was another field within which the YMCA became conspicuously active from the 1910s onwards and which was inextricably linked both to visions of 'progress' and modernity, and to the debates around citizenship, namely, the broad range of initiatives and activities that can be subsumed under the headings of humanitarianism, philanthropy and social service. Philanthropic schemes were by no means a novel phenomenon in South Asia or a mere response to colonial impulses. Rather, all major religions of the subcontinent have time-honoured traditions of charity that long predate any colonial or missionary impact.[67] Nonetheless, from the nineteenth century onwards, the protracted exchanges with imperial administrators and Christian missionaries did have an undeniable effect on the ways in which social service and philanthropy were conceived, organized and financed. Hindu reform organizations like the Brahmo Samaj in Calcutta and the Prarthana Samaj in Bombay pioneered new, more collective-based approaches to charity in mid-nineteenth century.[68] One of the most significant Hindu organizations that interpreted the notion of *sevā*, or service, not primarily as a means to gain spiritual merit but rather in a modern sense, as a social service effort arising from civic consciousness, was the Ramakrishna Mission. It was launched by Swami Vivekananda in Bengal in 1897 and soon spread to other parts of India.[69] Around the same time, the Hindu reformist Arya Samaj also became active in the field of organized philanthropy in the Punjab and all of North India. The 'spirit of service'[70] that had been implanted by the movement's founder Swami Dayananda Saraswati in his followers expressed itself first and foremost in the establishment of orphanages for Hindu children, with a view to save young famine victims from the care of Christian missionaries and, thereby, potential conversion.[71] Later on, the Arya Samajis' activities widened and included, amongst other things, various educational schemes, women's work, 'untouchable uplift' programmes targeted at the Dalit population and catastrophe relief campaigns. The schemes were soon emulated by the Samaj's orthodox opponents, the Sanatan Dharma Sabha, and by Hindu merchant communities seeking to enhance their status and reputation.[72]

While a rich associational culture, and philanthropic endeavours in particular, played a prominent part in the 'Bourgeois Hinduism' that emerged in urban and small-town middle-class circles over the nineteenth century,[73] other religious communities also engaged in organized charitable activities. In Sikhism, for instance, the reformist Singh

Sabhas propagated the ideal of *parūpkār* (benevolence) and the Chief Khalsa Diwan, a new umbrella organization founded in 1902 with a view to forge a more coherent and uniform Sikh identity, ostentatiously promoted public welfare in their community by opening an entire network of philanthropic institutions including orphanages, hospitals and schools.[74] Muslims, too, founded associations that contributed to the emerging civil society through an entire range of benevolent activities that ranged from educational schemes and debating clubs to direct philanthropic interventions like famine relief and orphanages.[75] By the 1920s, the boom of philanthropic and social service organizations translated into the staggering figure of more than 1,500 different bodies in British India and the princely states. Almost 700 of them were represented in Bombay alone.[76]

Whereas older literature has tended to highlight the radically 'modern' character of such formations and underscore the 'democratic yearnings' of their leaders as well as their reliance on European templates of organization,[77] recent research has somewhat revised such an undifferentiated paradigm of 'Westernization'. Several scholars point instead to the enduring impact of South Asian traditions and practices of association and charity. Canadian historian Carey Watt, for example, has shown how new forms of associational philanthropy were carefully grafted on Hindu notions like *sevā* (service) and *dāna* (donation),[78] while Gwilym Beckerlege has highlighted the new social and political function of the *saṃnyāsin* (renouncer).[79] This emphasis on the continuing significance of such 'organic living traditions'[80] and their simultaneity with 'modern' practices supports the argument made earlier by C. A. Bayly, who has pointed to the persistent bonding strength of religion.[81] Finally, it is worth mentioning that these outreach endeavours by various Indian religious organizations were often closely connected to processes of community building within the respective religious group. The focus on orphanages suggests that this aspect was reinforced by the fact that proselytizing Christian missionaries had criticized South Asian religions for their alleged neglect of social responsibility and *caritas* from early on, and that they served as a point of comparison for the emerging social service organizations. Missionary criticism and, for that matter, missionary philanthropy were also important in stimulating the interest of upper-caste and middle-class reformers in the fate of India's 'depressed classes'.[82] The 'Christian threat', it was hoped by all these associations, could be countered by integrating particularly effective or useful elements of missionary work into their own arsenal. As we have already seen, one of those elements was the establishment of youth wings and associations that specifically targeted children and young adolescents and were often modelled after the YMCA.

While most of the mushrooming social service organizations had a religious, and sometimes narrowly sectarian, outlook, a few initiatives also displayed a more all-encompassing, even ostensibly national, perspective on social service and philanthropy. The National Social Conference, launched by moderate politician M. G. Ranade in 1887 as a complement to the INC, was the first platform that at least officially followed such an all-embracing, secular approach to social service. As the nationalist agitation in connection with the Swadeshi movement intensified, many other groups followed suit in the first three decades of the twentieth century, with some of them taking secularism very seriously. The Servants of India Society, established by Gopal Krishna Gokhale

(1866–1915), an arch-liberal and one of the most prominent 'moderate' nationalists, is a particularly interesting case in point as it demonstrates the porous boundaries between social engagement, political commitment and quasi-religious devotion to 'the nation'.[83] The society was founded in 1905 in Poona (also known as Pune) and subsequently opened branches in several other cities. It never had more than two dozen members as it was conceived by its founder as an 'educated Platonic elite in the service of the motherland',[84] devoted to the cause of 'building up in the country a higher type of character and capacity'.[85] Revealingly, Gokhale wanted his highbrow 'servants' – it was mandatory for members to have a university degree – to tackle their volunteer work precisely 'in the spirit in which religious work is undertaken'.[86] This work ranged from promoting amicable relations between India's different religious communities to supporting projects of female education and untouchable uplift, to participating in famine relief operations.[87] That said, despite their noble intentions, the volunteers of the Servants of India Society and similar organizations often created distance between themselves and the groups they were targeting through their discriminatory approach and paternalist rhetoric. Mohandas Gandhi, in fact, pointed out in 1910 that their snobbish self-fashioning was in stark contrast to their liberal and democratic aspirations.[88]

All in all, such organizations were established to prove the organizational capacities and high moral standards – otherwise mostly denied in colonial discourse and orientalist depictions – of which Indians were capable, thus making implicit arguments for political autonomy. Despite differences of opinion about the right methods, their members generally enjoyed a high status, at least among the 'lettered' sections of the local population.[89] As a rule, the colonial authorities remained somewhat ambivalent about Indian social service associations overall but often perceived them in a predominantly positive light. While some officials viewed the Indian do-gooders as 'troublemakers', pointing to their alleged hidden political agenda, most colonial administrators and Western missionaries welcomed self-help initiatives from 'educated native gentlemen' as they aligned with the goals of their own imperial or Christian civilizing missions.[90]

Official recognition was initially more grudging vis-à-vis new currents of 'native charity' that went beyond philanthropic community engagement and expanded South Asian benevolence into the realm of global humanitarianism.[91] Hindu intellectuals and reformers like Bankim Chandra Chatterjee (1838–94) and Swami Vivekananda (1863–1901), who despised the 'little humanitarianism of the West', were the first to construct an indigenous tradition of a universal approach to compassion and charity based on elements from Hindu religion and philosophy.[92] However, it was South Asian Muslim societies that materially supported humanitarian interventions overseas for the first time. Islamic organizations and individuals sustained relief efforts and medical missions overseas during the Balkan Wars (1875–8 and 1912–13) and in Libya (1911– 12).[93] While the colonial authorities in British India feared a pan-Islamic conspiracy and remained suspicious of these transnational assistance campaigns, they lauded the generous Indian support of international relief organizations like the Red Cross and the St John Ambulance during the Great War without reservation.[94] Particular praise was reserved for the myriad humanitarian organizations and campaigns launched by South Asians themselves during 1914–19 in support of the allied war effort.[95] Clearly, the First

World War constituted a first peak of this new globally conscious Indian humanitarian engagement. The Indian YMCA's own war work, which we will scrutinize in the next chapter, must be located within this broader constellation.

During the interwar years, a more sinister facet of the vibrant associational culture came to the fore. After 1922, one observes a growing militarization and 'communalization' of volunteer organizations against the backdrop of rising religious tensions and violent Hindu–Muslim riots. Newly founded militant Hindu groups like the Hindu Mahasabha (HMS, first founded 1915, reactivated 1921),[96] the Rashtriya Swayamsewak Sangh (RSS, founded 1925) and the Arya Vir Dal (founded 1927) and Muslim bodies such as the Khaksars (founded 1931) and even the allegedly 'secular' INC's Hindustani Seva Dal (founded 1923)[97] displayed a hitherto unprecedented militaristic outlook. All groups became preoccupied with the 'double task of defence against external aggression and internal disorder'[98] whilst purely philanthropic and humanitarian agendas receded to the background.

As we shall see in the following chapters, both the widely felt need for social service schemes and the public prestige and political support connected to philanthropic and humanitarian activities greatly facilitated the American YMCA workers' quest for acceptance into the public realm of late colonial India. This holds particularly true after 1905, when the Indian branch gradually adopted a programme inspired by the social gospel that foregrounded this-worldly social responsibility at the expense of its previously dominant proselytization agenda. As will also become apparent, the Christian Association's work displays a very similar convergence of the religious, social and political that was characteristic (albeit in different and varying measures) of Indian non-state actors like the Arya Samaj or the Servants of India Society. Before examining the various strands of the Indian YMCA's modernizing mission in detail, however, it is indispensable to provide the broad strokes of the Association's institutional history from the 1890s, when the American element became dominant, to the early Nehruvian years when its influence waned in the new postcolonial constellation.[99]

The Y's passage to India: A brief institutional history of the Indian YMCA

It is ironic that a non-governmental organization that came to represent a liberal (read: American) alternative to colonial modernity in South Asia had its roots in Britain. The original Young Men's Christian Association was founded in London in 1844 in response to the rapid cultural transformations and social disruptions taking place in industrializing Britain during the first half of the nineteenth century. The subsequent spread and growth of the organization, which had the avowed aim of providing young (mostly middle-class) men with a healthy, moral and religious environment in the heart of the fast-growing and allegedly 'debauched' urban centres in the West,[100] was nothing short of spectacular. Countless branches opened in various European countries and also in the United States and Canada, where the new lay Association met with immediate success. As early as 1855, its spokesmen laid claim to its being a universal organization at the first YMCA world conference held in Paris.[101] In 1878, the YMCA World Organization established its permanent headquarters in Geneva.

Using primarily the 'imperial highways' of the European and American colonial empires, the Association also made inroads into the non-Western world, particularly Asia.[102] By 1905, a network of more than 5,000 YMCAs connected twenty-four countries.[103] The Association kept growing rapidly despite unfavourable geopolitical developments: in 1916, the North American YMCA's International Committee alone employed 157 'secretaries', as the fully paid YMCA workers were then called, in no fewer than fifty-five countries.[104] A sister organization, the Young Women's Christian Association (YWCA), had also been established in 1855, and its World YWCA was created in 1894. The YWCA would achieve a global reach similar to the YMCA's, especially after the North American branch launched its foreign programme in 1906.[105]

Even though Britain was its country of origin and the headquarters of the Universal Union of YMCAs was situated in Switzerland, North America soon became the movement's most important stronghold and its undisputed gravitational centre. It was here that the famous YMCA triangle, which became the worldwide symbol of the Association's holistic approach to developing 'mind, body and spirit' of young men, was first designed, and here that a fourth element – social responsibility – was added to this trinity. As mentioned earlier, the YMCA and YWCA's 'secular' programme was partly rooted in American notions of the 'social gospel', which became popular during the 1890s.[106] In a nutshell, pioneers of the social gospel approach, like the Rochester theologian Walter Rauschenbusch (1861–1918), argued that the expected consummation of the Kingdom of Christ had to be preceded by a thorough 'social reconstruction'[107] aimed at the removal of harsh inequalities created by industrialization, urbanization and the overall transformation of living conditions in the last third of the nineteenth century. These social gospel ideals increasingly influenced the North American YMCA's activities from the last decades of the nineteenth century onwards. The Y movement, which – much like its British role model – now increasingly promoted its vision of a liberal 'Protestant modernity' across the social scale and even among the 'underclasses and the down-at-heel',[108] targeting, in particular, white workers, African Americans and immigrant communities.[109] It remains open to debate, however, if the new focus on 'practical Christianity' and social work can indeed be interpreted as an indicator of secularization or rather as a 'tactical retreat' such as C. A. Bayly has described, typical of the 'new style religion' that emerged from the late nineteenth century onwards. According to Bayly, these retreats cannot be understood as evidence of the erosion of the power of religion but rather as a sign of the growing entanglement of religious and secular agendas that ultimately aimed to conquer 'new areas' of 'cultural and social life' so as to spread the old religious message more efficiently.[110]

Following the new, more inclusive, agenda, the Association embarked on a wide range of 'secular' activities that included education, urban social hygiene, 'industrial work' and rural development schemes, as well as various philanthropic and humanitarian programmes.[111] As will be discussed in greater detail in Chapter 3, one of the core features that distinguished the North American Y branches from the British original was the conspicuous emphasis on sports, physical education and fitness schemes, which were regarded as ideal vehicles to instil Christian/Bourgeois norms and values in members of the target groups. The North American YMCA thus became a 'priesthood of believers in the gospel of muscular Christianity' from the 1860s onwards.[112] It rapidly developed its physical programme and played a key role in the scientization and standardization of physical education and training in the United States,[113] whereas sports remained 'completely off the radar' in the British branch for a long time.[114] It is important to underscore here that it was the YMCA in this specifically American *avatār* that had a tangible impact in colonial South Asia.

This impact is all the more remarkable because YMCA branches had existed in India decades before the American influence became visible. In 1854, Englishmen in Calcutta founded the first short-lived outlet in South Asia.[115] It survived less than two years and even though it reopened in 1857, the movement grew slowly in the region over the next two decades. The Indian tour of A. N. Somerville, an eloquent minister of the Scottish Free Church, revived the stagnant Calcutta branch and led to the inauguration of new YMCA headquarters in Bombay and Lahore in 1875.[116] Around the same time, several new branches were also inaugurated in southern India. The southward expansion foreshadowed a phenomenon that persisted over the first half of the twentieth century: the spread of the Association was very uneven and had a strong bias towards the southern Tamil- and Malayalam-speaking regions, where Indian Christians were already a significant minority.[117] This latter fact not only contributed to the general acceptance of the Christian Association by the local population but also facilitated local fundraising, which was crucial for the survival of smaller branches. In 1882, Ceylon followed suit when a separate YMCA head office was opened in Colombo. The Y's expansion in British territories in South Asia was complete when its first branch opened in Burma in 1899.[118]

The rapid growth of the Association was hampered during the first three decades of its existence on the Indian subcontinent due to the fact that early South Asian branches were mostly run by British members and open only to members of the Protestant Church.[119] The resulting close association with colonial power hugely limited the YMCA's appeal for South Asian youth. This limitation was additionally reinforced by the fact that the responsible Y workers in India 'had not yet discovered that young men had interests and needs over and above those that could be satisfied by prayer meetings, Bible study classes and lectures'.[120] In other words, the 'secular' offerings that would become the Association's biggest attractions from the 1900s – that is, sport facilities, leisure programmes and educational schemes – were not yet available. Even more importantly, the local associations perfectly followed the imperial politics of social distancing between the rulers and the ruled. British-run YMCA branches, almost without exception, were at pains to exclude 'natives' from their ranks and catered exclusively to the small communities of 'Europeans' and 'Eurasians'[121] residing in South Asia.[122]

Thus, it was only around 1890 that the spread of the YMCA movement in South Asia gained any momentum. This shift occurred under the energetic leadership of young American missionaries, who were part of a widespread evangelical revivalist movement in North America that culminated in the establishment of the Student Volunteer Movement (SVM) in Northfield, Massachusetts, in 1886.[123] Three years later, the YMCA of the United States and Canada launched an International Committee and started its 'foreign work' scheme.[124] Though formally under the umbrella of the World Alliance in Geneva, the North American Association was largely independent in actual practice over the next decades, not least because it had vast funds of its own at its disposal.[125] A member of the Madras Missionaries' Conference, who had experienced the Y's work during his furlough in the United States put out a call for workers, following which the American branch's zealous student missionaries arrived in India in 1889.[126]

Several of the enthusiastic men who followed over the next five decades, determined to achieve 'the evangelization of the world in this generation',[127] were graduates of the best US colleges. These young and dynamic American secretaries made it a point to 'democratize' the Association. David McConaughy (1860–1946) from Philadelphia, founder of the Madras YMCA and the first trained US secretary working for the Association in India, declared from the outset that the Y would now afford 'its privileges alike to all young men without distinction of race, rank and religion'.[128] Overcoming the opposition of conservative British Association members, some of whom were reluctant to give up the politics of social distance between the so-called natives and 'the ruling race', took some time.[129] Matters were complicated by the fact that divisions existed between branches under the control of the US-financed International Committee and those under the British YMCA well into the twentieth century. Of the more significant urban branches in South Asia, American secretaries controlled Madras, Calcutta, Allahabad, Bangalore (now Bengaluru) and Colombo, whilst British YMCA workers were in charge at Bombay, Shimla, Lahore and Rangoon (now Yangon) into the interwar years.[130] McConaughy even noted that the American methods he propagated provoked overtly hostile reactions in the Bombay branch, which was financially supported by the British YMCA and led by a Scotsman afraid of 'American spies'.[131] As Australian historian Ian Tyrrell has noted, the rivalries were fuelled by the American YMCA workers' often overzealous attitudes, which made them speak in the 'polarizing language of "American" and "British" missionaries, where the latter symbolized conservative resistance to change'.[132] Indeed, though North American Y secretaries stressed in the in-house publications that circulated among their donors in the United States and Canada that their work in India met with 'high recognition' from the European establishment in the subcontinent and even found 'the approval of the Imperial Government itself',[133] the ground reality was often less harmonious. Although the colonial authorities and American-led YMCA branches cooperated on a variety of levels, there is also strong evidence that British fears of an 'American invasion' persisted into the 1910s, leading to frequent clashes and occasionally even 'grave difficulties' for the Association.[134]

In spite of such internal friction, the democratization strategy pushed by the North American secretaries soon yielded positive results: the number of subcontinental Associations rose from 35 in 1891 to 151 in 1901, and 241 in 1921, while the total membership grew from less than 2,000 to more than 10,000 during the same period.[135] The period of growth ended in the late 1920s, and the numbers remained fairly stable for a few decades thereafter.[136] Due to this significant expansion, South Asia became the most important 'foreign mission field' in Asia at the beginning of the twentieth century, before China displaced it in 1907.[137] Financial problems in the wake of the Great Depression eventually led to the gradual decline of American presence in South Asia. Before the early 1930s, however, the impact of the American YMCA in India remained much bigger than that of the World Association in Geneva: in 1925, for example, forty-two out of around seventy 'foreign secretaries' working in India, Burma and Ceylon were exclusively on the payroll of North American YMCAs, whose members annually channelled up to USD 220,000 into the project of morally and materially 'uplifting' the subcontinental population.[138] Arguably, these impressive results are related to some structural reforms and methodological innovations adopted by the North American Y secretaries that made the Association stand out from other missionary bodies and hence deserve a closer look.

'American methods': Innovation in organization and dissemination

In his 1957 discussion of the trajectory of the Indian YMCA, the official historian of the Association's International Committee observes that 'it was North Americans who had given the Movement a national organization and put up the major buildings'.[139] As mentioned above, it was indeed the first American in charge, David McConaughy, who completely restructured the organization from 1890 onwards, ushering in continuing and massive growth rates over the next thirty years.[140] In the spirit of his home country's YMCA, McConaughy promoted the professionalization of the Association's work in the subcontinent during his tenure as General Secretary (1891–1902) by pressing for more trained workers from the United States and also prepared the ground for the creation of special training schools for European and 'native' secretaries. His successors eventually implemented these plans in 1908 (in Landour) and 1911 (in Calcutta).[141] At the same time, the dynamic Madras secretary implemented various measures to overcome the isolation typical of the few YMCA branches that existed in British India before the American influence could be felt. Under his leadership – and despite the resistance of some British-led branches – a national umbrella organization of Indian YMCAs was formed in 1891 and a permanent National Committee (from 1894: National Council) that featured McConaughy as the national secretary was elected.[142] To further strengthen the union and foster the newly found *esprit de corps*, national conventions were held every three years starting in 1896, with delegates in attendance from all branches in India and Burma. From 1907 onwards, the Ceylonese YMCA also joined in, and the Indian YMCA's activities also covered the present-day Myanmar and Sri Lanka well into the age of decolonization in the 1950s and 1960s.[143]

Perhaps even more significant and long-lasting than the effect of such administrative reforms was the skilful use of various types of media to spread the American YMCA's message effectively. The intense use of print media started soon after David McConaughy launched the Madras Association. From 1890 onwards, he published two monthlies titled *The Young Men of India* and *The Inquirer*, the first of which became the official organ of the Indian National Council three years later.[144] Several regional periodicals aimed at YMCA members followed in the next decade, some of them in 'vernacular' languages like Tamil, Bengali and Malayalam.[145] The Indian Y's Literature Department with its Calcutta-based Association Press was founded in 1910–11.[146] An internal report written in 1932 celebrated the department as one of the Association's greatest assets in South Asia, as it allegedly left a lasting impression on the Indian public.[147] In addition to Christian tracts to be used in the Y's Bible classes and Army education programmes,[148] it launched several widely circulated quasi-academic book series. The books published in these series were written in a 'popular scientific' style and were concerned with the study of South Asian cultures and religions.

American YMCA leader John R. Mott (1865–1955) had prepared the ground for this novel Christian-Orientalist knowledge production two years earlier when proposing a new programme of 'mission study'.[149] Among other things, the scheme that Mott presented at a March 1907 workshop for leading Y secretaries in Yokohama involved a deeper engagement with other faiths and included producing state-of-the-art literature on non-Christian religions.[150] One of the delegates at the Yokohama meeting was the Scottish Sanskrit scholar John Nicol Farquhar (1861–1929), who was a secretary for the Calcutta YMCA and would become the *spiritus rector* of the incipient 'Y orientalism'. When the Scotsman brought up his detailed publication plans for several series of books on various facets of religious life in South Asia, Mott supported the project enthusiastically and raised the necessary seed money within a few months.[151] Thus, even before his official appointment as head of the newly founded Literature Department in late 1911, Farquhar started building a small group of academically inclined YMCA workers around him and began to translate his vision into reality.[152]

The fifty-plus monographs that came out before the series were eventually discontinued in the early 1940s due to the redirection of funds towards war-related work can be understood as examples of a 'third-stream' approach to the study of South Asia and its religions. As the third-stream, 'Y Orientalism' was at pains to differentiate itself from the strictly philologically inclined academic orientalism of Sanskrit departments of Western universities, as well as from the popular second stream of 'spiritual orientalism' advocated by the Theosophical Society and comparable esoteric bodies.[153] They did this by treading a fine line that would address their various concerns. On the one hand, the (mostly amateur) scholars contributing to the YMCA book series carefully adhered to the quality standards set by professional Indologists and Sanskritists; on the other, they were dissatisfied both with the elitist bias and the thematic and disciplinary limitations of academic Orientalism and tried to push the disciplinary boundaries accordingly. They managed this by focusing predominantly on various aspects of lived religion, popular culture and the 'vernacular' literatures of South Asia rather than merely on the Sanskritic tradition of Brahmanical Hinduism. As I have argued elsewhere, their unorthodox approach in many ways paved the way for the methods and perspectives that gained prominence in the 'area studies' programmes on South Asia launched in the United States during the Cold War.[154]

Significantly, most authors in the series were liberal Protestants who were highly critical of the older polemical (and often aggressive) Christian missionary literature on South Asian religious traditions. While clearly marking themselves as Christians, the authors selected by Farquhar and his successors also tried to popularize a more tolerant, dialogue-oriented tone in missionary writings on non-Christian religions. This change of tone was necessary not least because members of Hindu, Sikh and Muslim reform bodies reacted in increasingly hostile and sometimes even violent ways towards the cultural arrogance displayed by many missionaries.[155] Farquhar and other authors, on the other hand, declared that their hope was to reach not only Western readers but also a large audience of 'educated natives' to whom they wanted to present their own traditions in a different light, emphasizing its fundamental compatibility with the tenets of Christianity. Many Y Orientalists thus saw themselves – and were often publicly perceived – as 'able and sympathetic interpreters of the spirit of India'.[156]

Finally, another feature of the entire literary enterprise deserves to be mentioned. It pertains less to the actual methodological innovations of Y Orientalist scholarship or its underlying Christian ideology than to the novel ways in which their 'South Asia Studies' series (if one may call it that) was marketed and distributed. It is perhaps in those aspects that the business acumen and pragmatism that were so typical of many activities of the American-dominated Indian YMCA become most apparent. Firstly, the new books were very competitively priced so as to make them attractive to a broad South Asian audience: these low Indian rates were possible not least because the volumes sold in Europe and North America were priced significantly higher.[157] Secondly, the Association's Literature Department deployed innovative methods of advertising to make the series known to a non-specialist audience. The volumes from several of the Orientalist book series were displayed not only in the showrooms of the Association Press in ten major Indian cities but also in railway bookstalls all over the subcontinent.[158] In addition, sample copies were sent to student camps and shown at various *melās*[159] and exhibitions, where there 'was a steady run on … [YMCA] books on Indian topics'.[160]

The Publication Department, while eager to emphasize the value of its series 'to the missionary and the administrator',[161] apparently also did a good job bringing its products to the attention of the educational authorities in several provincial governments and some princely states. Some titles were adopted as textbooks in local colleges and universities,[162] while others were even used in colonial law courts to decide on matters of religious orthodoxy.[163] As a result, the Association Press became one of the large publishers of books and pamphlets in South Asia by the end of the First World War, selling more than 220,000 copies of the forty-one titles in their publication portfolio in 1919 alone.[164]

Books, pamphlets and periodicals aside, the YMCA also pioneered the systematic use of audio and especially visual media for religious propaganda as well as for educational and recreational purposes. The role of gramophone records and films will be discussed in greater depth in the next chapter, but it may be instructive here to say a few words about another important medium regularly deployed by the Indian YMCA: the magic lantern slideshow. To be sure, this medium has a long history of missionary use, especially within the British Empire,[165] but it was particularly prominent in the work of the media-savvy American YMCA employees. Right from the beginning, in the 1890s, individual Y secretaries brought their magic lanterns and collections of slides from the United States to India, where they used them extensively. The circulation of slides through the entire network of YMCA posts in South Asia intensified after 1909, when A. C. Harte became the general secretary of the Indian branch. When his tenure ended four years later, Harte donated fifteen sets of slides to the National Council's office at Calcutta,[166] which became the nucleus of a rapidly expanding collection. Soon after the outbreak of war in 1914, it was recognized that audiovisual media were ideal for the Indian YMCA's army work, leading to the establishment of a separate lecture department in 1915.[167] American YMCA worker Waldo H. Heinrichs (1891–1959), whom we shall meet again in connection with his scout work in Lahore,[168] was first employed as a 'technical and media adviser'. He expanded the existing collection by gathering about 100 additional sets of slides 'from old go-downs, store-houses, Associations and from various [other] sources'.[169] In 1920, Heinrichs eventually took over the newly created lecture department and became responsible in this capacity not only for procuring new slides and shellac records but also for repairing the audiovisual equipment.[170]

By 1921, the YMCA's slide collection had grown to 396 different sets, containing a total of 14,594 slides.[171] They were sent around the subcontinent in boxes 'which were bought in New York, after they have been used for the shipment of similar equipment to the stations of the American Army'.[172] According to in-house statistics, between 1924 and 1926, the Indian Y's Lecture Department organized no less than 3,205 slide show lectures annually, reaching a total audience of more than 500,000 people.[173] The magic lantern slide lectures covered a very wide range of topics. Predictably, many focused on religious subjects or the documentation of various types of YMCA work for an internal audience. In a number of cases, the medium's emotive power was also used to reach out to potential donors in North America.[174] Still other sets of slides illustrated edifying talks on history, art and literature for an audience of Europeans or 'educated natives'. The list of the most popular slide sets for the year 1920 reveals the colourful mix of religious, scientific and even military topics that the Lecture Department had on offer. The top five sets were *Indian Ascetics*, *Peep into Nature through the Microscope*, *Aerial Warfare*, *Story of Flying* and *Kashmir*. The single most popular set – the lecture on *Indian Ascetics* prepared by J. N. Farquhar – travelled more than 12,000 miles that year alone.[175]

Towards the end of the 1920s, the Lecture Department was renamed 'Department of Visual Instruction' and focused more strongly on didactic lectures considered invaluable for 'use in a land where illiteracy runs beyond 90 per cent'.[176] A secretary of the Indian YMCA declared in 1926 that the medium, which suffered increasingly from the competition posed by moving pictures, continued to be ideally suited to spread the Association's multiple messages: 'Religious meetings, propaganda of various kinds, study groups and lectures', he maintained, could be made 'so much more interesting and effective by the use of lantern slides'; he ended with a fervent appeal to local Associations 'to call on [the] lecture department for help'.[177] This conviction was due in part to the fact that as early as the 1920s, the magic lantern equipment was used in rural contexts to introduce South Indian peasants to the latest methods of scientific agriculture, showing, amongst other things, 'several interesting processes of cultivation of new and profitable crops'.[178] Last but not least, slides were seen as a 'very valuable contribution to the solution of the Adult education problem in India', and specially prepared sets with Urdu, Hindi and Tamil reading lessons were used during literacy campaigns in urban slums as well as in the countryside.[179]

An additional, particularly striking, example of the YMCA's propensity to experiment with the latest media technology to disseminate its 'man-making' message through all sections of Indian society is provided by the Lahore YMCA's setting up of its own licensed radio station. The broadcasting station VUL was launched in 1931 by the American Y secretary Harold H. Peterson, who was convinced that 'the ether waves' were the perfect medium to 'carry enlightenment to the darkest corners of India'.[180] In a report written in 1933, the General Secretary of the Lahore branch proudly reported as follows:

> We are on the [sic] air an average of sixteen hours per week and letters of appreciation are constantly received from widely scattered places. We broadcaste [sic] our regular lecture program. We have musical evenings and even an Amos and Andy night. This latter is in the Punjabi dialect and deals humorously but constructively with problems of the Indian villager. The educational and uplift possibilities of this effort are legion. Imagine the thousands of villages within the reach of our station where newspapers are scarcely known and where there are but few to read them even though they were.[181]

Amos 'n' Andy was an American radio sitcom in the blackface tradition popular in the 1920s and 1930s. It was about the adventures of two African Americans who had migrated from Deep South to Chicago and New York;[182] that this programme was recreated in India with Punjabi villagers as objects of benevolent ridicule is remarkable. It shows in stark relief the existence of a transcultural flow of racial stereotypes, cultural symbols and modes of expression brought by Americans to the South Asian Mission field. We shall come back to this pattern in some of the case studies discussed in the following chapters.

Another idiosyncrasy of the American-led Indian YMCAs in South Asia that enhanced their public visibility was their penchant for occupying public spaces by constructing imposing buildings. American art historian Paula Lupkin has described how the architecture, equipment and location of the YMCA headquarters in the United States were crucial in attracting a greater audience and spreading its religious and secular messages across various sections of American society.[183] That the North American YMCA's ways of using architecture to make space and meaning had export potential becomes obvious from her discussion of how the American template was transferred to the YMCA's mission fields in China.[184] Similar considerations were at work in South Asia. The securing of prestigious real estate in colonial metropoles like Calcutta and Madras was a key element of the organization's expansion strategy. For one thing, the plan to build a magnificent headquarters 'gave YMCA affiliates funding targets to focus organizing at home', as Ian Tyrrell has rightly observed.[185] Simultaneously, the resulting bricks-and-mortar signifiers of American modernity and practicality were calculated to lure the more open-minded, English-educated South Asian youth into the orbit of the Y. As in China, the hope in India too was that each new YMCA building would turn into 'a physical space dedicated to fostering the education of a citizenry and enlightened public opinion' that was 'essential to the functioning of a democratic civil society'.[186] At the same time, Indian architectural elements are clearly

'A Mission to Modernize' 35

Figure 1.1 Postcard from 1910, showing the YMCA's headquarters in Madras. The building was financed by the department store tycoon and philanthropist John Wanamaker and opened in 1900. It is a perfect example of the YMCA's architectural shock and awe strategy and became the model for similar structures erected by the Y in South Asia. Courtesy Digital Commonwealth (https://ark.digitalcommonwealth.org/ark:/50959/6w929798k).

recognizable in the Madras edifice, and it is safe to assume that they were designed to convey the message that this educational mission was untainted by racial prejudices or Western cultural arrogance (see Figure 1.1).

In fact, the creation of this physical space for encounters and interactions was a top priority of the American-led YMCA branches. One of YMCA pioneer David McConnaughy's earliest initiatives after founding the Madras chapter was to secure a donation of USD 30,000 by department store tycoon and fellow Philadelphian John Wanamaker.[187] On the basis of this solid financing, he planned to erect the iconic YMCA building in the heart of Madras 'close to the crowded business quarter and in the very centre of the student population'.[188] The chosen spot was also, as McConaughy did not fail to mention, ideal for tackling the Association's foes and rivals heads on, because 'in Madras' Center such great movements as the National Congress, the Social Reform Party, the Hindoo Tract Preaching Society, and the Theosophical Society' all had their headquarters.[189] The prospectus for the proposed building, circulated in 1892, also celebrated the potential of the construction site on the city's Esplanade, in somewhat overly optimistic tones:

> Past this spot there daily flows a stream of young men who have come from all parts of India to study in the Hindu and the Christian Colleges and in the Medical and Law Colleges, all situated within a five minutes' walk. ... In the city there are nearly 90,000 young men, thousands of whom have received Western

education and use the English language more than their own native tongues. The young Hindus do not need to be sought after for religious conversation, for they voluntarily put themselves under the influence of the Association.[190]

Arguably, the optimism regarding the 'young Hindus' derived mainly from two sources. Firstly, the Indian elements introduced into the building's design supposedly lowered the threshold to enter it. This was by no means a YMCA invention, but rather inspired by a well-rehearsed British imperial practice. In fact, McConnaughy had secured the services of George S. T. Harris (1852–1930), a renowned English architect for the purpose. Harris had earlier worked for the Maharaja of Gwalior and for the Government of Madras. He was specialized in fusing Western architectural elements with a lush 'Indo-Saracenic' style.[191] Secondly, the YMCA leadership in Madras was convinced that the projected headquarters offered facilities that were completely unheard of and immensely attractive to the members of the target groups. In addition to a well-equipped library and spacious reading rooms that housed the newest books and periodicals from the United States, the building also had a restaurant and lecture halls and classrooms for the regularly scheduled talks and seminars on cultural, scientific or religious topics. The edifice could even provide lodgings for up to forty-eight young men and offered access to fancy indoor and outdoor sports facilities, including a fully equipped gym and 'Bowling Alleys'.[192] Taken together, the amenities of the headquarters allowed the English-speaking 'native' young men of Madras to experience Protestant modernity in its American *avatār* first-hand. Indeed, the bourgeois respectability of the spacious and dignified parlour and reading rooms was as much part of the YMCA world as were the library's newest scientific journals or the state-of-the-art sports facilities, the billiard room, or the up-to-date audiovisual equipment that also included film screens and projectors from the 1910s onwards. American secretaries working for the Indian YMCA – much like their counterparts in China – were advocating regular film exhibitions as 'wholesome and healthful' forms of entertainment from early on.[193] It is, thus, perhaps not completely coincidental that the headquarters shared some similarities with other buildings that came to symbolize American liberal modernity in the 'white towns' of India's major cities during the interwar years. The ultra-modern 'picture palaces' that screened Hollywood movies for an audience of Europeans and 'educated natives' likewise 'exhibit[ed] modernity' that had an American inflection, and they too became magnets for the local cosmopolitan-minded youth.[194]

There is strong evidence that the 'model building' in Madras, eventually inaugurated in January 1900,[195] did have the intended effect. The new headquarters succeeded in making the project of liberal and muscular Christianity hugely visible in the public space of one of the most vibrant colonial metropoles in South Asia. Although the popularity of the new building among the educated Indian youth in Madras did not translate into spectacular rates of religious conversion, the Y leadership was confident that it would enable important elements of both modernity and Christianity to reach even those who were opposed to the proselytizing activities of Protestant missionaries (see Figure 1.2). That this optimism was not completely unfounded can be gathered from the fact that some of the Indian youth organizations mentioned above, which

'A Mission to Modernize' 37

Figure 1.2 A cosmopolitan urban middle-class avant-garde? Indian student residents at the Madras YMCA Hostel (*c.* 1910s). Courtesy Springfield College Archives, Special Collections (Digital Collection LA-NT 08-03).

replicated much of the Association's activities and organizational principles, also mimicked the American YMCA's architectural practices, constructing headquarters complete with a hostel, library, reading rooms and sports facilities.[196] Small wonder, then, that McConaughy's strategy fulfilled the local American Secretaries' 'most sanguine hopes'.[197]

The Association building in Madras was soon copied by the Y branches in other towns and cities, perhaps unsurprisingly. In 1910, General Secretary A. C. Harte launched a campaign asking the International Committee in New York for USD 215,000 to finance new structures in Calcutta, Colombo, Bangalore, Allahabad and a number of smaller places.[198] Given the growing importance of construction work and the acquisition of existing buildings for the Y's Association's work in South Asia, the Y.M.C.A.'s Indian National Council created the new position of 'National Architect' in 1910. This office was first filled by Henry Schaetti, a Swiss national from Fehraltorf in the Canton of Zurich, who continued to serve the Indian YMCA until his retirement in 1943 and designed dozens of buildings along the way.[199] The speed of the construction activities especially between 1910 and 1925 is remarkable. By 1916, the Association owned a total of thirty-one buildings in twenty-one South Asian cities, altogether valued at over USD 665,000.[200] It goes without saying that this rapid expansion would not have been possible without the active support of the colonial authorities who frequently sold the YMCA government-owned building land and sometimes even provided financial subsidies for the construction projects. This protracted government support once again underscores the fact that, in spite of noticeable ideological differences when it came to the Association's 'American methods', the colonial regime had great sympathy for the Y's overarching project of keeping Indian youth 'in harness'.[201] As we shall presently see, this sympathetic attitude wavered during the 1920s, when the colonial authorities increasingly asked questions about the Indian YMCA's position with regard to the radicalizing anti-colonial national movement.

The difficult relationship with Indian nationalism

As we have seen, the Indian YMCA's priorities and the strategies it adopted to achieve its mission underwent a number of changes over time. As the following pages will show, these changes had a tangible impact on various core schemes implemented by the Association. The early period of expansion, preceding the First World War, was characterized by a strong focus on the creamy layer of 'anglicized' South Asian college students in big cities.[202] This elitism coincided with the period when the British Empire and its civilizing mission were still widely admired by the first generation of American YMCA secretaries, as they were, for that matter, by US presidents.[203] While British methods were often criticized as outdated and the imperial power's conservatism and racial arrogance repeatedly drew caustic comments, most American and Canadian YMCA secretaries nonetheless shared a belief in the overall beneficent effects of colonial rule in South Asia into the 1920s. Even a liberal with leftist leanings such as George Sherwood Eddy (1871–1963), who spent fifteen years in India (from 1896 to 1915) before becoming the secretary for Asia in the organization's International Committee, was convinced that 'a strong, benevolent foreign government' was the best option for India, and that there could be no doubt that 'Britain's wise policy [wa]s making for the uplift of India and the ultimate education and contentment of the people'.[204] The Christian Association's imperial romance found expression in a large number of Anglo-American joint ventures and, as we shall explore in the next chapter, reached its peak during the Great War. The North American workers of the Indian Y together with their British and Indian colleagues supported the British war effort through a comprehensive 'army work' scheme, which in turn was heavily subsidized by the Imperial Indian and British governments.[205]

As already indicated, there is strong evidence that the Anglo-American alliance was increasingly eroded after the end of the Great War, and it seems plausible that this was at least partly because of the growing influence of Indian secretaries with robust nationalist leanings. In theory, the YMCA's International Committees had pursued an indigenization strategy from the outset; however, it was mainly during and after the Great War that South Asians actually rose to positions of prominence and power in the Indian YMCA. Some of them, like K. T. Paul (1876–1931) and S. K. Datta (1878–1927), who served as the first Indian general secretaries between 1916 and 1927, had connections both to the Gandhi-led INC and to the broad array of Indian social service organizations that mushroomed in the political ferment of the 1910s and 1920s (discussed above).[206] It is difficult to assess the extent to which they were acting independently as the Indian Y continued to rely on American money, know-how and manpower under their leadership. Even in-house historian M. D. David, who generally paints a rather euphemistic picture of 'race relations' in the Indian

YMCA, admits that 'the YMCA's indigenization was only partial' during the interwar years, as the new Indian leaders 'were dependent on contributions from the YMCA bodies in the West'.[207] There is evidence that this tension frequently led to conflicts and internal power struggles. One of the most direct references to such problems is provided by Edgar M. Robinson (1867–1951), the Boys' Work Secretary of the YMCA's International Committee in New York. He had inspected the Association's South Asian branches in early 1921 and candidly described the relationship of the American ex-General Secretary E. C. Carter, who served between 1902 and 1916 and remained influential for years afterwards, with his Indian successors:

> Carter is an autocrat. He 'breaks' any man he cannot dominate. He carried the National Council in his pocket. He does not believe in or develop democracy or local autonomy. He trained K.T. Paul to see things as he did. The Council by its appropriations keeps the Indian secretaries in a state of submission. They know the hand that feeds them. They listen for the central voice rather than do their own thinking.[208]

The extent to which Robinson's somewhat impressionistic account – he spent less than two months in India and Ceylon over February and March 1921 – adequately describes the complex interaction between North American and Indian Y secretaries is hard to assess. However, as we shall presently see, other evidence would seem to suggest that figures like K. T. Paul and S. K. Datta were too charismatic and independent to be 'broken' or dominated by their American colleagues and that they also did not refrain from articulating unpleasant truths. Nonetheless, it is safe to assume that Robinson's observations capture some of the tensions and controversy involved in the everyday collaboration between North American and South Asian YMCA workers. Unsurprisingly, this facet is mostly elided in the self-congratulatory in-house reports that claimed that the Association was an epitome of exemplary racial equality and successful collaboration with 'native leaders'.

Although it is unclear how much room the emerging Indian leadership had to manoeuvre during the interwar period, there can also be no doubt that their influence and efforts among urban students considerably broadened the Association's reach in the subcontinent. It certainly helped that this turn to 'practical Christianity' in the South Asian mission converged with the broader shift 'from evangelism to general service' that occurred in the North American Y over the interwar period.[209] This trend led some influential American and European YMCA secretaries in India to follow the example of Indian secretaries such as K. T. Paul and Daniel Swamidoss, who preached and practised a more intense engagement with less privileged sections of the population in big cities as well as in rural areas, especially through their newly devised 'industrial work' and 'rural reconstruction' schemes (see Figure 1.3).[210]

The sudden emphasis on 'hands-on' programmes in the 1920s suggests the dwindling importance of religious conversion and a considerable growth of the organization's agenda in the seemingly more secular realm of constructive social work and community development. By the end of the decade, this change led to a crisis

Figure 1.3 'Practical Christianity' with a 'hands-on' approach: Rural secretary Daniel Swamidoss at work in a vegetable garden at one of the YMCA's new agricultural demonstration centres (1919). Courtesy Springfield College Archives, Special Collections (Digital Collection LA-NT 08-03).

of identity, reflected in several heated exchanges in the pages of the *Young Men of India*. The first bone of contention was the 'foreign' character of the YMCA and the question of whether or not it ought to be completely indigenized. There were even more controversial topics, which cut down to the identity of the group itself:

> A second challenge which is brought to the Association … is this: *It does not yet seem to know its own mind. Is it an Evangelistic Agency, or an Organization for Social Service? Is it both?* … When the Y.M.C.A. first came to India, it was obviously an 'evangelistic agency' in that sense. But to-day, within the Association there are divergent attitudes with regards to this policy. The majority of its Secretaries are not engaging to any large extent in 'evangelistic activities' of this type. The change has come gradually, but has been far-reaching; it has won for the Indian Y.M.C.A. much support which would not have been forthcoming in an 'evangelistic agency'; but it has distressed some of its old friends (emphasis added).[211]

At any rate, this new 'social' outlook potentially entailed encroaching upon the territory already occupied by colonial officials, Indian nationalists and social reformers. The concrete ways in which the Y nonetheless intensified its 'secular' agenda, and how various sides reacted to these programmes, will be the focus of subsequent chapters.

The political allegiance of the Protestant lay organization was also affected by its general reorientation. By the early 1920s, some of the Indian YMCA leaders started to openly show their sympathies for the Gandhi-led INC and other currents of the national movement. Even some Western Y representatives showed their solidarity with the anticolonial cause. An American Boy's work specialist, for instance, declared in 1921 that Gandhi's 'appeal to the unselfish and the spiritual' made 'Indian boys and young men by the tens of thousands rise up and follow … [the] call'.[212] He concluded that Gandhi's methods and rhetoric could therefore serve as models for the YMCA itself.

This strong inclination to emphasize social rather than religious work along with the new tolerance of Indian nationalist agendas occasionally resulted in concrete collaborations with Indian activists who advocated for a constructive nationalism. The most spectacular such case was the Association's collaboration with the Servants of India Society in the aftermath of the so-called Mappila Rebellion in the autumn of 1921. The Mappilas (or 'Moplahs' in contemporaneous administrative terminology) were a plebeian agrarian Muslim community in the Southern Indian region of Malabar. They had been mobilized in the early phase of the Khilafat Campaign (1919–24) to the point of attacking both representatives and symbols of the colonial regime. Before long, their aggression was also directed at the prosperous Hindu landlords and moneylenders who controlled or exploited many of them.[213] Dozens of people were killed in the ensuing riots and according to sensationalist press reports, riots, rape and ruin were the order of the day in the short-lived millenarian Islamic kingdom established by the Mappila leaders.[214] Allegedly, hundreds of Hindus were also forcibly converted to Islam in the aftermath of the uprising. By October 1921, thousands of Hindu families fled their villages and lived in refugee camps, often under appalling conditions.

The Mappila emergency not only ended the short-lived harmony between the Muslim League and the INC, it also became a showcase for the social service organizations and activists flourishing amidst the various currents of Indian nationalism. The Arya Samaj, for instance, sent several *updeśak*s (missionaries) to Malabar in October 1921. Their primary aim was not humanitarian relief but rather the launching of a reconversion campaign. They used the novel instrument of *śuddhi* (purification) to reclaim the forcibly converted back into the Hindu fold: this was a practice that had originally been developed by the Samaj for 'untouchable uplift' (i.e. the admission of Dalits to the Hindu community) and was unheard of in Brahmanical Hinduism.[215] Similar goals were pursued by the more conservative HMS, which was almost defunct by 1920. Its spokesmen B. S. Moonje (1872–1948) and M. M. Malaviya (1861–1946) tried to exploit the Mappila riots to launch its comeback by evoking the scenario of a Hindu community under siege by Muslims.[216] As a matter of course, the ostensibly Hindu-oriented and at times even openly anti-Christian Samaj and HMS were out of the question as potential allies of the YMCA. However, the more moderate and secular Servants of India Society sent a small delegation to the region for relief work in the refugee camps, and it was this group that was selected by several YMCA workers to form a joint 'Malabar Central Relief Committee'.[217] The Association members involved in this joint venture were afraid of criticism along the lines 'that an idle mob was being bred on public charity', and hence implemented the 'working principle that no able-bodied man or woman is given food if he or she does not show work in return'.[218] In terms of their practical contribution to the relief work, it is noteworthy that, besides the implementation of a strict hygiene regime in the 'concentration camps' that were opened for refugees around Calicut,[219] the YMCA focused on its areas of strength and concentrated its activities on recreational schemes for the riot-affected communities living there.[220] A contemporary report published by the Servants of India Society describes the YMCA's contribution to the relief work as a splendid success:

> In the evenings, pleasant entertainments were arranged in the camps with gramaphone [sic] and magic lanterns by the Y.M.C.A. and by demonstrators of the Agricultural Department who showed on the screen several interesting processes of cultivation of new and profitable crops. Gentlemen like H. A. Popley of the Y.M.C.A. cheered the hearts of the people in the camps by occasional musical entertainments. In December a sports competition was held for the refugee boys in which the youngsters took very great delight. Distinguished visitors like … Dr. Annie Besant, Bishop Whitehead … Messrs. K.T. Paul, and C.F. Andrews, to mention just a few, visited the camps and their presence cheered up not a little the gloomy and despondent hearts of the people there.[221]

After the end of the actual relief operation, the YMCA continued its work in Ariakode, a small station about 30 miles (50 kilometres) from Calicut, where workers established a rural reconstruction centre in the former headquarters of the rebels.[222] Seeking to achieve their goal of 'training up the boys and young men of to-day into a nobler type of manhood', the YMCA workers continued a close collaboration with the Servants of India for several years.[223]

This cooperation with one of the best-known and publicly visible 'patriotic' Indian volunteer organizations was certainly not a coincidence. The internal correspondence of American YMCA workers is full of references to Indian philanthropic groups with which the secretaries compared their Association, and an internal survey conducted in 1932–3[224] provided a list of eleven Indian organizations engaged 'in activities similar to those of the Y.M.C.A.'.[225] This list featured, amongst others, the Arya Samaj, the Ramakrishna Mission, the Servants of India Society and even the Young Men's Indian Association founded by Theosophist leader Annie Besant.[226] This clearly shows that the North American Y secretaries saw themselves as competing with local social service organizations with nationalist or communalist leanings.

As stated above, leading Indian YMCA secretaries like S. K. Datta, V. S. Azariah and, especially, K. T. Paul were conspicuous as particularly vocal supporters of a 'Christian nationalism' in India despite the institutional and financial constraints within which they operated.[227] Not surprisingly, their statements on these lines alienated quite a few British Association members, and the old tensions between British and American approaches towards Y work in India quickly resurfaced in the ensuing controversy. This was particularly true whenever YMCA fora were used to openly criticize the colonial regime. For example, a speech by S. K. Datta on 'India and Racial Relationship' at the

Lahore YMCA in 1924 that castigated the existence of widespread racism throughout the British Empire provoked divided reactions. Whilst it was well received by liberal US secretaries, most British officials found it offensive.[228]

The new critical attitude if many North American Y workers vis-à-vis British imperialism also reflected a profound shift in the general political climate in the United States, where the Indian case was pushed by a small lobby of Irish and South Asian expatriates and discussed sympathetically in the US Congress as well as in the American labour movement.[229] This trend was further reinforced by the massive media coverage of Gandhi's Civil Disobedience campaign of the early 1930s, which increased the number of sympathizers of Indian nationalism in the United States.[230] The impact was perhaps the strongest within the African American community, wherein the Mahatma's famous Salt March fuelled an interest in the methods of passive resistance, and Gandhi himself was viewed as a 'second Moses' who would 'lead all of the darker races from the wilderness of bondage into the light of freedom'.[231]

Even before this wave of solidarity with the nationalist cause swept over the United States, many British residents of India, including YMCA members, had started to criticize the Association's heavy reliance on American funding. According to M. D. David, about 45 per cent of the Indian National Council's budget was covered by American subsidies in the mid-1920s.[232] Ironically, the dependence on American money grew further after numerous European businessmen in India 'stopped contributing ... – because they did not appreciate [the YMCA's] nationalist leanings'.[233] Simultaneously, more religiously minded European members lamented that a once-respectable Christian institution was not only becoming increasingly secularized but was apparently also under the influence of 'an insidious type of agitation'.[234]

As early as 1923, *The Englishman*, a newspaper widely read among the British expats in the Indian subcontinent, launched a frontal attack on the extra-religious activities of the Indian Y and its alleged political stance:

> In India the movement is following a line which must sooner or later lead into antagonism with the very community upon which it relies for funds. The reading rooms and lecture halls designed for the study of the Scriptures and for such teaching as would turn the young men professing Christianity into useful citizens, are now employed for the dissemination of political views ... borrowed not from divines, but from persons who deny a divinity. We do not, of course, assert that the Y.M.C.A. organization in India has been captured by the Bolsheviks, but it is in great danger of being captured by a party which is not very friendly towards the continuance of British rule in India and which in any case seems to be determined to champion the extreme claims of Labour against the Capitalist.[235]

The latter reproach was mainly referring to the controversial speech given by none other than the YMCA secretary George Sherwood Eddy at the Calcutta Rotary Club in 1923. Due to his decades-long relationships with Asian church leaders, nationalists and intellectuals, and his engagement with leftist US theologians like Roland Niebuhr, a great admirer of Gandhi,[236] Eddy transformed from a zealous Protestant crusader to a Christian socialist, advocating a liberal 'anti-imperialism for Jesus' line after the end of the Great War.[237] In his speech at the Rotary Club he denounced, amongst other things, the exploitative practices in Bombay's cotton mills.[238] Much like Eddy, K. J. Saunders, another prominent YMCA veteran who had spent a decade in India as a secretary in the Literary Department (1912–21), was also attacked by members of the conservative European Association within the pages of *The Englishman*. Saunders, who was introduced to the newspaper's readers as 'a distinguished American scholar', had lectured on 'The International Mind' at the Rotary Club. The article summarizes the gist of his talk in rather caustic words:

> Professor Saunders began by stating that he was a Canadian, educated at the Berkeley University, California, and from dwelling on the beauties of brotherly love he expressed the deep sympathy of a bleeding heart for the downtrodden Indian in his struggle for freedom. … [We] eventually made him confess that he was a funk-hole Christian of the Y.M.C.A.[239]

The situation was somewhat defused when S. K. Datta, the General Secretary of the Indian YMCA at the time, explained in a rejoinder that Saunders, far from being an American or Canadian 'funk-hole Christian', was actually a South Africa born and Cambridge-trained British citizen who had done patriotic service during the war.[240] However, speculations that the Indian Y had become a platform for people who were 'not only anti-British, but actually Bolshevist in aims and ideals' resurfaced after an incident dubbed 'the Bombay Y.M.C.A. sensation' by the British press.[241] For the better part of 1927, when official distrust of the Indian YMCA was at its peak, Philipp Spratt, a British Communist and Cambridge graduate, stayed in the hostel of the Bombay YMCA. Spratt, who is today mostly remembered as one of three British defendants in the notorious *Meerut Conspiracy* case,[242] had been sent to India by the Comintern to help build revolutionary networks in the subcontinent.[243] The Criminal Investigation Department (CID) raided the hostel in September 1927 and Spratt was arrested for sedition. Even though a search for incriminatory material in Spratt's hostel room was unsuccessful and he was highly unlikely to have spread his propaganda in Y circles, the Bombay YMCA branch was declared to be 'out of bounds' for British troops for months afterwards.[244] Given the long history of cooperation between the YMCA and the British Indian Army, this was a fairly drastic measure clearly showing how deep the fissures between the imperial establishment and the Association had become. The YMCA itself was now perceived by many as having been hijacked by a coalition of American leftists and Indian nationalist firebrands. Although an official enquiry committee acquitted the Indian YMCA of most charges, General Secretary S. K. Datta had to admit 'that in certain cases mistakes, though very few in number, ha[d] occurred'. After these developments, the YMCA's relations with the colonial establishment were never as friendly and unencumbered as during the Great War.[245] Unimpressed by the growing official distrust, some American Y workers continued to condemn the 'methods of irresponsible violence on the part of Government agents',[246] while others extolled the empowerment of women through the 'Gandhi movement'.[247] Still others openly celebrated the intensification of the nationalist campaign in the 1930s as an 'hour of opportunity' for the YMCA and its agenda, observing that[248]

India has perhaps the greatest claim in the world today for American help. ... The association should be at the forefront of analyzing the present and growing needs along the lines of citizenship-training, training in inter-national [sic] thinking and relationships ... a new leadership is being born and India is one [sic] the move. ... It is the association's hour of opportunity. ... The crest of the tide is coming soon. Are we ready?[249]

Although the Second World War brought about a short-lived revival of official collaboration with the colonial government through the YMCA's 'war work',[250] the political shift was more or less complete by the early 1940s. The message in a strategy paper on the YMCA's post-war policy that the Association's 'primary concern [was] for the human element rather than forms and systems' was an oblique way of stating that the Y's loyalty support would henceforth be with the future Indian national leaders and no longer with the imperial government.[251] The promised development aid 'along the lines of citizenship training and international thinking' was closely linked to the social service programmes and developed by the YMCA, because of which we must zoom in next on the role of the Association's philanthropic and humanitarian activities, particularly its 'army work', which aimed to train better civilians who were fully prepared for political participation.

Summing up

The purpose of this chapter has been twofold. The first section illustrated that the North American YMCA secretaries, who are the protagonists of the following chapters, did not operate in vacuum. Their modernizing programme inserted itself into a complex landscape rife with similar endeavours that were either already in progress or emerging alongside the Y's activities. The second section highlighted how the American-led branches of the Association felt the pulse of Indian society especially when experiencing the evolution of the anticolonial national movement and social reform agendas, and how they took advantage of the available opportunity to promise a blueprint for a different, more inclusive and egalitarian, modernity than the one embodied and propagated by the colonizers. The skilful use of print, audio and visual media played a momentous role here. Simultaneously, North American-led Associations also deftly employed the politics of making space and meaning through architecture in an attempt to exhibit their muscular Christian project in public urban spaces. Finally, the shift of the YMCA towards the Indian national movement that appeared after the end of the First World War created significant tensions with the colonial government. This change was made possible not only because of young American missionaries with liberal worldviews but also as a result of the pressure from 'native' YMCA members in South Asia, who were active agents in the process of 'secularizing' and 'nationalizing' the Association's activities rather than passive receptacles of practices and ideas from their American supervisors.

2

'Make them pure, fit and brotherly!': The Indian YMCA's welfare work for railwaymen and soldiers (c. 1904–1945)

John R. Mott, president of the World Alliance of YMCAs, toured India in early 1929. In various welcome speeches and dinner receptions organized by the Indian branch of the YMCA and frequented by the upper strata of Europeans and Indians, the future awardee of the Nobel Peace Prize from New York was repeatedly reminded of what was still regarded as the YMCA's greatest contribution to the public good in the Indian subcontinent: its 'army work' during and immediately after the First World War. At a reception in Calcutta, for instance, the editor of the important English-language daily *The Statesman* explained to Mott: 'If today we hear how the type of soldier has changed and how the soldier is a clean living athletic man who reads and thinks and is a credit to the country he serves, it is because of the work the YMCA did in his camp and barracks.'[1] Even outspoken critics of the Indian Y like the conservative British administrator Harry Hobbs, who – as we have seen in the previous chapter – suspected that the American-dominated Christian Association on the subcontinent had been infiltrated by Bolshevists, acknowledged its remarkable achievements during the Great War.[2]

This little vignette confirms the findings of an official survey on the activities of the Indian YMCA published a few years later. According to this report, the multifarious services offered by the Protestant lay organization during the war years 'greatly increased the prestige of the whole movement in the eyes of the general public and tended to give it the character of an agency for community service'.[3] At the same time, the emphasis on the transformation of the soldier into 'a clean living athletic man who reads and thinks' that was ostensibly achieved by the YMCA's army work would seem to suggest that the goals of this programme were much more ambitious than simply providing caregiving and entertainment for war-weary troops.

What, then, did the Y's 'war work' schemes mean for the Christian Association itself, for the British Empire and for the British and South Asian rank-and-file soldiers at the receiving end? This chapter addresses the Association's philanthropic activities primarily by studying its most visible contribution in this department. It takes stock of the wide spectrum of the Y's army work during the Great War and its immediate aftermath. After providing a brief sketch of the Indian YMCA's first systematic philanthropic campaign targeted at European and Eurasian railwaymen, the chapter analyses programmes developed for British troops stationed in India and for South Asian sepoys[4] deployed overseas from 1914 onwards. This analysis is followed by a discussion of the wider political and social impact of the YMCA's war work schemes, which explores the role played by the YMCA's religious agenda in its wartime activities and examines the extent to which pre-existing racial and cultural stereotypes influenced its services for European and South Asian soldiers.

The chapter contributes to several broader historiographical debates. For one, it adds to a line of research that has recently regained prominence due to the centenary of the Great War. Over the past decade, there have been a number of attempts to write a truly global history of the First World War with a focus beyond Europe.[5] Additionally, the case study enriches the growing field of the history of humanitarianism. Although most activities included in the Indian Y's war scheme would probably not be considered 'humanitarian' by the somewhat narrow definitions prevalent today, there was definitely some overlap. More importantly, observers and historical actors of the time themselves often referred to the organization's charitable aid schemes as 'humanitarian work'. In fact, following Abigail Greene's appeal to rid the historiography of humanitarianism from its presentism and include a greater variety of organizations and individuals within its scope,[6] I would argue that the case study presented in this chapter is instructive and gives us a better understanding of the broader transnational history of caregiving, philanthropy and humanitarianism in the early twentieth century.[7]

Towards war work: Early philanthropic efforts (1890–1914)

Given the Association's emphasis on 'democratization' and outreach to the South Asian populace, it is remarkable that the YMCA's first major philanthropic campaigns were developed with a view to 'save' or 'uplift' two segments of the British India's 'European' population that both imperial administrators and Christian missionaries usually regarded as disquieting – namely, railwaymen and soldiers.

Recent scholarship has discussed how the 'Tommies' serving in British India as well as European and Eurasian railwaymen were groups who could potentially undermine imperial claims to civilizational superiority through their plebeian status and notoriously 'unruly' behaviour.[8] As a result, both groups frequently became the targets of various 'internal civilizing missions' designed to bring them into the fold of white respectability from the early nineteenth century onwards.[9] Many missionaries were likewise concerned that the Europeans from the lower social orders would 'leave his religion behind him at Aden' as the imperial pun had it.[10] In fact, a leading American YMCA secretary writing in 1912 warned:

> The life of most of these men is a hindrance to the progress of Christian faith and morals among the Hindus, who regard all Westerners as Christians. Among

these, they see with bewilderment and scorn, drunkenness, profanity, gambling and immorality abound.[11]

The prevalence of such views was the major reason why railway workers became the target of the YMCA's first organized philanthropic programme in South Asia. And this programme, in turn, was part of the Association's broader strategy to curry favour with the imperial government. Although the YMCA's protracted railway work scheme was initially largely paid for by voluntary contributions from donors in the United States and Canada and essentially modelled on existing schemes in North America and Mexico,[12] it fit perfectly into the agenda of imperial self-civilizing efforts. This was not least because it was predicated on a number of British prejudices regarding the character of 'low Europeans' in colonial settings, as the above quote also indicates. It was likewise based on shared assumptions about the effects of the Indian climate and the exposure to 'native culture'.[13] Thus, F. J. Michel, the expert 'secretary' recruited in Kentucky by the Indian YMCA in 1904 to investigate the possibility of a special Railway Department in the subcontinent, was only replicating well-established colonial stereotypes in his report. Much like colonial officials, he diagnosed 'marked weaknesses among a large class of [European and Eurasian] railway servants' when it came to 'purity, honesty and high idealism'. He also subscribed to the well-worn imperial explanation for the 'degeneration' of the white working classes in India, observing that a long-term exposure to Indian climes 'encourages apathy and eliminates push and energy' and adding that exposure to the native bazars (where many of the poorly paid railway employees found cheap accommodation) was outright dangerous as the 'effect of such an environment is inevitably degrading'.[14] In the eyes of Michel and other Y secretaries, the environmental and cultural specificities of South Asian railway colonies only aggravated what they saw as the more general predilections of European railway men as a class. Most of them, it was believed, showed complete 'indifference ... to all except the grosser physical needs' and had a natural 'predisposition to irreligion, and consequent licentiousness, unfaithfulness to duty and other vices'.[15]

This sombre diagnosis notwithstanding, Michel introduced an important argument (and a metaphor) with regard to the YMCA's army work that would constantly resurface in the years to come. He pointed to the 'open door of opportunity' that the problems of the white subalterns working for the railways purportedly created, declaring that the Y alone would be able to handle the situation and thus become an indispensable partner of the colonial authorities:

> With its experience, and with its wise leadership of eminent professional and business men ... and energized by spirit of philanthropy and altruism more liberal and at the same time more exacting than perhaps any other organization, the Association is in a position to cope with these problems in a way which must bring ultimate success.[16]

The philanthropic 'railway work' thus promised to support the YMCA's mission in South Asia in important ways. For one, it would discipline plebeian elements of 'white' society in British India, aligning their behaviour with what was seen as 'proper

Christian conduct'. This was considered an essential goal, not only for its own sake but also because these elements allegedly endangered the credibility of proselytization efforts targeted at the indigenous population through their 'uncivilized' behaviour. Simultaneously, and equally importantly, this work also demonstrated the usefulness of the US-dominated Association's work to the imperial government, thus potentially opening up new sources of funding.

Considering the frequent tensions between the American Y missionaries and the colonial government discussed above, the significance of this collaborative manoeuvre can hardly be overemphasized, especially as the envisaged 'public–private partnership' did indeed materialize. The most important outcome of this joint venture was the takeover of the Railway Institute in Jamalpur by the YMCA in order to set up a recreational centre specifically for railway men.[17] Jamalpur is a small town in central Bihar that is regarded by historians as 'the quintessential Railway colony' of the Raj.[18] As one of India's most important railway junctions and home of the subcontinent's largest locomotive workshops, it had a significant population of low-class Europeans and Eurasians.[19] Importantly, the desired 'improvement in the physical, mental and moral tone of the employé'[20] was to be achieved by the Railway YMCA in Jamalpur by essentially the same means that were later used for European soldiers, as will be examined in greater detail in sections that follow. However, what was perhaps most unique about the Y's Railway work and hence deserves to be emphasized is that the YMCA workers thought it crucial to reinforce the existing racialized spatial segregation. In Jamalpur, fewer than 1,000 Europeans and Eurasians lived and worked in very close proximity to more than 16,000 Indians.[21] As railway secretary Michel's reports reveal, the activities in the YMCA-led Railway Institute were designed in part to keep the two communities separate so as to prevent the further 'moral degradation' of the former group. The 'presence of native women of ill-repute' in the Indian bazar, for instance, was considered as a particularly dangerous threat, potentially able to destroy 'the best that there is in [white] men'.[22]

Many of these motives also underlay the YMCA's desire 'to help the young men of the army units to remain loyal to the moral standards that had been part of their upbringing in the United Kingdom'.[23] This concern eventually led to the commencement of the Indian YMCA's army work scheme a mere year after the Christian Association took over the management of the Railway Institute in Jamalpur. The leadership of the Indian YMCA undertook its first small-scale pilot programmes among European regiments stationed in Madras and Bangalore (now Bengaluru) in response to the requests of high-ranking British officers.[24] After the Y secretary Joseph C. Callan (an Englishman on the payroll of the Association's International Committee in New York)[25] demonstrated successfully that British soldiers were receptive to the Association's message of temperance, purity and 'healthy recreation', the National Council of the Indian YMCA decided in 1907 to set up a special 'Army Department'.[26] The following years saw the establishment of full-fledged YMCA army centres in three of South Asia's major garrison towns, such as Bangalore, Poona and Maymyo (in British Burma), as well as the launching of annual 'Army Camps'. These centres also provided 'counter-attractions' to the perceived temptations of life in the cantonments through a range of educational and spiritual activities, and offered games and athletic events to improve soldiers' health and fitness.²⁷ Predictably, the new programme was generously supported by the British-Indian Government, whose representatives welcomed the Y's offer to care for the moral and physical well-being of the 70,000-plus British troops stationed in South Asia. As a symbolic expression of his gratitude for the YMCA's imperial service, Lord Hardinge, the British Viceroy, personally laid the cornerstone for a new army centre in Bangalore in November 1913.²⁸ However, with only three permanent centres that catered exclusively to European regiments, the Y's Army Department was only just beginning to find its footing. The outbreak of the First World War would, however, change the situation dramatically, and by the summer of 1915, the work of the fledgling new department would be considered seminal to the imperial war effort.

Entertainment, caregiving and 'intercultural training': The Association's service on the home front

That the Great War had a massive influence not only on the army work scheme but also on the Indian YMCA in general is evident from even a cursory glance at a few figures. The number of YMCA army centres for British troops in India increased from three to seventeen just three months after the outbreak of hostilities in Europe.²⁹ By the armistice in late 1918, there were fifty-six centres for British regiments, not counting over two dozen headquarters and huts catering exclusively to Indian soldiers were also established in the meantime.³⁰ Throughout the war, 412 men and women, many of them full-time paid workers, were engaged in YMCA army work on the subcontinent.³¹ The impact of the war on the Christian Association's finances was even more spectacular. In 1914, the Indian Y had a rather modest budget of Indian Rs 63,925. Owing to public subscriptions, donations from foreign YMCAs³² and official grants from the provincial governments as well as the central government of India, its budget grew more than thirtyfold to a staggering Rs 2,006,835 five years later.³³ According to Earl Ronaldshay, the Governor of Bengal, the wealthy citizens of Calcutta alone donated Rs 200,000 for the organization's war work during a single fundraising event in 1916.³⁴

The sudden influx of money and volunteers triggered by the general wave of solidarity with the imperial war effort that swept over India,³⁵ the British Empire and the United States after 1914 aroused great expectations in some of the YMCA secretaries working in the subcontinent. Before their efforts started, General Secretary E. C. Carter appealed to his fellow workers saying that 'if we … undertake really first class work on a national scale, it is not unlikely that we will be able to secure eventually substantial financial help from Government sources'.³⁶ Writing to the head of the Association's booming Army Department in January 1915, Y secretary S. S. Day likewise celebrated the war for creating 'unparalleled opportunities' to further the organization's broader proselytizing mission.³⁷ In a similar vein, the 1914 annual report of the YMCA's Ceylon branch began with the observation that 'never in the history of the world, during a great war has the same emphasis been placed on fitness as at present'. Its author somewhat cynically concluded that the 'year 1914 marked a great advance throughout the world' of the YMCA's core ideals of fitness and 'all-around manhood'.³⁸ Three years later, in 1917, the feverish excitement was still palpable when American Secretary D. F. McClelland admitted in his report on the Association's progress in Madras: 'I find it difficult to express the magnitude of the opportunity that opens up before us', while also indulging in visions of 'more time, more money, more power, more workers'.³⁹ At the same time, self-laudatory statements to the effect that the organization played an 'almost indispensable' role in the imperial war effort and that the Indian Y's humanitarian intervention 'had met with continued success and public favour' over the previous three years were already being coupled with expressions of anxiety about the predictable loss of money and manpower in a post-war scenario.⁴⁰ These anxieties were, indeed, not entirely unfounded: The YMCA suffered tremendously from the sudden withdrawal of financial support and concessions to sell food and drinks to troops in the wake of the armistice, especially in Mesopotamia and France.⁴¹

With its dramatically increased resources, the Indian Y's war work in the subcontinent supported the empire in a variety of ways. By 1919, no less than twenty-eight army huts had been erected to cater to Indian soldiers, offering the same blend of entertainment, sports and educational programmes that was characteristic of its 'sepoy work' overseas, which will be discussed in greater detail in the next section. Alongside this, YMCA representatives were also heavily involved in 'war hospitals' and 'convalescent depots' that had been set up in several Indian cities. In Bombay, the most important centre, the organization's hospitals work was done partly in cooperation with the British Red Cross and Indian St. John Ambulance.⁴² This work consisted mainly of letter-writing for the invalid or illiterate, and organizing entertainments for the British and Indian sick and wounded from fronts in Mesopotamia and East Africa.⁴³ The YMCA's caregiving work was supported by its sister organization YWCA, which trained nurses and offered first-aid courses to young Indian women.⁴⁴ Another task the Association's secretaries volunteered for was the care of prisoners of war (POWs) and so-called enemy aliens. This endeavour was made possible in part because, shortly after the outbreak of war, a huge detainment camp was set up in Ahmednagar, Central India.⁴⁵ It mainly housed combatant POWs from German East Africa, and also the German and Austrian civilians who had been arrested and interned in 1914. Throughout the war, the YMCA secretaries supplied detainees with books and journals, extra food, and little gifts, or organized theatre plays and sports competitions in the camp (Figure 2.1).⁴⁶

However, the bulk of the Y's work in South Asia was targeted at the so-called Territorials or 'Terriers'. The Territorial regiments were manned by volunteers from all over Britain who had only received a very short military training.⁴⁷ In October 1914, a batch of 30,000 'Terriers' arrived in Bombay to replace the regular British troops stationed in India, who had been sent to the battlefields in Europe, East Africa and the Middle East. Thousands more would follow over the next three years. The newly created YMCA army centres as well as the established Y headquarters in the seaports and garrison towns offered the men the usual conveniences of libraries, table games, writing materials, snack bars, concerts, cinema shows, theatrical performances, lantern lectures, musical entertainment and sports facilities.⁴⁸ They appear to have been very

Figure 2.1 A British YMCA poster advertising its newly opened army centres in India (c. 1915). Courtesy Hoover Institution Archives, Stanford, CA.

popular with the newly arrived troops. An American graduate of the YMCA training college at Springfield who visited India in 1916 even reported that the 'soldiers look upon the sign of the Red Triangle as a veritable God-send'.[49]

In the eyes of the YMCA leadership, the war presented a unique chance to demonstrate that the British Army could 'become not only a magnificent fighting machine, but a great factor in national education' and in citizenship training.[50] The Terriers, in particular, were ideal targets for the Association's 'bio-moral-spiritual-uplift' programme. Significantly, the secretaries' image of freshly arrived 'amateur soldiers' differed from that of the 'hardened Tommy' who had already served in India for years. Echoing the discourse on European railwaymen from before the war, the latter was seen as particularly prone to debauchery, racism and violence. Implicitly or explicitly, such tendencies were attributed to the rank-and-file soldiers' working-class backgrounds and the supposedly related lack of education and 'civilized' manners. The Terriers, by contrast, were often white-collar workers or students in civil life, perceived as a 'fine friendly lot'.[51] According to Y functionaries, they 'represented, better than the regular Army, a wide average of the English nation' and also tended to be more receptive to the Association's moral and spiritual message.[52] Whereas the work with 'regular Tommies' was largely restricted to the customary provision of comforts and attempts at minimizing 'the soldiers' temptations … to drunkenness and immorality',[53] schemes for Terriers were far more ambitious. In the latter case, the YMCA played a go-between, a mediator between two very different cultures, embarking on a mission with clear political overtones:

> It is desirable that India see the best side of English life. It is equally important that these thousands of men see the best side of Indian life, and that they gain an adequate conception of the greatness of India in religion, in art, and in commerce. What would it not mean from the point of view of racial, political and religious problems … for large numbers of the Territorials to become intimately acquainted with some of the finest Indian gentlemen in the different Indian cities?[54]

The unmistakable objective of the YMCA's efforts thus was to prepare for a peaceful post-war order by educating an influential 'lobby group'. The hope was that members of this group would embrace a role model of masculinity that was less rough and aggressive than the 'warrior-as-hero' ideal that prevailed in the British Army throughout the first half of the twentieth century.[55] At the same time, they could be sympathetic towards South Asian culture(s) and hence more amenable to Indian claims for greater political participation after their return to the UK. In order to achieve this, a comprehensive programme to foster cultural sensitivity in British troops was developed from early 1915 onwards, especially for the newly arrived. The most popular methods for achieving the envisaged intercultural rapprochement consisted of offering language courses (mostly in Hindustani) and organizing lectures by 'educated Indians' for the troops.[56] In their effort 'to interpret to the … [Territorials] the life and needs of the people amongst whom their lot is cast',[57] the Y workers even organized excursions for interested soldiers to sacred spots like the Sikh Golden Temple in Amritsar, the Burning Ghats of the holy town of Benares or Hindu religious festivals like the Allahabad Kumbh Mela (see Figure 2.2).[58]

On the face of it, these developments suggest that the primary goal of the YMCA's army work was to promote racial harmony and religious tolerance. And indeed, the Y publications were quick to declare that 'a new sense of race-brotherhood [wa]s taking the place of the old antagonism and prejudice' in the garrisons and cantonments due to the group's efforts.[59] Sharing this view, the YMCA Secretary Staunchfield reported to his superior that 'one Indian told [him] that "the only soldiers who know how to treat an Indian are the ones who had been in touch with the Army branch Y.M.C.A".[60] Nonetheless, one must bear an important caveat in mind: In spite of the emphasis on cultural sensitivity and broad-mindedness in matters of religion, a subtle but

Figure 2.2 Territorials posing for the cover photo of a YMCA brochure at the most iconic YMCA building in South Asia, namely, the Association's headquarters in Madras (November 1914). Courtesy Yale Divinity College Special Collections.

all-pervading Protestant missionary zeal was discernible in the army work scheme. Guest speakers were almost exclusively Indian Christians, and, for that matter, so were YMCA members recruited as intermediaries and experts on Indian life, culture and religion. Significantly, 'leading Indian Christians' and YMCA secretaries like S. K. Datta and Bishop Azariah were part of this programme.[61] Even K. T. Paul, the YMCA's first Indian General Secretary, contributed by addressing military audiences. In early December 1914, for instance, he gave a series of lectures on 'Indian Social Life' attended by almost 1,000 British Terriers.[62] The fact that Paul actively supported the imperial war effort is especially noteworthy as he later on repeatedly confessed that the experience of the Great War severely shattered his belief in the moral integrity of the British Empire and 'Western civilization' at large.[63] One may well speculate if such tensions or even outright conflicts between Indian and Western YMCA secretaries might have also arisen while the conflict lasted; however, perhaps not surprisingly, they cannot be traced in the available sources.

Other lecture titles like 'What Christ Has Done for India', 'The Work of the YMCA around the World', 'Indian Superstitions' and 'The Outcaste's Hope', as well as the organized tours carrying parties of soldiers to mission stations 'to see with their own eyes what … has been accomplished by missionary enterprise', leave no doubt that the Y secretaries managed to skilfully weave their own designs and ends into the tapestry of their humanitarian mission among imperial troops.[64] Indeed, critical voices raising internal doubt as to 'whether the Army YMCA ha[d] enough to show for its "C"' were reassured that, in spite of its official policy of religious impartiality, the entire war work scheme was designed 'to give expression to the fundamental belief that only by the following of Jesus Christ can the evils of the world in war or peace be overcome.'[65]

At the same time, however, the secretaries of the Indian YMCA remained convinced that their combined work for 'intercultural education', moral guidance and Christian propaganda directed at British troops was 'of enduring value and service for the British Army in India'.[66] By teaching soldiers to respect Indians and their culture, they believed, they would help reduce incidents of provocative displays of cultural and racial arrogance or even acts of interracial violence and thus do 'good service … towards the mitigation of a serious source of Indian discontent'.[67] The war was seen to have already catalysed the 'spirit of unrest and dissatisfaction with existing conditions' among parts of the Indian population,[68] so this work was perceived to be a vital contribution to the stability and longevity of British dominion in South Asia.

Targeting the sepoy: The YMCA triangle on the battlefields of Europe and the Middle East

Let us now shift gears and explore the war work programmes targeted at Indian troops serving overseas.[69] Although this aspect is still often neglected in many standard accounts of the First World War, the *Urkatastrophe* of 1914–18 was an imperial conflict involving more than four million soldiers and workers from Africa and Asia.[70] Whereas the role of the British and American YMCA on various European fronts and in refugee work has been highlighted by a number of recent studies,[71] historians have largely overlooked the activities of these agencies for non-Western soldiers; even the role of the Indian YMCA has been almost completely elided. Even the otherwise excellent recent anthology *The YMCA at War*, focuses largely on the Y's services for European, North American and Australian and New Zealand Army Corps (ANZAC) troops and barely mentions the Indian Y's pioneering work.[72] This omission is all the more regrettable as the Indian YMCA contributed significantly to the British imperial war effort on three continents.

Between 1914 and 1920, the Association served in a total of about 180 different centres in France (12 centres), Mesopotamia (102), East Africa (51) as well as in Egypt, Palestine (10) and a few other places.[73] Almost from the outset, the Indian branch of the ubiquitous Christian organization became intricately enmeshed in the imperial war effort. In fact, the humble pioneering delegation comprising twelve secretaries of the Indian Y that reached Marseille with the first major convoy of Indian troops in early November 1914, even before the Government of India had officially granted permission,[74] were the first YMCA representatives of any country to arrive at a war theatre. The members were a mix of American, British and South Asian secretaries who were carefully selected for their qualifications, with even some of the 'Europeans' having a solid grasp of Punjabi, Hindi or Urdu.[75] According to the famous US journalist Katherine Mayo, it was their success that paved the way for the large-scale engagement of the American YMCA work for US troops after 1917.[76] The delegation to France was headed by the YMCA's army work pioneer Joseph Callan, who proudly reported after a couple of weeks that the YMCA secretaries were already 'well established and recognized' by grateful British officers.[77] The evidence for such official accolades is momentous, as the imperial military had initially articulated strong concerns about whether a Christian missionary body would be accepted by Hindu, Sikh and Muslim soldiers and had imposed a 'strict obligation of silence regarding the propagation of Christianity' on the Y secretaries working with non-Christian troops.[78] Even while accepting Joseph Callan's offer to send a YMCA delegation to France 'to be of assistance to the troops of the Expeditionary From India in various ways', the Commander-in-Chief of the British-Indian Army issued a clear warning that 'there must be no attempt at proselytising among Indian Troops [sic], for the fact of your making even a few converts would have a disastrous effect on the caste status of their comrades on their return to India'.[79] Callan accepted this condition and did his utmost to make a virtue of necessity. In one of his earliest reports back to India in December 1914, he wrote:

> Forbidden to preach, but permitted to serve in the spirit of Jesus. Already, this has caught the imagination of the sepoy. ... It is my firm conviction that when this great Indian Army returns to its innumerable village homes, our service here will have prepared the way in those homes for the Christian missionary.[80]

Like Rouen and Boulogne, Marseille, the main port of arrival for South Asian regiments, was one of the major centres of the Indian YMCA' activities in the European war theatre before they were all finally dissolved in the autumn of 1920 (see Figure 2.3). An 'Indian Club and Hostel' exclusively for South Asian officers was also opened at Paris in 1917.[81] During the five years that the mission in Europe lasted, a total of eighty-three secretaries (forty-nine of whom were Indians) served in recreational centres, 'huts' and hospitals in France, Belgium and Germany.[82] The most popular services demanded by the Indian soldiers in the Y huts were letter-writing facilities (which we will return to) and the free barbershops.[83] The sports events organized by YMCA secretaries – consisting mostly of football, hockey and cricket tournaments but occasionally also including badminton, volleyball, races and 'track-meets' – likewise proved very popular.[84] This was particularly true of the occasional competitions involving 'interracial tournaments'[85] or even mixed-race teams as they allowed the Indian soldiers to momentarily escape the strict racial segregation that otherwise structured their everyday experience.[86]

Unlike in non-Western theatres of war, where the Indian YMCA catered to both European and 'native' regiments, activities in France focused almost exclusively on South Asians.[87] After Indian infantry contingents left France in late 1915, the bulk of its work was targeted at the fighting soldiers of the Punjabi Cavalry regiments serving in Northern France and Belgium.[88] From 1917 onwards, specially calibrated services were also offered to Indian Labour Corps concentrated in the *départements* Somme and Pas-de-Calais in Northern France.[89] The porters (or *coolies*) serving in this auxiliary unit were mostly recruited from among Dalit ('outcaste') groups, 'the aborigines of the Indian jungles'[90] and 'weird looking Nagas from the higher mountains of Assam'.[91] According to the responsible secretaries, the 'coolies' needed to be kept amused with particularly 'simple libraries and ... lantern entertainments'.[92] For this purpose, special

Figure 2.3 Five members of the pioneering first detachment of Indian YMCA secretaries in Rouen, France (1915). Courtesy Cadbury Research Library Special Collections, University of Birmingham, UK.

material in tribal languages 'as far removed as Lushai and Khasi' was produced by the YMCA.[93]

Mesopotamia became the single most important field of service for the organization soon after the first Y secretaries landed there in summer 1915. For more than a year, work was exclusively focused on British troops, before military authorities granted permission to extend it to Indian regiments in late 1916.[94] It was not just the fact that by far the highest numbers of Indian troops and 'coolies' were serving in the land of the two rivers that attracted the attention of the YMCA leadership in India.[95] It was also widely believed that there was a pressing need for philanthropic intervention because of the harsh conditions of warfare prevailing in that region.[96] By the beginning of 1918, seventy-eight secretaries (Americans, Indians, Britons and Canadians) had worked in dozens of different Y headquarters stretching from Basra to Mosul as well as in the more modest 'huts'. As in India, the volunteers were also attached to hospitals for British as well as Indian troops.[97] They would offer their letter-writing services, distribute 'tea, hot Bovril, cigarettes and other comforts' to the patients, and occasionally amuse them by organizing concerts, staging theatre plays, provide for 'bioscope entertainments' or a performance by a party of jugglers imported from the subcontinent.[98] Even the well-being of South Asian POWs living in German camps was taken care of. On the initiative of E. C. Carter from the Indian YMCA, Ceylon tea, curry powder and 'phonograph records from India'[99] were shipped into Germany by the British to raise the spirits of Indian and Nepali POWs who suffered from the flavourless rations dished out by the German military.[100]

The ranks of the secretaries serving in Mesopotamia were initially exclusively filled by 'using British subjects of non-military age'.[101] By 1916, however, when the military authorities decided that the work would be extended to South Asian regiments whose morale had suffered and whose loyalty was regarded as uncertain after the disastrous beginnings of the campaign characterized by poor planning and bad logistics,[102] it became obvious that there were simply not enough men who fitted this description. Consequently, a large number of Americans who had volunteered for war work were accommodated.[103] The British military authorities in Mesopotamia were initially reluctant to do so, insisting that 'precautions against possible espionage and the disclosure of useful military information' be taken.[104] To appease the military leadership, the Government of India eventually developed a special application form asking detailed questions 'connected with the nationality of the parents ... and possible contributions to journals and newspapers'.[105] The information thus collected on the applicants' biographical background ensured that the prospective Y workers had no personal loyalties to or politically motivated sympathies for the Central Powers.[106] This precautionary measure, together with the Indian YMCA's leading functionaries' repeated assurance that only US secretaries 'who are proved to be pro-Ally in their political sympathies' would be selected,[107] eventually eased the concerns raised by the army command. That being said, it is intriguing that the distrust of the British authorities apparently never completely vanished. In October 1917, for instance, the British ambassador in Washington warned the Indian Government about the YMCA missionary Howard Walter from Hartford, CT, who had recently reached Lahore. According to an informer, Walter was 'a pacifist who ha[d] caused considerable embarrassment' and hence required close surveillance.[108]

The rare cases of supposed 'black sheep' notwithstanding, the number of US volunteers arriving in Mesopotamia via India continually grew from early 1917 onwards (see Figure 2.4). The constant stream of American volunteers for army work in the East was not least due to the propaganda efforts of prominent YMCA leaders back in the United States. John Mott, for example, toured American colleges and universities, giving fervent speeches to entice the students to enlist for the Y's humanitarian mission in India and Mesopotamia.[109] He was particularly successful in the most renowned Ivy League institutions, where many young men responded to

Figure 2.4 The Indian YMCA's expanding army work in Mesopotamia in early 1917. The map clearly shows the segregationist logic underlying the scheme. Courtesy Cadbury Research Library Special Collections, University of Birmingham, UK.

his appeal. Thus, the Association opened the 'Princeton Hut' in Baghdad in spring 1917.[110]

The following excerpt from a YMCA pamphlet written in 1918 gives a vivid impression of the imperial logistics required to move not only the men but also tons of material from the port town of Basra to the dozens of its centres that were by then scattered all over Mesopotamia.

> Railway trains, motor cars, motor boats, mule cars, *gufars* (Arab boats), and other local means of transport carry huge supplies both of canteen stores and hut equipment: Letter heads and envelopes at the rate of four lakhs [i.e. Indian Rupees

400,000] a month, gramophones, pianos, folding harmoniums, violins, horns and other instruments, cinemas and films, outdoor and indoor games by the gross, billiard tables, books and magazines, pictures, war-maps, flags and other such impedimenta.[111]

This short passage throws light on not only the complicated logistics but also the nature of the actual services provided to the soldiers. By and large, the Y's offerings for Indian troops deployed in Mesopotamia (or their compatriots serving in Europe or East Africa) were not too different from those designed for the British Terriers in India. However, some features deserve to be underscored when we look specifically at YMCA programmes for the South Asian regiments. First, there is the importance of letter-writing services, which were a key part of Y work for the sepoys due to the high illiteracy rates in 'native regiments'.[112] The fact that the Y secretaries played a pivotal role as mediators between the Indian troops and their families back home over the course of the entire military campaign in France and Mesopotamia (1914–20) is remarkable. This mediatory role was also more generally extended to the realm of presenting 'news from India'. The distribution of newspapers and booklets as well as provision of regular briefings or lectures on current political developments in India (as well as in other war theatres) gave the YMCA a virtual monopoly in that department too.[113]

In light of last chapter's discussion of the Indian Y's propensity to use all available media to reach their target groups, it is perhaps not surprising that army work in both war theatres included intense use of the latest communication and entertainment technologies even in the remotest areas. It is possible that no other element of the YMCA's service was appreciated by the common Indian soldier as much as the daily use of the gramophone. Mostly, shellac records of Indian music were imported from various regions of the subcontinent to cater to the sepoys' preferences. A sentimental fondness for 'native' music united the ethnically diverse South Asian soldiery fighting in the Great War, at least in the perception of Western YMCA secretaries, and allowed them to forget the quotidian hardships of military service 'across the black waters'.[114] One of the secretaries describes the magical effect of a regular 'gramophone concert' in a YMCA tent for Indian troops in France using strong orientalist overtones:

> The gramophone is going and the sound of a common music holds all in its thrall. It is the only time the *sipahi* is voiceless, when he listens, dreamy eyed, to the songs of old Hindustan: and Buta Singh and Muhammad Din [*two typical Sikh and Muslim names, H.F.-T.*], as they sway rhythmically, all unconscious, are far away, back in her gay bazaars or out in her sunny fields ... Great is the power of music, great our debt to him who has made it possible thus to carry to exiles in far lands the songs of home.[115]

A similar effect was achieved by the regular film screenings, widely held within Y circles to be the 'strongest factor to keep men content in camp'.[116] The role of the YMCA's cinemas during the Great War as a momentous means of providing 'morale-boosting entertainment and moral-strengthening guidance' for British soldiers on the Western front has already been highlighted by recent research.[117] That said, scholars have failed to mention that moving picture shows were extremely popular with South Asian troops too.

The majority of the Indian and Nepali soldiers, who were mostly uneducated and hailed almost exclusively from rural areas,[118] came into contact with these technical devices for the first time in their lives. Here too, the YMCA volunteers fulfilled an important function as mediators, introducing Indians from lower social classes to some of the elements of modern everyday (entertainment) technology that had thus far only been available to a minuscule urban elite on the Indian subcontinent. In the three decades following the outbreak of war, films and gramophone records would gradually become mass media, facilitating the smooth flow of political propaganda and transforming the lives and leisure practices of millions of South Asians.[119] It might even be claimed that their acceptance among the rural population was catalysed by the YMCA's war work. The same holds true for magic lantern slideshows. To be sure, Christian missionaries working in the subcontinent had occasionally tested this technology from the late nineteenth century onwards. Lisa Trivedi has argued some time ago that, these limited experiments aside, most rural Indians would not have had a chance to encounter this new entertainment machinery before the Indian National Congress's mass campaigns of the late 1920s and early 1930s;[120] however, this argument ignores the hundreds of thousands of illiterate country-dwellers who had already seen magic lantern slideshows during the war through the army work of the YMCA. As both written and visual sources suggest (see Figure 2.5), much like some of the sports events, the YMCA's illustrated lectures and film exhibitions created micro-heterotopias, as it were, in that they provided a shared space of encounter and recreation that transcended military and racial hierarchies.

These micro-heterotopias indicated the existence of another dimension during this period. Even without the use of technical gadgets, the presence of South Asian secretaries (or, for that matter, Europeans and Americans speaking South Asian languages) was conceived as having a positive influence that could prevent tensions and conflicts arising out of the transcontinental mobility of subaltern soldiers. Many of the Indian servicemen had never travelled except from their village to a garrison town and would have suffered from homesickness or even what we today call a culture shock after arriving in the Middle East or Europe.[121] Prominent YMCA functionary Sherwood Eddy, who toured various theatres of war in 1916–17, elaborates on the significance of 'sepoy work' under these circumstances:

> The [YMCA] hut must stand as the friendly home that gathers up all the best traditions of Indian life. It takes the place of the banyan tree in the heat of the day, the village well and the meeting place for the men in the cool of the evening. Even beyond all hopes it has proved a potent factor for unity, harmony and peace in a time of unrest. It draws the British officers and men closer together, and the Indian secretaries have served time and again as the mediators between the two, who could so easily have misunderstood each other.[122]

This quote is momentous in that it clearly indicates the benefits to the imperial military from the Indian Y's engagement in war work: The Y facilities served as a comfort

Figure 2.5 The front cover illustration of a YMCA brochure published in 1916 shows an open air film projection for Indian and British troops in Mesopotamia. Note the presence of both British and South Asian troops and officers. Courtesy Cadbury Research Library Special Collections, University of Birmingham, UK.

zone of sorts, a buffer softening the hardships of military hierarchy and service in a culturally and climatically alien environment. The secretaries in charge of the overseas 'sepoy work', much like their equivalents in South Asia, were at pains to 'show the best side of Indian life' to the British Terriers, and thus fulfilled a crucial task as mediators or 'cultural brokers'. Overall, the YMCA's wartime work can be understood as a sort of stabilizer, significantly reducing the potential for conflict resulting from overseas military service under extremely difficult conditions (see Figure 2.6).

The fourth and final noteworthy aspect of the war work designed for Indian troops in Mesopotamia and France was its strong emphasis on educational programmes. In France, Marseille became the most important centre where 'a good deal of elementary educational work' was done. A 1920 report by a senior Indian YMCA secretary provides some clues as to the substance of this educational work:[123]

> Many men have been taught to read and write English as well as their own language. Courses in French conversation have been conducted for Indian clerks and others. One very helpful piece of work was a series of lectures given by one of the Y.M.C.A. staff at the request of the Camp medical officers on personal and sex hygiene. The doctors were of opinion that advice and suggestions along this line would be more appreciated by and acceptable to the men when coming from Indian Y.M.C.A. secretaries than from anyone else.[124]

Figure 2.6 The YMCA hut in Amara (Mesopotamia, 1916) as a harmonious space of male comradeship, leisure and cross-cultural encounter. Courtesy Cadbury Research Library Special Collections, University of Birmingham, UK.

It should be noted here that, in addition to the popular language courses,[125] the sepoys could also take classes in history, geography and other subjects.[126]

The last point in the above quote is important, as it highlights yet another way that YMCA secretaries acted as cultural translators between the South Asian soldiers and their British officers. According to military authorities, the Y's Indian volunteers were critical in avoiding cultural clashes, as the sepoys apparently were more amenable to advice concerning the thorny issue of 'sex hygiene' from persons familiar with their own religious and cultural idiosyncrasies. That said, an altruistic concern about the soldiers' health was not the only motive behind the YMCA lectures on sexual hygiene, at least in France. The YMCA workers' anxieties about potential sexual transgressions by British soldiers in India paled into insignificance when compared with the outright panic of *métissage* (miscegenation) involving South Asian sepoys in Europe. Such fears were additionally fanned by the fact that French women were apparently easily available to Indian servicemen near their camps and bases.[127] In two letters to the General Secretary of the Indian Y in Delhi, Joseph Callan expressed his bewilderment regarding the alleged lack of moral restraint among French women:

> On the arrival here of the Sepoy army a strange passion took hold of the women of France. Traditionally they are somewhat loose in morals, but in this crisis they are surpassing all their traditions. They have been literally throwing themselves at the sepoys.[128]

In a letter to a British colleague, Callan conjured up a rather gloomy scenario. If the Indian Corps returned with 'such an idea of the Christian West', he wrote, there would 'scarcely be a village in North India where the missionary will not be hindered in his work'.[129] Shortly afterwards, however, the British Y secretary noted some positive aspects resulting from the prevalence of 'immorality' in and around the camps by connecting his embarrassed observations with the well-worn 'unparalleled opportunities' approach. He highlights how the expertise and services of YMCA men were indispensable for the British military authorities:

> The officers of the Indian Army feel the need of us very deeply. I cannot give you much information as this is sure to be censored. But already the moral problem has become one of grave seriousness. Officers ... have told us that nothing will keep women out of the camps of Indian troops. They will get over any obstacle round a camp. These women are not the professional prostitutes but women of a better class. The officers are face to face with the gravest issues in this matter and have told us they will grant any facility if we can aid them.[130]

In Mesopotamia, too, educational schemes gained momentum by 1917. In the Basra Base Depot, for instance, Indian students from Punjab University in Lahore worked for the YMCA as teachers, engaging their mostly Punjabi-speaking audience through their 'simple popular lectures in the vernacular' on a broad variety of topics. These lectures included hygiene-related presentations such as 'Life, Light and Cleanliness', and 'Health and Sanitation' and also talks relating to self-improvement of a different kind, like 'Booker T. Washington, a Man with a Vision'.[131] The African American reformer and activist Washington was well-known in South Asia at the time. His educational schemes for Black Americans were considered an ideal model for South Asians by some 'progressive' imperial administrators and quite a few Indian social reformers.[132]

In October 1917, Professor J. C. Archer from Yale University arrived in Basra with the aim of professionalizing the Y's didactic mission in the land of two rivers by establishing 'an elaborate educational system of regular classes, popular lectures and Khaki Universities', complete with examinations and diploma.[133] However, it should be emphasized that very few sepoys benefitted from this particular scheme. While a small number of South Asians managed to take advantage of the offerings and learnt to read and write during the war,[134] most educational resources were used for advanced classes and lectures on the history and culture of Mesopotamia or topics like 'How to Recognize the Different Classes of Arabs', tailored to the British soldiers rather than Indian servicemen.[135] Following the logic of racial difference that already undergirded the two-tier system of YMCA huts (discussed later), it was believed that the 'education, outlook, customs, and preferences of the sepoy are so vastly different from those of "Tommy" that special methods of work had to be devised, and all material presented in lectures and classes had to be greatly simplified'.[136] This led, among other things, to a stronger emphasis on visual teaching aids in the courses designed for sepoys and also measures like basic French classes with teaching materials that used Hindustani transliterations of French words as well as writing courses in 'Roman Urdu' (i.e.

Hindustani in Roman script) to increase the literacy rate among the troops (see Figure 2.7).[137]

Such basic educational programmes were seen as beneficial on two planes. On the most obvious level, lectures, classes and educational films (much like sports and entertainment programmes) were seen as a means of keeping 'the sepoys employed for all their leisure time',[138] thus putatively helping Indian servicemen steer clear of the temptations of camp life. As it was considered 'impossible to keep vice out' of the army camps, the YMCA was 'needed as a counter-attraction.'[139] In a 1917 article penned

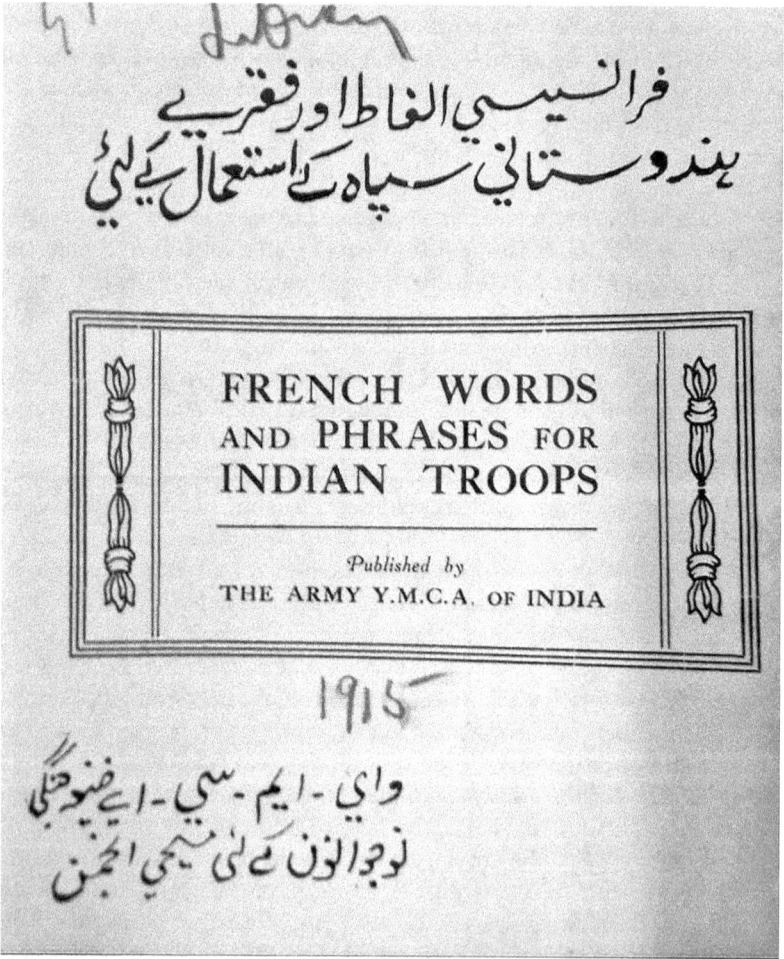

Figure 2.7 Dictionary of French words and phrases in Urdu transliteration (1915) that was distributed to the South Asian troops in France and Belgium and used in conversation classes taught by YMCA secretaries. Courtesy Kautz Family YMCA Archives, University of Minnesota, Minneapolis.

for the Indian Y's mouthpiece *Young Men of India* in 1917, American secretary R. D. Whitehorn provides what is probably the most expressive summary of this argument:

> The suggestion and leadership of a Y.M.C.A. secretary are often what keeps men from acquiescing in boredom which is good for neither man nor beast. The proverb about Satan and the idle hands might have been made by one who knew Army life.[140]

Besides the perceived need 'to keep the men employed and happy',[141] the Y's classes were also believed to have a much deeper effect. Its rudimentary education programme was conceived as a bait of sorts that could potentially affect durable changes inasmuch as it made the sepoy 'see the value of learning for his own sake'.[142] YMCA Secretary W. H. Moore explains the 'downward filtration theory' that underlay the educational programme for sepoys:

> It … seeks to ground them in the rudiments of the three R's and to teach progressive ideals about sanitation, the education of children, the position of women etc. … when [the Indian soldier] returns he is a leader in the community and … a much traveled man. His word goes, and just as the ideals of the West are being brought back to North India by returning soldiers, and are fermenting there, so the movement can be guided and spread more widely by a sustained policy of Association work.[143]

Ultimately, the fundamental goals of the YMCA schemes for South Asian troops were thus not too different from those connected with those directed at 'Regulars' and Terriers of the British Army. Both types were designed 'to maintain the magnificent morale' of the troops and simultaneously 'prepare men to be better citizens after the war'.[144] The fact that soldiers and sepoys were understood and treated as future civilians in this context ties in perfectly with an argument recently made by Tammy Proctor some time ago, namely, that the Great War blurred the boundaries between military and civilian spheres in a variety of ways.[145] That said, it is also obvious from the examples presented thus far that, in spite of the organization's lofty goals, racial thinking, cultural arrogance and orientalist clichés affected how civilian members of the Indian YMCA perceived Indian society and organized their army work for South Asian and British troops. This problem deserves closer attention and will be discussed in the next section.

The contradictions of Y philanthropy: Issues of sexual purity and racial hierarchies

At first sight, the YMCA's efforts at translation as well as its creation of spaces of intercultural encounter appears to provide a more liberal and egalitarian order than the authoritarian and strictly enforced racial hierarchy prevailing in the imperial army.[146] This self-representation as a liberating and democratizing force was especially cultivated by leading American YMCA functionaries in India, some of whom ridiculed the race-conscious British rulers as hopelessly out of touch with reality[147] while others anticipated 'epoch-making shifts in race relationships' as a result of the war work performed by Indian secretaries.[148] The single detail that an Indian, K. T. Paul, held the highest position in the Indian YMCA for the first time from 1916 onwards, seemingly confirms this view. Such an interpretation would also be in line with recent literature, which discusses the activities of some American YMCA workers in the interwar period as part of a broader 'anti-imperialism for Jesus' campaign.[149] However, as we have already seen in the previous chapter, American secretaries like E. C. Carter remained at least partly in control despite the official hierarchies. Further, there is evidence that the appointment of a South Asian to the highest position the Indian Y had to offer was largely a strategic move and did not mean that power indeed changed hands. Thus, in 1918, literary secretary J. F. Farquhar expressed his satisfaction that the manoeuvre had given the Indian YMCA a progressive image and palpably increased its credibility among South Asian communities, celebrating the appointment of K. T. Paul as 'a brilliant piece of policy'.[150] While it certainly cannot be denied that an element of a critique toward imperialism was already discernible in many South Asian and some American members of the Indian YMCA by the 1910s (the story of the 'pacifist' troublemaker Howard Walter in Lahore is an example), such an attitude seems to have still been the exception rather than the rule. For one thing, the official policy of accepting only US volunteers who had 'proved to be pro-Ally in their political sympathies'[151] certainly limited the number of critical minds. Nevertheless, there was an astonishingly widespread identification with Britain's imperial enterprise. Even an African American YMCA secretary, working in Bangalore for a few months in 1916, praised the 'liberal and wise politics of the British government' and expressed his admiration for its imperial project.[152] The official history of the American Y's war engagement, too, discusses the British role in conquered Mesopotamia in a way that shows the full endorsement of the imperial civilizing mission:

> Fair-minded persons, least sympathetic with the British Imperial idea, were bound to admit that Britain's colossal programme of reconstructive, administrative, and humanitarian effort in Mesopotamia was conceived on a magnanimous scale and was a great work of civilization in a country that has suffered the unprogressive rule of the Turk.[153]

In fact, I would argue that the example of Americans engaged in the Indian YMCA's wartime work provides particularly powerful evidence for the continued enmeshment of the Y agenda with imperial ideologies, practices and epistemes. In the remainder of this chapter, I will illustrate this point with a few examples pertaining to the Association's war work directed at both Indian and British troops.

To take the case of British soldiers first, I would like to return to the rather unique cultural training programme directed at the Territorials that was briefly sketched out above. It is striking how the ideal of a 'new sense of race-brotherhood' the programme was designed to create stood in stark contrast with some of the messaging simultaneously directed at the Terriers.[154] The Y secretaries typically started their propaganda well before the new arrivals set foot on Indian soil. As soon as a troopship carrying British territorials reached Bombay (the usual port of arrival), YMCA secretaries on boats would visit, providing them with tea, sweets, newspapers and information leaflets while still aboard ship.[155] One of these brochures is particularly intriguing because of the light it sheds on the thorny issue of the Y's imperial complicity.[156] Created for the Territorials, it equipped them with information about how to behave as a British soldier in India; at the same time, it was intended to contribute to the YMCA's overarching mission to 'safeguard them from the temptations of intemperance and immorality'.[157]

The anti-vice agenda of the organization is reflected in a list of '20 Don'ts for India', which included 'Don't forget to play the game', 'Don't forget your best girl – honour her by your conduct' and 'Don't forget that it takes a good judge of whisky to let it alone'.[158] This classical Y strategy of promoting the cultivation of physical fitness while at the same time advocating temperance and chastity acquires a particular meaning in an imperial military context. Next to the obvious concern that alcohol abuse and venereal disease might affect the troops' fitness for combat, drinking and interracial sex had for a long time been regarded as threatening imperial prestige and thus undermining the stability of colonial rule.[159] The attempt to prevent the potential transgression of 'going native' through the choice of sex or drinking partners and thus losing the imperial self, as it were, was accompanied by a strong element of racial and religious self-assertion. The commandments 'Don't be ashamed of your religion', 'Don't forget to write home' and 'Don't forget that you are British' sent out strong messages against a possible dissolution in an alien cultural environment that appear to be in tension with the official agenda of internationalism and cultural rapprochement. At the very least, they clearly show its limits.[160] The fear of miscegenation, in particular, seems to have haunted the authors of the brochure: In medicalized language that was unusually explicit for the period, the leaflet also provided 'sex information'.[161] The newly arrived territorials were reminded that 'sexual intercourse [wa]s not a physical necessity' and hence from 'a physiological standpoint', there was no need 'for a young man to "sow wild oats"'.[162]

That eugenic concerns related to sexually transmitted diseases were apparently inseparable from moral objections would explain the fact that the brochure also featured a text by popular American author Ella Wheeler Wilcox (1850–1919).[163] Her melodramatic poem 'The Price He Paid' tells the story of a young man who, after years of 'hotfooting the road of vice', eventually marries and tries to start a family. However, his young wife gives birth to a son who is 'blind and crippled and weak and sore' because he infects her with venereal disease, while she herself is 'left a wreck'. The poem ends with a flaming appeal to warn young men more outspokenly about the actual physical consequences of venereal diseases:

Folks talk too much of a soul,
From heavenly joys debarred
And not enough of the babes unborn
By the sins of their fathers scarred.[164]

Admittedly, this medico-moral policing of the empire's sexual frontiers might also be interpreted from the perspective of the YMCA's general anti-vice stance and its vision of ideal masculinity, and hence need not necessarily be undergirded by racialist preconceptions. However, the small dictionary of Hindustani words and sentences which also formed part of the leaflet unmistakably shows how deeply the YMCA's agenda was tangled up in the imperial everyday racism that was characteristic of the military in India. Among the elementary thirty phrases and grammatical hints for the use of European soldiers in India, one finds, amongst others, the following:

> Make haste – *Juldy kurro*
> Clean this properly – *Berarber sarf kurro* …
> Hold your tongue, remain silent – *Choop rou*
> Stop all that noise – *Woo sub arwarz bund kurro*
> Take off my boots – *Humarar boots nikar lo* …
> You are a fool! – *Toom pargle waller ho*!
> Oh, you clown! – *Ar-eh Jungly*! (Don't say 'jungly waller'. Either 'jungly' alone or 'jungle waller'.)[165]

This harsh and high-handed language was part of the linguistic repertoire typically associated with both the 'hardened Tommy' when talking to South Asian camp followers and even the more arrogant members of British India's white elites when addressing their 'native' servants. Polite formulaic greetings to express gratitude, by contrast, were not among the phrases included.

Admittedly, it is impossible to establish if and to what extent British military authorities were involved in the production of the brochure. However, there are many other examples of latent racism where interference by imperial agencies can be discounted in the European and American Y secretaries' description of South Asian troops and labourers. Several also toyed with the cliché of the 'jungle waller' (literally: savage, primitive), which featured in the mini-dictionary, as the perfect object of ridicule. English YMCA leader A. K. Yapp, for example, describes his experience of familiarizing a 'native' regiment stationed in Burma with the products of the latest Western entertainment technology as follows:

> Most of the men are from the deep jungle, and very few of them can read or write. The gramophone interests them enormously, and they look inside it to see who is producing the sound, and will sit round in a circle listening to it for hours. Picture papers interest them, but usually they prefer holding the pictures upside down.[166]

The semi-serious engagement with exotic illiterate 'tribesmen' seems to echo the attitude of British officers, who were likewise fascinated by the 'very engaging savages' serving in the Indian Labour Corps.[167] The assumption of essential differences between Indians and Westerners also manifested itself in forms of structural racism. To give but one example: as a rule, the centres for the Territorial regiments were quite luxurious and much better equipped than the rather austere huts simultaneously opened for Indian units (see Figures 2.8 and 2.9).

'Make Them Pure, Fit and Brotherly!'

Figure 2.8 Home away from (European) home: A YMCA centre for 'Terriers' near Bangalore (*c.* 1916), typically equipped with piano, newspaper library and billiards. Courtesy Kautz Family YMCA Archives, University of Minnesota, Minneapolis.

Figure 2.9 Home away from ('native') home: A YMCA hut for Indian sepoys in Central India (*c.* 1916). The Indian huts were usually much simpler and featured neither pianos nor billiards. In this case, the Y centre offers table games and a gramophone instead. Courtesy Kautz Family YMCA Archives, University of Minnesota, Minneapolis.

While it may seem predictable that Englishmen working for the Y (e.g. Callan or Yapp) would lack distance from imperial racial rhetoric, it has to be emphasized that many American Y workers articulated similar views. The fact that even 'progressive' US YMCA secretaries shared basic racist assumptions should not come as a surprise if we consider the attitudes prevailing in the United States and, for that matter, in the US military, at the time.[168] What is important here is that they exhibited many elements of the specifically British imperial variety of racial prejudice that they were denouncing at the same time. In fact, the US secretaries' debasement of South Asians often went hand in hand with their near-total identification with the representatives of British imperialism. The American Y worker D. Spencer Hatch, whom we will meet again in Chapter 5 as the architect of the Indian YMCA's village development programme, is a case in point.[169] The Cornell graduate served with British and Indian regiments in Northern India and Mesopotamia between 1916 and 1919 and wrote extensively about his war experiences. Dwelling on his stint in India's North-West Frontier Province, Hatch mentions in his diary that he had prepared his mission on the Afghan frontier by relying on colonial knowledge and thoroughly studying Winston Churchill's account on warfare in that region.[170] Hatch repeatedly voices his admiration for British officers and makes it a point to mention that he was treated like one of them, noting that he enjoyed 'officer's status without definitive rank'.[171] His tacit admiration of the British Empire (which by no means excluded occasional articulations of a sense of American superiority) also translated into how the Y volunteer from New York State styled himself for a souvenir photo as a 'pucca sahib',[172] on camel back complete with Indian servant and *solar topee* (see Figure 2.10).[173]

Hatch came in contact with many different ethnic groups during the course of his war work and occasionally even criticized the 'ridiculous race prejudice' that was ubiquitous in the imperial army.[174] Nevertheless, his diaries reveal that he himself was influenced by precisely this prejudice. Thus, he observed in late 1916 during a fire alarm in his camp at the Afghan border that such an emergency could reveal 'great difference in cultures: the Englishmen working frantically but quietly, and the natives yelling excitedly *paani lao, chelloa* [sic],[175] like crazy men'.[176]

Hatch not only noted the cultural dissimilarities but also believed in significant fundamental physical differences between Westerners and 'natives'. His views are apparent in another anecdote from his posting on the Afghan frontier, which he relates in his unfinished and unpublished memoirs:[177] Without the slightest indication of disapproval or disgust vis à vis an obvious act of desecration of a corpse, he accepted the gift of skulls from a clergyman and medical doctor who was, like himself, engaged in special services for the imperial troops in Waziristan. The skulls belonged to dead bodies of Mahsuds, members of a local ethnic group that the British considered one of the most dangerous 'rebellious hill tribes'.[178] Recycling entrenched colonial stereotypes about the alleged existence of 'criminals by birth',[179] Hatch explains as a matter of course in his memoirs that the Mahsuds were 'a race of robbers and murderers' and that such 'wild tribes … had to be kept in order'.[180] Twenty-nine of them had been killed during a punitive expedition by a British regiment a few days previously, and Hatch seems to fully understand that his medically trained friend left the camp secretly to decapitate two of the 'great stalwart fellows':[181]

Figure 2.10 A 'Pucca Sahib': American YMCA secretary Duane Spencer Hatch doing army work at Risalpur, North-West Frontier Province, India (1916). Courtesy Kautz Family YMCA Archives, University of Minnesota, Minneapolis.

Every Doctor, he told me, always wanted a mounted skull in his office. Now these giant Mahsuds had the finest heads anyone has ever seen in all the world. He wanted one of those, as I suppose every medical officer who passed them did.[182]

This instance of Hatch's collecting combat trophies under the guise of scientific interest was fully in line with long-established British practices in frontier warfare.[183] This example may be extreme, but there is plenty of anecdotal evidence that other American secretaries too constantly reproduced the standard repertoire of colonial ethnic clichés and stereotypes about 'martial' and 'effeminate' races passed on to them by imperial officers and administrators. Waldo H. Heinrichs, a Columbia history graduate whom we have met already in the previous chapter as the head of the Indian Y's Lecture Department (1919–24), was involved in organizing cultural and social gatherings for Terriers in Madras and Calcutta in 1916. In his diary, he replicates typical imperial prejudices when describing a 'Eurasian' woman he met at one of those events:[184] 'The young lady is not a bad looker, like a great many half castes [*sic*],'[185] but she has a refinement and culture that the vast mass of them do not have.'[186] But negative clichés were not the only ones adopted. Sherwood Eddy, in depicting the Indian expeditionary forces in France, repeatedly talked appreciatively about 'stalwart Pathans', whom he contrasted with the 'big bearded Sikhs with a soldier's religion' and the Nepalese Gurkhas, predictably described as 'brave little hill men'.[187] In a similar vein, A. L. Miller, a YMCA worker from Sioux City, Iowa, serving in Lahore, even combined his endorsement of the imperial martial race theory with speculations about a potential 'Indian advance' in a post-war political order when he observed that two-thirds of the soldiers serving in the imperial army during the Great War came from the Punjab, concluding as follows:

> This fact alone shows the type of man that we have here and the importance of winning this section of India to our cause. Much of the new leadership in the new realms of Indian advance must come from this northern race of stalwart leaders.[188]

That such statements could be made not merely in private chats or correspondence, but even, as in this case, in the context of an official report to the headquarters of the American YMCA's International Division in New York, indicates the degree to which racial thought in its British imperial variety had pervaded the mindset of American Y secretaries. This seems ironic given the fact that they at the same time projected visions of a liberal alternative to the existing imperial order.

Unlike the other chapters in this book, the present one has focused on a rather short span of time, concentrating mainly on developments between 1904 and 1921. Before wrapping up the main findings of our case study, it might therefore be helpful to provide an epilogue of sorts in the form of a brief sketch of the further evolution of the Indian Y's Army Department up until the end of the Second World War.

As indicated above, the euphoria among many North American YMCA secretaries about the 'unprecedented opportunities' created by the war came to a somewhat abrupt end when the financial resources provided by the British and British-Indian government dried up rather quickly following the armistice.[189] In the subsequent years, the Army Department had to drastically reduce the scope of its activities due to a substantial reduction in its budget. As a result, it concentrated exclusively on the welfare of British troops, whereas the facilities and programmes targeted at South Asian soldiers came to a complete halt by the mid-1920s. The financial situation of the Department was rather precarious by this time[190] and the number of army centres catering to European regiments was also reduced. Of the dozens of such bodies that existed at the time of the armistice, only eight remained in 1926.[191] While the First World War certainly constituted a decisive flashpoint for organized forms of voluntary charity and philanthropy all over the world, there was an equally wide-ranging and pervasive trend during the interwar years for direct state intervention, which curtailed the role of such civil society organizations.[192] In the United Kingdom, for example, British servicemen were taken care of by the Navy, Army and Air Force Institute (NAAFI), founded in 1921. The NAAFI ran shops, restaurants, cafés, bars, clubs, supermarkets and other facilities on most British military bases and aboard Royal Navy ships.[193] In British

India, too, state-sponsored institutions increasingly appropriated the important field of caregiving and troop entertainment. Adam Scott, the Indian YMCA's National Army Secretary, somewhat frustratedly noted in 1926 that 'much more is now done for the welfare of the Soldiers by the Army Authorities [sic] than ever before, through sports, games [and] educational classes'.[194] One may well speculate that the tensions resulting from the allegations and rumours that the Y had become a 'disloyal' organization will have additionally reinforced this trend.

While the overall significance of the YMCA's army work thus was clearly dwindling, new opportunities opened up occasionally. In the spring of 1926, for instance, a new programme was launched with a view to assist servicemen with 'making the right choices and right contacts' in the critical moment of their return to a civilian life. The National Army Secretary Scott was

> invited by Army Headquarters to undertake an experimental voyage to England on a home-going transport carrying men leaving India on discharge. Throughout the voyage, a programme of lantern lectures, concerts, informal conferences and interviews filled the days and everyone on board was reached with such information … as he cared to have.[195]

By and large, however, the Army Department was reduced in size and significance throughout the 1920s and 1930s. When the Second World War broke out in September 1939, the Association was hence ill-prepared to play a role similar to the one it did in the Great War.[196] There simply were not enough Y workers to volunteer for what was now called 'war emergency work'. Consequently, the Association had to recruit new men from India, the United Kingdom, the United States, Canada and a few other countries. As there was neither time nor staff to establish a training programme through which the newly recruited volunteers 'could be initiated into the mysteries of the many and varied tasks they were called upon to perform',[197] the large majority of the 254 secretaries (23 of whom were American and 10 Canadian) involved between 1939 and 1947 had to be trained on the job.[198] This meant that the overall number of secretaries was about half of what it had been during the First World War, while the number of soldiers they had to care for had effectively doubled.

In addition, the small group of YMCA volunteers serving outside the Indian subcontinent was even more widely dispersed than had been the case from 1914 to 1920. Y army secretaries were deployed in no less than fifteen different countries ranging from Italy to Iraq and from French Indochina to Japan. At the peak of their work in early 1945, a total of thirty secretaries were serving with Indian troops overseas.[199] The majority, however, remained in South Asia where they worked in welfare centres for British, Indian and West African troops stationed in India, Burma and Ceylon, or provided services to Italian and Japanese POWs.[200] Particularly noteworthy is the role of the Madras College of Physical Education (MCPE) during the war years. On the request of military authorities, a huge 'recreation hut for allied forces' was erected on the premises of the MCPE. This was one of the rare cases in which Indian YMCA facilities could also be used by American and Canadian troops, and consequently large sums of money were spent to keep them up to date.[201]

Amongst other things, a large swimming pool was constructed for the soldiers' amusement at the cost of Rs. 125,000.[202]

In sum then, the impact and visibility of the Indian YMCA was markedly lower during the Second World War as compared a quarter century earlier. This change was not only due to the smaller number of men involved and the more modest funding available. More importantly, the Association's Army Department had much less room to manoeuvre. This was because, following the global trend of more direct state intervention in philanthropic and humanitarian aspects of armed conflicts and the military in general, the imperial, provincial and military authorities in British India had not only created their own institutions, whose offerings competed with the YMCA's services, they also acted in a more *dirigiste* manner. Either the Government of India or provincial governments fully controlled the distribution of funds, and state officials decided in minute detail where and how Y secretaries were allowed to provide which type of services. This novel constellation made it difficult this time for even the most optimistic YMCA worker to cultivate lofty dreams about Y-sponsored large-scale citizenship training programmes that would affect the post-war order.

Summing up

This chapter has argued that the military welfare schemes launched to great effect during the Great War were part of a broader strategy of the US-dominated elements in the Indian Y to win the trust and support of the imperial Indian Government. This tactic was first applied to the programmes for European and Eurasian railway men, which can be understood as the direct predecessors of the army work schemes. It has next focused specifically on the Christian NGO's programmes directed at the tens of thousands British 'Territorials' who arrived in India after the outbreak of hostilities, and at the hundreds of thousands of Indian soldiers and labourers serving in France and Mesopotamia from 1914 to 1920. It has become evident that the YMCA's wartime services on the Indian home front were conceived of as a way to support the imperial war effort in a number of ways. Homesickness, boredom and potential cultural clashes resulting from the mass arrival of barely trained British soldiers were reduced by typical sports and entertainment programmes offered by Y secretaries in more than fifty huts and centres scattered all over the subcontinent. The shock of exposure to an unfamiliar environment often perceived as hostile was also cushioned by the YMCA's ambitious 'intercultural training scheme', which translated India and her people for the newly arrived Terriers. Apart from reducing the actual conflict potential between European troops and the indigenous population, the scheme also had a far-reaching political dimension: it was seen as preparation for establishing a more egalitarian post-war order in South Asia, softening the existing 'racial antagonism' and instilling into representatives of a new generation of young Britons' sympathy for South Asian cultures and people. In that sense, there were clear elements pertaining to the emancipatory project of modernity discernible in the Y's programmes, although they were targeted not primarily at South Asian or

European soldiers from a low-class background but rather at the educated middle-class Terriers.

Cultural mediation and conflict reduction were also key elements of the Association's work for Indian soldiers and labourers deployed in Europe and Mesopotamia, albeit in a less egalitarian setting. In both theatres of war, the Y huts functioned as spaces of leisure and masculine comradeship. Significantly, they were also sites of education, where Indian YMCA secretaries provided the sepoys with language skills and basic information about the war and the country in which they were stationed. Some American Y workers, serving in the sepoy camps and barracks, also pointed to the value of the educational programmes as a citizenship training of sorts that could prepare the ex-servicemen for future democratic participation (and potentially conversion to Christianity!). More importantly, however, the YMCA huts and classes were crucial communication hubs, where Y men would act as intermediaries between the South Asian rank-and-file soldiers and their European officers, thus helping avoid cultural misunderstandings and stabilize an often conflict-ridden relationship. In this case, too, the popular entertainment, sports and educational programmes were equally vital to boost the morale of battle-weary South Asian soldiers who were frequently treated 'second class' by their British superiors and in most cases insufficiently trained and equipped for the kind of mechanical warfare they were confronted with.[203] It is certainly not too bold to conclude that, given the tremendous potential for interracial strife and conflict, the various facets of the Y's sepoy work overseas helped substantially in keeping the imperial war machinery going.

Superficially, then, it appears that the Indian YMCA's war work was an important and fruitful philanthropic endeavour. In all probability, it contributed to the victory over the Central Powers by making the hardships of war more bearable to both South Asian and British troops and auxiliaries. This goal was achieved not least through watering down the rigid racial/cultural hierarchies prevailing in the imperial military. The popularity of the Indian Y's army work programme with South Asian subalterns, its panegyric appreciation by high-ranking imperial officers and government officials, as well as the stunning financial support it received from the Indian public thus become understandable.

However, alongside these undeniable achievements of the Y workers, some more problematic aspects of the Christian Association's war work have also become apparent. Firstly, its philanthropic activities like the army work scheme were shaped from the very beginning by the rather self-seeking motives of a Protestant Christian organization whose primary goal it remained to 'evangelise the world'. This agenda was already obvious in its pioneering pre-war small-scale experiments with European railwaymen and soldiers. These pre-war programmes were designed to bring plebeian elements of 'white' society in British India in line with what was seen as 'proper Christian conduct' and bourgeois standards of masculinity, as deviations allegedly endangered the credibility of proselytization efforts through their 'uncivilized' behaviour. At the same time, the reclamation of 'white subalterns' also demonstrated the usefulness of the US-dominated Association's work to the imperial government, thus opening up new sources of funding. This strategy was developed to perfection during the Great War. Its financial success at this time led to some YMCA secretaries fantasizing about future proselytization campaigns in South Asia: some of these workers in fact viewed the war almost as a blessing in disguise as it significantly boosted the organization's monetary resources, visibility, popularity and influence. As we have seen, even explicitly 'non-religious' work for Indian troops was affected by the overarching strategic consideration to push the YMCA's missionary agenda.

Secondly, it is notable that the novel social spaces that were created in an imperial army context – YMCA huts, canteens, playing fields, make-shift cinema halls and so on – were advertised as 'democratic' microcosms,[204] and might indeed have looked less rigidly hierarchic and segregated on the outside. They were nonetheless profoundly informed by imperial racialist ideologies and practices. The message of cultural arrogance and high-handedness communicated by the 'conduct book' and mini-dictionary distributed to British Territorials, for example, was hard to reconcile with the Association's self-declared objective of bringing about 'epoch-making shifts in race relationships'.[205] The same holds true for the skull-collecting activities of American Y secretary Spencer Hatch and his medically inclined colleague, and for the milder forms of everyday racism displayed by some of his fellow secretaries in their dealings with South Asian soldiers and 'coolies'. Strikingly, some British officials' distrust against the alleged 'egalitarian leanings' of YMCA secretaries from the United States notwithstanding, there seems to have been little difference between British YMCA members and the growing number of American volunteers when it came to cultural prejudices or outright racism.

Lastly, it is difficult to make an authoritative claim about the actual meaning and relevance of the YMCA's army work for the South Asian sepoys and 'coolies' on the basis of the sources used for this chapter. A comprehensive and systematic analysis of soldier's letters and other ego documents in Indian languages for their description of and engagement with leisure activities remains an important desideratum in the growing literature on the social history of the South Asian soldiery deployed in the Great War. What has become clear, however, is that hundreds of thousands of Indian and Nepali subalterns appreciated the YMCA's letter-writing services, and many of them developed a fondness for 'Western' sports. Even more used the opportunity to grow familiar to the latest western entertainment technologies such as the gramophone, the 'bioscope,' and the magic lantern slideshow. The Indian YMCA's pivotal role in disseminating these novel forms of mass communication and entertainment among South Asian non-elites turned the Association into an important agent of modernization and is a fascinating topic begging fuller exploration.

Whereas the Y's 'secular' modernizing mission was certainly effective to a certain degree, the extent to which the Association was successful in disseminating its template of 'ideal masculinity' remains unclear, as does the effect of the bio-moral appeals of the YMCA secretaries on their South Asian addressees. Even though YMCA functionaries claimed that 'the Association was ... tacitly recognized by all as the dominant moral force' in the army camps,[206] there is reason to doubt such boastful statements. The expected moralizing effect of the language classes offered to South Asian soldiers, for example, appears to have been limited. One secretary complained that 'in the French classes we are holding, we are continually being asked by the sepoys the French words having reference to immoral relations!'[207] The fact that the South Asian soldiers usually referred to the YMCA hut as the *tamāśā ghar* (house of spectacles)[208] and to the Y secretaries as *tamāśāvāle* (showmen),[209] and that many of them were quite obviously entirely ignorant of the organization's religious background would also seem to point in a different direction.

3

'Physical ministry': The Indian YMCA's sports and physical education programmes (c. 1900–1950)

This chapter enhances our understanding of a key element of the YMCA's citizenship training agenda and arguably its most successful field of activity in general by shedding light on its physical education and fitness programmes in South Asia. At the same time, it addresses an obvious lacuna in the global history of sports by contributing to a better understanding of the transfer and reception of American fitness ideologies and practices in a vast region outside the West. By underscoring the significance of the specific South Asian context and highlighting the agency of those at the receiving end of the American 'sportizing missions',[1] this case study challenges facile notions of both 'cultural imperialism' and a 'ludic diffusion' from North America to the global South.[2]

Many historians have pointed out that the introduction of modern forms of sports and physical culture has had a particularly noteworthy impact on the political history of late colonial South Asia.[3] As we have already seen, Western notions of fitness found their way into both the rhetoric and the practice of educational and political projects of a wide range of actors, including religious reformers from various backgrounds as well as political leaders ranging from Indian revolutionary 'terrorists' to apostles of non-violence like M. K. Gandhi, especially during the first three decades of the twentieth century.[4] In spite of all their ideological differences, these actors shared the belief that physical training would render South Asians fit for the challenges of a modern age perceived as hostile, 'effeminating', and corrupting, and would thus prepare them for the hardships of the political struggles ahead of them if self-rule was to be a realistic objective.

With very few exceptions, however (and the pioneering work of social anthropologist Joseph Alter must be acknowledged here),[5] the existing literature on the region has addressed the transfer of the notions and practices of physical and moral fitness almost exclusively within a rather narrow imperial frame of reference, focussing either on the role of the colonial state or the handful of British missionaries who targeted an equally minuscule group of Indian aristocrats in imperial colleges.[6] While there exists a copious literature on the dissemination of US games and sports all over the world, and particularly in Latin America and East Asia,[7] one finds very little scholarly work on the influence of the American-style 'empire of sports' on the Indian subcontinent.[8]

Through the case study presented in this chapter, I seek to demonstrate that the intensification of American economic and cultural influences in the realm of sports and physical culture did not *eo ipso* mean that North American models could be transplanted in a simple or straightforward manner into non-Western contexts. Rather, the 'American' physical fitness programmes implemented by the Indian Y in South Asia were products of complex local interactions and negotiations between distinct (and often oppositional) groups of actors, including both British colonial administrators and Indian nationalists. Under these circumstances, the programmes eventually acquired very specific 'pidginized' forms, drawing as they did on highly diverse cultural resources.

The chapter builds on the observation that the new 'body language' and modern physical practices that took root in late colonial India were closely connected to the 'great acceleration' of economic and cultural globalization processes,[9] and particularly to the increasingly intense worldwide circulation of American 'mass culture'. As recent research has documented, the subcontinental enthusiasm for all things American that was discernible especially after the First World War, when the United States had acquired the role of a 'great power' on the global political stage, included a fancy for Hollywood movies, Jazz records and Ford automobiles.[10] What is less known is that the 'excessive Americanism' that British officials observed in early twentieth-century South Asia[11] also extended to ideals of fitness, beauty and masculinity. This is proven by the fact that a huge market existed for 'lurid physical culture magazines usually emanating from America' at precisely the same time, filled with posed photographs of well-trained body builders.[12]

To be sure, Americans were not the only ones to export sports-related physical practices to the Indian subcontinent. Physical culture and fitness had become something of a global obsession by the turn of the twentieth century and a broad variety of training regimes and 'systems' – ranging from German *Turnen* via Scandinavian calisthenics and Japanese jiu-jitsu to bodybuilding regimes advocated by the famous Anglo-German strongman Eugen Sandow – were disseminated in the subcontinent as well as in the rest of Asia.[13] By focusing on the YMCA and its North American physical educators, the present case study sheds light on some of the most important global players in the transnational circulation of fitness ideals and practices.[14] As historians working on other world regions have amply demonstrated, the YMCA was 'an institution equipped to carry the gospel of sports all over the world', an important factor in its becoming a mainstay of America's 'moral empire'.[15] To be sure, the (often transnationally constructed) sports and fitness schemes it attempted to disseminate in South Asia were undoubtedly represented to the local recipients as *modern* or *Western*, they were at the same time frequently advertised as being specifically *American*. In fact, the emphasis on the 'progressive', 'liberal' and 'egalitarian' image of the United States and its supposed compatibility with Indian nationalism were arguably their biggest selling points as these marked the programmes as being distinct from the kind of 'Westernness' and modernity that South Asians associated with the colonial rulers.

This chapter is divided into four sections. It starts with a short sketch of physical education and fitness programmes in colonial South Asia before the YMCA became active in this field. The second section explores the emergence and development of the Y's specific 'scientific', 'playful' and 'democratic' programme of fitness training and physical education in North America (already briefly touched upon in Chapter 1). The third section is the centrepiece of the chapter. It explores in detail how the physical education and fitness schemes designed by North American sports experts were implemented in South Asia and reconstructs the multifarious transformations that they underwent in the process. The bulk of this section focuses on the activities of John H. Gray, Arthur G. Noehren and Harry C. Buck, three leading American 'physical directors' who worked for the Indian YMCA, and analyses the role of the pioneering MCPE, which was founded in 1920. This institution soon became an icon of the YMCA's ideal of Muscular Christianity and an important hub for the transmission of the Association's sports and physical culture programmes. It was largely through the activities of the MCPE that the Y's engagement with physical fitness achieved region-wide visibility and was soon emulated by both British colonial officials and Indian nationalist politicians. The fourth and final section eventually complicates the apparent success story of the Indian YMCA's Physical Department. It does so by switching the focus from the reconstruction of the Y's agenda and self-representations to a close analysis of the quasi-imperial ideological underpinnings of its programmes, thus revealing the inconsistency of its liberal rhetoric and the tensions arising from the emancipatory aspects of modernity.

In quest of strength and manhood: The place of sports and physical culture in British India

Let us briefly revisit the discussion in Chapter 1 and commence with looking at the role of physical education and other forms of 'embodied knowledge' in South Asia before the American lay Association became a key player and started co-shaping them. Four decades ago, a pioneering article by John Rosselli first pointed to the crucial importance of physical culture programmes in fostering Indian patriotism and anti-colonial sentiment.[16] Especially in Bengal, constant confrontation with the imperial stereotype of the alleged 'effeminacy' of the 'natives'[17] triggered a movement among certain segments of the Indian population to revive traditional forms of physical culture, so as to recuperate the beleaguered masculinity of the colonized.[18] This included as rediscovery of physical activities such as yoga,[19] but also a cultivation of various kinds of martial arts. In this process, the new significance attributed to rediscovery of Indian wrestling (*kuśtī* or *pahalvānī*) as a particularly potent symbol of Indian manhood and martiality and the new function of *akhāṛā*s or *vyayāmśālā*s (gymnasiums in which wrestlers used to train), as crucial sites for cultural self-assertion played a particularly conspicuous role.[20] This is not to say that this was a completely 'invented' tradition, but what was new especially in the context of big cities such as Calcutta, Bombay or Pune, was the fact that in the atmosphere of budding nationalism, many educated middle-class males participated in games and exercises, hitherto mostly considered as rustic and/or low-class pastimes.[21] While traditional Indian forms of play and physical culture thus acquired a new popularity in the modern context of nationalism as an effective means to 'stave off the harmful effects of modernity and ensure the continuation a healthy Indian race',[22] more contemporary physical activities that had no roots in the

Indian subcontinent also became tremendously popular during the final decades of the nineteenth and the first quarter of the twentieth century.

The colonizers, of course, cannot be left out of the equation and much has been written about Indian appropriations and subversions of typical British games like cricket and football.[23] While the circulation of these British team sports undeniably plays an important role – though it remains doubtful whether it can indeed be described as a purposeful 'ludic diffusion' –[24] recent studies have emphasized that the borrowing and adaptation of modern forms of sports and physical exercise in South Asia cannot be reduced to the colonial connection. German historian Sebastian Conrad, for example, has persuasively argued that the turn of the twentieth century constituted a global moment of sorts. During the *fin de siècle*, writes Conrad, a strong interest in physical culture coalesced with a rising consciousness of the collective health of 'the nation', a novel ideal of male beauty and a new 'scientific' approach to bodily training. Taken together, these factors ensured that exercises for the (male) body gained worldwide currency.[25] South Asia was no exception to this trend. International fitness entrepreneurs – or 'strength peddlers'[26] – like the Anglo-Prussian strongman Eugen Sandow, the American health apostle Bernarr MacFadden and the Danish Body builder Jørg Peter Müller all had a presence in the subcontinent via the sales of their books, training equipment and workout devices.[27] Sandow even visited India in person. During his world tour in 1904–5, the eminent bodybuilder spent eight months in India where his sold-out shows 'created a physical culture craze' and even made him 'the hero of intellectual Bengal'.[28] Simultaneously, East Asian sports and martial arts were reshaped, standardized and prepared for export in their countries of origin.[29] The late Meiji and Taisho regimes officially promoted the international dissemination of Japanese sports like judo and jiu-jitsu, and these martial arts started to generate a keen interest not only in Europe but also in colonized Asia. The fascination with Japanese martial arts was further catalysed by Japan's military triumph against a European power in the Russo-Japanese War of 1904–5.[30] Such was the public interest in the methods of corporeal self-empowerment that John H. Gray, one of the leading physical educators of the YMCA in South Asia, even claimed in the 1920s that there were 'a larger number of the so-called "systems" and "brands" of physical … culture, or training being exploited and urged at this time in India than in any other country in the world'.[31]

As we have seen in Chapter 1, leading Indian nationalists were also deeply concerned by the neglect of physical education and instruction in 'personal and sex hygiene' in the country's schools, colleges and universities. Several of them sought for international role models to help overcome the existing defects of the colonial educational system. Arya Samaj member and INC activist Lala Lajpat Rai, for example, complained in 1920 as follows:

> We have every year about a hundred thousand young men engaged in mastering Milton, Shakespeare, Southey, Shelley, Kalidasa and Firdausi, who have never been told, either at home or at school, how to cultivate an erect posture, how to take care of their bodies, hands, legs, noses, eyes, teeth, ears, organs, muscles and nerves. They know nothing about the hygiene of living, of housing, of food, of dress and of

mating. The curriculum of studies takes no cognizance of these things, nor of those, which provide recreation and amusement of a healthy and edifying character.[32]

According to Lajpat Rai, the solution to this 'national problem of the first magnitude'[33] could be found in the 'Bulletin of the United States Bureau of Education (No. 50, of 1917) on the subject of "Physical Education in Secondary Schools."'[34] In his opinion, studying this brochure, which he had acquired during his long stint in New York (1914–19), would be 'of more practical use to our educational leaders, teachers and students than volumes of high-class English and Sanskrit poetry'.[35]

In sum, then, one can observe that the new interest of South Asians in sports, physical culture and physical education expressed itself in a variety of ways. For one thing, this interest led to an intensification of colonial borrowings and mimetic appropriations. Simultaneously, it spurred the 'nativist' rediscovery and revival of indigenous physical and martial traditions. And finally, it triggered the increasing consumption and adaptation of Western and Asian bodily practices and regimes as well as related educational schemes that were available on the global market. As mentioned already, this latter phenomenon was embedded in a broader trend of consuming global commodities and cultural artefacts, which was particularly prominent among the intermediate social strata in India's cities.[36] What, then, was the specific variety of sports, physical education and physical culture that the YMCA brought to the table, and why was it so successful in South Asia? This question is at the heart of the following section, which starts the investigation by looking again in greater detail at the trajectories of the Y's physical work' in North America.

Preparing for the 'modern strain': Science and physical education in the American YMCA

Chapter 1 has indicated how, in its initial British and continental European *avatārs*, the YMCA was conceived as an 'evangelical antidote to urban vice', providing solely for the spiritual needs of middle-class bachelors.[37] It was only in the 1860s, after the YMCA branches began to mushroom in the United States and Canada that sports became an integral component of the organization's work and the gym a standard feature of the average YMCA headquarters.[38] While the recreational physical activities were accepted somewhat slowly in the movement's country of origin,[39] the provision of physical culture facilities soon proved to be the expanding Christian lay organization's single biggest attraction in North America.[40] The resulting need for 'physical instructors' was met through the opening of the International YMCA Training School (later renamed Springfield College) in Springfield, Massachusetts, in 1885. In 1887, it became the first Christian academic institution to offer an organized course in physical education.[41] Under the aegis of sporting pioneer Luther H. Gulick (1865–1918), New England colleges like Springfield and neighbouring Holyoke soon became famous as sites where older evangelical conceptions that were hostile of physicality were discarded and sports and religion began to be integrated 'around the concept of body-building'.[42] In the process, the freshly trained 'physical directors' of the YMCA invented and popularized new safe and sanitized team games like basketball and volleyball.[43] Somewhat ironically, the success of the physical programme indicated a shift that gradually transformed the Association from a protective shield against a 'godless' modernity into an agency obsessed with 'physical efficiency' that prepared Christians for precisely the same 'modern strain', teaching them how to cope with the stiff competition prevailing in capitalist societies and ensuring that they could 'do the most and the best work', as Gulick put it (see Figure 3.1).[44]

For the purpose of this chapter, it is important to note that the peculiar kind of sports, fitness and physical education that was cultivated in Springfield differed in important ways from the more conventional practices believed to be still prevalent in Britain, at least according to the self-perception of its inventors. In a nutshell, their methods were regarded as being more playful, more 'democratic' and more 'scientific' than British exercises and games. Clifford Putney has shown, for instance, that the new team sports promoted in the Massachusetts colleges were advertised as being different from established 'solitary and antisocial' physical activities like dumbbell exercises and drills; the advertisements instead emphasized sociability and the recreational aspect of fitness training.[45] The fact that Luther Gulick regarded play and pleasure as 'the most character determining force within a people'[46] also explains the YMCA's sports philosopher's political and social engagement in endeavours that were typical of the social engineering projects undertaken in the Progressive Era. As we shall discuss in

Figure 3.1 Scientizing sports: Luther H. Gulick (bearded, in the centre of the second row) and students of the YMCA Training College (today's Springfield College) at a summer training camp for physical educators, 1890. Note the callipers in Gulick's hands. Courtesy Springfield College Archives, Special Collections.

the next chapter, Gulick served as chairman of the Playground Extension Committee and founder of the Camp Fire Girls and Boy Scouts of America in the first decades of the twentieth century.[47] His strong emphasis on play also entailed a condemnation of sports professionalism and one-sided or extreme forms of training. Physical fitness as propagated by the Y was after all not primarily built to produce winning athletes but rather to create better citizens and more moral men and fathers.[48] This stress on symmetry, balance and the 'earnest desire … to develop thoroughly rounded manly character' rather than muscle-bound bodies is crucial in understanding the nature of the physical education and 'leadership-training' programmes adopted later in the Association's South Asian mission fields.[49] Here too, the training of morally impeccable and efficient citizens was the main objective of the scheme. In fact, in 1933, one of the main protagonists of the Indian Y's Physical Department used almost exactly the same wording as Gulick when he reassured the Association members that their primary aim was 'not to develop star athletes, winning teams, expert performers, or physical marvels, but a national vitality based on character values'.[50]

In the United States and Canada, sports definitely played a pivotal role in the training of Y cadres as early as the 1890s. The YMCA Leader's Corps and high school fraternities recruited their members not primarily on the basis of their academic brilliance and exemplary conduct but rather according to their athletic accomplishments.[51] This facet, too, would later resurface in the South Asian context where it was taken for granted that 'boys who are trained and grow up under efficient physical supervision, are the boys who … prove to be leaders in their walks of life'.[52]

Another key aspect of the sports-oriented YMCA that was promoted by Gulick and his associates consisted of what could be termed a 'scientific' approach to issues of fitness and physical education. The Springfield school connected physical training to broader schemes of public health, social hygiene and even eugenics. In an article published in 1890, Gulick celebrated the new 'science' of physical education for being

> in line with the most thorough modern physiological psychology … and with our modern conception of evolution, as it works to develop a superior race. This profession offers to its students a large and broad field for intellectual activity, involving for its fullest appreciation a profound knowledge of man through physiology, anatomy, psychology, history and philosophy.[53]

Consequently, he regarded schemes of physical education as particularly 'fundamental in the up-building of the nation'. Such large-scale, bio-moral engineering, however, could only be achieved by fitness programmes implemented by professional experts, by 'men of collegiate training, philosophical minds, broad purposes and earnest hearts'.[54] In other words, the physical directors trained in Springfield and similar places were thought to hold the key to both the crafting of citizenries and 'racial improvement' because of their novel training method, which they sometimes referred to as 'scientific man-making'.[55] As Clifford Putney has observed, the techniques of corporeal citizen-crafting developed in Massachusetts were soon not only applied to the lower classes and immigrants in the United States but also 'affected natives in the "foreign field"'.[56]

Gulick, who came from a missionary family himself, pushed for extending his muscular missionaries' work to overseas regions from the very beginning.[57] As early as 1901, the first Springfield graduate reached Asia.[58] From the late 1900s onwards, the international assignments of Springfield-trained physical educators became more frequent and more regular, with China and India being the most important destinations.[59] In 1933, no less than 186 Springfield graduates (142 of whom were US citizens) were serving in forty-seven countries (see Figure 3.2).[60]

That the impact of the International YMCA Training College in South Asia had become very strong by the end of the interwar period can be gathered from the travelogue of Laurence Doggett, long-term president of the Springfield institution. Doggett visited the subcontinent in 1936–7 and proudly mentioned that altogether 'some twenty' Springfield alumni were 'giving spiritual leadership to the youth of India, Burma and Ceylon'.[61] This observation begs the question about their actual role in South Asia and thus leads to the next section.

Working out India: American physical educators and their programmes

First experiments with 'physical work'

Not surprisingly, the creation of training facilities and the organization of sports events became regular features of most Y branches in South Asia almost immediately after North American influence became palpable in the region. A November 1890 editorial in the *Young Men of India* proclaimed the founding of an athletic club in Madras as an important event that would mark the first step in turning the Indian YMCA into the 'most powerful factor in the field of athletics'.[62] A few months after that the Madras branch was granted a piece of land by the colonial authorities near its headquarters for use as athletic grounds, where 'the American Game of Baseball, for which a nice outfit was sent by friends from the New York City YMCA', was played for the first time on Indian soil.[63] Before long, the Madras Y endeavoured to lure young Indians with the advantages of a potential membership, starting its list of benefits with the observation that 'for physical culture, athletic grounds specially set apart by Government are used by the members for Cricket, Badminton, Tennis, Base-Ball and Foot-Ball'.[64] Baseball failed to garner the attention of the cricket-crazy Indian elite youth over the long term, the 'nice outfit' notwithstanding, but another YMCA innovation was an immediate success. In October 1897, four years after the first historic college basketball match had taken place in the United States,[65] an 'exhibition match' was organized on the Y's premises in Madras. As per a report in a local newspaper, the game was introduced as being 'less rough and more scientific' than football, which 'awakened lively interest among the spectators'.[66]

However, even the interest in basketball could not match the tremendous popularity of another Y innovation. In Chapter 1, we dwelt at length on the imposing four-storey YMCA headquarters in Madras that was opened in 1900. We also mentioned that it

Figure 3.2 Promotional poster from 1932 showing the global assignments of educators trained at the YMCA's International Training College at Springfield, MA. Courtesy Springfield College Archives, Special Collections.

contained not only affordable accommodation, a well-stocked library, lecture halls and rooms for social activities but also a 'Gymnasium fully equipped with up-to date apparatus'.[67] This gym, in particular, became a magnet for Madras's Indian middle-class youths from various religious and linguistic backgrounds. Before long, other branches in the subcontinent copied this model just as they did the other sports facilities and physical culture classes, so that they could be on par with the pioneers in Madras. Within less than two decades, bodybuilding equipment and other sports gear became staple items in the Indian YMCA in the same way that they were in North America and other places like Puerto Rico, China and Brazil.[68] Clearly, the early sports and fitness initiatives in South Asia were strategically calculated to draw more 'native' youngsters into the organization with a view to their future conversion.[69] Given that fitness training was regarded as the major attraction, the sites for gyms and athletic grounds were sometimes explicitly chosen to guarantee maximum public visibility of the Y's sporting activities.[70]

The available statistical evidence seems to confirm that this strategy was at least partly successful. It is no exaggeration to state that the YMCA's role as an agency specializing in spreading the gospel of physical fitness and health began to outshine its work as a religious body aiming to proselytize to India's 'teeming masses' by the end of the 1910s. A table published in its 1919 Annual Report suggests that South Asians were evidently more interested in the sports programmes offered by the organization than in its religious activities. In Calcutta, for instance, the 'physical sessions' of the local Y were frequented 30,552 times, whereas the bible classes only had 5,337 attendees. In Colombo, the figures were 6,594 and 807, respectively.[71]

Some of the more conservative European YMCA members saw the tremendous success of sports and fitness programmes as a mixed blessing and 'did not grasp the value' of the physical dimension 'for the furtherance of the Kingdom of God in India'.[72] However, others recognized the potential in using fitness schemes and, even more importantly, physical education as more than a decoy to prepare the ground for the large-scale evangelization of India. Throughout the 1910s and 1920s, advocates of the Y's 'physical ministry'[73] relentlessly lobbied for its use as an effective instrument of citizenship training instead of merely focusing on South Asia's spiritual salvation,[74] thus promoting political empowerment and societal betterment on the subcontinent. This holds particularly true for physical education, which was much broader than mere sports and fitness schemes in conception as it had to 'take cognizance of rules of hygiene and sanitation' and needed to be imparted 'under the direction of trained experts' if it was 'to serve its highest purpose'.[75]

Colonial complicity, cultural distance and the emergence of a pedagogic fitness scheme

The Indian YMCA's in-depth engagement not only with games and sports as healthy leisure activities but with comprehensive schemes of physical training and hygiene education began in earnest when Dr John Henry Gray (1879–1964) took up his position in India as the first proponent of what he himself referred to as the Y's 'fully qualified scientific leadership'.[76] Gray was born in India and was the son of American medical missionaries. He was sent to the United States for his education when he was four. He joined the YMCA at the age of ten and graduated from the YMCA International Training College in Springfield, where he attracted attention as 'captain of the football team and a star in all forms of athletics', before getting an MD from Columbia University's medical school.[77] He eventually returned to India in 1908 to take over the post of physical director at the Calcutta YMCA.[78] From 1910 to 1919, he also filled the newly created post of the first National Physical Director of the YMCAs of India, Burma and Ceylon. From 1920 to 1927, he held a similar position in China where he was instrumental in setting up a school for physical education and played a momentous role in the development of modern sports in that country.[79]

The creation of a separate Physical Department within the Indian YMCA in 1910 bears testimony to the fact that Gray had managed to convince the more religious-minded YMCA functionaries in most South Asian branches of the manifold advantages emanating from sports events and the newly devised fitness programmes. His most powerful argument apparently was that 'physical work is one of the best iconoclastic means at our command'.[80] In a programmatic article penned in 1910, John Gray contended that the transformative power of sports could arouse the supposedly inert Indian society and cure one of its fundamental problems, namely, the rivalry and tensions between various religious and social groups:

> Men cannot come into physical contact and keep caste, religious or social … Men cannot form pyramids and do combination work on the floor and remember or really care whether they are Brahmins or Mahomedans [sic], mercantile or tradesmen. … But one must indeed really love his Indian brother if he is going to be smeared with his perspiration in tumbling and Basketball. Come with me some hot June night to the College Branch [of the Calcutta Y.M.C.A.] and I will show you what I mean.[81]

The YMCA's first professional physical director in India was convinced that bodily activity would 'smash … its way into time-hoary religious and social customs', and thereby eventually achieve the Christian Association's long-term goal of 'breaking down Hinduism'.[82] That said, the expected benefits were not limited to the collapse of 'Oriental superstitions' and the resulting opportunities for proselytization. Much like Gulick's quasi-eugenic argument, Gray's firm belief was that the YMCA's fitness programme would have an equally positive impact in the political realm and would incite India to wake from its 'state of semi-hibernation' and assume a more 'prominent place in the family of Nations'.[83] Particularly basketball and baseball, the Y's signature games, he declared, could open up new horizons as they were by 'giving the Indian a real taste of democracy in play, synchronising with foretastes of democracy in many other lines'.[84]

Last, but not least, John Henry Gray believed that physical activity could also solve the most immediate health problems of Indians, who, he said, deserved the unflattering title of being 'the sickest nation of the world'.[85] Combining Luther Gulick's scientific approach to physical culture with the insights from his medical training at Columbia, Gray regularly 'gave hygiene and sex talks in many parts of the country'.[86] On such occasions, he usually emphasized that the knowledge of hygiene and sanitation was an indispensable part of the fitness package. His combined programme of 'character-building, sports and scientific health education'[87] soon caught the attention of the British imperial administration, which eventually offered its 'hearty cooperation and financial support'.[88] Within a year after Gray's arrival in Calcutta, British officials from the provincial government approached him with an offer to take over the training school for gymnastics masters and drill instructors who served in public educational institutions. Between 1909 and 1914, he worked part-time as an official advisor for physical education for the Government of Bengal and was invested with an astounding power to influence colonial body politics in India's most important province.[89] He even pioneered the establishment of public swimming pools in Calcutta.[90] His tasks in this official capacity were manifold: he served on an enquiry committee into school and college hygiene, trained teachers, lectured in schools and universities, developed curricula and wrote textbooks as well as handbooks with standardized rules for various sports and games.[91] Imperial approval soon also came from the new capital Delhi: in 1914, the Government of India supported Gray's work for the propagation of physical and health education in schools with a grant of Rs 4,000 in a deal described by the responsible government official as 'a good thing, cheaply got'.[92]

In a letter written to his former classmates in the YMCA International Training School in Springfield shortly before the outbreak of the First World War, Gray gives a positive assessment of his first five years in India. Despite the heavy workload that his multiple responsibilities entailed, he had managed to spread the Association's 'physical gospel' successfully and, even more importantly, win the trust of the imperial government:

> I had to start in on about twenty-five classes a week, and work my head off for about two years at that speed, organize the work in the Association and travel about inspecting schools all over Bengal. The time was well spent and it has been an up-hill game, but a successful one, till now the Association physical director is the one recognized expert on physical education not only in Bengal, but has been suggested a useful person for other provinces to get in touch with by the Government of India. India is in a new great swirl of physical life and opportunities are thicker than peas in a pod.[93]

Indeed, impressed by Gray's success, other provincial governments followed suit with 'eight provinces in all requesting trained physical directors from America'.[94] Arthur Noehren, who later succeeded Gray as National Physical Director (1922–8), likewise had a degree in medicine, which apparently increased his prestige with the colonial authorities.[95] Like Gray in Bengal, Noehren was employed by the provincial government of Madras from 1915 to 1921 as an advisor on physical education. In this role, he 'reorganized the entire department of physical education in the Presidency' and conducted physical examinations of over 2,000 Indian university students. He hailed the latter task in particular as a 'welcome opportunity for personal evangelistic effort'.[96]

By the 1920s, the joint venture between the British colonial state and the American-led Christian lay organization had even spilled over to Burma and Ceylon. The YMCA's branch in Colombo, especially, became an important centre for physical activities for over a decade. In 1916, Robert W. Cammack, another Springfield graduate and personal protégé of Gray's, took over the post of physical director in Ceylon and started manifold activities, including the introduction of 'Swedish Drill',[97] the establishment of several athletic leagues and protracted collaborations with the colonial authorities.[98] A few Indian princely states with a reputation for a 'progressive' style of administration such as Travancore and Baroda likewise employed foreign fitness experts who were trained by the Y.[99] Thus by 1917 no less than eighteen YMCA physical directors worked for various administrations.[100] Most of them were American, and the few non-Americans like the Englishman Donald Munro (who became physical director in Bombay in 1913) were culturally and ideologically assimilated by having attended Springfield for their degree in physical education.[101] There were even efforts to ensure that the US industry benefit from the American bias in India's physical education schemes. In a plan for sports facilities that Gray designed in 1914, to be set up at Nagpur University, he made it a point that 'all heavy apparatus should be American goods' and only 'balls, nets etc.' be of British manufacture.[102] All in all, it was no exaggeration when K. T. Paul (1876–1931), the first Indian general secretary of the subcontinental YMCA, proudly declared that the Association was 'dominating the physical education of the high school boys in the entire country'.[103]

Highlighting the role of the Y, however, should by no means make us forget the fact that other influential organizations and individuals from a broad array of backgrounds tried simultaneously to spread the gospel of fitness in India. It is important to note, however, that few, if any, could count on a similar degree of acceptance and support from the British colonial government. The ultimate evidence of the YMCA's extraordinary reputation in the realm of sports and fitness is provided by the fact that, even after the viceroy initially withheld his support 'due to suspicions of a political nature',[104] the Government of India eventually selected two YMCA directors to coach the first Indian Olympic teams in the 1920s.[105]

This infrastructural support and financial backing that the YMCA received from the imperial authorities rested largely on the latter's conviction that 'scientific physical education' as promoted by Gray and other Y secretaries[106] was markedly superior to the established British (let alone indigenous!) forms of physical exercise for students.[107] If sports classes existed at all in government schools, they consisted merely of tedious drill and were constantly criticized by YMCA spokesmen. The 'gymnastics masters' (often ex-servicemen trained in the colonial army), it was maintained, were 'as a whole not selected because of any particular qualification' and failed to 'take into consideration the educational and moral value of exercise and play' that was so central to the Springfield scheme.[108] It is also intriguing that, despite being on the payroll of the Government of Bengal for years, Gray himself stressed his distance from the British colonial administration, which he dismissed as anachronistic 'paternalistic autocracy'.[109] The Columbia-trained doctor repeatedly highlighted his own 'American-ness' as well as that of his specific approach to physical education. In a paper written in the 1950s, he recalled his first encounter with status-conscious British officials in 1908:

> The fact that I was an M.D. and from a Medical School recognized by the British, gave me without question a place in the British Colonial order. One of my secret joys was to watch the British try to classify me. They never really did. I was a new specie.[110]

Thirty years later, during a lecture tour in the United States in 1938, Gray put 'America's pioneering role in India's awakening' into stark relief and dwelled at length on how his own efforts were undertaken with a view to 'enlisting the sympathetic cooperation of Governments, in order to make possible the introduction of North American conceptions of physical education, recreation and sanitation'.[111] Even conceding that a part of his rhetoric was due to the fact that Gray needed to impress potential American donors, one can hardly doubt that he saw himself as representative of a superior modern and scientific variety of fitness education. He had developed a strong sense of mission not only vis-à-vis the 'natives' of South Asia but also towards their supposedly outmoded colonial masters, who were often ridiculed by the American YMCA secretaries.[112] This trajectory ties in with the more general observation recently made by Mark Dyreson and others, who argue that according to the popular American self-perception of the 1920s, the United States had surpassed its erstwhile role model on the playing field, with Britain being widely viewed 'as a veteran athlete who had passed the champion's crown to a younger and worthier successor'.[113] That this new self-perception as 'great power' in the fields of international sports coalesced with the role the United States had acquired in the international political system after the Great War needs little elaboration.

The Madras College of Physical Education

During the First World War, the 'old paternalistic authorities' of British India were so impressed with the YMCA's innovative sports programme (which, as we have seen in the previous chapter, also formed an important part of the Y's army work) that they announced a grant of Rs 300,000 for the establishment of a Central College of Physical Education in Bangalore. This college was to be run by the YMCA but controlled by the colonial administration. The plan, however, was cancelled after the political turmoil that followed the Amritsar Massacre of 1919.[114] Not surprisingly, the YMCA leadership in India (which now included more Indians in high and middle positions) had also become extremely sensitive to the political atmosphere of the time and tried to avoid an all-too-conspicuous association with the colonial authorities.[115]

It was at this juncture that the organization's most ambitious project to further India's moral character and physical fitness was launched. The proposed College of Physical Education was eventually established in the Y's South Indian stronghold of Madras – considered by the Y leaders to be 'the Boston of India', due to the heavy concentration of high schools, colleges and universities in the city.[116] It was not run-in cooperation with the colonial state but rather solely by the YMCA, reflecting the organization's growing self-confidence and changing political outlook. The new institution was decisively shaped by its charismatic American founder Harry Crowe Buck (1884–1943), remembered even today as one of the outstanding pioneers of modern sports in India.[117] Buck, too, was a Springfield-trained enthusiast of scientific fitness education. Only in his early thirties when he arrived in Madras in 1919, he had far-reaching visions of what the right type of 'somatic engineering' could do for India.[118] He was convinced that the Association could make a much greater contribution to the country's advancement 'by training the sons of India to take upon their own shoulders the task of the physical regeneration of their people,[119] and went on to develop a plan for a new institution exclusively concerned with the training of 'native' physical instructors. Buck's experiment started in August 1920 with a mere five students on the premises of the Madras YMCA, but within a decade the MCPE acquired a subcontinental visibility.[120]

The MCPE relocated to the Madras suburb of Royapettah in 1923.[121] The new site offered more room for outdoor games and exercises, and mud huts were built as hostels.[122] The growth of the institution was such that even the new home of the pioneering institution became too small after a few years. The institution then moved to its final location in Saidapet in 1932,[123] thanks to a generous grant of 65 acres of land by the Government of Madras.[124] Both student housing and sports facilities had been very basic in Royapettah, but a donation of USD 35,000, received from Vincent Massey, scion of the famous Canadian tractor manufacturers, philanthropist and future Governor General of Canada, changed this. The donation allowed for the construction of permanent brick buildings, a huge hall (aptly christened Massey Hall), a swimming pool, gymnasiums and separate fields for cricket, football, basketball, volleyball, hockey and 'indigenous sports' on the new site.[125] The School of Physical Education had by now grown into a recognized college officially affiliated to the University of Madras.[126] The number of its students also rose from five in the pioneering class of 1920 to sixty-four in 1930.[127] By the end of the 1930s, the college attracted around one hundred students every year from all parts of the subcontinent because of its one year diploma programme and 'developed into a fine all-India institution' recognized by the imperial government.[128] The most spectacular act of official recognition of the MCPE came in 1932, when Harry Buck and his wife Marie received the prestigious *Kaiser-i-Hind* medal from the viceroy.[129] On the initiative of the Government of Madras,[130] the MCPE's first training course for women was launched in July 1940 under the aegis of Marie Buck, a 'frontier-thinker leader in her own right',[131] who also served as 'women specialist in Physical education to the Government of Madras'.[132] After this expansion, the average student body grew to about 140 students in the 1940s (see Figure 3.3).[133]

In spite of being decorated with one of the highest orders of the British Indian Empire, Harry C. Buck, like the pioneer Gray before him, underscored the specifically *American* character of the new institution as expressed in its combination of playful voluntarism and the sound scientificity of the fitness education it offered. Buck, described by a contemporary as 'a typical American',[134] stressed that the new college was unique in the subcontinent in that it was a direct outcome of the YMCA's scientific physical programme and had been developed especially for India 'backed by American leadership and aid'. Its main goal was to catalyse the 'desirable transfer of emphasis' from the 'meaningless drills' of the earlier British efforts in physical education to activities 'better suited to the nature and needs of the Indian young men'.[135] He thus purposely continued the strategy of distancing the YMCA's programme from what was regarded as an outdated approach associated with the colonial regime. For instance, in a report on the inauguration of the Saidapet facility in 1932, he reiterated that the Y's programme was 'based on the fundamental urge for play' and proudly declared that due to the successful spread of this gospel through the dozens of graduates that the MCPE had already produced, it was no longer necessary 'to use the word "compulsory"

Figure 3.3 A period of substantial growth: Harry Buck (eighth from left in the second row) with the seventy-two graduates of the MCPE's class of 1935. Courtesy Kautz Family YMCA Archives, University of Minnesota, Minneapolis.

in connection with physical education in schools and colleges'.[136] In Buck's view, their natural attractiveness made the Y methods vastly superior to the 'artificial' German, Swedish and Danish systems, which 'fail[ed] utterly to shape men to be good citizens of any social order'.[137] Buck thus also followed his predecessor John Gray in drawing direct connections between fitness training and democracy, possibly guided by the emphasis on the importance of voluntary participation in fitness activities. The fact that the Madras College drew students from all over South Asia who spoke different languages and represented a wide range of social and religious backgrounds further reinforced the self-representation of the Indian YMCA, in general, and the MCPE, in particular, as a 'school for democracy', an image that became popular by the end of the interwar period.[138] This view is particularly strongly articulated in the institution's 1940 prospectus, which highlighted the reconciliatory capacity of the institution:

> The fact that the Y.M.C.A. College is an All-India Institution makes it unique in its cosmopolitan nature, and the opportunity it presents for social education, and in helping to build up inter-sectional and inter-religious friendships. Our students come to us from all parts of India, Burmah [sic] and Ceylon. We also had them from Egypt, Siam, and Africa and have visions of the College becoming *the* College of Physical Education for the Orient. ... This opportunity of learning to live happily with others of totally different backgrounds is an experience that we crave for larger and larger numbers of the youth of this country.[139]

The message was reinforced through an illustration placing the MCPE prominently on a map of the Indian subcontinent. Such a visual representation, of course, had strong nationalistic overtones, as the physical shape of India had been invested with manifold political meanings since the early 1900s and had become an almost-omnipresent icon in the Congress's nationalistic mass campaigns during the interwar years.[140] It is worthwhile having a closer look at this remarkable image. The beneficent impact of the physical education imparted at Saidapet, it suggests, radiates across the entire region. The implication was that the spread across India of physical directors trained in the college could ensure that their internalized values of democratic citizenship and the capacity to mediate conflicts in a non-violent fashion would reach thousands of students in schools and colleges in each and every province of a country that would soon deserve to be free of the shackles of British colonial rule under the Y's tutelage. This 'preparation for democracy' strategy thus perfectly corresponded to the ones implemented by American YMCA secretaries Charles McCloy in China and by Elwood Brown in America's own Asian colony, the Philippines (see Figure 3.4).[141]

The great expectations from MCPE's graduates can also be inferred from the bombastic prose of Harry Buck and John H. Gray, who described the college's alumni as 'leaders with vision, initiative, resourcefulness [and] intelligence', as a 'stalwart group of ... men, India's finest' and 'apostles' who would 'go forth as physical directors in universities and colleges all over India' to 'render a high type of patriotic service' by taking on the 'necessary work of the physical regeneration of their people.'[142] Indeed, as a 'directory of students' in the MCPE's monthly mouthpiece *Vyayam* notes, more than 200 of the college graduates found active employment. Several worked for local YMCA branches but the majority of them served as physical instructors in colleges, high schools or some other educational institution, or as advisors to a provincial government or princely state.[143] A fairly typical example can illustrate that at least some of them did indeed exert a palpable influence in the development of sports and physical education in the subcontinent. Harbail Singh, a Punjabi graduate of the class of 1931, found a job as Director of Physical Education in the Khalsa College, Amritsar, immediately after graduation. Once in office, he established a gym, systematized the methods of physical instruction and introduced a new style of 'scientific Hockey'. The success of the latter allowed him to lead the college's hockey team to a number of regional and national titles and coach it on a widely reported tour to Australia and New Zealand in 1934.[144] After fifteen fruitful years in the Khalsa College, Harbail Singh reached a position of even greater influence when he became the 'Chief Organiser of Sports in the Faridkot State' in 1946.[145]

As stated above, the physical regeneration advocated by the MCPE was achieved not solely through team sports and exercise but also through the spread of knowledge on hygiene and sanitation.[146] Besides classes in anatomy and physiology, the curriculum of the Madras College, therefore, also contained compulsory courses in 'Tropical Hygiene and Sanitation', 'Personal Hygiene', as well as 'Sex Hygiene'.[147] The last, in particular, was highlighted as being important preparation for the service the graduates could later offer to the country's adolescent youth through their 'instructional and guiding influence'.[148] Even before graduation, the MCPE students had opportunities to apply their expertise in integrated community projects like the Saidapet health project. This venture was aimed at bettering the living conditions of communities living in the Madras suburb in which the college was situated.[149] It seems safe to assume that this

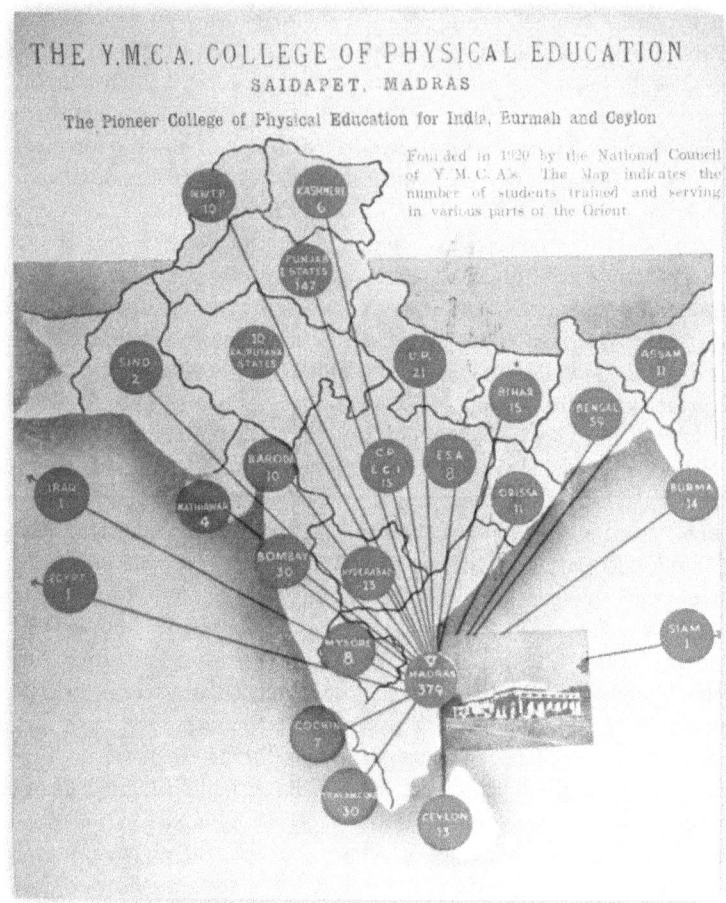

Figure 3.4 Map indicating the region of origin of the MCPE graduates (1937). Courtesy Kautz Family YMCA Archives, University of Minnesota, Minneapolis.

type of direct practical engagement further enhanced the acceptance of the Christian College not only among the local population but also within the Gandhian movement, which was almost simultaneously carrying out experiments with 'constructive programs' of community development with a similar bio-moral focus.[150]

It is important in this context to keep in mind that the foundation of the MCPE took place at a time when the Indian provincial governments were no longer controlled by nominated British officials but rather by elected Indian representatives due to the constitutional reforms implemented by the Government of India in the wake of the First World War.[151] This shift enabled an intense cooperation with local governments without risking losing the sympathy of the INC and other currents within the anticolonial movement. Long after his retirement, J. H. Gray had an original explanation for the appeal that the Y's physical education programme had for India's nationalist activists and politicians, many of whom were otherwise ostentatiously critical of the 'aping' of Western ways and instead stressed the value of all things *svadeśī*.[152] According to Gray, the patriotic leaders of the national movement were aware that India was 'physically the poorest country of the world', and therefore 'naturally recognized the need for racial vitality and gave their full support'.[153] It should be added that the wide acceptance of the YMCA's programme of spreading the value of hygiene and generally improving South Asia's 'human material' was fairly predictable given the popularity of eugenic thought prevailing in the subcontinent, particularly during the interwar period.[154]

The INC indeed clearly approved of the Y's efforts in cultivating the health and fitness of India's future citizens, and the MCPE soon found Indian emulators in Hyderabad and other places, especially after the next round of constitutional reforms and the India-wide elections of 1937 propelled Congress governments into power in most provinces.[155] The INC Minister of Education B. G. Kher appointed a Committee on Physical Education in Bombay in 1937. The committee recommended 'the establishment of an Institute at Kandivli for the training of teachers of physical education'.[156] The institution, clearly modelled on the MCPE and featuring a YMCA-trained director (P. M. Joseph), was opened in the following year. C. J. Varkey, Minister of Law and Education in the INC-led provincial government of Madras, visited the MCPE in Saidapet in July 1939 and celebrated the college as a lighthouse institution for the entire South Asian region. Perhaps unsurprisingly, the minister singled out the collectivizing aspect of the Y's fitness scheme as being the most praiseworthy. Varkey was particularly impressed by the mass callisthenics demonstration he had witnessed and declared in his address to the college's students and faculty that, through the contribution of the MCPE, physical education had become a 'subject of study of social value' as the institution's approach to sports was no longer 'selfish and individualistic' but 'scientific and socialistic'.[157]

In the turbulent years around India's independence, the official appreciation of the MCPE's value for the education of future generations of citizens even led to protracted attempts by the Government of Madras to take over the college completely. The Director of Public Instruction of the Madras Province put pressure on the MCPE principal and the National Council of the Indian YMCA to grant government officials far-reaching control over college affairs, including the selection of students, the appointment of staff and the curricular design.[158] The YMCA leadership, anxious that their 'very considerable investment' might go to waste,[159] sent a high-profile delegation to meet the responsible minister and present him with a memorandum so as to stop the 'hostile takeover' at the last minute.[160] The mission was successful, but the price was high: the Y delegation eventually accepted most of the government conditions, and the college lost much of its independence, being subsequently affiliated to Madras University.[161]

In sum, the appreciation (through appropriation) of the YMCA's fitness programme by prominent nationalist politicians might be read as a confirmation of the claim made by in-house histories that the Christian lay organization had not only grown more 'secular' in its outlook but had 'become truly national', even becoming 'in complete agreement with the patriotic aspirations of India'.[162] The YMCA's scientific-cum-democratic fitness scheme, or so it would appear, functioned as a dynamic tool of empowerment for young South Asians, who were to be thoroughly physically and mentally in a way that would lend authority and credibility to their ambitions for political self-government, or, to use the rather more gendered language of a contemporary American YMCA secretary, that 'would encourage the evolution of a virile manhood more consistent with national aspirations'.[163] The Y institutions, free from the Britons' 'unconscious racial arrogance',[164] thus professed the ability to train an élite community of responsible young leaders well able to guide their country into a modernity resembling the American model rather than that of the British colonial masters.

However, I argue that such an interpretation is simplistic and overlooks important facets of the Y programme that need to be addressed. In order to understand the limits of physical education's emancipatory potential and better grasp the ambiguities of the YMCA's body politics, it is instructive to look closer at the ideological underpinnings of the project of 'working out India' that evolved from the strange convergence of evangelical missionary zeal, considerations of colonial governance and the concerns of anticolonial nationalists.

Somatic orientalism and Indian *Eigensinn*: Limitations and modifications of the YMCA's 'democratizing fitness' project

The focus of this chapter, thus far, has been on the programmatic aspect of the YMCA's physical work, or in other words, on what North American fitness pioneers like Gray and Buck *wanted* to do and less on what they *actually achieved*, or indeed how Indians reacted to their schemes. In the remaining few pages of this chapter, I will argue that the success of the Y's specifically North American 'democratizing fitness' programme was severely curtailed by powerful influences coming from the two opposite ends of the political spectrum in late colonial India. Firstly, in spite of their continued efforts to distance themselves from the 'paternalistic authoritarianism' of the British Raj, North American YMCA secretaries remained heavily indebted to the colonial rulers on an epistemic and discursive level. Sharing what I call the 'somatic Orientalism' of the Raj,[165] they constructed native bodies (and, for that matter, societies) as fundamentally different and 'hopelessly defective', as the influential Y secretary George Sherwood Eddy put it.[166] While this discursive overlap might have made it easy for colonial administrators to identify with and support the YMCA's project of keeping 'youth in harness',[167] it seems plausible that it simultaneously undermined their purportedly egalitarian and inclusive democratizing agenda, although, of course, it is difficult to assess the effects that this ideological inconsistency had on the Indian target groups.

Secondly, the 'physical renaissance' of India, and the experiments in nationalistic subject formation that went hand in hand with it, cannot be understood as the results of a mere absorption of Western influences as they were profoundly shaped by local Indian actors and the persistence of existing traditions of physical activities and games.

Even modernist fitness experts like Harry C. Buck, who were otherwise extremely optimistic about the societal effects of the Association's physical work, had to admit that 'one cannot bring a purely Western programme of physical training to the Orient and expect it to be a huge success'.[168] His observation reminds us of the importance of Indian agency and *Eigensinn*,[169] and perfectly reinforces a point widely accepted among sports historians, that the transfer of Western forms of games and physical exercise to the non-Western world can be better understood as process of translation or remaking rather than a unilateral diffusion or dissemination.[170] But let us turn to the persistence of imperial somatic orientalism first.

Like generations of British colonial administrators before them, on whose shoulders they stood when it came to 'knowing the country', leading American Y activists perceived India as 'stationary' and standing in need of 'awakening'.[171] On the basis of this general assessment, they provided discriminatory and condescending commentaries on Indian groups and individuals that were almost interchangeable with the familiar imperial original. Predictably, the YMCA secretaries tended to reproduce the entire range of existing stereotypes about educated Bengalis in the province's urban centres, describing them as 'terribly indolent' and 'effeminate' people who seemed like 'incomplete editions of the English'.[172] In a similar vein, the 50,000 plus college and high school students living in Calcutta's 'poorly supervised messes' were collectively introduced as ignorant, weak and degenerate victims of immoral influences and unhygienic living conditions in an annual report written in 1917:

> Immoral influences are around them and the low physical vitality of the average school boy or college man is also due to malnutrition … or ignorance in matters of personal hygiene. Their ignorance of the simple rules of health, such as eating, sleeping, the care of the body etc. is appalling.[173]

An author writing in the Y's journal *Foreign Mail* underscored the beneficial impact of medical check-ups that were compulsory for everyone who wanted to attend the Association's sports facilities, observing that the physical examinations allowed

> not only to combat weakness and disease, but to show the way to victory over the sin that is almost invariably inducing physical difficulties. It is seldom an Indian is examined who could be pronounced normal; either he suffers from chronic malarial attacks, hook-worm, alimentary troubles, diabetes, nephritis and the like, or shows marks of malnutrition.[174]

The 'sin' alluded to in the *Foreign Mail* article refers in all likelihood to masturbation. The quote thus illustrates the convergence of moral with medical, social hygienic and eugenic concerns that was typical for the approach of the YMCA's physical directors.

According to J. H. Gray, the 'abnormal' state of Indian bodies was aggravated by the corrupting influence of Hinduism. The Hindu propensity to asceticism, he especially noted, had led to 'incalculable losses in impaired racial vitality [and] physical suffering'.[175] He was firmly convinced that this practice of self-denial and consequent 'low racial vitality' was the main reason that the Spanish influenza pandemic had taken such a heavy toll in the country in 1918–19.[176] In a paper read before the annual congress of the American Physical Education Association in Chicago in 1919, he enlightened the expert audience about his reading of the complex material and religio-cultural reasons for this sad state of affairs:

> The children of India have been born of physical immature mothers and fathers almost as bad. Take their food, for instance. They are vegetarians there, and yet the diet of the Bengalis ... is the most insufficient in the world. You cannot bring up a strong, vigorous race on an insufficient diet. In addition to that, as I suggested, the social and religious customs are all tied together in that country. They believe in reincarnation, they will not kill animals. They will not kill a cow, because the cow is sacred. If I believed that, I do not think I would kill one, either, or I would be committing murder if I believed that my old grandmother was in that cow. That is the way they regard such things there.[177]

Even if one allows for the fact that Gray was addressing an audience largely unfamiliar with the specificities of the South Asian context, the superficiality and *naiveté* of his platitudes are astounding for a man of science. Having spent eleven years in the country, he must have been aware of the fact that merely two-thirds of the South Asian population were Hindus and that not all Hindus were vegetarian. One is tempted to conclude that the lack of nuance was part of a deliberate strategy to discredit Hinduism by making it responsible for the perceived physical deficiencies of the Indian populace.

The Madras physical director Arthur Noehren was even more extreme, maintaining that 'venereal diseases, including syphilis, are very common and often traced to semi-religious practices.'[178] Not surprisingly, he repeatedly reminded his audiences of Indian high school and college students in his speeches of the 'necessity for full surrender to Christ as the only means of living a clean victorious life in pagan atmosphere reeking with corruption'.[179] Even a sober rationalist like Harry Buck subscribed to the fundamental otherness (read: deficiency) of Oriental bodies. The discursive repertoire of the colonial politics of difference is a recognizable subtext in his rhetoric when he lists the specificities that supposedly made his work with South Asian students different from the training of Western undergraduates, making it 'more of an exercise in preventive medicine'. Among the features he regarded as typical of Oriental students, he mentions amongst others the 'disinclination to exercise', 'lack of activities that develop hardihood', 'improper diet' and the 'widespread use of drugs'.[180]

It has already been pointed out that such a diagnosis of individual bodies went in tandem with equally negative assessments of allegedly backward and static South Asian societies and belief systems. In this context, too, the pervasive influence of deep-seated colonial attributes and stereotypes is ubiquitous. Whereas the 'scourges' of Hinduism with its stark hierarchies and the caste system were obvious and logical targets of the harshest criticisms from North American Y secretaries,[181] it might come as a surprise that the Buddhist society in Burma was seen as equally degenerate. Because the dominant philosophy in Burma was 'Buddhist un-social' (i.e. concerned with individual spiritual salvation rather than societal betterment), as Warren D. Healy, the Y physical director in Rangoon, declared in 1931, the entire Burmese population was said to lack 'social consciousness' and therefore be incapable of nation-building without the YMCA's help.[182] Thus, the aims of the Association's brand of physical education were perceived as the perfect antidote against Eastern 'un-social' attitudes:

> By properly conducted team games, group consciousness is awakened and the individual learns to sacrifice his selfish interests for the greater advantage of the group. He learns to play the game according to the rules, thus developing the spirit of loyalty and obedience to authority. Submission to group opinion, co-operation, courtesy and thoughtfulness for others should become his every-day habits.[183]

Thus, orientalist clichés were critical in defining the role of the MCPE graduates and portraying them as leaders in educating their 'physically illiterate' South Asian countrymen, thereby building up their weak and feeble bodies and reorganizing their fragmented and heterogeneous societies. The improvement and refinement of the bodies and characters of the institution's South Asian graduates were crucial for the success of this mission. It is striking how precise a vision Buck and his fellow instructors had of the end product of their nation-building workout in Saidapet:

> The model of man that modern Physical Education aims to build is slender in type, graceful, not heavy muscularly, clear-eyed, supple not tense, alert, erect, easy on his feet, enthusiastic, happy, forceful, imaginative, self-controlled, true, clean, with a sense of fair play, who loves the companionship of his fellows and who has the fear of God in his heart.[184]

Interestingly, collective spirit and group solidarity are strongly emphasized even when the programme's effect on a single individual is described. This quote also allows us a glimpse into the ideals of the specific bodies and masculinities that were envisaged as resulting from Buck's ambitious endeavour in somatic engineering. The 'model of man' and the capable leader embodied by the MCPE-educated physical directors, it seems, was to be brought into full congruence with North American Protestant ideals of health, beauty, efficiency and morality. In the process, he was also purged of all physical and mental traits that marked his 'Oriental' origins.

The interpretation of the Y's fitness training as an exercise in 'de-Orientalization' is supported by a rare photograph showing the participants of a 'Perfect Physique Competition' that was organized by the physical director of the Colombo YMCA in 1939. Given the multi-ethnic composition of Ceylonese society, it can hardly be a coincidence that exclusively light-skinned young men with what would probably have been described by contemporaries as 'European features' were chosen to represent the perfect physique of Ceylonese youth. Moreover, the poses adopted by the young sportsmen bring to mind Greek and Roman sculptures, corroborating the interpretation that the Y's physical work in South Asia was inspired by the same aesthetic ideal that has been famously described by George Mosse as the 'positive stereotype' of Western masculinity.[185] The transformation brought about in the gyms, pitches and athletic grounds patronized by the YMCA in South Asia seems to have amounted to a process of 'bleaching' as it were, diminishing the gulf between Oriental bodies and Western physiques.¹⁸⁶ By shaping their bodies along Western lines, and consequently physically inscribing them within a normative code of masculinity, the YMCA-trained South Asian youth could thus also hope to partake in the prestige ascribed to 'whiteness'. This option was clearly attractive given the prevailing imperial world order, sarcastically described by a contemporary Indian intellectual as 'albinocracy' (see Figure 3.5).¹⁸⁷

In sum, then, one can conclude that in spite of the North American Y secretaries' protracted efforts to present themselves as an egalitarian and inclusive force clearly distinct from and superior to the British, and as embodying an imperially untainted alternative model of modernity to be emulated by 'Young India', their schemes rested on ideological foundations that shared much in common with the discursive repertoire of the British imperial civilizing mission. If this obvious tension between inclusive rhetoric and the persistence of deep-seated racial prejudice seems incongruous, it has to be noted that a very similar racialist logic undergirded the YMCA's physical work programmes in East Asia and the Philippines.¹⁸⁸ It may also be helpful to look at a comparable phenomenon in the United States: in spite of all the lip service paid to 'Christian brotherhood', 'egalitarianism' and 'interracial dialogue', YMCAs for African Americans remained strictly segregated from those catering to a white clientele until the late 1940s.¹⁸⁹

As stated previously, the North American 'athletic crusade' in India did not quite work out as per the original design of the first generation of the YMCA's sports experts

Figure 3.5 'De-orientalized bodies?' – Participants of the 'perfect physique competition' organized by the Colombo YMCA, 1939. Courtesy Kautz Family YMCA Archives, University of Minnesota, Minneapolis.

for other reasons as well. Springfield-trained physical directors like John Gray had a deep contempt for existing South Asian traditions of games and physical exercise whose 'methods and practices' they regarded as 'contrary to those based on modern scientific knowledge'.[190] Even though the Association's fitness experts left no opportunity to stress that they were trying to replace the existing 'archaic' and 'individualistic' system of 'physical torture' that they saw as characterizing Hindu traditions with a rational, scientific and socially beneficent system of 'physical culture',[191] the local practices so dismissed turned out to be surprisingly resilient. Following the inclusion of non-elite groups in the YMCA schemes, it was impossible to completely ignore what had been labelled as 'native' or indigenous sports. For instance, the sports programme designed for the millhands of central Indian textile factories that were part of the YMCA industrial work scheme prominently included *pahalvānī* (a.k.a. *bhāratīya kuśtī*), a traditional Indian form of wrestling.[192] This inclusion is noteworthy, because, as we have seen, this particular martial art had been rediscovered and cultivated by Hindu nationalists and revolutionaries since the last decade of the nineteenth century and acquired slightly more nativist and nationalistic overtones by the interwar period.[193]

One major reason why the YMCA leadership could not ignore the popularity of 'patriotic' indigenous sports and physical culture schemes was the growing competition from various Indian agencies. The high-caste, middle-class and predominantly English-educated leadership of the INC adopted a positive stance towards the Christian Association's fitness schemes, but this was not the case for the entire political and religious spectrum.

Chapter 1 has already discussed how, as soon as the reinvigorated Indian YMCA had its first limited accomplishments in converting high-status Indian, Ceylonese and Burmese youths to Christianity, religious authorities and self-proclaimed spokesmen of a wide array of faiths and denominations prevalent in South Asia (namely, Hinduism, Buddhism, Sikhism, Islam and Jainism) reacted by founding their own youth organizations in a mimetic impulse of self-defence. In many cases – Swami Kuvalayananda's yoga scheme is a case in point[194] – there was direct contact between the Indian physical programmes and the YMCA's physical work, but this is not clear in other cases. Nonetheless, even without direct influence, there were many other instances of local projects aiming to develop alternative masculinities and biomoral modernities that competed with the Christian Association's offerings.[195] Consequently, if the YMCA's fitness experts wanted to attract a growing number of Indian students and at the same time retain their credibility as an ally of (moderate) Indian nationalism, they had to include, at least to a certain extent, Indian games and exercises into their physical fitness schemes.

A more direct form of pressure to align their training programmes to local demands resulted from the cooperation of the YMCA physical directors with the Congress-led provincial governments. Thus, Arthur G. Noehren, who served as Director of Physical Education for the Government of Bombay in the late 1920s, was asked to write a physical education syllabus for the schools in that province. While preparing the proposed publication, he visited dozens 'native' gymnasiums and *akhāṛās*, hoping to acquire 'some concrete knowledge of exercises ... that would represent the genius of Western India'.[196] Almost simultaneously, Harry Buck, who held a similar position in Madras, sat on an expert committee on physical education. Since seventeen out of the twenty-three committee members were Indians, it is not surprising that one of the resolutions framed in the concluding session prescribed that the new scheme of physical education to be adopted in the province's schools and colleges 'should be so framed as to suit local conditions' and hence include 'local games of an indigenous nature in revival of the past glory of India'.[197] Even in the YMCA flagship institution at Saidapet, Indian exercises and games became part of an ever more eclectic curriculum, but only if they proved compatible with 'all the truths brought to us by the study of such sciences as biology, psychology, sociology and allied subjects'.[198] Whether Buck can indeed be meaningfully understood as the open minded and cosmopolitan 'cultural frontiersman' that Vertinsky and Ramachandran view him as[199] remains doubtful. But nevertheless, by the end of the 1940s, *Buck's Book of Rules*, a serial publication pioneered by Harry Buck in 1929, contained chapters on no less than four different Indian games: *Atya-Patya, Kho-Kho, Hututu* and *Kabaddi*.[200] Needless to say that they had become thoroughly 'sportified' in the process.

Not all YMCA members were happy about these new tendencies to 'go native'. Arthur Noehren, for example, contended that Indian forms of bodybuilding and muscle control were anachronistic and might perhaps 'be featured in a circus tent', whereas they seemed completely 'out of place on a school compound'.[201] Another expert insisted that the newly adopted Indian callisthenic exercises like *danda*s and *baithak*s, were 'individualistic in type' and consequently held 'no inherent social development value', 'besides putting an undue strain on the physical organs'.[202] However, such protests had little effect at a time when the leadership of the Indian YMCA increasingly shifted towards Indian secretaries who made no secret of their patriotic propensities. Far from merely disseminating a ready-made American blueprint of fitness and physical culture, the YMCA ultimately contributed to the creation of what has been aptly described by Mark Singleton as a 'hybridized though distinctly Indian culture of sport and exercise'.[203] As Singleton has shown, this hybridization cut in two directions. While Harry Buck somewhat reluctantly introduced modified forms of yoga *āsana*s (postures) into the MCPE's curriculum in the 1920s despite his concerns about their 'subjective nature', Swami Kuvalayananda (1883–1966), arguably the single most important Indian advocate of 'modern Yoga exercise', developed his rigorous posture work at least in part to refute Buck's assertion of the inadequacy of *āsana*s as a complete physical programme.[204] It seems plausible that this recalibration of South Asian yogic traditions, which brought this bodily practice closer to the YMCA's 'scientific approach' and its well-established holistic 'mind-body-spirit' ideal, considerably increased its export potential for Western markets in the following years and decades.[205]

Summing up

This chapter has demonstrated that the spread of the global idiom of fitness and modern forms of sports in late colonial South Asia cannot be fruitfully understood as an act of transfer solely undertaken by the British rulers. It has demonstrated that the activities of the Indian YMCA were also seminal in this respect. The Y's physical programme was initially used as an iconoclastic device and subordinated to the overarching goal of winning Indian, Ceylonese and Burmese converts. After the First World War, however, sports and fitness schemes became the most important components of the broader liberal modernization project that the YMCA had meanwhile adopted in its Asian mission fields. The ultimate objective was no longer to achieve a large-scale religious conversion, but rather a conversion to what one might call a modernity in an American inflection. This agenda was reflected in the fact that the first generation of YMCA physical directors in South Asia relentlessly stressed the putatively superior American (read: progressive and egalitarian) character of their training programme. The type of fitness education that had been developed in the pioneering physical training college in Springfield seemed to lend itself perfectly to the needs of the Indian national movement with which the Y leadership increasingly sympathized. It focused on the training of responsible and self-controlled leaders and citizens, it was 'scientific' and therefore supposedly more efficient than existing programmes, it integrated physical culture and team sports into a wider project of societal improvement that also included hygiene and sanitation, and it promised to achieve nothing less than 'the development of a superior race'. Perhaps most importantly, the emphasis on playfulness and voluntarism that was cultivated by the Y turned the Association's physical work schemes into supposedly ideal 'schools of democracy' that (it was hoped) would entice Indians, Ceylonese and Burmese into following the American model when it came to state-building. Although there was stiff competition from other fitness systems, the YMCA exercised a considerable influence in its heyday, directly by attracting tens of thousands of South Asian youth to colleges, training classes and tournaments, and indirectly through the physical directors who had been trained by the Y programmes and served as advisors to several provincial and 'princely' governments. Last but not least, the organization also had a significant impact through the many subcontinental 'mimics', which offered vernacularized versions of the Association's fitness scheme. The national significance of the YMCA's 'physical ministry' reached its peak in the 1930s and 1940s with the success of the MCPE in Saidapet and the autonomy of Congress-led provincial governments. The college's graduates went on to serve as amplifiers of the norms and values that they had internalized through games and exercise, sharing them with tens of thousands of pupils and students all over the subcontinent. After independence, there were even attempts by provincial governments to 'hijack' successful YMCA institutions such as the MCPE.

Whereas the overall significance of the physical activities campaigns certainly cannot be denied, the limitations, contradictions and problematic aspects of the scheme have also become apparent through our analysis. The last section has demonstrated how the Y's supposedly inclusive and emancipatory discourses and practices of physical fitness were overdetermined by the powerful influences of racialized colonial discourse of difference on the one hand and the *Eigensinn* of Indian nationalists as expressed in their agenda of discovering indigenous sports on the other. As a result of these twin influences, the fitness programme of the Indian YMCA incorporated elements of the imperial and nationalist agendas.

Finally, a brief look at the practical operations of the Association has suggested that it was less of an '*American* crusade' or establishment of an *American* cultural hegemony than the established literature might lead us to believe. 'Sportified' versions of local games and physical exercises played an ever-increasing role in the numerous Y establishments in South Asia, leading eventually to the thorough 'pidginization' of its fitness regime. By the 1940s, the Indian *avatār* of the YMCA's physical work scheme differed substantially from the North American blueprint, and the kind of modernity it embodied was as 'muscular' as it was idiosyncratic.

4

'One-fifth of the world's boyhood': American 'boyology' and the Indian YMCA's work with early adolescents (c. 1900–1950)

Echoing a global tendency among Christian and secular organizations that became discernible shortly before the First World War, the Indian YMCA launched a separate Boys' Department in the first decade of the twentieth century. The new department gradually widened the scope of its activities in subsequent years in order to attract young males aged ten to seventeen. This trend gained further momentum during the interwar period, when boys' work became increasingly popular not only in North America but in various ideological and political quarters all over the globe. In the South Asian YMCA branches, it reached the peak of its influence in the two decades preceding the independence of India and Pakistan in 1947.

In this chapter, I will first reconstruct the wider transnational trends that led to the new focus on boys. I will then flesh out the genesis and specificities of the Indian YMCA's boys' work schemes. The four main pillars of the Association's secular programme for boys will be introduced in this context and their ambivalent relationship with Indian nationalism will be discussed.[1] Three of these pillars were camping and scouting, social service schemes and educational activities. The fourth key element, 'physical work', is closely connected to the observations made in Chapter 3, and we shall see that Springfield College and its graduates played a key role in the Boys' Department as well. As has become evident in the chapters devoted to army work and physical education, the rhetoric and practice of the Indian Y were shot through with contradictions. This also holds true for the Association's boy's work scheme. This analysis of the Indian YMCA's 'adult-sponsored children's leisure activities'[2] laid particular emphasis on the ways in which YMCA boy experts oscillated between an idiom of universalism on the one hand and cultural and racial stereotyping on the other. As a result, Indian boys were either considered as equal or inferior to their European and North American peers, the latter position being congruent with the widespread views of the British officials and 'domiciled European' population in colonial South Asia. While the significance of colonial discourses thus cannot be denied, the YMCA's boys' work in India, Burma and Ceylon was not simply an extension of British imperialism. As was the case in the field of physical education and sport, North American Y workers in the boys' branches also tried to promote the YMCA's own profile by implying that it was not only distinct but even superior to British imperial practices.

Most obviously, the medico-sociological American discourse of 'boyology' can be found in contemporary manuals designed for social workers and educators as well as in the practical programmes targeted at South Asian youngsters.[3] This quasi-scientific approach to working with adolescents was seen as more advanced than imperial schemes because, much like the Y's physical education scheme or educational army work discussed in the previous chapters, it supposedly fostered the boys' capacity for 'self-government' and prepared them for democracy. In the eyes of some US boy experts, this purported superiority of American methods brought new responsibilities. As one YMCA 'boyologist' put it, 'As our country is the home of democracy other countries are constantly looking to us for the solution of the world's problems.'[4] In this respect, the Y secretaries involved in boys' work in South Asia were part and parcel of the wider phenomenon of the *messianisme démocratique* that increasingly pervaded US civil society and politics from the late 1890s onwards.[5]

On a more abstract level, and with obvious relevance for debates among historians of childhood and youth, the close analysis of Indo-US entanglements in the field of 'informal education'[6] undertaken in the following pages allows one to assess multiple aspects of youth work in the early twentieth century. It also reveals how global currents in the perception of 'boyhood' and male adolescence as well as transnational models of 'harnessing youth' through character building, habit formation and citizenship training schemes played out in a specific colonial context, and how they all left traces in the postcolonial societies of the region.

Contours of the 'Boy Problem' in the United States and India

In the history of boys' work programmes organized by the YMCA's Foreign Department, India plays a distinguished role among the dozens of the Association's overseas branches, not least because it was in the South Indian city of Madras that the very first overseas Boys' Department was opened in 1901.[7] However, the new attention to children in the (pre)puberty age range was by no means an idiosyncratic Indian affair. It reflected at least two trends that went beyond the South Asian setting. For one, this attention to children must be seen in the context of the imperial mobilization of youth that was typical of the late Victorian and Edwardian British Empire. It radiated from the imperial metropole across the Atlantic and to the wider world, including, of course, the British colonies.[8] Of all the manifestations of this imperial concern for the young, the establishment of the Boy Scout and Girl Guide Movements by Boer War veteran Baden-Powell in 1908 and 1910 respectively has received the most scholarly attention.[9] However, another organization preceded the Boy Scouts by two-and-a-half decades, one which is less well-studied despite the fact that it too played a significant role as a template for youth organizations all over the 'Anglosphere' and beyond: the

Boys' Brigade, first founded in Glasgow in 1883.[10] The Brigade was arguably 'the first youth group to emphasize the specific nature of boyhood and to develop a programme and philosophy for this stage of life,'[11] and was soon copied in several British colonies. About a decade after its founding, it was also adopted in the United States, where it enjoyed a certain popularity in the two decades preceding the outbreak of the Great War.[12] Much like the Boy Scouts, the Boys' Brigades developed their global appeal not least through their use of flamboyant uniforms, paramilitary drills and outdoor leisure programmes. Existing research leaves little doubt that the influence of such 'crypto-imperial' youth organizations that were established with a view to nurturing civic virtues and inculcating the spirit of service for nation and empire was also strongly felt in North America.[13]

However, there was another important current at play at the same time: the quasi-scientific discourse of 'boyology'. Embedded in the transformations of the broader understanding of childhood and fuelled by a motley crew of educators, psychologists, sociologists and social commentators of various backgrounds on both sides of the Atlantic, a vivid debate had crystallized around (male) children as a potential risk for society.[14] The so-called boy problem soon became a media-hyped phenomenon that generated sensationalist press reports, which in turn triggered 'cultural anxiety and concentrated reforms in society and education and juvenile justice'.[15] According to the self-proclaimed experts, this new peril was partly due to the youngsters' lack of moral grounding in an urban world that simultaneously contained dwindling physical challenges and ever-increasing temptations through the lurid attractions of consumerism and the emerging leisure and entertainment industries.[16] As a result, the negative figures of 'degenerate' or 'deviant' youths such as 'the hooligan' or the 'juvenile delinquent' were seen as imminent.

While there were some influential British publications on the 'boy problem',[17] the concern about the male child was particularly strong in the United States, which was a country, after all, that had had to cope with the loss of its 'frontier' and the 'character-forming' challenges it provided. It is unsurprising, therefore, that American scholars, youth organizations and 'boy workers' had a massive impact on the emerging field of 'boyology'.[18] In addition, there was a specific Protestant variety of the popular 'boy-problem' debate in America. Whereas psychologists and sociologists tended to stress crime, delinquency and vice as the main perils for adolescents, a number of influential religious educators emphasized the dangers of 'effeminization' and 'over-refinement' that were allegedly threatening the younger generation, often blaming the dominance of women in the education system. With increasingly popular cultural commentators sharing this concern about the potentially devastating effects of 'over-civilization', the 'boy problem grew into a national epidemic' around the turn of the twentieth century.[19] As a result, 'boyology' became the undergirding element of 'informal middle-class character building' efforts all over the country.[20] Even future US president, Teddy Roosevelt (1858–1919), jumped on the 'boyology' bandwagon. Roosevelt, a hunter and 'a lover of nature and the American West', who 'looked like a bear and roared like lion', himself embodied a rough and virile type of masculinity quite unusual in American elite politics.[21] From the late 1890s onwards, he occasionally issued public warnings against American youth leading a 'life of slothful ease'.[22]

After 1900, Christian boy workers increasingly cited the work of scientifically minded youth experts like the tremendously influential psychologist G. Stanley Hall (1846–1924). Strongly shaped by the popular social Darwinist theories of the day, Hall's eponymously titled book ushered in the age of psychosocial *adolescence* studies in 1904.[23] Christian boy workers also referred to the more practically oriented writings of YMCA activists such as Luther Halsey Gulick (1865–1918), who popularized Hall's 'recapitulation theory' in his publications, lectures and speeches. This theory posited a correlation between the stages of child development and the epochs of human evolutionary history: according to Hall and his epigones, every individual passed through the various stages from savagery to civilization.[24] George Walter Fiske, another popular YMCA boyologist, explained this journey as follows:

> In many senses it is true that the savage is a child and the child a savage. … Both live self-centered, egoistic lives and are little influenced by public opinion. … Both are apt to shun labor, responsibility and care; having little foresight, worrying little and laughing much. Creatures of physical appetite, they are seeking for the creature comforts and the untrammelled delights of an out-of-door life.[25]

Leisure activities such as swimming, sitting around campfires and 'playing Indians' acquired an entirely new significance in view of this model.[26] In the genre-defining book *Boyology*, first published in 1916, YMCA boys' worker Henry W. Gibson explains the psyche of early adolescents using a similar logic. Thus, for example, Gibson emphasizes the 'uncivilized' conflict resolution strategies normally resorted to among his charges, namely, 'the battle of words followed by the battle of fists'. He elaborates that a twelve- or thirteen-year-old boy 'like his savage ancestry' saw no alternative to settling 'his disputes in the primitive physical fashion', because 'arbitration ha[d] not yet come into his vocabulary or understanding'.[27] According to Gibson and other Y experts, it was the task of the YMCA boys' workers to apply their educational and disciplinary knowledge with a view to transforming this potentially destructive savage fighting spirit into 'a strong impulse to do great things', thus ultimately producing a man who would be able to act as 'defender of home, church, and country'.[28]

To a considerable extent, these various agendas and strands of knowledge, which can only be broadly summarized here, shaped the North American YMCA's perspective and approach to the 'boy problem', and influenced the public debates and policies related to it. Luther H. Gulick, whom we have encountered in the previous chapter as a pioneer of the scientific approach to sport and physical education, disseminated the insights of 'boyology' to a broader audience in his capacity as a professor at the YMCA International Training School in Massachusetts for more than fifteen years.[29] His contemporaries describe Gulick as a missionary 'by instinct and inheritance', who left no stone unturned in spreading the 'new gospel of health, happiness, wholesome living and efficiency' developed for America's youth to wider audiences even after he had left the college in 1901.[30] Meanwhile, his home institution in Springfield not only produced the first Boys' Work Secretary of the YMCA's International Committee, appointed in 1900,[31] it also trained scores of educators who would later work around the world, not least in South Asia.[32] In the early 1920s, the training of experts in this rapidly expanding field was further professionalized when a special four-year BSc programme was designed by the college authorities in Massachusetts with a view to attracting 'men of unquestioned character ... [and] genuine aptitude' and educating them to become boys' workers.[33] At least half dozen Springfield-trained Y volunteers served in the Boys' departments of Indian and Ceylonese cities. As we have seen in the previous chapter, many more worked as physical directors in the subcontinent, where they also had a formative influence on Indian pupils and high school students with their 'scientific program of body building and character building'.[34] It was mainly through men like John H. Gray (class of 1904), John W. Storey (class of 1906), Harry Crowe Buck (class of 1910), Harold Gething Beall (class of 1911) and other graduates of the YMCA International Training School that this particular type of knowledge first reached the Indian subcontinent.[35] 'Scientific Boyology' was taught at the International Training College well into the 1930s, as is evident from some of the theses submitted at Springfield. G. Stanley Hall's recapitulation theory, for instance, featured prominently in the 1932 master's thesis of a Springfield alumnus from Madras, while Gibson's standard work informed the teaching material used for training Boys' workers at Springfield.[36] Moreover, long-term Springfield College President Laurence Doggett (1896–1936) and G. Stanley Hall frequently communicated directly. In 1917, for example, Doggett contacted the prominent psychologist, who at the time was also president of Clarke University, to recommend an alumnus serving in the Indian YMCA for a scholarship at Clarke.[37] It is also quite safe to assume that the writings of professional American boys' workers as well as those of other popular and academic boyologists of various backgrounds also circulated in South Asia at the same time, through the libraries that were staple features of all urban YMCA branches in India, Burma and Ceylon. That said, the fact that Western experts and missionaries strove to transfer their educational knowledge to South Asia does not necessarily mean that those at the receiving end were interested in it. Let us, therefore, now briefly explore the situation that the aspiring boys' workers from the United States and Canada confronted in the Indian subcontinent.

As already indicated in Chapter 1, the colonial state had pervasive anxieties regarding the allegedly deviant and criminal propensities of low-caste children.[38] However, the public controversy about the best way to channel the potentially destructive energy of boys and early adolescents between ten and seventeen years in British India was largely restricted to the minuscule elite minority who received an English education. Predictably, the question of colonial imposition and the supposed risk of 'de-nationalization' through Western-style educational institutions for male children and adolescents[39] loomed large in discussions of the Indian variety of 'boyology'.[40] The humiliating fact of colonial subjugation together with the imperial discursive strategy of representing colonized subjects as either childlike or effeminate played a crucial role in this context. It persuaded many Indian reformers and political activists from the last two decades of the nineteenth century onwards that it was not only vital to stop the 'degeneration' of the race by reinvigorating the younger generations but also to do so in specifically indigenous ways.[41] In spite of the fundamental differences in power separating the colonizers from the colonized, some of the concerns that had triggered the transatlantic discourse on the 'boy problem' resurfaced in the elite debate around the effects of 'Western education' in the Indian subcontinent. As a result, contemporaneous South Asian intellectuals, reformers and political activists frequently framed their polemics in confrontational East–West dichotomies.[42] Especially in the half-century between the 1880s and the 1930s, countless articles in English and vernacular Indian newspapers and journals were devoted to reflections on how to acquire scientific and technical knowledge from the West and at the same time stop the combined processes of cultural alienation and moral corruption. The corruption and alienation were regularly depicted as inevitable side effects of a 'Western education', which was perceived as materialistic and superficial.[43]

The alienating, 'artificial' and unhealthy character of student life was stressed by many of the emancipatory indigenous elites organized in the INC from 1885 onwards.[44] The exclusive focus on book learning, the 'corrupting' influence of the urban environment in which institutions of higher education were usually situated and the complete lack of physical education characteristic of colonial schools and high schools were other items that featured regularly in the 'snagging lists' of Indian critics of formal education under the Raj.[45] Speaking in Lahore 1913 and using a vocabulary strikingly similar to Teddy Roosevelt's a few years previously, Lala Lajpat Rai (1865–1928), whom we have met in the previous chapter as a staunch champion of compulsory physical education in colleges and universities, tried to persuade a much younger audience of local high school students of the necessity 'to develop grit and determination'.[46] According to him, 'building character', 'leading a strenuous life' and the cultivation of 'good habits' were indispensable, because 'discipline [wa]s the secret of success' both for one's own personal development and 'for the progress of the country'.[47]

Rai's stance was fairly typical, as we saw in Chapter 1. As Carey Watt has observed, 'emergent definitions of the ideal Indian citizen' articulated by Indian nationalists and social reformers from the 1900s onwards were 'rather conservative and tended to stress expectations of obedience, self-discipline and self-sacrifice'.[48] Very often they represented an amalgam of liberal principles of individual self-improvement with local upper-caste values. German historian Franziska Roy shares his view and emphasizes that youth movements and organizations in late colonial India were 'permeated' by a 'sense of necessary self-purification to counter a perceived decadence or 'lack of modernity', and this was to be achieved through selfless service'.[49]

Thus, ironically, both the diagnosis and cure proposed by the emancipatory elites in India were astonishingly similar to the ones advocated by social reformers in Britain and North America, and even, for that matter, by Western purity activists and temperance campaigners already active in South Asia.[50] Firstly, this nationalistic project of inculcating civic virtues into the wider population explains the popularity of 'moral uplift' and citizen-training schemes in general, and of Hindi translations of Victorian 'character forming' advisory literature in particular during the 1910 and 1920s.[51] Secondly, and more importantly, the self-targeted 'middle-class civilizing mission'[52] agenda advocated by South Asian nationalists and reformers helps us understand why extracurricular learning and structured leisure activities of the kind offered by the practice-oriented 'boyologists' of the Indian YMCA converged with quite a number of similar indigenous revitalization endeavours. Clearly, these efforts were seen as potentially healthy and much-needed supplements to the one-sided and 'bookish' instruction imparted in high schools and colleges.[53] A partial overlap, at least, with the overarching Y project of 'harnessing the power of youth'[54] could be expected from the small minority segment of the predominantly high-caste, middle-class, urban elites. Significantly, this social group not only produced the principal carriers of the Indian nationalist movement but also constituted the main target group for the American YMCA secretaries in South Asia. It is to the latter's background and agendas that we turn next.

The development of boys' work in the Indian YMCA

In the early 1900s, some of the larger YMCA city branches began to broaden the usual age group of youngsters that they targeted, usually of college age (roughly between eighteen and twenty-five years), by setting up a distinct Boys' Division, especially designed to cater to the needs of younger patrons. As has already been indicated, the Madras YMCA authorities led this reorientation towards the young and established its Boys' branch as early as 1901. Its membership rose from 38 to 100 boys during the first decade, reaching 169 in 1914.[55] In 1902, the Y's Rangoon branch opened a Boys' Brigade, which offered Bible classes as well as outdoor sports and 'drill' for over fifty boys.[56] However, it was initially targeted only at European and 'Anglo-Indian' children. It became a full-fledged Boys' Department, accommodating Burmese, Chinese and Indian teenagers, too, in 1906.[57] The third branch to offer 'Boys' work on the American plan' was Calcutta in 1903,[58] where a new building was erected for the purpose.[59] Once again, this had become possible through a generous donation of Rs 50,000 by the department store tycoon (and former US postmaster general) John Wanamaker from Philadelphia, whom we have met earlier as the main financier of the YMCA's headquarters in Madras.[60] C. S. Paterson from Montreal was the very first full-time 'boys' secretary' in Asia, and assumed office at the Calcutta boys' branch in December 1904.[61] The boy membership doubled to 124 within the first four years of its existence, reached about 300 by 1915 and peaked at more than 450 in the mid-1920s.[62]

The relatively rapid success of these pioneering branches convinced the National Council of Indian YMCAs to promote boys' work on a larger scale. At its annual convention in 1905, a resolution was passed that boys' work would 'become a regular as well as most important feature of the larger centres, at least where schoolboys are accessible'.[63] This specification clearly shows the elitist bias in the early phase of the programme: throughout the 1900s and 1910s, the YMCA leadership held that only high school boys (preferably those with a sound knowledge of English) constituted a worthy target group for their 'character building' efforts. Referring to the residents of the Boys' Department's hostel in Calcutta, C. S. Paterson declared in 1912 that 'the boys all come from the wealthy middle-class Bengali families and must necessarily do so as the fees are rather high.'[64] Y secretary W. B. Hilton, who was in charge of the boys' branch at the Rangoon YMCA a decade later, wrote that early adolescents in South Asia could be subdivided into four classes, namely, 'A. Coolie Class, B. Servant Class, C. Clerk Class; D. Wealthy Class', and explained that 'Y.M.C.A. branches for

Indian boys in Calcutta Madras and Rangoon carry on work for' the high school boys stemming from class D almost exclusively.[65] Accordingly, the next Y branches that launched special boys' programmes were also situated in big cities with sizeable communities of 'native' pupils in English-medium educational institutions. Bangalore, Bombay, Lahore, Allahabad, Colombo, Delhi, Calicut and Jubbulpore all started boys' work schemes before 1919.[66] Following the same logic, an internal report lamented that the YMCA had not managed to offer boys' work in Poona despite the fact that in the western Indian city

> 4,797 high school boys challenge the Young Men's Christian Association. Fifteen hundred of them are sons of the influential people of the higher classes … No other agency is making any attempt to direct the lives of these potential leaders of Indian affairs. The Association has in this open field a big opportunity to prove its value to the community and help make clean and strong and honest the youth of this old land.[67]

In 1915, the National Council even established a separate YMCA High School Department, but it had to be shut down again after six years owing to 'financial stringency'.[68] The fate of the short-lived 'National High School Department' was not atypical. Not all the local ventures related to boys' work were successful either. In fact, most of the boys' branches founded between 1906 and 1918 had to be closed down after two or three years either because the membership figures remained too low or for the simple reason that no suitable 'boys' secretary' could be recruited. The various branches' reports therefore constantly reiterated that 'the work suffered from the lack of trained, permanent leadership'.[69] This happened in most cases because the high-salaried Americans, Canadians or Europeans who were considered qualified for the job were too expensive for the smaller Y branches, and the 'native leaders' were either reluctant to perform the task or viewed as insufficiently trained.[70] We will return to this point later.

To be sure, the developments on the Indian 'mission field' were strongly shaped by such internal dynamics. At the same time, however, they cannot be understood without taking into account the broader global trends and shifting international strategies of the YMCA. Partly driven by the surge of 'boyology' debates in the United States, boys' work had acquired a central place in the YMCA's activities on a global scale by the 1910s. In 1914, the first *World Conference of Y.M.C.A. Workers among Boys* was held in Oxford, with seventy-five international delegates in attendance.[71] One of its resolutions underscored that it was 'essential for the YMCA work to begin when the life of the growing man can be most surely influenced; that is, during boyhood and adolescence' and accordingly stipulated that 'the World's Committee should give an adequate place to Junior Work and develop means by which its interest may be best served'.[72] However, these ambitious plans were scuppered by the outbreak of the Great War and the subsequent reallocation of Y funds for 'army work'. This shift in focus with the start of war was especially palpable in the Indian YMCA, which was (as we have seen in Chapter 2) heavily involved in supporting the allied forces during the war and its aftermath until 1920.

It was therefore only in the 1920s that the new prominence given to the global 'boy problem' finally translated into concrete action. This move towards the practical implementation of boyology became most visible in the organization of the second *World Conference of Y.M.C.A. Workers among Boys* on the shores of the bucolic Lake Wörth at Pörtschach, Austria in 1923, described by American Y officials as 'the outstanding event of the period'.[73] The conference was manifestly shaped by the upsurge of internationalism and the general quest for a stable world order that characterized the early interwar years,[74] and was designed to map the 'place of boyhood in the world'.[75] It was much bigger than the original gathering in Oxford and attracted more than 950 delegates from fifty-one countries, including three representatives from India and Burma.[76] In a well-received address, the American Y leader John R. Mott famously declared 'Boyhood' to be 'the greatest asset of any nation', reminding his audience 'not only of the primacy of ... [boys'] work, but also of its immediacy'.[77] The general enthusiasm that spread among the Y workers in the wake of Mott's speech – and the huge gathering more generally – catalysed efforts to develop more numerous and more sophisticated boys' work schemes in most countries where the YMCA was present.

At least in India, it was apparent that such a boost was sorely needed. Three years before the Pörtschach conference underscored the significance of boys' work in a post-war world order and nurtured the general expectations about the YMCA's leading role in it, the author of a 1920 report published by the YMCA's International Committee expressed his utter disappointment about the 'meagreness and the scattered character of the work accomplished' thus far. By 1920, there were 'only eleven boys' work secretaries on the field sent out by the New York Committee', a mere four of whom worked in India.[78] The efforts were hence intensified over the next two decades, and the approaches became more nuanced and diverse. As a result, in Southern India, various schemes of work were developed that specially targeted illiterate village boys.[79] Alongside these programmes, several local YMCAs became involved in scouting, occasionally cooperating with a number of provincial, national and international Boy Scout Associations (of which more will be said later).[80] In the second half of the 1930s, Canadian boys' work secretary John Dunderdale enriched the boys' work programme in South Asia with a specially developed 'leadership' training course for early adolescents. The course design reflected the increased emphasis placed on 'the problem of leadership training' by the World Alliance of YMCAs from 1929 onwards,[81] and was offered annually in Madras before most resources of the Indian Y were, once again, reallocated to 'war emergency work' from 1940 onwards.[82]

In sum, one can observe that the Indian YMCA's boys' work scheme was significantly expanded during the interwar period. However, unlike other activities of the Association, the history of the boys' work programmes was not a straightforward success story. Growth was interrupted by repeated local failures and severely hampered by the chronic shortage of staff and funding. The latter problem became serious especially after the Great Depression had significantly dried out the donations from the United States and Canada in the early 1930s.[83] All such difficulties notwithstanding, in 1940, no less than twenty-one local Associations all over India, Burma and Ceylon conducted boys' work of some kind or the other.[84]

Having a precise idea about the theoretical undergirding of the programme and its overall scale, we can now zoom in more closely on the concrete motives that led to the establishment of boys' branches and explore the various types of activities subsumed under the somewhat vague label 'boys' work'. The next section will shed light on these aspects and examine the broader agendas behind the programme in some of the more important YMCA branches in South Asia. Of particular interest in this context is the extent to which the disciplinary and educational knowledge of North American Y 'boyologists' were considered suitable for a sociocultural environment perceived as fundamentally different.

'The field of action': Motives and methods of YMCA boys' work in South Asia

The debates following the inauguration of the first separate boys' branches in Madras, Rangoon and especially the colonial capital Calcutta allow an interesting glimpse into the YMCA secretaries' perceptions of the boy problem in India. Most notably, they address the question of whether or not schemes of informal education developed in the West soon after this innovation had spread to the subcontinent 'under American influence' were universally applicable.[85]

Malleable lads, modern menaces and 'native' suspicions

The prospects of the new boys' branches were a major topic of discussion during a 1907 meeting of YMCA secretaries working in South Asia that was held in Lanauli, a small hill station near Bombay. P. E. Curtis, a YMCA secretary representing a branch with a majority of British members, stressed the importance of devising special programmes for European Boys in the subcontinent, observing that the white boy was 'neglected in India and we get hold of him only when practices detrimental to his moral, intellectual and spiritual life have taken root in him'.[86]

Although Curtis does not mention the class background of the envisaged target group with a single word, his intervention clearly points to the aforementioned problem of the so-called domiciled community or poor whites in British India.[87] As colonial administrators, well-heeled business men and high-ranking military officers normally sent their sons to Britain for the entirety of their education,[88] only European families from the lower middle classes, the working class (e.g. railway employees), and the 'white subalterns' in the imperial bottom drawer[89] faced a 'boy problem' in British India. The practices regarded as detrimental to European 'moral, intellectual and spiritual life' are not specified, but many other contemporaneous statements made by YMCA workers and other Western missionaries suggest that the proximity to the Indian population with their supposedly immoral religious and recreational practices are alluded to here.[90] As we have already noted with respect to the Y's philanthropic schemes for railway workers, the combination of intermingling with 'natives' and the tropical climate was widely held to create 'a thirst of that thrilling recklessness of absolute self-abandonment' in Europeans, tempting them into leading 'lives as purely animal as the most sensual rajah'.[91] It was this common belief in 'the degenerative impact of the tropics',[92] which had both orientalist and environmentalist overtones that rendered the 'white boy problem' particularly pressing in colonial South Asia.

Curtis was not quite sure about the best method to save the endangered white boy from these pernicious influences. While he showed some sympathy for the British 'Boys' Brigades system' with its 'military training',[93] he also acknowledged that the original could not be transferred unaltered to the context of a colonial society without the risk of potentially embarrassing cultural misunderstandings:

> The [Boys' Brigade's] uniform as laid down by the authorities at Glasgow is not suitable for India. Apart from the fact that the cap is no protection from the heat of the sun, its style is not unlike the headgear worn by one of our native troops. No lad wants to be a butt for the ridicule of others, and no plan is more effective in driving away a boy than to ridicule him. He objects to being called a Goorkha.[94]

Being confused with a 'native' soldier, then, was regarded as humiliation for a European boy and the Boys' Brigade cap did not adequately protect him from 'the perils of the midday sun'.[95] Curtis ultimately rejected the British Boys' Brigade template because of this combination of cultural and climatic incompatibility and instead supported the Boys' Club model that was booming in the United States, championed by American Y secretaries.[96] This example clearly brings out the tensions that still existed between the older British-dominated YMCA branches in India, which were at pains to uphold the social distance between the rulers and the ruled, and the more liberal Associations led by US secretaries. At the same time, it demonstrates the growing importance of the theoretical 'superstructure' of American boyology as well as its applied methods.

The second speaker who addressed the 'boy problem' at the Lanauli meeting was the Indian Christian H. G. Banurji, who worked with C. S. Paterson in Calcutta. Unlike Curtis, he focused exclusively on the prime target of the newly created branch in the 'second city' of the empire: the Indian high school boy.[97] It is fascinating how Banurji, on the one hand, stresses the equality of boys all the world over, underscoring that 'the Bengali boy [wa]s no exception'. The Y secretary from Calcutta nevertheless finds it necessary to mention that 'the same boyish elasticity and impressionableness of character that are so common in other lands and climes' were also typical of the Bengali boy. This is particularly revealing as he underscores that this malleability was by no means based on innate 'racial traits' of the Bengali, but emanated from the fact that Bengali lads shared 'universal boyish qualities'.[98] Such statements betray the felt need to resist the colonial gaze and counter widespread colonial stereotypes that directly blamed the climate for rendering 'the Bengali male' soft, weak and 'effeminate'.[99] However, in a slip in the same paragraph, the author nevertheless concedes that 'the prominence given to the mind' in Bengal interfered with the 'proper development of the body' of the Bengali lads. It was, therefore, one of the main objectives of the newly opened boys' branch 'to remove this defect in the life of the Calcutta boys'.[100] The trope of the Bengalis' alleged physical deficiency, weakness and effeminacy thus re-entered through the back door, as it were.

Banurji's speech, also, is one of the few sources that dwell in some detail on the concrete social evils against which the urban boys' work was supposed to serve as a protective shield. The 'wholesome recreation' offered at the boys' branch was meant to do more than merely guard pubescent teenagers against the 'multitudinous temptations' of 'impurity' in the city (the usual oblique phrase of the period that referred to prostitution). Nor was its sole purpose to counteract 'evil companionship, the theatre, and the perusal of obscene books',[101] which would otherwise have filled up the spare time and corrupted the character of boys in the colonial metropolis. The boys' branches were in fact designed to fight against more devastating temptations. As Banurji elaborates, a newly emerging drug problem threatened the health and morals of high school boys and hence required immediate action:

> Besides the very common and pernicious habit of smoking, Cocaine has gradually made its influence felt amongst our boys and can now count its victims in scores, if not hundreds. It seems an almost helpless task to stamp out this disease … so strong is its hold upon those whom it can once bring into its clutches.[102]

It is striking how this description of the local problems and constellations reminds one of similar contemporary accounts about the drug menace in the big North American cities.[103] From this perspective, at least, the Canadian and American boyologists serving in Calcutta and Rangoon would have been well prepared for the local challenges.

Apart from illustrating the persistence and power of colonial stereotypes and bringing the commonalities between American and Indian urban boys' work schemes into stark relief, Banurji's speech is valuable for yet another reason. Towards the end of his talk, he mentions 'one of the great barriers to the work in Calcutta',[104] namely, the reluctance of local parents to send their children to the YMCA because of its identity as a Christian and Western institution. Given the spirit of patriotism accompanying the anticolonial Swadeshi movement that took shape precisely around this time,[105] such an open collaboration with Westerners – even ones unrelated to the colonial rulers – would have been frowned upon by many. Besides, the fear that the Christian Association would use its influence over the boys to convert them loomed large in the minds of many Hindu and Muslim parents. Although the actual conversion figures remained extremely low, such anxieties were not completely unfounded. For instance, an internal 1909 report triumphantly mentions that 'the first convert from Hinduism was baptised' in the Calcutta branch.[106] In order to dispel such concerns of patriotic and/or religiously conservative South Asian clients, the boys' secretaries and other YMCA authorities increasingly appeased parents over the coming decades by stating that they could rest assured 'that while their boys [we]re spending leisure hours at the Y.M.C.A., they [we]re surrounded by an environment that [wa]s healthy, congenial and uplifting', but not proselytizing.[107] They reiterated – though with varying degrees of success – that their mission was not primarily a religious one and that 'training for productive citizenship' was 'the ultimate goal of the programme'.[108] It was hoped that the anxieties of nationalistically inclined South Asian elites about the ostensible lack of 'grit' and 'character' among Indian youth would make them turn to the Y's boyologists, who made grandiose promises about the effects of their methods on national progress and the prospect of gaining political autonomy. Calcutta boys' work pioneer C. S. Paterson even declared in 1936 that Indian independence would necessarily end in a disaster 'until courageous, well-trained and public minded leaders [we]re developed' with the help of the YMCA.[109]

However, the Association did not have to grapple only with widespread parental distrust and nationalist suspicions. As the brief sketch of the institutional history of the YMCA's boys' branches has shown, finding suitable Indian Y members who were willing to work as boys' secretaries proved to be difficult throughout the entire period under study. The experienced boys' worker and General Secretary of the World Committee of YMCAs in Geneva, Tracy Strong, spent several months in India in 1933 inspecting the Association's boys' branches. Summarizing impressions gathered over the tour, Strong provides an interesting cultural interpretation of the problem of 'native leadership' (see Figure 4.1):

> Men who see the unique opportunity for work with boys in the Young Men's Christian Association are not numerous. In a country like India, the situation is still more difficult. Boys' Work is new. Many persons are suspicious of the intentions of a man who associates with boys. Parents fail to appreciate what a man outside the family can do to help them with their sons. There is neither prestige nor security in the position of a Boys' Work Secretary, so that men hesitate to specialise … On the other hand, it is almost essential that the leadership of the Indian boys must be given by Indians who understand the language of the boy and the social background of which he comes.[110]

According to Tracy, then, a commitment to boys' work was often misread in the Indian cultural milieu as a sign of paedophilic propensities. In addition, career prospects were much more attractive in other fields of specialization. This interpretation seems plausible, but the extent to which American experiences and motives were projected onto the Indian secretaries is unclear. In the United States, the image of the YMCA had been tarnished by a long history of 'sex scandals' that gained national notoriety, one of them involving a member of the Chicago Association who was expelled for 'encouraging immoral practices among boys at the gym' and another involving a YMCA boys' worker from Wellsburg, WV, who sexually harassed a number of boys in the supposedly protected space of a rural summer camp.[111] It is possible that word about the growing notoriety of YMCAs in American cities as popular 'cruising spots' and 'points of entry for many rural young men into an urban homosexual subculture' had reached India by the 1920s.[112] This would also partly explain the reservations of Indian Y members vis-à-vis boys' work. Given the fact that same-sex relationships and sexual abuse played such a prominent role in the history of the North American Y movement, it is both conspicuous and regrettable that available sources are silent about those issues in the South Asian context. Ultimately, however, there can be no doubt that the recruitment of Indian boys' workers was challenging, irrespective of the correctness and adequacy of Tracy's interpretation. The Y authorities undertook various (and at times quite costly) steps to try and address this persistent problem: for example, a 'training fellowship' was

Figure 4.1 A problematic position *in loco parentis*: An Indian YMCA secretary with a high school student (Madras, c. 1924). Courtesy Kautz Family YMCA Archives, University of Minnesota, Minneapolis.

introduced in the 1940s to allow selected Indian candidates to undergo specialized boys' work training in the United States.[113]

Let us now move from the motives that led to the setting up of the scheme and the intrinsic problems that it faced over the decades, to the precise methods that were developed and implemented in the boys' branches. Given their enormous popularity, it may be appropriate to begin with the element that we have already analysed in the context of the YMCA' schemes for adults, namely, programmes related to fitness, health and hygiene.

Muscling in on Indian boyhood: Sports, games and physical culture

As demonstrated in Chapter 3, sports, games and physical education played a vital role in the Indian YMCA's work with male adults. Available sources leave no doubt that Y secretaries regarded the 'physical programme' as the centrepiece of boys' work too. This focus on 'native' physiques is completely not only in line with the more general insight that power is primarily exercised by enacting rituals on and through the body[114] but also consistent with the general strategy of the YMCA's International Committee in New York. In a report on the latter's 'Boys work in the Foreign field', Secretary Donald Dutcher singled out the 'attraction of up-to-date physical equipment' – that is, modern gyms and swimming pools – as a particularly efficient method of spreading the gospel of Y boyology across the world. Writing in 1920, he opined that

> The physical privileges, which have been developed as a specialized contribution of the Association to the community, meet the need just as much and are as popular with boys abroad as they are in North America. The gymnasium and bath controlled by a trained physical director are as much needed and as much appreciated in foreign communities as they are at home. Herein is an opening wedge to the confidence of any community in our work.[115]

The belief that sports and physical culture functioned as an 'opening wedge', at least for the bigger Indian Y branches able to provide the necessary facilities, led to a close collaboration between the boys' work secretaries and the 'physical directors' from the end of the 1900s onwards. Like some of the boys' secretaries, almost all the early physical directors in the Indian mission field had been trained at Springfield college.[116] After 1920, additional sports experts were trained locally in the MCPE. The Calcutta branch pioneered the trend of professionalizing its sports offerings for boys, first in 1903 through the installation of 'up-to date physical equipment' imported from the United States in the new building, and again in 1908, when John H. Gray 'took over the charge of gymnasium work' for the boys.[117] A few years later, Gray also pioneered the popularization of 'scientific' playgrounds in India. It was under his aegis that a fully equipped demonstration playground was inaugurated in the Calcutta suburb of Ballighata. As the official journal of the American playground movement emphasized a few years later, it was 'opened along the lines of similar demonstration playgrounds in America', its object being 'to influence all India to adopt the best from our American playgrounds'. In the long run, it was hoped that 'these transplanted American institutions' would play a significant part 'in the up-building of the new India, as they are also in the new China'.[118] By the mid-1920s, YMCA leaders could proudly report that their 'supervised playground programme' had 'suddenly become successful due to enthusiastic support from Municipal bodies'.[119] Bombay was a particularly striking example of the successful public–private partnership:

> The first Bombay experiment was made ... on a small ground, less than the size of a football field, in one of the most congested Chawl sections of the city. This ground had been a notorious rendezvous for badmashes [hoodlums, HFT] and respectable children were warned to give it a wide berth ... It was fortunate that a Mohamedan [sic] trained by the Y.M.C.A. in Madras was available for the post ... [The] ground has now an average daily attendance of 1000 children of all communities, an achievement made possible only by expert supervision and organization.[120]

Their playground expertise allowed some of the Y's boys' workers to find lucrative positions in yet another long-term public–private joint venture. In a report published on the eve of Indian independence, the Board of Physical Education established by the Government of Bombay praised the YMCA secretaries for the establishment and running of supervised public playgrounds in the city. It was a contribution that lasted for decades:

> In 1923 the Bombay Municipal Corporation took the initiative and started three play centres in the most congested areas of the city. The Y. M. C. A. undertook the general supervision of these centres and appointed Physical Directors to be in charge of each centre. The cost of maintenance, apparatus and the pay of these Physical Directors is borne by the Municipality and it gives an annual grant of approximately Rs. 5000. Experience has shown that these centres have been a great boon to the inhabitants of these localities. An improved health, a higher civic sense and morale has been noticed among those who have constantly utilized these centres for their recreation.[121]

However, the introduction of 'scientific' playgrounds was by no means the only Y innovation. It was also owing to the influence of Gray that regular physical examinations of all boys who wanted to become members of the Calcutta YMCA's boys' branch were introduced in 1915.[122] This should not come as a surprise, as Springfield Professor Luther Gulick had pioneered anthropometric measurements and medical examinations for the Y's work in America.[123] His methods became firmly anchored within the curriculum of the YMCA Training College by the 1890s.[124] Physical tests also played a role in the Allahabad branch, where the responsible boys' secretary introduced a selection process for applicants that was inspired in part by the Canadian Standard Efficiency Tests (CSET).[125]

In light of the observations made in the previous chapter about the medical tests of college students, it should come as no surprise that the boys' work done by medically trained physical directors also had a racist dimension. Some of the prominent physical directors working for the YMCA in South Asia actively spread their 'somatic Orientalism', which included racial stereotypes held by the white establishment of British India. For instance, Arthur G. Noehren, who was the National Physical Director of the Indian YMCA at the time,[126] made a sweeping generalization in a 1926 report that 'the average [Indian] student is muscularly flabby, and since such weakness depresses the normal working of all physiological systems, he builds up no power of resistance to chronic ailments and bacterial infections.'[127] His 'expert' opinion was clearly shaped by imperial race science, as can be seen in his claims that South Indian adolescents 'must still be considered subnormal', whereas pupils in the Bombay Presidency were 'an example of actual physical deterioration' when contrasted with their ancestor 'Shivaji and his martial followers'.[128] Canadian physical director and Springfield graduate Harold G. Beall, employed at Secunderabad, a city in the princely state of Hyderabad, seconded Noehren's gloomy assessment. After conducting a 'graded physical efficiency test' in fourteen schools near the city of Secunderabad, he confirmed that 'the average South Indian is twenty pounds lighter and 50 per cent weaker muscularly than the average Englishman or American'.[129] This tendency toward medicalization seems to have grown in the 1930s and 1940s. A bulletin handed out to boys' workers in 1941, for example, advised group leaders to arrange for a 'thorough medical examination' of each group member. In case no medical doctor was available, the group leaders were expected to record the height and weight of the children at least, and compare the results with an official table compiled by the Public Health Department of the Government of Bihar and Orissa.[130]

Due to financial constraints, many branches could not afford the construction of a modern gym, let alone a swimming pool. As a result, 'non-equipment' work in the forms of gymnastics, 'drill', and especially team sports played a major role in the scheme. Established British sports like field hockey, badminton, cricket and especially football (soccer) could be offered even by the smaller branches, and proved to be extremely popular with South Asian boys.[131] Much like the sport programmes targeted at adults, American pastimes were actively promoted. These sports included, most notably, the YMCA-invented signature games of volleyball and basketball, which were, as discussed previously, widely touted as 'the true forerunners of democracy'.[132] Indian teenagers seemed to be particularly interested in the latter, and it was not without pride that Calcutta's long-term boys' secretary C. S. Paterson reported in 1906 that his branch had conducted 'the first basket ball [sic] tournament in India'.[133] That individual 'manly' sports such as boxing also enjoyed a growing popularity among the YMCA's young clientele seems perfectly plausible given that the urban Hindu middle classes especially were fighting back against the persistence of colonial stereotypes and 'self-images of effeteness'; the same group provided the bulk of 'native' YMCA members. At the same time, one should not underestimate the attraction that the various games and sports had for many adolescents in South Asia (as elsewhere in the world) regardless of political constellations, simply because they were fun to practice and offered a welcome opportunity to fill their leisure time (see Figure 4.2).

Moreover, as already indicated, the pursuit of martial leisure activities tied in perfectly with the 'man-making mission' advocated by some of the more influential Indian nationalists in the period under survey.[134] Subsequently some of them supported the Indian Y's method of using sport and physical culture in their programmes for boys with a view 'to try and direct their mentality, their activities and their lives in the right channels'.[135] Ideas, what precisely were 'the right channels', however, could differ hugely. Whereas most YMCA secretaries regarded 'all these political movements and tremendous upheavals' of the interwar period as a threat to Indian boyhood,[136] many Indian reformers and political activists used their programmes to make male adolescents part of such movements.

Experiencing modernity outdoors: Camping and scouting

As one might have expected, given the close interlinkages of Y boyology and G. Stanley Hall's social Darwinist-flavoured recapitulation theory, camping, scouting and related outdoor activities were other crucial components of the programme offered by the various boys' branches in India, Burma and Ceylon. In 1910, the Madras branch organized 'the first boys' camp in India' at Pallavaram,[137] and in 1920 Frank V. Slack, one of the leading American YMCA functionaries working in India, stated that scouting and 'the camp of four or five days' had become the Association's main means to attract Indian high school students.[138] The YMCA Training School prided itself on

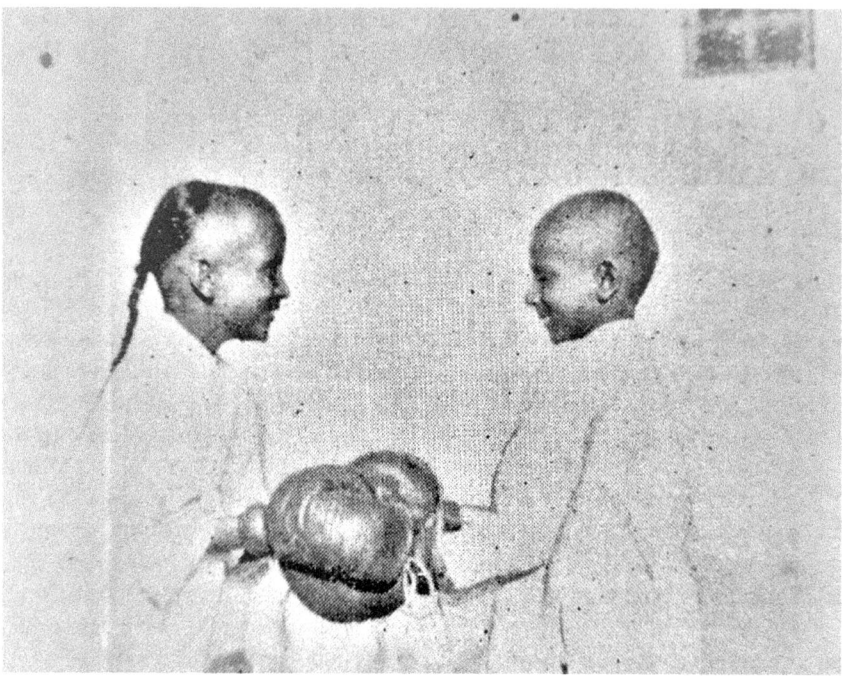

Figure 4.2 Box training at the Madras YMCA boys' branch (c. 1926). Courtesy Kautz Family YMCA Archives, University of Minnesota, Minneapolis.

the fact that 'Springfield ha[d] introduced American Camping methods in all parts of the world',[139] and India was no exception. A leading Association functionary declared in 1933 that scouting and camping were still regarded as the 'most effective methods for developing character' in the Indian boy.[140]

The chief advantage of these outdoor activities, according to Strong, was that the boys could be isolated from their families and the cultural influences they usually were exposed to. This was deemed to be necessary 'because of the nature of the Indian boy', allegedly shaped by 'collective living and thinking, with all its dangers.' This mindset, Strong claimed, dismissed individual ideas, ambitions and achievements as being of secondary importance and made Indian adolescents constantly expect control 'from the home, the school, the caste, the religious community and the government'.[141] It was, therefore, only in the isolation of the camp, under the purportedly benevolent guidance of professionally trained Y boyologists, that the Indian or Burmese teenagers could be 'given ... an opportunity for self-expression, for participating in all kinds of wholesome activities and in learning how to live with those of other castes and religious communities'.[142]

It is somewhat ironic that scouting and camping practically had opposite connotations in 'the east' as compared to 'the west'. These activities enabled Western boys to re-enact the 'primitive' civilizational stages of their forebears, but for 'eastern' boys, they provided a closed, decidedly 'modern', social space. The mixed-race camps occasionally organized by the YMCA, therefore, simultaneously had different temporalities at work. While the European boy took in homoeopathic doses of the 'savagery' of past generations, the camp supposedly prepared the Indian boy for his future by providing a sanctuary of sorts, shielding him from the pressures and prejudices of his own backward, deeply hierarchical, 'semi-civilized' society. The protected and purportedly culturally neutral space of the camp, in the eyes of the YMCA workers, allowed him to encounter a 'progressive' world that valued equality and social responsibility as much as it cherished 'self-expression, self-development' and 'the individual's growth'.[143] From the late 1920s onwards, Y experts working in India often used the maxim '*for* boys and *by* boys' to underscore the importance of 'self-help' and individual commitment.[144] Taking responsibility and expressing personal preferences were key goals of the programme. According to J. H. Dunderdale, another influential Y boyologist working in India, the 'choices a boy makes when he is free to do as he pleases are the ones that count in character development.'[145]

It must be mentioned here that the YMCA boyologists' high esteem for the multiple outcomes of camping had an impact on the educational policies of the postcolonial state. In Bombay, at least, an expert committee (of which one member was the American Springfield graduate Frank Weber) recommended in 1946 that 'camping should form an essential part of school programme', specifying that 'no pupil should be allowed to complete the High School Course without completing at least one month of camping'.[146] The experts explained their recommendation using rhetoric that might have been straight out of a YMCA manual:

> All our boys and girls should experience group living under camping conditions. This would help our youth to learn to put up with inconveniences, withstand hardships, be more self-reliant, develop close friendships and mutual appreciation, and above all, help them to adjust their actions in terms of common group interests. Camping is a very useful and valuable educational experience.[147]

In contrast to the organizing of occasional camps, the Y's engagement in full-fledged scouting activities proved to be problematic in the South Asian colonial setting. As Carey Watt has explained, the rapid spread of scouting in British India in the 1910s and 1920s was accompanied by utter 'chaos and confusion'.[148] The reason for the uncontrolled growth between 1908 and 1920 of more than a dozen major scouting organizations that competed with one another was that the Government of India was reluctant to support the movement. Its hostile stance was caused by widespread anxiety among colonial officials that Indian adolescents might use the paramilitary training that was part of the scout programme to organize an open rebellion against British rule.[149] The shock of 'terrorist outrages' conducted by members of secret revolutionary societies still loomed large after the Great War. Most of these secret society members were former high school or college boys with a penchant for physical culture and martial arts, which had attracted thousands of adolescents, especially in Bengal, between 1908 and 1914.[150] From the mid-1920s onwards, new threats emerged in the form of openly militant bodies like the Hindustan Socialist Republican Army and similar revolutionary organizations.[151] The resulting anxieties concerning Indian 'anarchy' and 'terrorism' were mostly projected onto the country's youth and continued to haunt the British in India well into the 1930s.[152] It was against this backdrop that the Boy Scout Association of India, founded in 1912, adopted a policy of admitting only Europeans and 'Anglo-Indians' while strictly excluding Indian boys, leading to the founding of several independent Indian Scout Associations throughout the 1910s and early 1920s. Even after a superficial amalgamation took place in 1921, racial segregation remained the order of the day well into the 1930s.[153]

In contrast to the persisting segregationist tendencies of the colonial authorities, the Indian YMCA's scout work was outright groundbreaking. It started as early as 1909, when the Bombay branch established the first YMCA Scout troop 'on the foreign field'. Most troops were initially racially segregated. The Rangoon boys' branch, for instance, had three separate Scout units by 1915, for European and Eurasian, Chinese and Indian boys.[154] After the end of the First World War, however, more and more branches under North American leadership offered mixed-race scouting events. The Lahore branch became particularly active in this respect.[155] The first 'united camp for Indian and English boys' was organized in the Punjab in 1922 despite the suspicions expressed by 'both the Indian and English public'.[156] Daniel Swamidoss, one of the Indian delegates at the Pörtschach conference held the subsequent year, reassured his international audience that the Indian and European boys participating in this experiment knew 'no racial barriers, and by their noble conduct dispelled the scepticism of their elders'.[157] In like vein, a 1926 report proudly mentions that the Lahore branch's annual Scout camps in Murree were 'attended by boys of all Communities, Indian, Anglo-Indian and European, and have done much to promote Fraternity and Fellow Feeling [sic]'.[158] Along similar lines, the Indian YMCA's monthly mouthpiece extolled a Boys' camp organized in Madras for Christian, Hindu and Muslim boys in 1928, during the peak of communal tensions in India, as "a demonstration of the possibility of these communities living together in an atmosphere of brotherhood" (see Figure 4.3).[159]

Scouting excursions thus served as experimental spaces where new, more egalitarian, forms of living together could be tried out to prepare future citizens. The Y's boys' secretaries were eager to demonstrate these beneficial effects not only to the parents of the boys and the inhabitants of the cities in which they had their branches 'but to a large number of officials as well.'[160] In 1929, Lahore Boys' worker Waldo Huntley Heinrichs (1891–1959) was particularly successful in demonstrating these benefits to members of the British military, who still observed the YMCA's scouting activities involving 'native' boys with mixed feelings. He had invited several high-ranking British officers to the annual scout camp, which he had had decorated alternately with the Star-Spangled Banner and Union Jack flags. In his diary, he writes dryly:

> 'Brigadier Mathew Lannowe inspected camp for us this A.M. All boys were in their element and best form. We had massed yell assembly and then inspection, flag

Figure 4.3 Teatime at the 'united scout camp' organized by the Lahore YMCA (1922). Courtesy Springfield College Archives, Special Collections.

signals, football, fencing, wrestling & swimming finals. Old Boy and Mr. Duncan were very pleased with the show.'[161]

Due to his military credentials, Heinrichs, a former pilot of the US Air Force and a highly decorated war hero,[162] was in the perfect position to impress and appease the British officers. He shrewdly put on a 'show' highlighting the martial aspects of scouting. This was to demonstrate that the American method of working with 'racially mixed' troops was best-suited to transform Indian adolescents into disciplined, obedient and socially responsible future citizens, potentially even reliable soldiers, who would be loyal beyond religious and caste affiliations.[163] In private, however, Heinrichs made no bones about his belief in American superiority. Convinced that 'indecision, lack of push and pigheadedness' were quintessential British qualities,[164] he regarded the 'old boys' (i.e. colonial army officers) as hopelessly old-fashioned and out of touch with reality, occasionally even ridiculing them as 'foolish old bull-headed lime juicers' (see Figures 4.4 and 4.5).[165]

Heinrich's 'show' at Murree was by no means the first case in which YMCA-led scout troops had received acclaim from the highest colonial officialdom. Official approval was particularly visible during the First World War, when many 'native' Scout units displayed their solidarity with the imperial war effort: many Indian Scouts had taken first aid courses with the St. John Ambulance, and it was also highly appreciated that the scout troop for Indian Boys at the Rangoon YMCA

Figure 4.4 An Indian Scout patrol from Patiala (Punjab) posing in front of the British and American flags in Murree Hills (1929). The group participated in a scouting contest staged during the Lahore YMCA's annual camp. Courtesy Yale Divinity School Library, Special Collections.

Figure 4.5 A show for 'foolish lime juicers'? – British army officers inspect a tent pitching during a scouting contest. Courtesy Yale Divinity School Library, Special Collections.

branch 'spent much time in aiding the Red Cross by packing parcels, distributing pamphlets etc.'[166]

Selfless service to the community: City cleaning and welfare work for 'bustee boys'

This example of voluntary social service leads straight to another major field of the boys' branches' activities: the so-called 'welfare work'. As elucidated in Chapter 1, there had been an outright explosion of non-state social service activities in the Indian subcontinent from around 1900, especially in British India. As we have also noted, the Indian YMCA had become a serious player in this area by the First World War and even inaugurated sustained social service schemes.[167] In the Y's boys' branches, this new social commitment took on various shapes. One of the most visible efforts was the work it did with homeless street children, which was launched in some of the bigger YMCA centres during the 1920s. The Calcutta branch, for example, started a regular programme directed at the so-called 'bustee boys'[168] shortly after the end of the Great War.[169] Activities for these underprivileged slum children and early adolescents 'of the poorest type' included 'supervised play and night school on five or six evenings a week and occasional illustrated lectures, sports excursions' as well as other forms of light entertainment like the army work-tested 'bioscope shows'.[170] Similarly, the Rangoon branch inaugurated its Street Boys' Refuge in 1929, which provided 'lodging, food, clothing and education' for up to fifty boys at a time.[171]

In the 1940s, the 'welfare work' efforts directed at slum children intensified. Most notably, the YMCAs in Madras and Bangalore established so-called boys' towns and boys' clubs, respectively, which provided shelter and education specifically for Indian 'waifs' and 'street urchins'.[172] Unlike many other YMCA institutions that were quickly Indianized after independence, the Madras Boys' Town, the most durable of these branches, remained under American leadership for years. It was modelled on a Christian orphanage in Omaha, NE, and founded in May 1947 by the African American 'fraternity secretary' Lawrence Burr (1913–87), who had earlier served in the YMCA's Wabash Avenue branch in Chicago.[173] It got off to a difficult start, as Burr and his assistants 'had to prowl the empty basaar [sic] streets at dawn' in a car, 'virtually kidnapping the homeless orphan boys from the sidewalks'.[174] However, any initial resistance was overcome under the able guidance of the Indian YMCA's only 'Negro secretary' and the 'boys' town' soon became 'India's model youth work project', synonymous with the Association's chosen task 'of educating 400 million Indians in the rights and duties of citizenship.'[175] It received substantial publicity in Nehruvian India due to Burr's media savviness that, amongst other things, garnered him an invitation to speak on an All India Radio show on the subject of 'the social service program among youth in the United States'.[176] Local newspapers also covered the countless fundraising talks he gave during his regular visits to the United States and Canada. On these occasions, Burr used to explain, in detail, the secrets of the 'transformation wrought in underprivileged boys from juvenile delinquents to conscientious citizens.'[177] Due to the general excitement in the media,[178] the Madras Boys' Town continued to attract Indian and American VIPs as visitors throughout the 1950s, from the commander-in-chief of

Figure 4.6 The Indian army commander greeting YMCA workers at Boys Town in Madras (1950). Lawrence Burr is standing at the extreme left. Courtesy Kautz Family YMCA Archives, University of Minnesota, Minneapolis.

the Indian Army in 1950 to the famous Hollywood director Frank Capra in 1952 (see Figure 4.6).[179]

Another activity worth mentioning in the context of the welfare programmes are the 'city cleaning campaigns' launched in Madras and four smaller South Indian towns in the early 1930s. Over the course of these campaigns, members of the local Y boys' branches could demonstrate their public spirit by scrubbing and polishing their local *muhalla* (quarter).[180] As a matter of course, hygiene was one of the core values taught to the boys on an individual basis by the boys' secretaries and group leaders. The step from individual to social responsibility (as well as to social discipline and, one might say, social hygiene) was the logical progression in the Y's educational scheme. This agenda was reflected in the Madras cleaning campaign, as the following account of the responsible boys' secretary clearly shows:

> The members were drawn largely from underprivileged classes. Each night they used to meet, take their beds, together, and rise at 5-30 a.m. when their leader blew his whistle. By 6-30 a.m., they had gone to their places of work, and were busily engaged teaching people habits of hygiene, pointing out to them the dangers of converting streets into lavatories, and directing them in the proper use of the public latrines.[181]

The peculiarity of this scheme lay in its socially transgressive character. The fact that the modern gospel of hygiene was spread through the agency of members of the

Figure 4.7 Demonstrating public spirit: Members of the Madras boys' branch at work during the city cleaning campaign (1938). Courtesy Kautz Family YMCA Archives, University of Minnesota, Minneapolis.

'underprivileged classes' (i.e. low-caste and Dalit children, whose communities were usually associated with ritual impurity and bodily filthiness in 'orthodox' Hinduism) must have been provocative to many. This twist, one suspects, must have made the message the campaign sent out even stronger (see Figure 4.7).

Shaping up for democracy: Education, debating culture and anti-vice activism

Along with inculcating public spirit through social service schemes, education and vocational training were also crucial elements of the YMCA's holistic boys' work schemes from their very inception. According to the programme-guiding boyology theories, the development of the boys' intellectual faculties was as important as cultivating their physical prowess and acting out their 'primitive' impulses as long as they were not fostered in a one-sided fashion. Indeed, given the reluctance and distrust shown by most middle-class or elite Indian parents towards the Christian Association's boys' work, educational offerings were another 'opening wedge,' almost as important as the Association's physical programmes and popular outdoor activities. The North American Y secretaries recognized the potential of educational programmes in the organization's portfolio in making their religio-moral message more palatable to Indian audiences.

In this field, too, the Calcutta branch not only led the way, it also offered the most comprehensive and variegated programme. In fact, we can analyse the YMCA's educational scheme as a whole by looking *pars pro toto* at this example. Thanks to a 'munificent gift' from the New York-based philanthropist Helen Miller Gould (1868–1936), the Calcutta branch became the first to establish its own boys' library in June 1907, which immediately became 'a great attraction to the Branch …, much appreciated by the members as well as by their guardians'.[182] The library comprised a reading room equipped with the latest newspapers, journals and magazines, and contained books in English, Urdu and Bengali. It was repeatedly expanded over the following years. By 1922, the Calcutta's boys' branch library included more than 1,200 books, and the facility was used by no less than 481 members in that year (see Figure 4.8).

Concurrent to the opening of the library, a regular educational course was also initiated by the boys' secretary. Whereas the Bible classes mostly attracted a small number of Christian youths to the Y (or the 'bustee boys' in the improvised slum *pāṭhśālā*s, who seem to have been grateful for any diversion), the 'secular' evening classes were immensely popular with the lower middle-class constituency. These classes were taught by YMCA secretaries and were free for branch members. They were oriented along the high school curricula and helped the students to prepare their regular morning lessons. They were a great success as they 'undoubtedly attracted many of the poorer boys', who could not afford private tutors, to join the Association.[183] There were additional evening lectures for older boys on a variety of topics, held either by YMCA secretaries or by professors from local colleges. Lantern-slide lectures and

Figure 4.8 Library and reading room of the Calcutta YMCA, boys' branch (1920). Courtesy Springfield College Archives, Special Collections.

talks on science-related topics, which were 'illustrated with diagrams and experiments', tended to be especially popular.[184]

It needs to be emphasized that the YMCA's anti-vice agenda also played a significant role in these educational schemes. The Association regularly disseminated its message of abstinence, bodily cleanliness and physical fitness in various educational formats. Thus, lectures at the Calcutta branch over the following decade often included talks on 'health and hygiene', and 'lectures on temperance and smoking' were given on a regular basis.[185] In 1931, for example, the biannual temperance lectures were on the somewhat predictable topics 'Fight Against Drink' and 'Alcohol: The Enemy of Physical Fitness'.[186] They were supported by a lantern slide show and 'given to the boys by the Organiser [sic] of the Calcutta Temperance Federation'.[187] The boys' branch, moreover, repeatedly collaborated with the Women's Christian Temperance Union to organize 'temperance recitation' competitions,[188] where 'silver medals were distributed to the successful contestants.'[189] Temperance was also a favourite topic in the branch's thriving 'literary and debating society'. Debating clubs, established with a view to preparing young 'citizens in the making' for the orderly deliberations that formed the backbone of a modern democracy, had become standard features of the YMCA's major boys' branches in South Asia even before the outbreak of the Great War. For instance, most of the thirty members of the Calcutta debating society, were also active in the temperance club as early as 1908, and had taken 'a triple pledge against drinking, smoking and swearing.'[190] This is another example of the fact that the civic virtues inculcated through the YMCA's programmes were undergirded by moral values that often overlapped with those championed both by the colonial authorities and by South Asia's aspiring political elite.

Summing up

This chapter has analysed a facet of the Indian YMCA's work on the Indian subcontinent that was added in the early 1900s with a view to enhancing the Association's outreach. As shown above, the transatlantic boyology discourse was particularly prominent in North America, and US and Canadian scholars and boys' workers dominated the debates and designed the actual programmes. This chapter has demonstrated that the transfer of such programmes to South Asia was made possible not, as one might have expected, by the British colonial state but by a US-sponsored Christian lay organization, which became the most important player in the dissemination of such 'scientifically' informed boys' work in the region. It has also become apparent that North American experts and their know-how aside, US and Canadian donors pumped a good deal of capital into projects concerned with the moral and physical 'uplift' of early adolescents in South Asia.

The YMCA's political position in the Indian subcontinent during the last decades of the Raj was ambivalent. On the one hand, the impact of the broader 'Anglo-Saxonist' sentiment that informed public debates in North America in the early 1900s is evident.[191] Many American and Canadian YMCA secretaries working in the region also clearly sympathized with the British imperial 'civilizing mission'. Besides, the

Association needed the approval of the colonial authorities for its work and there were many instances of close cooperation with colonial officialdom. Tendencies of a sense of American superiority became stronger after the end of the First World War for the same two reasons that we have already observed in other fields of YMCA activity. Firstly, more Indians openly sympathizing with the anticolonial nationalist movement came into positions of influence in the YMCA and advocated for the Association spreading the 'dharma of citizenship'.[192] Secondly, the United States' newly acquired geopolitical significance palpably boosted American self-confidence in the interwar years. The shift of foci in the work of the YMCA's boys' branches in India, Burma and Ceylon clearly reflects these developments. As this case study has demonstrated, there were constant attempts to recruit patriotic Indians for the kind of early citizenship training that the boys' branches offered. The concerted efforts to overcome the religious and caste differences that undermined political mobilization and national unity expressed themselves in the ostentatious egalitarianism in the microcosm of the boys' branches. The YMCA's broader citizen-making agenda foresaw an independent India in the not-too-distant future. This agenda, which already dominated the YMCA's army work and its physical education schemes, was equally noticeable in how 'Indian boyhood' was prepared for political participation through physical empowerment, the inculcation of civic virtues and training in a democratic debating culture.

However, the case study has also left little doubt that, in spite of its undeniable liberal aspirations (and potentially liberating effects), the YMCA's boys' work programme contained 'traces of empire'.[193] For instance, the paramilitary elements of the crypto-imperial scout movement had a strong impact on the YMCA's programmes. Imperial racialism, imperial medicine and the practices of 'social distancing' and ethnic segregation remained ubiquitous in the YCMA microcosms despite the lip service paid to racial equality and meritocracy. Likewise, as shown by their discussions of the 'nature of the Indian Boy', YMCA boys' workers were also not free of the cultural and racial prejudices that viewed 'natives' as generally inferior, stereotypes that were widespread among British officials and the 'domiciled European' population in the region. Ironically, the quasi-imperial scouting scheme made the YMCA particularly attractive to patriotic Indian parents in search of ways to instil manliness and morality in their sons.

A second point deserves to be mentioned here. Due to the paucity of other sources, the case study is based to a large extent on material produced by the YMCA itself. Predictably enough, such in-house sources tell us a lot about the agendas, visions and plans of the YMCA functionaries and boys' work experts. They say much less about their actual implementation on the ground and almost nothing about the perspective of their main targets: Indian, Ceylonese and Burmese boys. In fact, the boys appear to have been more acted upon than acting, if the copious documentation pertaining to the various programmes studied is anything to go by. The question of Indian agency in this story is indeed a dicey one, but there are at least some hints one can get by reading the one-sided source material against the grain. Thus the difficulties faced by Lawrence Burr, for example, which made him resort to kidnapping 'street urchins' in Madras to fill the beds in his Boys Town, would seem to suggest that there might very well have been outright resistance to the boys' branches' welfare programmes and that the boys made conscious choices. The nature of the educational offerings also points in the same direction. Apart from the entertaining lantern slide lectures, the most popular courses at the Calcutta boys' branch were tutorials for regular school classes. This format was a service offered in response to the demands of Indian students and their parents. Rather than remedying the oft-criticized penchant for cramming among Indian students, it possibly reinforced it and left virtually no space for the 'character building' message the YMCA actually wanted to convey. On a different level, the refusal of many Indian Y members to work as 'boys' secretaries' also indicates that indigenous members remained autonomous and took decisions based on cultural preferences and individual career prospects rather than on the basis of considerations pertaining to the Association's needs or its touted ideologies. There were, in other words, clear limits to the imposition of an American programme on South Asian societies.

This leads me to a much larger question: How successful and how significant, ultimately, was the transcultural circulation of the boyology programme through a Christian civil society organization? Was it, after all, not a mere footnote in a story largely written by colonial administrators and Indian nationalists? The sheer figures for the peak year 1941, when twenty-one boys' branches with between 50 and 450 members were operational, would seem to give a clear answer when compared with the demographic realities. Claims by Y officials of reaching '400 million Indians' with a view to 'educating them in the rights and duties of citizenship'[194] would appear to be megalomaniac fantasies that were completely out of touch with reality. Yet, it would be misleading to reduce the impact of YMCA's intervention in the Indian subcontinent to only those of the population that it directly reached. In the realm of boys' work, as in a number of other fields, the YMCA's greatest programmatic achievements in India and its neighbouring countries were not so much owing to direct intervention as they were to the fact that the Y ideologies and methods were validated by the colonial state, adopted by competing indigenous and international NGOs, and even by several postcolonial governments. Its primary goal of 'harnessing the power of youth', at least, was quickly endorsed by the representatives of the Nehruvian state. We have seen, for instance, that the Government of Bombay made camping compulsory for high school students on the basis of an expert recommendation involving a YMCA boyologist. In a similar vein, Rajendra Prasad, the first president of the Indian Republic, reassured the leading American YMCA functionary Dalton McClelland in 1949 that the 'YMCA ha[d] a definite future and an important place in the new era' and that the Government of India, in its broader nation-building efforts, relied heavily on its 'programme to build good citizenship and its emphasis on character-building'.[195]

5

'The gospel of rural reconstruction': The YMCA's rural development programmes in South Asia (*c.* 1916–1955)

This final chapter takes the analysis of the Indian YMCA's modernizing endeavours to another level in an attempt to capture their repercussions beyond the Indian subcontinent and to assess their legacy in the region after the end of colonial rule. It does so by exploring the Y's activities as an agent in promoting rural reconstruction schemes in South Asia and beyond from the 1920s to the 1950s. Its main purpose is to demonstrate that during the interwar years, the group of religiously inclined civil-society actors from North America serving in the Indian YMCA played a crucial role in shaping the norms, practices and epistemes that would characterize later secular development schemes in the region. Alongside this general argument, it also aims to intervene in broader debates within the history of knowledge and development studies by shedding some light on the emergence and global dissemination of a new 'gospel of rural reconstruction'.[1] It argues that a body of knowledge and practices that developed in South Asia by the mingling of American scientific agricultural expertise and the specific Protestant missionary impulse that characterized the YMCA's vision of 'practical Christianity' with various strands of colonial, 'local' Indian and global knowledge enjoyed a worldwide circulation from the mid-1930s onwards. There is reason to believe that this new development knowledge shaped the transnational aid regime that would begin to flourish during the early Cold War era to some extent.

Historicizing rural development schemes in India

Historical research has typically addressed American rural development programmes in Asia as powerful political weapons that enabled the 'establishment of American global hegemony' during the decades characterized by an all-pervasive East–West antagonism.[2] Most available studies emphasize the role of various academically trained US 'development experts' in spreading agricultural 'high modernism' to the third world together with the impact of wealthy non-state donors such as the Ford and Rockefeller Foundations, which are often represented as quasi-auxiliaries of the US State Department.[3] Historians of agricultural uplift programmes in the Indian subcontinent have, however, only rather superficially contextualized the post-Second World War phenomenon of American rural development schemes, discussing them perfunctorily as part of the history of earlier schemes in the region promoted either by the colonial state or by Indian nationalists like Mohandas K. Gandhi and Rabindranath Tagore, who carried out much publicized village experiments.⁴ An important group of actors and their ideological agenda have thus been completely edited out of the prehistory of development programmes. Revealingly, while it is often taken for granted that the rural experiments of Indian activists like Gandhi or Tagore were informed by their individual religio-cultural world views, the question of the extent to which religious tenets and agendas might have shaped the seemingly secular village uplift schemes of Western and especially American 'experts' is rarely asked.⁵ Nicole Sackley has pointed to the 'transnational roots' of rural reconstruction programmes in the first three decades of the twentieth century and acknowledged that 'Anglo-American protestant missionaries' indeed played a role in the development of such schemes.⁶ However, with very few exceptions, existing research still focuses strongly on secular experts coming to South Asia from the mid-1940s onwards,⁷ and hardly helps us understand how these earlier transnational flows and American Protestant influences moulded the way in which knowledge about the Indian peasant and the village/rural economy came to be conceptualized in the decades that preceded the heyday of the age of development in the 1950s and 1960s.

Inspired by the few authors who have challenged this dominant narrative,⁸ this case study closely examines the Indian YMCA as one of the most conspicuous actors in the field of agricultural reform. The period surveyed begins in the 1910s, when the first rural reconstruction programmes designed by Indian YMCA secretaries were tested in Southern India.⁹ The better part of the chapter looks at the period between the mid-1920s and the early 1950s, when rural development schemes were launched by the Indian YMCA under American guidance. The discussion focuses strongly on the activities of Duane Spencer Hatch (1888–1963), arguably the single most important expert on rural reconstruction connected with the Association. The Cornell-trained agronomist, celebrated by contemporaries as 'India's double-your-income-man',¹⁰ worked for various international and national institutions and achieved worldwide acclaim in the 1940s and 1950s. The Rural Demonstration Centre that he opened in 1924 in the south Indian village of Martandam¹¹ (henceforth MRDC) inspired later architects of community development, both Indian and foreign,¹² and its influence soon extended all over Asia and beyond. The chapter ends with a brief discussion of Hatch's subsequent global career as a village development expert, which helps demonstrate how knowledge about rural populations and economies, originally generated by the YMCA in colonial South Asia, circulated on a global scale.

Based on this case study, I intend to make a number of wider historiographical arguments. The first is rather predictable and relates to a noticeable lacuna in South Asian history: While the YMCA's crucial contribution to secular agricultural and social reform projects in other parts of Asia has been analysed at length by historians,¹³ scholars have hitherto discussed the Christian lay organization's role in the Indian subcontinent rather uncritically.¹⁴ In addition to filling the obvious gap of providing a critical history of this momentous facet of the Y's work in South Asia, an in-depth study of the Association's rural work in Travancore can significantly contribute to the overarching goal of this book, namely, to overcome the fixation on colonialism (and particularly the colonial state) and anticolonial nationalism, which still pervade much of the historiography on early twentieth-century modernization and development schemes in the region. It sheds light, instead, on how an internationally oriented Christian civil society organization contributed to such endeavours, and particularly highlights the crucial significance of American actors and capital in this context during the late colonial period. The third is that historians of development and foreign aid initiatives have tended to concentrate almost exclusively on the period between the late 1940s and the 1980s.[15] Their selective focus on post-Second World War phenomena downplays or completely omits essential aspects of the prehistory of the age of development from their narratives.[16] Most importantly, the fact that 'progressive' and 'secular' village uplift schemes involving US experts were intricately enmeshed not only with colonial ideologies and designs[17] but also with Christian missionary agendas is obfuscated by the acceptance of the Cold War and decolonization as seemingly 'natural' caesurae, validating the primary emphasis on wider geopolitical contexts and large-scale government-driven aid programmes after President Truman's famous Point IV speech of 1949.[18] A detailed microstudy of the YMCA's early rural work in interwar India, by contrast, reminds us of the importance of regional and local contexts while also rendering these entanglements visible.[19]

Finally, from a more abstract history-of-knowledge perspective, focusing on the actual processes of production, transmission and application of scientific knowledge about South Asian (and by extension, 'third world') peasants and villages, agricultural practices, and rural economies can correct widespread misconceptions about US rural development expertise as exported to the global south. The early America-sponsored village uplift schemes studied here, at least, cannot be productively understood as direct precursors of later 'high-modernist' development aid schemes or large-scale 'techno-politics' propelled by 'the Great American Mission'.[20] This is because, firstly, they were designed for small communities and were therefore ostentatiously 'low modernist' in their approach. They should thus be seen rather as predecessors of later sustainable development schemes.[21] Secondly, they were not simply transferred ready-made from US universities, laboratories or government offices to South Asian hinterlands. Rather, they emerged in complex negotiations and exchanges involving not only colonial administrators, 'progressive' South Asian princes and nationalist elites but also the local subaltern target population. Additionally, they were significantly enriched through eclectic borrowings from disparate sources worldwide. The resulting 'pidgin-knowledge'[22] was not only applied on the spot but also re-exported to the wider world. In other words, notions of rural development produced under very specific conditions in a tiny south Indian village came to be seen as being universally valid. Pioneers like Spencer Hatch disseminated this scientific template of rural reconstruction to the nascent 'epistemic community'[23] of Western as well as non-Western agricultural development professionals, convinced that it could be applied 'even to the most isolated parts of the world'.[24] All of this suggests that the interwar years must be acknowledged as 'a germination period of development … theory and practice',[25] as it was during *this* era that rural reconstruction experts learned to think globally and borrow from multiple sources prior to and independent of the Cold War constellation.[26] As I shall argue, this was not least because some of them – including our protagonist Spencer

Hatch – were rooted in the religiously tinged modernizing mission of a Christian Association aptly portrayed as one of the first INGOs: the YMCA.[27]

In order to situate the Indian YMCA's rural experiment in its specific context, it is helpful to first have a glimpse of competing village development schemes. As has already been discussed in Chapter 1, agricultural knowledge and its application were considered vital by both the colonial administrators and their nationalist critics due to the recurring food crises in India. We have also seen that the Y's 'rural work' schemes, which came into being against the backdrop of these broader ideological changes, were by no means exceptional or unique. The pioneering impulse, again, came from the colonial state. Serious attempts by the colonial rulers at affecting improvements in Indian agriculture had been going on, however fitfully, since the 1860s. They gained further momentum in the wake of a large-scale enquiry conducted by a governmental committee that had published a highly critical report in 1892.[28] Most importantly, these government initiatives led to the inauguration of the Imperial Agricultural Research Institute in Pusa, Bihar, a decade later.[29] The more grassroots approaches introduced after the Great War by colonial experts like Frank L. Brayne and Malcolm Darling were followed later by various non-government actors, including Indian Nationalists, religiously motivated Indian social reformers and also Christian missionaries.[30] Indeed, missionary bodies were active in this field years before the Indian YMCA commenced its first forays into the field of 'rural reconstruction'. For example, Protestant missionaries from the Scottish Free Church's Madras Mission and the American Arcot Mission in Southern India attempted to liberate converts from the Panchama (a.k.a. 'Pariah') community from their bonded labour obligations by providing them with both education and land from the 1870s onwards.[31] The English Church Missionary Society had started Christian 'model villages' in the irrigated canal colonies of the Punjab even earlier, in the late 1860s.[32] Belgian Capuchins would follow suit over two decades later with the foundation of the Catholic rural settlement of Maryabad, in which they applied infrastructural innovations that had been designed and tested a few years previously in rural Belgian parishes.[33] The American Presbyterian Mission, too, shared the Belgian Capuchin's pioneering spirit and the colonial government's view that scientific agricultural research and training was the best remedy against the perceived 'rural decay' and, therefore, established an Agricultural Institute in Allahabad in 1910 under the aegis of the US-trained Welsh agronomist Sam Higginbottom.[34]

Almost simultaneously with the YMCA activities, Indian intellectuals and activists connected to one of the many socio-religious reform movements discussed in Chapter 1 also became involved in the general efforts for rural uplift. Disaffection with the state of agriculture in India and especially the failure of the colonial government to increase food production through a modernization of agricultural methods was repeatedly articulated in the vernacular press in the 1900s and 1910s.[35] In an attempt to translate such criticism into practice, some Indian reformist colleges began to include agricultural studies in their curriculum and even started small demonstration farms to show the superiority of modern 'scientific' methods of agriculture and husbandry.[36] The most famous such village reform project was initiated by Bengali poet and intellectual Rabindranath Tagore (1861–1941) in Sriniketan after the end of the Great War, with the help of the (equally US-trained) British agronomist Leonhard Elmhirst.[37] In the

Madras Presidency and several princely states of South India, local reformers of various shades and colours were convinced that 'the only way to bring the rural citizens into the national fold on an equal footing with other citizens' was to inculcate the 'values of civics and align them with agricultural development'.[38] They endeavoured to do so by advocating the creation of agricultural cooperatives (a strategy also encouraged by the colonial authorities who passed an Act to promote co-operative credit societies in 1904)[39] and launching a network of agricultural schools.

It has been convincingly argued that 'developmentalism was central for the definition of Indian nationalism from the start', and that rural reforms in particular were at the very heart of nationalist schemes.[40] It is unsurprising, therefore, that more or less simultaneously, Mohandas K. Gandhi and other Congress leaders developed their own 'rural uplift' schemes.[41] The Mahatma, especially, considered the village to be the very centrepiece of the new India he envisioned, and the individual peasant the centrepiece of the village. The success of his reform scheme did not rely on increased agricultural production through the use of chemical fertilizers and tractors but rather aimed at a thorough and holistic re-education of the rural population. In Gandhi's view, the peasants of a future India needed to be transformed into 'intelligent human beings' who did no longer 'live in dirt and darkness as animals'.[42]

In sum then, 'rural reconstruction' clearly was a ubiquitous buzzword by the 1930s,[43] even though it was variably defined, and the idea of village development had become the prime site of contestation between different groups claiming moral and political authority in India. It is striking that despite the obvious differences between colonial officials, missionaries, reformers and nationalists (and their respective agendas), almost all initiatives combined the modernization and scientization of agriculture with the schooling and 'moral uplift' of the rural population and their preparation for responsible citizenship.

As we have seen in Chapter 1, rural reconstruction and village development were not originally part of the Y's activities in South Asia. However, shortly before and during the First World War, many South Asians reached positions of influence in the Association and began to initiate changes, with the result that YMCA secretaries, who had thus far targeted only the English-educated urban youth, started a more intense engagement with the less privileged segments of the population in rural areas. Their newly devised rural reconstruction schemes initially centred around the establishment of agricultural cooperatives and the distribution of microcredits.[44] Although these early pioneering initiatives had economic betterment at their centre, they also had a much more far-reaching agenda, as prominent Y secretary Sherwood Eddy underscored in an article written for the American journal *Rural Manhood* in 1919. The 'able young Indian college graduates of strong moral character'[45] who were chosen as rural secretaries would ensure that the

> cooperative society and the economic benefits are made the leverage for lifting the entire life of the village – moral, social, educational, and religious. In the first place, the people are taught that no loans will be advanced unless there is better sanitation; the filthy cesspools must be filled and the village cleaned up and made healthful. In the next place, the society insists upon the opening of a village school

... The cooperative society becomes also a great moral leverage. The relation of drink to poverty and debt is proverbial. Men who drink are not likely to pay their obligations and the community therefore makes strict rules with regard to sobriety for its members. A new moral standard is soon discernible in the village.[46]

After the end of the war, the rural reconstruction and village development schemes expanded considerably, becoming a prominent part of the YMCA's 'peace programme' during the 1920s.[47] As we have seen, this shift towards practical development work undergirded by a strong moral agenda certainly reflected the growing importance of the 'social gospel' back in the United States,[48] but it was also prompted by local circumstances. The mass conversions of peasants in southern India from the lowly Dalit (or 'untouchable') segments of Hindu society had fundamentally changed the organization's constituency, and the Y leadership had to respond by offering programmes suitable for this new membership.[49] Their new rural work schemes also benefited tremendously from the general scramble for rural development that had started in the last decade of the nineteenth century and intensified during the 1910s. What, then, was the specific contribution of American YMCA secretaries to this polyphonic concert? The next section will help answer this question.

A man with a mission: Duane Spencer Hatch and the Martandam Rural Demonstration Centre

As we have seen already in Chapter 2, Duane Spencer Hatch, the man who came to personify the seemingly neutral American alternative to both nationalist village uplift schemes and official colonial agricultural reform programmes, first came to India on a quasi-imperial mission. Hatch was born in a modest farming family near Greenwich, NY, in 1888. Between 1909 and 1915, he studied agriculture, rural sociology and economics at Cornell University and subsequently acquired practical experience in a local rural extension programme.[50] He became active in the YMCA in college and volunteered to support the British war effort.[51] He threw himself into the Y army work on India's turbulent North-West Frontier Province (NWFP) and later with the British expeditionary forces in Mesopotamia over the next two and a half years.[52]

As we have seen already in Chapter 2, Hatch's autobiography and diaries leave no doubt that he essentially identified with the British imperial project and was particularly impressed with soldierly life and the military prowess of the British forces in Asia. This is not surprising, as the evidence suggests an almost natural identification of North American YMCA secretaries with fellow 'whites' in a colonial setting often initially experienced as hostile. The shared culture between 'Europeans and allied races', as the Colonial Census termed it,[53] was also responsible for a largely sympathetic attitude among most North American members of the YMCA towards the British imperial project. As indicated above, this attitude changed a little during the interwar period, but the emotional enmeshment that resulted from the status of Americans as an 'allied race' was difficult to overcome. Not only did Americans benefit from the 'racial dividends' of whiteness,[54] as I already observed elsewhere, there was also a kind of epistemic enmeshment as YMCA secretaries hailing from the United States and Canada relied mostly on British colonial knowledge of South Asia in order to make sense of the country, its inhabitants and their customs.[55] To be sure, after some time spent in the mission field, secretaries like Hatch would interact directly with South Asians too, thus getting access to alternative sources of information. Nevertheless, the initial imperial socialization seems to have been a formative influence, which might explain why Hatch continued to reproduce orientalist stereotypes without any apparent critical reflection even after spending two and a half decades in South Asia.[56]

Spencer Hatch fell ill during his long, exhausting stint in Mesopotamia and was repatriated to the United States in 1919. He used his two years of convalescence to obtain another degree in 'public philanthropy' at Yale and married Emily Gilchriest, a graduate of Syracuse University and an energetic actor-playwright whom he knew from his days at Cornell.[57] Over the next four decades, Emily Gilchriest Hatch would also become his partner in planning and implementing new schemes in rural development with global impact. On their arrival in South Asia in 1921, the newly-weds were assigned to serve the Association in the southern Indian state of Travancore by K. T. Paul, the first non-American General Secretary of the Indian YMCA.[58] Hatch's professional background in agriculture caught Paul's eye because of the latter's personal interest in rural reform, and he convinced the Hatches that a conspicuous Rural Demonstration Centre would be most useful in the region. Hatch, influenced by his training at Cornell, which is famous as a pioneering institution in agricultural extension schemes in the United States,[59] wanted to launch a similar programme in Travancore, in a 'real rural' setting.[60] Martandam, a small village halfway between the cities of Trivandrum and Nagercoil, fitted the bill perfectly.[61] K. T. Paul had already named the new programme in Martandam 'Rural Reconstruction' in a speech he gave at Coimbatore.[62] Hatch initially resisted this designation because of Paul's nationalistic reputation and his own colonial sympathies, fearing that 'it had in it a bit of political sting against the British'.[63] Paul nonetheless insisted, and the name was adopted, though it appears to have led to the souring of relations between Hatch and Paul.[64] However, Hatch curried favour with both, the colonial rulers[65] as well as the rulers of Travancore. The resulting closeness paid dividends in the form of practical and financial support to the YMCA and especially to the rural experiment in Martandam.[66]

These details remind us of the very complex set of relationships that characterized the Martandam experiment. Not only had Indian agency grown palpably in the Association since the Great War to the extent that K. T. Paul ultimately decided the location and name of the project, but also Hatch and his fellow workers were dependent on the goodwill of the local aristocracy in Travancore, which was, in turn, unobtrusively controlled by the British. There is no evidence, however, that Hatch viewed this co-operation with the ruling elites as particularly problematic. His minimal to non-existent criticism of imperial autocratic rule and Travancore's aristocracy appears at odds with the rural reconstruction programme's professed goal of preparing the local population for democracy.[67] This tension is at least partly resolved when one considers that, to him, democracy in India was a long-term goal rather than something that lay in the foreseeable future. Thus, in October 1941, at a time when many other American spokesmen of the YMCA in India openly sided with the national movement, Hatch still wanted to relegate the country to the proverbial waiting room of history[68] 'until we have a much more orderly and sane world'.[69] Going back to the differentiation made earlier, one can, therefore, argue that rural reconstruction as envisaged by Hatch and his fellow Y workers was ultimately more about *modernization* as a technocratic process of infrastructural improvement and less about *modernity* as a project of societal and political liberation.

In the MRDC, in the meantime, the new programme came into existence after an initial evaluation of the local villagers' requirements. Spencer Hatch noted that the 'Spiritual, Mental, Physical, Social, and Economic needs' that were identified as part of the rural reconstruction programmes came to be symbolically represented in a five-sided triangle developed by his 'ingenious' wife Emily, who simply added two more sides (social and economic) to the well-established YMCA signature triangle (see Figure 5.1).[70]

In contrast to his exclusive reliance on British sources during his army work, both Hatch and his wife followed the missionary practice of acquiring linguistic skills and in-depth local knowledge once they were in Travancore. By the time their training programme for rural leaders started in 1926, they were even able to converse and teach in both Malayalam and Tamil, the vernacular languages most spoken in the immediate vicinity of Martandam.[71] That the Hatches' interest in the regional culture was not merely strategic is highly probable, at least in the case of Emily, as she was fascinated by south Indian music and dance and wrote a dissertation about *Kathakali*, a local art form at the intersection of drama, dance and religious ritual.[72] Spencer Hatch, too, engaged quite intensely with his new environment and received his PhD in agricultural studies from Cornell in 1928 with a thesis based entirely on his fieldwork in Martandam.[73] The role of local South Asian know-how alongside scientific data-gathering and the tapping of global, colonial and other missionary sources in this process of knowledge formation is evident from his memoirs, where he describes the initial challenges of making sense of his new environment and starting the project, emphasizing that he had to 'learn from many people: natives and foreigners long in the country'.[74] Towards the end of his career, when he was part of the emerging establishment of international experts, Hatch reminded his future colleagues that it was pivotal for the success of village development programmes to integrate local knowledge into one's own repertoire:

> The teacher friend should not disregard or insult the local culture ... Instead of going to a village with the attitude that all is wrong there, one should and can find practices that are very good. He should praise these, should recognize that there is much for the outsider to learn here; that there can be a sincere pooling of knowledge. There should be a cross fertilization [*sic*] of ancient wisdom with the new.[75]

This appreciation of local expertise seems rather vague and general, and hard evidence of what he viewed as 'cross-fertilization' is difficult to find. However, at least one example can be reconstructed from the available sources. In 1939, Hatch told *Reader's Digest* reporter Jerome Beatty that 'even though you have agricultural degrees from big

Figure 5.1 Symbolizing the shift to the 'social gospel': the Martandam Rural Demonstration Centre's unique logo designed by Emily Gilchriest Hatch. Courtesy Kautz Family YMCA Archives, University of Minnesota, Minneapolis.

colleges, there are things that an ignorant Indian farmer can tell you', and confessed that he had had to abandon part of his Cornellian principles of animal husbandry and instead adopt 'the Indian way'[76] to ensure the continuous milk production of cows that had lost their calves.[77]

In spite of such occasional nods towards the value of indigenous agricultural knowledge, however, a clear hierarchy is discernible in Hatch's collaborations with Indian co-workers, and he had a tendency to 'blow his own horn', as he himself phrased it.[78] K. T. Paul, the architect of the YMCA's first rural work scheme in the 1910s and General Secretary of the Indian Y until 1930, is only very rarely mentioned in Hatch's correspondence and publications. This is particularly noteworthy because an early plan sketched out by Paul in 1914 already contained many of the MRDC's key features and signature methods, which Hatch would later claim as his own innovations.[79] This 'borrowing' suggests that the American took a lot from his Indian superior who, after all, came from a family of experienced Tamil farmers.[80] Likewise, Hatch's copious writings rarely acknowledge the Indian rural secretaries, including Manuel, Jesudas and others, who had pioneered rural reconstruction initiatives in Travancore a few years previously and were doing most of the actual everyday work in the MRDC.[81] It is also revealing that 70 per cent of the USD 5,000 sent annually from New York to sustain the MRDC were spent on Hatch's salary, whereas most of his Indian assistants, 'fired by his leadership, work[ed] part time for nothing'.[82] Such asymmetries even permeate the visual representations of the relationship between the American expert and his South Asian co-workers: a photograph shows Hatch in discussion with Indian 'rural leaders', one of whom is ostentatiously placed at the head of the table as if to suggest the egalitarian character of the exchange, but nevertheless has a benevolent colonial flavour, largely because the central focus is very much on the American (see Figure 5.2). It perfectly captures the guiding principle of the entire Martandam project, which was, Hatch declared, to provide 'self-help with intimate, expert counsel'.[83]

The American agronomist repeats colonial and Indian elite stereotypes about the alleged passivity and ignorance of South Asian 'village folk' when justifying the need for expert counsel and outside leadership too.[84] His diagnosis of the problems and defects of the village society, agriculture and rural economy in Martandam and India

Figure 5.2 Providing 'intimate, expert counsel': Hatch and some of his Indian fellow workers during working session in Martandam (1927). Courtesy Kautz Family YMCA Archives, University of Minnesota, Minneapolis.

in general is harsh: livestock and poultry, he maintains, were 'generally poorly kept [and] unproductive' while cultivation methods could only be described as 'exceedingly primitive'. The food supply was 'insufficient' as a logical result, and the 'very evident lack of play life' in rural areas had a similarly deplorable effect on the rustic population's physical constitution.[85] To make things worse, as per Hatch, certain 'religious customs and uneconomic traditions definitely accentuate[d] the distress of the country and retarded its rise out of poverty',[86] and a whole array of 'superstitions' were 'powerful checks to the introduction of new, scientific, and more productive methods … in the Indian rural village'.[87] It is astonishing how closely the assessment of the American YMCA secretary mirrors both the 'discourse of deficiency' deployed by the British imperial administrators attempting to 'improve' the Indian countryside from the late eighteenth century and the Euro-American paternalism characteristic of post-Second World War development initiatives.[88]

However, though the diagnosis was similar, the suggested remedy was different. To improve the situation and overcome the 'uneconomic traditions' that he held responsible for the villagers' 'indisposition to effort',[89] Hatch advocated the demonstration method pioneered by the 'schoolmaster of American agriculture', Seaman A. Knapp, who introduced advanced cultivation methods in 'backward' southern states in the United States in the early 1900s.[90] Clearly, Hatch assumed that rural India had 'many features similar' to the American south and that what worked for African American sharecroppers in Tennessee or Alabama would work equally well for Tamil or Malayali villagers;[91] the presumed analogy is also visible in the title of Hatch's first monograph, *Up from Poverty in Rural India*, an obvious allusion to Tuskegee founder Booker T. Washington's *Up from Slavery*.[92]

Hatch's self-help scheme was predicated on the ideas that the new centre was not an 'impressive show place' but rather a modest, simple and inexpensive experiment station and that the YMCA's 'expert counsel' involved a 'maximum of living and doing and a minimum of verbal preaching'.[93] This approach was in stark contrast to the later 'authoritarian high modernism' projects described by James C. Scott,[94] and might be termed 'low modernism', a label applied to similar strategies that developed almost simultaneously in the United States during the New Deal years.[95] As recent research has demonstrated, such 'low modernist' programmes were not applied only in the American Deep South but were soon exported to the other side of the Rio Grande in an attempt to protect the collective landholdings of Mexican *campesinos* (small farmers) and improve their economic situation.[96] In Martandam, the claim to simplicity also included the lifestyle of the village workers themselves. In Hatch's words, rural reconstruction in India needed 'workers … rich in the things they can do without'; he even cited Gandhi as an exemplary pioneer of simple life in this context in a rare reference to contemporary politics.[97] Like the Mahatma, Hatch was convinced that simplicity would save scarce resources and help bridge the gap between the 'rural leader' on the one hand and the village population on the other. Sharing his view, one of Hatch's Indian rural co-workers in the Y.M.C.A. stressed that, in order to be successful, 'the attempts … to reform the rural areas should be done most cautiously and without the least possibility of being misunderstood as an act of generous patronizing.'[98] Acceptance by peasants was therefore crucial not least because rural reconstruction also included improving the 'spiritual and moral quality of the people', which, in turn, was regarded as a prerequisite for 'successful democracy'.[99] Of course, mutual trust was vital for effectively disseminating these salient messages.

The YMCA workers in Martandam designed variegated strategies of improvement to tackle its most pressing economic needs. A method that eventually became the core of the 'green revolution'-type of US development aid consisted of replacing purportedly inferior Indian varieties of seeds and livestock with imported ones.[100] Not surprisingly, Hatch's 'discourse of deficiency' also targeted the local fauna. For instance, he declared that India needed 'larger and more able bees' and acquired 'six hives of his best Italian' from an old Catholic priest in Lombardy during a long and adventurous journey.[101] He also tried to breed single-combed White Leghorn chickens, an attempt that he described in noticeably colour-coded terms. The white hens imported from New Jersey,[102] he maintained, produced 'twice as many eggs and twice as large ones' compared to the local 'mongrels'.[103] Hatch calculated precisely how the 'pure White Leghorn blood' could turn 'the tiny brown jungle fowl white': a 'progeny of seven-eighths, or practically pure White Leghorns' would be produced in less than three years by passing surplus cocks from family to family.[104] He was also not averse to using mild forms of coercion, 'insisting that the family kill all its jungle cocks' to achieve his ambitious purity target.[105] Ironically, the White Leghorn population was so quickly decimated by local birds of prey that Hatch gave orders to repaint them in brown to provide camouflage. Similarly, goats were 'upgraded' through cross-breeding and the 'tiny cows of the one tea cup of milk a day output' were replaced by 'bigger, stronger ... cattle, with the expected increase in milk'.[106] 'Special fast-growing fodder grasses like the Sudan, the Napier, the Guinea' were also imported into the area to feed the cattle. Importantly, close co-operation with the government and missionary institutions like the Government Agricultural Farm and the Allahabad Agricultural Institute made all these innovations possible.[107]

Besides the agricultural output, and in another overlap with Gandhian village uplift schemes, the centre also experimented with various village industries (or 'subsidiary cottage vocations',[108] as Hatch called them) that were practised in the MRDC, such as weaving, dyeing, carpentry and basketmaking. The YMCA's dense network of contacts helped sell the products and establish durable trade relations. Eggs, cashew nuts, honey, palmyra sugar and the output from cottage industries were produced and distributed by post all over India by newly founded co-operatives.[109] Like other emerging village development experts active in South Asia in the interwar period (irrespective of political agenda and ideological background),[110] Spencer Hatch deemed 'the co-operative method' a crucial 'matter of education' and a potential panacea for all kinds of rural defects.[111] Inspired by K. T. Paul's groundbreaking experiments so enthusiastically praised by Sherwood Eddy, micro-credit societies were established and became a particularly important aspect of the co-operative activities organized from Martandam in forty surrounding villages to alleviate the villagers' 'crushing load' of debt with local moneylenders.[112] Like a number of similar initiatives run by contemporaneous state and non-state bodies,[113] the Y co-operatives linked the measures for economic betterment with more far-reaching attempts to improve Indian society through the Association's 'socialization programme'. Hatch and his helpmates believed that they had to 'tackle India's fundamental problem, her divisions into religious and social castes ... which do not love and respect each other'. The Cornell agronomist developed the so-called intercommunity-committee plan[114] to actively break up existing social conventions and barriers, making it a point that all the major religious, social and caste groups were represented in each project committee in the village.[115] Further, the efficacy of inter-communal alliances was demonstrated by holding committee meetings publicly in front of Martandam's newly established village library, which soon became the gravitational centre for various modernizing activities. Inter-religious services that were staged at the same conspicuous site fulfilled a similar function. Last but not least, Boy Scout and Girl Guide activities of the type discussed in the previous chapter formed part of the 'socialization' scheme and were likewise practised in public, and were open to people from all castes and creeds.[116] Emily Gilchriest Hatch's engagement was crucial in this respect as she served as commissioner of the Travancore Girl Guides and served as the only female member of the Travancore State Council of the Boy Scouts.[117]

A combined strategy was also developed to improve the physical condition of the rural Indian population. On the one hand, conveying fundamental precepts of hygiene and basic facts of health and nutrition through an 'intensive educational programme to teach the people how to live cleanly' was considered effective.[118] Clean living, of course, crucially included the construction of latrines and the introduction of an entire 'new sanitary system'.[119] However, in another striking analogy with contemporaneous Gandhian campaigns,[120] clean living also included 'temperance teaching'. A special temperance survey conducted by Hatch's Indian co-workers in 1924/5 formed the basis for a targeted anti-alcohol crusade by the local YMCA in thirty neighbouring villages.[121] Given the prominent place that sport and games had in the YMCA portfolio, it will not come as a surprise that the third pillar of the 'physical uplift' programme comprised healthy recreational activities. As a result, two volleyball fields were constructed and badminton, tennis and swimming tournaments were organized near the village library, which apparently drew local youth.[122]

The question then arises as to how the YMCA conveyed its low-modernist message to the (predominantly illiterate) local population. Many observers regarded Hatch's method of reaching out to a village audience by means of educational plays as a most potent and yet culturally sensitive strategy of dissemination.[123] Once again, Emily Gilchriest Hatch's manifold talents were critical, as she was involved in the creation of these dramatic performances, which Spencer Hatch considered 'the most effective way of teaching' rural populations. The method had already been applied successfully in various agricultural communities in the United States[124] and had also been tested by the first generation of Indian rural secretaries in the 1910s,[125] demonstrating that dramatic performances attracted large crowds from all religious and social backgrounds. Further, Hatch believed that 'the dramatic tendency [wa]s inherent in the Indian nature'.[126] Emily Hatch, therefore, wrote more than a dozen educational plays, some of which were even published and enjoyed a wide circulation.[127] The anti-alcohol drama *Out of the Pot into the World*, for instance, was translated not only into nine different Indian languages but also into Mandarin.[128] One of her collections, *Little Plays*, written in the 1920s and published in the early 1930s, was used for 'reconstruction teaching' in the Philippines even after the Second World War.¹²⁹ These plays were, without exception, extremely simple and very didactic.¹³⁰ Their sole purpose was to convey a particular message or inculcate a specific value regarded as crucial for the YMCA's broader rural reconstruction project. *Cock a Doodle Doo*, for instance, demonstrated the superiority of White Leghorn chickens to encourage the villagers to become part of one of the Y's poultry co-operatives. *The Durbar of King Cereal* uses motifs from Indian epics to instruct the south Indian village population, whose diet was predominantly rice-based, about the nutritional advantages of 'northern grains' like wheat, corn or buckwheat. This attempt to improve 'native' food habits on the basis of scientific and rational arguments is particularly noteworthy as it overlapped and competed with both imperial and nationalist attempts at altering and regulating the diet of the Indian population.¹³¹ Such experiments, designed to improve food security and combat the newly discovered 'malnutrition', were quite popular in the period between the 1920s and 1950s.¹³² Finally, *Draughts* was a temperance play contrasting 'Toddymen' with 'Watermen', celebrating 'good clear cold water' as an infinitely better alternative to the local palm wine.¹³³

A particularly powerful example of the discursive strategies used to persuade villagers to change their lifestyle and dietary habits is provided by the drama *The Trial*, which itself deserves a brief analysis. This play was written in support of the YMCA's proposed physical improvement programme, to inculcate healthy dietary habits and stimulate physical exercise. To get its message across, the mini-drama invoked images of the colonial legal and police apparatus that must have been familiar to most people in the audience. Emily filmed portions of a performance for the documentary *The Martandam Story* in 1937 in order to present the YMCA's rural work in southern India to donors back home,¹³⁴ offering a rare opportunity to analyse the performative elements of the staging in addition to the text. The setting is the courtroom of 'Healthland', at the hearing of six offenders dressed as simple villagers. They are accused of having violated the fundamental laws of health, such as 'the Law of Fresh Air, the Law of Cleanliness, the Law of Exercise' and so on.¹³⁵ The judge – fittingly played by a fair-skinned student from North India who acts as arrogantly as he possibly can – wears Western clothes and displays the full paraphernalia of an imperial magistrate. The guards are clad in the familiar khaki uniforms worn by the colonial police.

The commentary in the documentary is provided by Spencer Hatch himself, who explains that the court scene is well understood even by uneducated peasants in this remote village since 'litigation ha[d] become a popular indoor sport in India'.¹³⁶ That the repressive machinery and authoritarian rhetoric of the colonial state were apparently key devices in convincing villagers to change their bodily practices is suggested by this short excerpt from a dialogue between the judge and offender 'No. 4', accused of overeating and lack of exercise:

Judge: Do you play tennis or Badminton?
No. 4:   No sir. It is too much running about. It makes one perspire.
Judge: That's good for you. Why don't you like it?
No. 4:   It is so uncomfortable to perspire.

Judge: You lazy glutton, what do you think your stomach is? A steamroller? What are the pores of your body for?
No. 4: I didn't know I had any. ...
Judge: Your punishment is severe because you don't have any sense at all. (*knocks on the table Heralds appear*) You shall be put in jail, fed frugal meals, quite the proper amount of frugal nourishing food, but a mere fraction of what you have been eating. Then you will undergo a system of physical exercises in the morning and be made to play tennis in the evening. When I consider you are again fit for society I will let you go.
No. 4: (*very crestfallen*): Very well, your Honor.[137]

It does not seem too far-fetched an interpretation to read such examples as evidence of the fact that the colonial setting in which the rural reform programme took shape (and possibly also the 'imperial past' of its main architect) exerted a tangible influence on the scheme itself. Despite all the rhetoric about a participatory, inclusivist and culturally sensitive approach, clear traces of a benevolent but strongly normative and moralizing paternalism remain, an attitude not altogether dissimilar from the one displayed by colonialist and nationalist advocates of rural reconstruction. In fact, the Hatches' perception of the villagers overlapped a great deal with that of high-handed imperial pioneers of rural reform such as Frank Brayne, who was appalled by the peasants' ignorance and apathy.[138] It was also not dissimilar to that of nationalist reformers such as Gandhi, who often reiterated that he was viscerally repelled by both rustic drinking habits and standards of hygiene, and famously denounced Indian villages as 'muck-heaps'.[139]

However, it was not only the shared 'language of physical cleanliness, rational productivity and disinterested social service'[140] that united these superficially different currents. Another pivotal aspect consisted of their all-encompassing holistic approaches. Rural reconstruction, Spencer Hatch wrote, could only succeed 'when it attack[ed] all sides of a villager's life simultaneously'.[141] Most importantly, as we have seen, it had to include the fundamental goal of effecting 'a change in the psychology of the peasant, and in his social and personal habits'.[142]

The extent to which the villagers concerned were indeed impressed by spectacles such as *The Trial* is, of course, difficult to establish. This thorny question raises the general issues of success and failure of the Y project. How much could Hatch and his fellow workers indeed achieve a hegemonic position in the MRDC and the surrounding villages? On the basis of the existing sources, it is not possible to reconstruct adequately the perspective of those at the receiving end of the Y's rural uplift scheme. However, even the usually very positive YMCA sources contain indications that the rural populace of Martandam and its vicinity occasionally evaded or resisted its educational efforts. The volleyball matches between different villages or communities, for instance, often led to quarrels, punch-ups and even court cases instead of turning the villagers into 'good sports' (and supporters of democracy) by inculcating a sense of fair play and a respect for constituted authority. Moreover, the account of Jerome Beatty, an American journalist who spent a week with Hatch in Travancore in 1939, makes apparent that even after a decade and a half of continuous fieldwork, Hatch's authority as an agricultural expert remained quite fragile among the local population. After the entire population of Italian bees imported to replace their allegedly inferior Indian cousins had perished within a few months, 'it was a crisis. Hatch's prestige began to fall. Perhaps, the natives decided, his ideas about chickens and goats and sugar weren't so good, either'.[143] The position of the foreign expert and his 'scientific knowledge', it seems, was always precarious: there was no wholesale conversion to the new methods, and the trust and respect of the locals needed to be constantly legitimized and defended.

Even if the actual impact on the ground was far more modest than Spencer Hatch's rather self-laudatory reports imply, it is suggestive that a thorough and comprehensive transformation of the village population remained the explicit objective of the YMCA's rural programme. The Martandam scheme perfectly illustrates the problems connected to the self-help approach that later not only became a pillar of Indian post-independence development planning[144] but also an essential part of the template for small-scale community development programmes worldwide. The concept of self-help, of course, has a long prehistory in social and pedagogical reform schemes.[145] As German historian Hubertus Büschel has argued, the developmentalist self-help programmes that gradually evolved after the First World War basically consist of the 'subtle entanglement of putative voluntarism on the one hand and [demand for] total surrender on the other'.[146] The pioneers of village development faced the fundamental dilemma of negotiating between the application of moral pressure on the target populations of such endeavours and cementing the structural asymmetries between 'experts' and 'backward village folk' that stood in tension with their egalitarian rhetoric.[147]

The Hatches' intense social interaction with educated Indians seems to have followed a similar transformative logic. Emulating the Western – or indeed, the Protestant American – way of life was seen to be the only means of improvement. In 1925, Spencer Hatch reported to the YMCA headquarters in New York that he was very pleased that the 'natives' in Trivandrum had started copying the ways of Westerners living in their midst and that 'every Tom, Dick and Harry' wanted to become a YMCA secretary:[148] 'especially among the Hindus we find them trying to make their houses like ours in ways such as copying our furniture and butting in plants, flowers and pictures to take away their former barrenness'.[149]

The move from 'barrenness' towards 'a more abundant life'[150] definitely had a socio-economic dimension that made it compatible with later Cold War development programmes designed to save Asian peasants from the pernicious influences of Communist propaganda. However, as Kevin Lowe has recently noted, this concept also had strong religious overtones and was deeply rooted in early twentieth-century US Christian agrarianism.[151] The goal of converting the local population that had first brought American Y secretaries to South Asia had by no means dissipated, even though the emphasis was now at least outwardly on 'conversions to modernity'[152] rather than on the formal acceptance of Protestant Christianity, and on material rather than spiritual uplift. This observation is perfectly in line with a recent body of research that underscores the 'merging of religious and secular goals within the sphere of development' and pointed to the 'roles played by Christian actors in laying the foundations for technocratic forms of development management'.[153] Accordingly,

Hatch was convinced that the manifold social contacts, sport, scouting activities and the 'socializing programme' he had developed would help increase the Indians' 'respect for Christ and Christianity', so that one distant day they 'actually may fully accept Christ'.[154] The most powerful aspect of the entire village uplift scheme – and here Hatch was in line with other Christian pioneers of rural reconstruction like Sam Higginbottom[155] – was its emphasis on 'action', as a 'hundred years of the word of mouth alone w[ould] neither evangelize India nor fill the hungry mouths of India'.[156] To critics who suspected that the original religious goals of the YMCA's foreign mission might be diluted through the increasing emphasis on social and economic improvement, he replied that rural reconstruction was the most spiritual method of presenting the gospel in a country such as India where 'direct proselytism' could not work and a programme had to be 'for the whole people and by the whole people'.[157]

Hatch's position reflected the deeper shift in the strategy of the YMCA in South Asia that has already been addressed in several of the previous chapters. By the mid-1920s, the Association's leadership had recognized that aggressive proselytizing and doctrinal purity were doomed to failure, especially at the height of anticolonial nationalism and anti-Western sentiment. The subtle distinction between proselytization (making converts) and evangelization (inducing people to accept and practise Christian values) was therefore officially introduced at an international YMCA meeting in Mysore in 1937.[158] The ground for such a move had been prepared, amongst others, by the influential American Christian crusader and agrarian expert Kenyon L. Butterfield, who had met Hatch in 1930.[159] In a number of publications, Butterfield described the task of softly 'permeating' the life of the rural masses in Asia and elsewhere through practical reconstruction work as key for Christian missionary work in the decades to come.[160] Clearly, even after becoming a prominent agent of rural development and social engineering, the Indian YMCA remained a faith-based organization.[161] It is, therefore, not surprising that even observers with no particular sympathy for Hatch's 'evangelizing' agenda described the transformative power of his work in quasi-religious terms. Louise Ouwerkerk, an Anglo-Dutch professor of economics teaching in Trivandrum in the 1930s,[162] noted that Spencer Hatch was successful in his mission to change minds because he had managed to evoke 'enthusiasm' and a strong 'desire to improve'[163] in the local peasants. Similarly, Jerome Beatty observed that, in contrast to the 'disgusting, cringing and dirty people' untouched by Hatch's work, villagers living near the MRDC were 'a different breed ... Their chins are up, their clothes may be rags, but they are clean rags, there are flowering vines over their huts and proudly they lead you to see their children exhibit the English they have learned in YMCA night schools'.[164]

Most of the centre's activities discussed thus far have been of an educational character in an indirect sense. However, one of the most influential and long-lasting activities at Martandam were the educational courses for training voluntary as well as professional full-time 'rural leaders', offered by the YMCA secretaries. A broad variety of short-term courses like weekend study groups, educational camps and summer schools for the village workers were available, as well as Sunday schools and exhibitions for villagers.[165] The Martandam Training College in Rural Reconstruction, set up in 1926, was the most important institution in this context. It offered six-week and four-month courses in agriculture and village development that emphasized a 'hands-on approach' and 'a maximum of practice and a minimum of theory', in line with Hatch's personal views on rural development.¹⁶⁶

From southern Travancore to southern Arizona: The regional and global circulation of 'low modernist' rural development knowledge

By the early 1930s, Martandam was known in Europe, America, China and Korea as the MRDC and its Training Colleges were 'claiming the attention of leading experts in rural reconstruction', inducing 'Government agencies, educational organizations, and missions and service groups ... to send men and women there for training'.¹⁶⁷ By the end of the decade, more than a thousand students from South Asia, and also from faraway places such as China, the Dutch East Indies and Egypt, had undergone training in the 'seven Dollar University' to become professional village workers.¹⁶⁸ Many alumni would go on to occupy influential positions in various missionary or government schools and in rural training institutions.¹⁶⁹ D. R. D. Souri, a graduate from the class of 1933, worked in the Government Rural Reconstruction Centre in the Princely State of Baroda that had been established by the local administration at Hatch's urging; C. K. Velayudan and A. W. Kannangara, both of the class of 1937, held leading positions in government-run agricultural centres in Cochin and Ceylon, respectively.¹⁷⁰ In a 1944 speech at a conference in Washington, DC, Hatch dwelt on the career of one 'Hussein Ali Orphy', a former student from Egypt who had become a leading rural development expert for the Egyptian government, to illustrate the universal success of his methods.¹⁷¹ It is thus safe to argue that village workers trained at Martandam's Practical Training School fulfilled important roles as experts or 'go-betweens' from the late 1940s onwards, when large-scale rural development programmes were initiated by state governments or as a part of UNESCO or foreign aid programmes.¹⁷²

The excellent reputation and popularity of the Training College was further enhanced by the astonishing success of Hatch's books. The highly respected Oxford University Press brought out all three of his major publications, and his first book, *Up from Poverty in Rural India* (1932), even contained a foreword by Lord Willingdon, the Viceroy of India (1931–6). Four editions of this work were released by 1938, a remarkable achievement for a semi-academic publication on so specialized a topic. It was even translated into several Asian languages including Gujarati, Malayalam, Sindhi and Chinese.¹⁷³ Its sequel *Further Upward in Rural India* (1938), though slightly less successful commercially, was equally well received by critics.¹⁷⁴ By the 1940s, Hatch's books as well as his practical work became the focus of articles in scientific journals in the United States.¹⁷⁵ The knowledge template created in the MRDC thus circulated widely among the emerging epistemic community of village workers and development experts.

The colonial as well as the missionary elements of the YMCA's rural reconstruction project in southern India became more difficult to detect once the expert knowledge produced by Spencer and Emily Hatch started flowing beyond the specific context of its production. As mentioned earlier, the development knowledge generated in the MRDC in the 1920s and 1930s was shaped by local systems of governance, but was also borrowed from a variety of other sources. Subir Sinha has persuasively argued that Hatch's writings must be understood as important contributions to an emerging transnational development regime unbound by national or imperial borders.[176] Throughout his career, Hatch undertook study tours to countries all over the world in a quest to supplement his knowledge on rural reconstruction. One of these tours led him to Germany and Denmark in 1927, where he spent several weeks studying 'Cooperatives, the Folk Schools, and the ways of rural life'.[177] Other destinations included the Tuskegee Institute in Alabama, where he witnessed 'a demonstration made for the whole community at one of the most run-down Negro homes' and obviously drew inspiration for the title of his book *Up from Poverty*. Asian destinations included the Philippines, where he studied the home gardening projects directed by the US Colonial Educational Department and China, where he examined experiments in co-operative egg production and marketing.[178]

By the mid-1930s, Hatch had acquired an international reputation as an expert in rural development in 'tropical' countries, which brought him increasing official attention. Having taken the 'lead in the particular field of service called rural reconstruction' by the late 1930s,[179] he received the accolades of imperial agriculturalists for his work at MRDC.[180] The centre was even honoured by official visits from the Viceroy of India and the Chief Minister of the Government of Ceylon, and both were full of praise for what they saw.[181] In 1936, the Government of Ceylon requested the American village development expert to help quell a rural malaria epidemic and give a lecture on rural reconstruction to the Ceylonese State Council.[182] While in Ceylon, Hatch received an invitation from a preparatory committee established by the League of Nations Health Organization (LNHO) to share his Martandam experiences.[183] In the wake of 'globalizing' debates on health issues, the LNHO committee had visited India and other Asian countries in 1936 to prepare for a conference in the Dutch East Indies on rural health, and were delighted to hear that 'rural reconstruction' was the topic of the day.[184] The eventual Intergovernmental Conference of Far-Eastern Countries on Rural Hygiene, held over two weeks in Bandung in August 1937, is regarded by historians as a milestone in the creation of health and development regimes that 'linked the local and the global, and Europe to Asia'.[185] The conference focus on extension work, nutrition and the training of rural workers meant that Spencer Hatch counted as an internationally renowned expert.[186] His grassroots approach in the MRDC fitted the LNHO's new paradigm perfectly, emphasized 'an awareness of the contextual and the vernacular'.[187]

Hatch subsequently visited various co-operatives and 'the world's most famous nutrition laboratory in Batavia' to learn more about the preparation of soya bean foods. He continued this study tour by visiting Australia, Tahiti and Nouvelle Calédonie (where he scrutinized the agricultural reform programmes of the French colonial administration) as well as a number of other places in the South Sea.[188] This growing international exposure further catalysed the popularity of the YMCA's rural reconstruction methods back in South Asia. The colonial government that had supported Hatch's Rural Demonstration Centre almost from its inception now further intensified its involvement. Next to the provision of financial aid, free lumber and the provision of bulls, cocks and other animals from government breeding farms, 'able officers from Government Departments' were now regularly sent to the 'Seven-Dollar University' to teach courses on sanitation, agriculture, economics, physics and other subjects.[189] This quasi-official recognition was also helpful in attracting third-party funding: from 1936 the MRDC was in receipt of an annual grant by John D. Rockefeller Jr's Davison Fund, and thus helped pave the way for the Rockefeller Foundation's massive intervention in agricultural development programmes in India after independence.[190] Roughly at the same time, the Association was contacted by the government of Madras province as well as several of the largest Indian princely states to establish rural centres in Hyderabad, Mysore, Pudokottai, Baroda and other places. These projects materialized, with Spencer Hatch playing a crucial part in starting each of the new institutions.[191] By 1940, when he left, an entire network of institutions modelled on the MRDC existed in India.[192] The 'Martandam Larger Team', too, had gone global, as the foreign alumni returned to their respective home regions to convey 'the knowledge of the more abundant life to their fellowmen'.[193]

Word about Hatch had spread to Washington a few years earlier. Upon arriving on furlough in 1941, he was sent to Mexico on an official five-year rural reconstruction mission. The US government followed a 'good neighbour' policy in Mexico at the time, and the Rockefeller Foundation famously planted the seeds of a 'green revolution' there.[194] Hatch established a Rural Demonstration Centre in a remote valley near Tepoztlan along lines very similar to the Martandam programme.[195] Indeed, Hatch noted explicitly that the Martandam template was applicable on a global scale and would 'work in every country'.[196] An article in *The Reader's Digest* likewise speculated in 1945 that Hatch's 'one man rural reconstruction program ... could be a model for raising the living standards of depressed peoples everywhere'.[197]

Given the Indian YMCA's affinity to visual media (discussed in Chapters 1 and 2), it is hardly surprising that the Association used it to further the popularity of the prominent rural reconstruction expert and his low-modernist approach. The YMCA had previously used the MRDC film footage for educational purposes and to satisfy its donors.[198] In 1947, Hatch's village uplift programme in Mexico was professionally filmed for an MGM documentary in a style that foreshadowed later Cold War propaganda. *Give Us the Earth* (see Figure 5.3) featured Hatch as protagonist and captures the spirit of benevolent paternalism that informed his earlier work in South Asia.

The Cold War made rural rehabilitation programmes an important political weapon for Washington. With the start of the Cold War, the spotlight turned on American do-gooders in an unprecedented manner even as enormous funding opportunities opened up for them. This new constellation gave the final stages of Hatch's career a definitive global twist. When the United Nation's Food and Agricultural Organization (FAO) came into being in Quebec City in October 1945,[199] the YMCA's 'Old India Hand' was a founding member of the new body and served as Secretary of the FAO's Education and Extension Panel (see Figure 5.4).

After the pioneering phase of the Mexico experiment ended, the Hatches received offers from various quarters.[200] Their specialized knowledge was especially attractive

'The Gospel of Rural Reconstruction' 159

GOOD NEIGHBORS

Dr. Spencer Hatch, YMCA rural rehabilitation expert and a young student of his scientific farming methods, as they appear in MGM's Theatre of Life fact-film "Give Us the Earth" now at the Theatre.

Figure 5.3 Promotional poster for the MGM 'Theater of Life' documentary *Give Us the Earth*, starring D. Spencer Hatch (1947). Picture in the public domain (available at: https://www.hindutamil.in/news/environment/145922--2.htm).

to the Inter-American Institute of Agricultural Sciences, which was sponsored by the Pan-American Union and set up in Costa Rica in 1944.[201] Hatch worked at the institute in Costa Rica for almost four years until 1950, teaching a course on 'Methods of Extension'.[202] Spencer and Emily briefly visited the MRDC again in the early 1950s as part of a third and final South Asian Mission on behalf of UNESCO and the Government of India, during which he had extensive discussions with Prime Minister Nehru and his cabinet.[203] He subsequently co-ordinated a large-scale project in Ceylon for UNESCO from 1951 to 1957.[204] Shortly after the end of his mission in Ceylon, Hatch celebrated the global proliferation of the 'Pillars of Policy' established in Martandam. They were so 'tried and true', he boasted, that they had meanwhile been applied 'over India, in Ceylon, in Burma, in China, in Egypt, in Mexico, in Latin America, in the Mid-East [sic] and in Indonesia'.[205] As the Cold War peaked, the Hatches' work became a part of the US State Department's anti-Communist propaganda. Spencer Hatch featured on

Figure 5.4 Spencer Hatch (third from the left in the front row) at the first FAO conference in Quebec (1945). Courtesy Kautz Family YMCA Archives, University of Minnesota, Minneapolis.

the cover of the magazine *Free World* in 1951, distributed freely in American Cultural Centres all over South and Southeast Asia (see Figure 5.5).[206] The former YMCA secretary had come to symbolize the American promise of a 'more abundant life' – this time stripped of all spiritual connotations – in a capitalist world system under 'mild American suzerainty'.[207]

Hatch's final assignment brought him back to the United States in the late 1950s, where he spent the last years of his life on a reservation for Native Americans near Tucson, AZ, using the knowledge he had gathered in southern India to promote community development schemes among a different type of 'Indians': members of the Mojave, Navajo and Hopi tribes.[208] This last post acquires a peculiar significance in light of the fact that quite a few American development experts who would later serve in ex-colonies in Asia and Africa during the 1950s and 1960s started their career with the US Bureau of Indian Affairs. In addition, the Department of Anthropology and Sociology at Hatch's *alma mater* Cornell conducted a special programme between 1949 and 1952 that involved the Hopis and Navajos of the American southwest. This graduate field seminar sought to provide applied anthropology training for experts and administrators 'actively involved in the introduction of new technology to underdeveloped regions of the world'.[209] It seems rather ironic that Spencer Hatch did it the other way around: the YMCA's leading development expert came back to apply

Figure 5.5 Cold War hero? – Spencer Hatch with American and Ceylonese village workers on the front page of the US propaganda magazine *Free World* (1951). Courtesy Kautz Family YMCA Archives, University of Minnesota, Minneapolis.

the knowledge about the cross-cultural dynamics of development work he had mostly gathered in colonial India to America's very own 'natives'. In spite of the different direction of the knowledge flow, however, Jacob Tropp's recent assessment of Cornell's development training in 'Native American laboratories' is also perfectly relevant to Hatch's rural reconstruction scheme. In both cases, resolving challenges and problems inherent in disseminating development knowledge to an allegedly 'backward' target group 'was approached fundamentally as a question of improving tactics of cross-cultural implementation rather than addressing underlying dynamics of power and inequality'.[210]

Summing up

In a widely circulated article, Fred Cooper argued forcefully some time ago that to write convincing histories of development, historians needed to abandon 'abstractions ... generalizations', and 'metacritique', and instead analyse concrete historical instances.[211] The case study presented in this chapter has attempted to do precisely this by focusing on the Indian YMCA's rural work. By adopting a biographical lens and providing a detailed discussion of the career of Spencer Hatch, who pioneered village development schemes in southern India, the analysis has embraced a rather narrow perspective. Nonetheless, this micro-(hi)story is clearly significant for the grand narratives of the history of development.[212] Most importantly, it underscores that the foreign-aid initiatives and the transnational development regime of the 1950s did not emerge in a vacuum, but rather had a prehistory in the interwar period that decisively shaped their methods and agendas. While the continuities between colonial administrative experts and Cold War development initiatives have been discussed at length by other scholars, an analysis of Duane Spencer Hatch's long and illustrious career highlights the neglected role of extra-imperial civil society actors connected to a global Christian lay movement.

Exploring Hatch's life and work has yielded some important insights. In spite of his association with the American YMCA, an organization at pains to stress its inclusive and non-imperial character in most of its Asian and African projects, Hatch was a hinge figure of sorts, shaped by the imperial culture he was exposed to for more than three decades. His earnest attempt to acquire linguistic skills, adapt a simple local lifestyle and tap indigenous knowledge systems links him to earlier generations of Christian missionaries. However, the deep emotional and epistemic enmeshment with imperial racialist thought, language and knowledge that we have also observed in a variety of other facets of the YMCA's work in South Asia is also apparent. As shown in this chapter, Hatch's (and the YMCA's) project of transforming the hearts and minds of 'native' peasants even included mild forms of coercion and intimidation through references to the repressive apparatus of the colonial state, which demonstrates that even low-modernist projects could be fairly authoritarian. Simultaneously, Hatch's inextricable links to the Christian Association's evangelizing agenda remained pivotal for the village workers, even though 'collecting scalps' (i.e. open proselytizing) was rarely emphasized as a primary YMCA goal in public from the 1920s onwards.[213]

That said, it would be misleading to represent the Y's rural work in South Asia as an all-powerful American neo-imperial or missionary machine of repression. The Hatch case study also makes clear that various South Asian actors co-shaped it from its very inception, and that evasion from and subversion of the Protestant pedagogic project continued to exist. Indian YMCA secretaries, Travancore's aristocracy, political leaders connected with the Indian national movement and even ordinary peasants who added their sometimes superior practical knowledge to the MRDC programme contributed to the Martandam experiment in a variety of ways. Taken with Hatch's global borrowings of agricultural, sociological and anthropological knowledge, the

MRDC was a heavily 'pidginized' rather than a strictly American programme, making the aid that Hatch and his fellow workers provided only partially foreign.

Spencer Hatch's global career as an influential member of the international epistemic community of rural development experts underscores that his expertise was influential, circulating as it did through various channels and in various directions from the late 1930s onwards. A detailed and authoritative assessment of the impact of post-Second World War development discourses and programmes would certainly require further research, but some interesting observations can be made even on the limited basis of this case study. Thus, alumni from the YMCA Rural Training College in Martandam and the various institutions that Hatch helped establish were part of several postcolonial community development schemes in the Indian subcontinent and postcolonial administrations in India, Ceylon, Burma and even Egypt. Simultaneously, new supranational institutions founded by the League of Nations and later the United Nations provided important platforms that facilitated the spread of his low-modernist approach across the globe. Hatch's postings in various Asian and Latin American countries during the 1940s and 1950s, widely publicized by US Cold War propaganda, further added to the worldwide circulation of the Y's gospel of rural reconstruction within an emerging transnational expert community. It would no doubt be a rewarding task to revisit the history of early Cold War village development schemes on a global scale in order to scrutinize precisely where the legacies of the Indian YMCA's pidginized rural reconstruction knowledge can be detected, how influential this current was, and how long it survived. Such a study, however, would be the subject of an entirely different project.

Conclusion: Modernization without modernity

Since the preceding chapters have all ended with exhaustive summaries, I shall restrict myself to a very brief wrap-up of the main findings here, before proceeding to more general reflections related to some of the issues raised in the introduction.

Chapter 1 laid the ground for the case studies presented in the later chapters of the book by shedding light on the complex forces and conditions in the context of which the Indian YMCA operated in colonial South Asia. More specifically, it situated the Y's secular schemes and programmes against the backdrop of the various other modernizing missions conducted by several groups of actors during the last five decades of the Raj. The general surge of philanthropic, humanitarian and social reform schemes that developed between the 1900s and the 1940s helps us understand why the 'secular' work of the Christian lay Association met with so much interest from different quarters. Responses to its work ranged from support to collaboration, or (hostile) appropriation. The varied reactions from British imperial officials as well as South Asian individuals and organizations amplified the impact of the Indian Y's educational and welfare schemes considerably and contributed to their disproportionate visibility. The use of what British officials somewhat derogatively called 'American methods' – that is, a set of state-of-the-art practices of professionalized training, management, medialization and communication – further enhanced their popularity as these practices were often regarded as superior to the existing ways and means and therefore widely emulated. All in all, Sumit Sarkar's observation that the influence of Christian missionaries under the Raj profoundly penetrated colonial South Asia and was much more far-reaching than the rather modest conversion statistics would seem to suggest[1] holds particularly true for the rather unorthodox Protestant lay organization we have discussed in this book.

Chapter 2 focused on the Indian YMCA's philanthropic work and particularly the programmes offered by its Railway and Army Departments, arguing that the welfare schemes for soldiers and railway workers launched before and during the Great War were designed by the US-dominated branches of the Indian Y primarily to win the trust and support of the imperial government. However, these schemes simultaneously provided the organization with a welcome opportunity to disseminate two of its core messages to 'risk groups' of hundreds of thousands young men in rather 'dangerous' professions that purportedly left them exposed to the constant temptations of idleness and vice. Thus, the programmes targeted at the British, South Asian and 'Eurasian' railway employees and military servicemen facilitated the extensive spread of the YMCA's ideal of a 'muscular' yet disciplined and restrained masculinity. At the same time, the group's army work in particular was geared towards the education of better and more responsible citizens. In other words, the undisguised objective of Y philanthropy in the 1910s and 1920s was 'civilizing subalterns' of various 'racial' and cultural backgrounds. Nevertheless, the methods used differed significantly depending on the ethnic composition of the respective target group. This chapter, as well as the rest of the book, provides ample evidence that racial and class prejudices and hierarchies played a major role in the concrete practice of such social engineering efforts, notwithstanding the constant emphasis on 'egalitarianism'. Ultimately, however, it did make a difference, irrespective of whether those at the receiving end of the Indian YMCA's citizenship training were South Asian, European or 'mixed-race', and of whether they were considered as 'cultured' or 'rough'.

It was mainly through its protracted promotion of (American) sports, fitness regimes and physical education schemes during the first half of the twentieth century that the YMCA came to epitomize muscular Christianity on a global scale. Chapter 3 amply demonstrated that significant segments of South Asia's colonized population, too, succumbed to the appeal of the Indian Y's 'physical ministry'. Besides illuminating the complex processes of transfer, translation and adaptation of such programmes, the chapter interrogated how they were significant to the Association's larger agenda concerned with promoting a liberal American version of modernization/modernity. At first sight, the offerings of the YMCA's Physical Department seem to have contributed to the empowerment of the South Asian target populations. The emphasis placed by the Y's 'physical directors' on playfulness and voluntarism turned the Association's sports schemes into conduits for the message of democracy that could entice Indians, Ceylonese and Burmese into emulating the American model; the hope was that this would continue to be the case when it came to embracing new societal norms and a particular political culture. That said, the chapter has also brought to light some striking tensions within the philanthropic schemes: much like the colonial racial (and racialized) discourse, the training regimes, physical education courses and body sculpting programmes that the North American physical directors (and their South Asian graduates) advocated were often heavily influenced by the same cultural stereotypes and orientalist clichés that characterized contemporary colonial rhetoric. Imperial tropes of *somatic Orientalism* predicated on the idea of fundamental racial differences between Westerners and South Asians generously infused the ideologies of the YMCA. The subtext of the Indian YMCA's 'physical work' thus was largely consistent with the Raj's ideologies and was in stark contrast to the democratic and liberating agenda that the Association's advocates chose to emphasize. Indeed, this ambivalence even serves as a concrete example of a phenomenon described by Paul Kramer as the reliance of international 'non-state actors' on the infrastructure, protection and ideological resources of imperial states that helps explain the seeming paradox of such non-state institutions 'reimagining and reforming but not dismantling colonialism'.[2]

Chapter 4 further developed the analysis of transnational knowledge circulation by retracing the emergence of 'boyology' and its transmission to Asia. This particular corpus of educational and disciplinary knowledge was developed with the goal of protecting supposedly 'malleable' young males (both children and teenagers) from the 'degenerating' effects of urban modernity. The discourse of boyology was particularly *en vogue* in the United States during the first two decades of the twentieth century, and it found its way to the Indian subcontinent through North American YMCA workers among others. As the chapter has demonstrated, this quasi-scientific approach to structuring leisure activities and providing informal education sought to establish the template of a virile yet controlled masculinity. Not surprisingly, this template was akin to the version disseminated to rank-and-file soldiers by the Army Department. Moreover, just like the physical education schemes targeted at adult 'natives', the miscellaneous offerings of the YMCA's boys' branches were portrayed as superior to comparable British colonial practices of youth work, because of how the YMCA schemes allegedly fostered South Asian boys' capacity for 'self-government' and democratic participation.

In sum, then, the close analysis of Indo-US entanglements in the field of 'informal education' has allowed us to reconstruct how the global currents in the perception of 'boyhood' and adolescence as well as transnationally circulating gender norms and models of character building, habit formation and citizenship training played out in the Indian subcontinent. The case study not only points to the important legacies and traces left by the YMCA's boys' work schemes in the region's postcolonial societies but also illustrates how the programmes could be evaded, resisted or subverted by members of the projected target groups (and their parents).

The YMCA's scientific views on sports and physical culture as well as its boyology schemes were already refined and well-developed when they were exported to India and its adjacent countries. In contrast, the case study on the YMCA's low modernist rural reconstruction programme, the focus of Chapter 5, offered us a glimpse into the actual (co-)production of a new body of knowledge in South Asia itself that involved a number of Indian actors. However, while Indian YMCA secretaries such as K. T. Paul were crucial in the early phase of the scheme and the practical experiences of Indian farmers shaped the 'pidgin knowledge' on sustainable agriculture and village development to some extent, our investigation leaves no doubt that their contribution was sidelined by the American agronomist and YMCA secretary Duane Spencer Hatch. Local knowledge and its carriers were largely erased in the canonized and codified versions of development knowledge disseminated by Hatch in the form of academic monographs published by renowned University presses or UNESCO-sponsored radio talks and documentary films in the 1940s, 1950s and 1960s.[3] While the paraphernalia of modern science and academia were thus deployed to mark the authority and universal validity of the Y's rural reconstruction scheme, the case study has also provided evidence that religion continued to be significant in the organization's social work. The discussion of Hatch's interpretation of rural reconstruction as the ultimate method of spreading the gospel effectively especially testifies to the fact that seemingly secular development knowledge was also undergirded by proselytization fantasies. The chapter has thus helped to better grasp and contextualize a specific current of knowledge that was widely adopted by the first generation of global development experts as well as by state-employed administrators and technocrats in postcolonial South Asia itself.

Taken together, then, the study has substantiated the claim that an interstitial space between the conflicting agendas of the colonial state and its nationalist detractors, in which civil society actors from the North America played a prominent role, did indeed exist. It has also shown that the philanthropic, educational and social engineering programmes launched by experts and voluntary workers occupying this in-between space exerted a palpable influence on the ways in which modernizing processes in late colonial India took shape. That being said, it is necessary to add two caveats. Firstly, it has not always been easy – indeed, it has sometimes been impossible – to filter out 'North American voices' within the Indian YMCA. On the one hand, the complex set-up of the organization, which had many South Asians and members from numerous other nationalities, and the close relationship between the Indian Y entertained with both the British YMCA and the International Association of YMCAs in Geneva, renders the identification of an American position a somewhat arbitrary exercise at times. This endeavour was further complicated by the existence of a broad spectrum of ideological, political and religious opinions within the seemingly manageable and homogeneous group of North American YMCA secretaries serving in South Asia. Therefore, as we have seen, a huge difference in the worldviews of various Y secretaries existed. The more conservative men like Duane Spencer Hatch were either outspoken or tacit admirers of British imperialism whereas fringe characters like the pacifist 'troublemaker' Howard Walter and even Sherwood Eddy with his 'Bolshevik' leanings did not shy away from openly criticizing imperial practices and policies. Besides the political differences, it has also become apparent that there were constant disagreements about the respective importance of *social* and *religious* service schemes in the Indian Y's work.

The second caveat is equally important. While acknowledging that American civil society actors related to the YMCA did play a conspicuous role in the modernization processes of South Asia, this study's interpretation of the YMCA's 'secular' interventions in the subcontinent emphasizes their ambiguous character and also points to their failures and unintended side effects. In other words, the variety of 'soft power' deployed by the YMCA only had limited success. Attempts at 'agenda setting', to use Joseph Nye's phrase, that were initiated by US Y secretaries were not always 'regarded as legitimate by the target' and hence 'native' compliance was not always forthcoming. Even if it was, any apparent acceptance rarely resulted in a wholesale approval of the programme in question and even less so of the norms and values behind it. More often, it stimulated a highly selective, idiosyncratic and often oppositional appropriation of certain elements by the South Asian target groups and even by British colonial officials. As a result, what was conceived as an (American) liberal alternative to the official imperial and nationalist modernization programmes eventually turned out to be heavily influenced and reinterpreted by their most important competitors, epistemically as well as ideologically. Without a doubt, the Indian YMCA's social engineering schemes *did* serve as efficient catalysts of change. Yet it remains important to stress that they largely failed in fulfilling their promises of securing access to a liberal American modernity at the same time. Most importantly, partly due to the imperial epistemic burden they carried and partly because of the racial and class biases they imported from home, American YMCA secretaries rarely succeeded in establishing spaces of true equality and democratic participation in colonial South Asia. Arguably, therefore, their interventions had more to do with a superficial modernization rather than with the societal transformations and 'flattening of hierarchies' that are the core elements of the political project of modernity.

Let us shift to a second issue raised in the introduction. To what extent has the global approach to South Asian history and the focus on transnational entanglements and the often-overlooked third space occupied by international actors enhanced our understanding of social, political and cultural change in late colonial India and beyond? In other words, what are the historiographical benefits and what are the risks and shortcomings of the 'global-microhistory' approach adopted here?[4]

Firstly, it is apparent that the widening of the lens and the overcoming of the entrenched fixation on the imperial and national framework were a necessary precondition for making visible, and appreciate the salience of, a set of actors that might otherwise have fallen through the cracks of historical analysis. There can be no doubt that the US-sponsored educational and philanthropic efforts of the Indian YMCA did have a significant impact in the region itself, even though it was not always the one intended. The focus on a comparatively small number of actors and the institutions that they set up in South India has allowed for a very thick description of the phenomenon under study. The sections on the MCPE and the MRDC are perhaps the best illustrations of this richness. The micro-perspective alone, however, would not have allowed for some of the fascinating insights summarized above, which require a more flexible *jeux d'échelles*.[5] Thus, for instance, the occasional distance from the South Asian context to retrace the origins of scientifically informed boys' work in Massachusetts, to follow YMCA army workers to Mesopotamia and France, and to accompany the agricultural expert Spencer Hatch through his various journeys and career stages has shown the contours of a much wider web of interactions and entanglements. Finally, one must reiterate that, on an empirical level, the focus on North American protagonists (and a partly US-financed organization) has opened up a body of extremely rich and often completely untapped new source materials that are normally beyond a South Asianist's purview. A large part of this material appears to be relevant to historians working on South Asia far beyond the narrow focus of this specific study, thus opening up exciting new prospects for future research. In certain respects, then, the experiment was successful and the global micro-historical approach taken in this book has clearly paid off.

However, it cannot be denied that, interesting though our case study may have been, some thorny issues remain. The most important one pertains to the above-mentioned one-sided character of the sources. The interaction between Western Y 'secretaries' and South Asians, be they Ceylonese school boys, Punjabi infantrymen or South Indian toddy tappers, could, for the most part, be reconstructed solely from often biased official YMCA sources and ego documents produced by the Association's leading protagonists in South Asia. Most of the Indian and Nepali servicemen enjoying the entertainment programmes in a YMCA hut during the Great War and the peasants affected by the Y's village development schemes were illiterate and therefore left no traces in the archives.[6] Even in instances where written sources could be found – potentially the case with young adolescents from the 'educated classes' drawn to the

MCPE and the multifarious programmes offered by the boys' branches – certain difficulties remain. Given the situation of the YMCA's regional strongholds in the subcontinent, it is likely that most of the sources are not in Hindi but rather in South Asian languages that I am not conversant with, like Bangla, Malayalam and Tamil. Depending on the specific research question and the wider project context, such a neglect of sources in the local languages can obviously be profoundly problematic. Especially considering the inclusionary and emancipatory potential of global history that is often propagated by its champions,[7] such concerns must be taken seriously. Otherwise, the inclusion of 'indigenous voices' must remain restricted to elite figures such as K. T. Paul and Lala Lajpat Rai, both of whom wrote mostly in English. Even apart from the recent criticism of global history being an inherently superficial and elite-centred variety of history writing, linguistic limitations are a genuine problem that clearly deserve attention.[8]

While this tension pertaining to the silencing of less-dominant linguistic groups must remain unresolved for the time being, it might be instructive to end this concluding section with a short epilogue offering a glimpse into the further fate of the YMCA on the Indian subcontinent in the two decades following the end of its 'American era' around 1950.[9]

Epilogue

The short forays into the independent years undertaken in some of the previous chapters have already indicated the main problem that the Indian YMCA had to face in the era of decolonization. While there was definitely an acknowledgement and appreciation of the Association and its educational and philanthropic work by prominent leaders of the Congress Party like Jawaharlal Nehru and Rajendra Prasad, dissenting voices also existed. Several prominent Congress politicians warned of a possible continuation of Western paternalism if the influence of Western missionaries was not curbed by the state. The Hindu nationalist camp voiced even harsher criticism. In 1952, mass conversions to Christianity by Adivasi groups in Central India sent shockwaves through ethnonational parties like the Bharatiya Jan Sangh and the HMS as well as 'cultural' organizations such as the RSS. Clearly, the Hindutva forces were afraid of a massive weakening of the 'Hindu fold' through the 'defection' of underprivileged groups.[10] The HMS, therefore, staged an 'Anti-Conversion Day' in Poona in April 1954 that was widely covered by the media. Reacting to the growing pressure from the Hindu right, the Congress-led state government in Madhya Pradesh set up an inquiry commission about the impact of foreign missionaries, in general, and their conversion practices, in particular. The 1956 publication of the so-called Niyogi Report on the results of the commission's investigation, which recommended a legal prohibition of conversion that was not entirely voluntary, further fuelled the rising anti-Christian sentiment in the country.[11] According to popular stereotypes, which had their origin mostly in the era of nationalist mobilization during the interwar period, foreign missionaries were widely perceived as the fifth column of Western imperialism. By extension, the patriotism and loyalty of Indian Christians was also frequently questioned as they were viewed as puppets of the foreign (i.e. Western) hand. Despite official reminders of the 'unity in diversity' ideal, reductionist views continued to fester in the decade after independence while the postcolonial nation was preoccupied with stabilizing its shaky identity.[12]

As a result of such entrenched prejudices, the work of foreign missionaries was severely hampered from the mid-1950s onwards by a number of bureaucratic hurdles on various levels. The YMCA's few remaining so-called fraternity secretaries from Canada and the United States were also affected by these measures.[13] The now-overwhelmingly Indian-led YMCA had serious difficulties in coping with the new situation and the multifarious challenges it entailed. Faced with a generally hostile atmosphere vis-à-vis Christian organizations of foreign origin, the seventy-seven Indian and eight foreign YMCA secretaries who remained in 1957 also felt the growing competition of the postcolonial state. Nehruvian developmentalism interfered much more deeply than the colonial state had done in education and social welfare activities. In doing so, it imperilled the 'ecological niches' in which the YMCA had operated relatively unmolested in the previous decades. Perhaps most devastating, however, was the rapid drying out of American funding after 1947. This was even more troubling as attempts to raise funds locally remained only moderately successful until the late 1950s. It is revealing that it took another American initiative (and large-scale investment!) to breathe new life into the Association, which, according to in-house historian M. D. David, remained in a state of lethargy and depression for over a decade after independence.[14] From the early 1960s onwards, a substantial amount of money from New York's International Committee's generous 'Buildings for Brotherhood' (B4B) programme[15] – partly matched by local funding – was pumped into forty-five different projects of the Indian YMCA, allowing the organization to re-enter the fields of philanthropy and social engineering with new self-confidence.

It ought to be mentioned, however, that not all YMCA activities had fallen out of government favour. As seen in Chapter 5, the rural reconstruction programme in Martandam and other YMCA centres was a major source of inspiration for the postcolonial Community Development scheme, which, in turn, was part and parcel of the First Five Year Plan endorsed by the Nehru administration in 1951. In a Martandam jubilee volume published in the mid-1960s, Emily Gilchriest Hatch, therefore, commented triumphantly that the vision of the MRDC pioneers had been 'greater than the needs of the hour' and that the work of the new Ministry of Community Development represented their actual fulfilment.[16]

The wish of the YMCA leadership to prove the Association's usefulness to the new regime had already become apparent a few years earlier. When the Sino-Indian War broke out in 1962, the Indian Y's new National Secretary, M. G. Dharmraj, contacted several ministers and eventually even approached Indira Gandhi and Prime Minister Nehru to offer the Association's services in support of the national war effort. In spite of the YMCA's considerable experience with welfare and caregiving work accrued over the two World Wars, Dharmraj did not even receive a proper reply, let alone the permission for the Y's now-reactivated 'Defence Department' to perform 'war emergency work'.[17] This unusual coldness left no doubt that the official distrust of the Association was deep seated and that the loyalty of the Indian Christians in the

YMCA was still in question, not only among representatives of the Hindu right and the extreme left, who repeatedly warned of the YMCA's American connections, but also within the ruling Congress Party itself.

Perhaps it was due to the protracted frustration with being excluded from the national mainstream that the Association's leadership took an unprecedented step a few years later. In an attempt to end the 'paternalistic relationship it had with the International Committee of U.S. YMCA',[18] the National Council announced at its 1970 meeting that it would no longer request the Americans for financial support in the future. Even if it remains open to debate if the official attitude towards the YMCA changed after this decision, there can be no doubt that the American romance with the Indian YMCA definitively came to an end with this profound, if largely symbolic, statement.

Notes

Introduction

1. Cf., for instance, Harald Fischer-Tiné, 'Global Civil Society and the Forces of Empire: The Salvation Army, British Imperialism and the "Pre-History" of NGOs (ca. 1880–1920)', in *Competing Visions of World Order: Global Moments and Movements, 1880s–1930s*, ed. Sebastian Conrad and Dominic Sachsenmaier (New York: Palgrave Macmillan, 2007), 29–67.
2. Cf., for example, G. Balachandran, 'History after the Global Turn: Perspectives from Rim and Region', *History Australia* 14 (2017): 6–12; Sanjay Subrahmanyam, 'One Asia or Many? Reflections from Connected History', *Modern Asian Studies* 50, no. 1 (2016): 5–43; David Arnold, 'Globalization and Contingent Colonialism: Towards a Transnational History of "British" India', *Journal of Colonialism and Colonial History* 16, no. 2 (2015), DOI: 10.1353/cch.2015.0019; Kris K. Manjapra, *Age of Entanglement: German and Indian Intellectuals across Empires* (Cambridge: Harvard University Press, 2014); Babli Sinha, *South Asian Transnationalism: Cultural Exchange in the Twentieth Century* (London: Routledge, 2014); David A. Washbrook, 'Problems of Global History', in *Writing the History of the Global: Challenges for the 21st Century*, ed. Maxine Berg (Oxford: Oxford University Press, 2013), 21–31; G. Balachandran, 'Claiming Histories Beyond Nations: Situating Global History', *Indian Economic & Social History Review* 49, no. 2 (2012): 247–72; Jon E. Wilson, 'Early Colonial India beyond Empire', *The Historical Journal* 50, no. 4 (2007): 951–70; Mrinalini Sinha, *Specters of Mother India: The Global Restructuring of an Empire* (Durham, NC: Duke University Press, 2006).
3. It should be noted, however, that the winds of change are blowing: just a few weeks before I gave the final touches on the manuscript for this book, the first comprehensive overview on modern South Asian history from a global perspective was released: Claude Markovits, *India and the World: A History of Connections, 1750–2000* (Cambridge: Cambridge University Press, 2021).
4. Harald Fischer-Tiné, *Shyamji Krishnavarma: Sanskrit, Sociology and Anti-Imperialism* (New Delhi: Routledge India, 2014).
5. Harald Fischer-Tiné, *Der Gurukul Kangri oder die Erziehung der Arya Nation: Kolonialismus, Hindureform und 'nationale Bildung' in Britisch-Indien (1897–1922)* (Würzburg: Ergon Verlag, 2003), 89, footnote 83.
6. Cf., for instance, John Boli and Gerald Thomas, *Constructing World Culture: International Nongovernmental Organisations since 1875* (Stanford, CA: Stanford University Press, 1999); Martin H. Geyer Johannes Paulmann, eds, *The Mechanics of Internationalism: Culture, Society, and Politics from the 1840s to the First World War* (Oxford: Oxford University Press, 2001); Akira Iriye, *Global Community: The Role of International Organizations in the Making of the Contemporary World* (Berkeley: University of California Press, 2002); François Mabille, *Approches de l'internationalisme Catholique* (Paris: L'Harmattan, 2002);

David P. Forsythe, *The Humanitarians: The International Committee of the Red Cross* (Cambridge: Cambridge University Press, 2005).
7. Among the more helpful volumes, cf. Davide Rodogno, Bernhard Struck and Jakob Vogel, eds, *Shaping the Transnational Sphere, Experts, Networks and Issues from the 1840s to the 1930s* (New York: Berghahn, 2015); Emily S. Rosenberg, Transnational Currents in a Shrinking World (Cambridge: Belknap Press of Harvard University Press, 2014); Abigail Greene and Vincent Viaene, eds, *Religious Internationals in the Modern World: Globalization and Faith Communities since 1750* (Basingstoke: Palgrave Macmillan, 2012).
8. Cf. Gene Zubovich, 'The Protestant Search for "the Universal Christian Community" between Decolonization and Communism', *Religions* 8, no. 2 (2017): 1–12; Michael G. Thompson, 'Sherwood Eddy, the Missionary Enterprise, and the Rise of Christian Internationalism in 1920s America', *Modern Intellectual History* 12, no. 1 (2015): 65–93; Christopher Clark and Michael Ledger-Lomas, 'The Protestant International', in *Religious Internationals in the Modern World: Globalization and Faith Communities since 1750*, ed. Abigail Greene and Vincent Viaene (Basingstoke: Palgrave Macmillan, 2012), 23–52; Daniel Gorman, 'Ecumenical Internationalism: Willoughby Dickinson, the League of Nations and the World Alliance for Promoting International Friendship through the Churches', *Journal of Contemporary History* 45, no. 1 (2010): 51–73; Dana L. Robert, 'The First Globalization: The Internationalization of the Protestant Missionary Movement between the World Wars', *International Bulletin of Missionary Research* 26, no. 2 (2002): 50–66.
9. The literature on modernization, social reform and nationalist mobilization in late colonial South Asia will be discussed *in extenso* in Chapter 1.
10. Two recent examples are provided by Kristin L. Hoganson and Jay Sexton, eds, *Crossing Empires: Taking U.S. History in Transimperial Terrain* (Durham, NC: Duke University Press, 2020); Andrew Preston and Doug Rossinow, eds, *Outside In: The Transnational Circuitry of US History* (New York: Oxford University Press, 2017).
11. Cf., for example, Andrew Preston, 'America's Global Imperium', in *The Oxford World History of Empire*, ed. Peter Fibiger Bang, C. A. Bayly and Walter Scheidel (Oxford: Oxford University Press, 2021), 1217–48; Abigail Green, 'Religious Internationalism', in *Internationalisms: A Twentieth-Century History*, ed. Glenda Sluga and Patricia Clavin (Cambridge: Cambridge University Press, 2017), 17–37; Ian R. Tyrrell, 'American Protestant Missionaries, Moral Reformers, and the Reinterpretation of American "Expansion" in the Late Nineteenth Century', in *Outside In: The Transnational Circuitry of US History*, ed. Andrew Preston and Doug Rossinow (New York: Oxford University Press, 2017), 96–122; Ian R. Tyrrell, *Reforming the World: The Creation of America's Moral Empire* (Princeton, NJ: Princeton University Press, 2010); Barbara Reeves-Ellington, Kathryn Kish and Connie A. Shemo Sklar, eds, *Competing Kingdoms: Women, Mission, Nation, and the American Protestant Empire, 1812–1960* (Durham, NC: Duke University Press, 2010).
12. David Ekbladh, *The Great American Mission: Modernization and the Construction of an American World Order* (Princeton, NJ: Princeton University Press, 2010); Nicole Sackley, 'The Village as Cold War Site: Experts, Development, and the History of Rural Reconstruction', *Journal of Global History* vi, no. 3 (2011), 481–504; Daniel Immerwahr, *Thinking Small: The United States and the Lure of Community Development* (Cambridge, MA: Harvard University Press, 2015).

13. In doing so, the study draws on an existing body of literature. See, most importantly, Talal Asad, *Formation of the Secular: Christianity, Islam, Modernity* (Stanford, CA: Stanford University Press, 2003).
14. For a thoughtful assessment of the complex role of Christianity in twentieth-century United States, cf. also David A. Hollinger, 'Christianity and Its American Fate: Where History Interrogates Secularization Theory', in *The Worlds of American Intellectual History*, ed. Joel Isaac (New York: Oxford University Press, 2017), 280–303.
15. A *locus classicus* is Björn Wittrock, 'Modernity: One, None, or Many? European Origins and Modernity as a Global Condition', *Daedalus* 129, no. 1 (2000): 31–60. For useful, though very different, surveys of the ensuing debates, see Peter Wagner, 'Introduction', in *African, American and European Trajectories of Modernity: Past Oppression, Future Justice?*, ed. Peter Wagner (Edinburgh: Edinburgh University Press, 2015), 1–18; Vittorio Cotesta, 'Three Critics of Weber's Thesis of the Uniqueness of the West: Jack Goody, Kenneth Pomeranz, and S. N. Eisenstadt. Strengths and Weaknesses', *Max Weber Studies* 14, no. 2 (2014): 147–67; Sasheej Hegde, 'Reassembling Modernity: Thinking at the Limit', *Social Scientist* 37, no. 9/10 (2009): 66–88. Cf. also Saurabh Dube and Ishita Banerjee-Dube, eds, *Unbecoming Modern: Colonialism, Modernity, Colonial Modernities* (New Delhi: Social Science Press, 2006).
16. Rana Mitter, 'Modernity', in *The Palgrave Dictionary of Transnational History*, ed. Akira Iriye and Pierre-Yves Saunier (Basingstoke: Palgrave Macmillan, 2009), 721.
17. Dipesh Chakrabarty, 'The Muddle of Modernity', *American Historical Review* 116, no. 3 (2011): 669.
18. Saurabh Dube, 'Makeovers of Modernity: An Introduction', in *Handbook of Modernity in South Asia: Modern Makeovers*, ed. Saurabh Dube (New Delhi: Oxford University Press, 2011), 6.
19. One of the earliest and most influential statements to that effect was made in Sanjay Subrahmanyam, 'Vignettes of Early Modernity in South Asia, 1400–1750', *Daedalus* 127, no. 3 (1998): 75–104.
20. Partha Chatterjee, *The Nation and Its Fragments: Colonial and Postcolonial Histories* (Princeton, NJ: Princeton University Press, 1993). Jane Burbank and Frederick Cooper use the related and perhaps more pertinent concept of the 'politics of difference'. Jane Burbank and Frederick Cooper, *Empires in World History: Power and Politics of Difference* (Princeton, NJ: Princeton University Press, 2010), cf. especially 11–13.
21. David Washbrook, 'Intimations of Modernity in South India', *South Asian History and Culture* 1, no. 1 (2009): 143.
22. Cf., for example, David Washbrook, 'Forms of Citizenship in Pre-modern South India', *Citizenship Studies* 23, no. 3 (2019): 224–39.
23. Carolien Stolte and Harald Fischer-Tiné, 'Imagining Asia in India: Nationalism and Internationalism (ca. 1905–1940)', *Comparative Studies in Society and History* 54, no. 1 (2012): 69–71.
24. Washbrook, 'Intimations of Modernity in South India', 128.
25. Daniel Roger Maul, 'The Rise of a Humanitarian Superpower: American NGOs and International Relief', in *Internationalism, Imperialism and the Formation of the Formation of the Contemporary World*, ed. M. B. Jernimo and J. P. Monteiro (Cham: Palgrave Macmillan, 2018), 127–46; A. G. Hopkins, *American Empire: A Global History* (Princeton, NJ: Princeton University Press, 2018), 443–538; Victoria

de Grazia, *Irresistible Empire: America's Advance through 20th Century Europe* (Cambridge, MA: Harvard University Press, 2005).

26. These series are henceforth cited as KFYA, IWI, IWB and IWC, respectively.
27. These series are henceforth cited as KFYA, SF, and KFYA, BF, respectively.
28. Material from the Springfield College Archives and Special Collections is henceforth cited as SCASC.
29. See, for instance, SCASC, R. Walter Cammack, 'Physical Education in Ceylon', unpublished graduation thesis, International Young Men's Christian Association College, Springfield, MA, 1920; SCASC, 'A Normal Course in Physical Training for Grade School Teachers', unpublished Master of Physical Education thesis, Springfield College, Springfield, MA, 1917.
30. Material from the MS 1282 Duane Spencer Hatch Collection at the University of Arizona, Tucson, AZ, collection will be cited as UATSHC.
31. Material from Yale University, Divinity School, Special Collections in New Haven, CT, will henceforth be cited as YDSPC.
32. Material from the two institutions will be cited as SSCWH and RAC, respectively.
33. Cited as BL/APAC/IOR/L/P&J and BL/APAC/IOR/L/MIL, respectively.
34. Cited as BL/APAC/IOR/Mss Eur F178/11.
35. Material from the Cadbury Library is cited as CRLSC.
36. Material found in this archive is cited as WAYAG.
37. The Indian Y's most important periodical is cited as *The Young Men of India* throughout the book.
38. Material from the National Archives of India in New Delhi is marked with the acronym NAI and sources from the Uttar Pradesh State Archives in Lucknow are cited as UPSAL.
39. Material found in this archive is cited as UTCAB.
40. The sources I found in this small collection in the Y's New Delhi headquarters located at Jai Singh Marg are cited as RYND.
41. Cf. Michel-Rolph Trouillot, *Silencing the Past: Power and the Production of History* (Boston, MA: Beacon Press, 1995), 52.
42. Cf. Ann Laura Stoler, *Along the Archival Grain: Epistemic Anxieties and Colonial Common Sense* (Princeton, NJ: Princeton University Press, 2008).
43. Cf. also Natalie Zemon-Davies, 'Foreword', in *The Allure of the Archives*, ed. Arlette Farge (New Haven, CT: Yale University Press, 2013), ix–xviii; and the classic Gayatri Chakravorty-Spivak, 'The Rani of Sirmur: An Essay in Reading the Archives', *History and Theory* 24, no. 3 (1985): 247–72; David M. Gordon, 'Reading Archives as Sources', *Oxford Research Encyclopedia of African History*, 20 November 2018, 1–19. Available online: https://doi.org/10.1093/acrefore/9780190277734.013.227 (accessed 31 August 2021).
44. Gordon, 'Reading Archives as Sources', 5.
45. See the discussion in Chapter 2.
46. Samuel W. D. Walburn, '"A Most Disgraceful, Sordid, Disreputable, Drunken Brawl": Paul Cadmus and the Politics of Queerness in the Early Twentieth Century', *The Purdue Historian* 8, no. 1 (2017): 3. Available online: http://docs.lib.purdue.edu/puhistorian/vol8/iss1/2 (accessed 2 September 2021). That the American YMCA has cemented this reputation in the more recent past is evident not least from the above-mentioned 1970s disco track. The fact that *Village People*, the first openly gay pop band to achieve global success, had their biggest hit with the single 'Y.M.C.A.' (taken from their bestselling album *Cruisin'*, 1978) is quite revealing in this respect.

47. Robert E. Frykenberg, *Christianity in India: From the Beginnings to the Present* (Oxford: Oxford University Press, 2008).
48. M. D. David, *The YMCA and the Making of Modern India (A Centenary History)* (New Delhi: National Council of YMCAs of India, 1991); M. D. David, *The YMCA and the Making of Modern India: A Saga of Selfless Sacrifice, Vol. II. 1991–2016* (New Delhi: The National Council of YMCAs of India, 2017).
49. Cf. J. H. Dunderdale, *The YMCA in India: 100 Years of Service with Youth* (New Delhi: YMCA Publishing House, 1962); Kenneth Scott Latourette, *World Service: A History of the Foreign Work and World Service of the Young Men's Christian Associations of the United States and Canada* (New York: Association Press, 1957), 105–63; A. E. Holt, *A Study of the Y.M.C.A. of India, Burma & Ceylon. Made as an Integral Part of the International Survey* (Calcutta: National Council Y.M.C.A., 1933).
50. Cf., for example, Sherwood Eddy, *Eighty Adventurous Years: An Autobiography* (New York: Harper & Brothers, 1955), 31–59.
51. Susan Billington Harper, *In the Shadow of the Mahatma: Bishop V. S. Azariah and the Travails of Christianity in British India* (Grand Rapids, MI: W. B. Eerdmans, 2000).
52. Nandini Chatterjee, *The Making of Indian Secularism: Empire Law and Christianity, 1830–1960* (Basingstoke: Palgrave Macmillan, 2011), 134–65.
53. Tyrrell, *Reforming the World*, 49–73; Ian Tyrrell, 'Vectors of Practicality: Social Gospel, the North American YMCA in Asia, and the Global Context', in *Spreading Protestant Modernity: Global Perspectives on the Social Work of the YMCA and YWCA, 1889–1970*, ed. Harald Fischer-Tiné, Stefan Huebner and Ian Tyrrell (Honolulu: University of Hawai'i Press, 2021), 45–52.
54. Karen Phoenix, 'A Social Gospel for India', *The Journal of the Gilded Age and Progressive Era* 13, no. 2 (2014): 200–22; Karen Phoenix, '"Not by Might, nor by Power, but by Spirit": The Global Reform Efforts of the Young Women's Christian Association of the United States 1895–1939', unpublished PhD dissertation, University of Illinois at Urbana-Champaign, 2010.
55. The most comprehensive general account of the YMCA in China is Jun Xing, *Baptized in the Fire of Revolution: The American Social Gospel and the YMCA in China, 1919–1937* (Bethlehem, PA: Lehigh University Press, 1996). Another thorough and sophisticated study of American Y work in China is unfortunately still unpublished: John E. Heavens, 'The International Committee of the North American Young Men's Christian Association and Its Foreign Work in China, 1895–1937', unpublished PhD dissertation, University of Cambridge, 2013. Specifically on the main fields of 'secular' work in China cf. also Kristin Mulready-Stone, 'Character Conservancy in Shanghai's Emergency: The YMCA in Shanghai, 1931–1942', in *The YMCA at War: Collaboration and Conflict during the World Wars*, ed. Jeffrey C. Copeland and Yan Xu (Lanham, MD: Lexington Books, 2018), 143–60; Walter Demel and Rotem Kowner, eds, 'Stefan Hübner,"Uplifting the Weak and Degenerated Races of East Asia": American and Indigenous Views of Sport and Body in Early Twentieth-Century East Asia', in *Race and Racism in Modern East Asia*, vol. 2 (Leiden: Brill, 2015), 196–217.
56. On the YMCA in Japan, cf. Jon Thares Davidann, *A World of Crisis and Progress, The American YMCA in Japan, 1890–1930* (Bethlehem, PA: Lehigh University Press, 1998); Jon Thares Davidann, 'The American YMCA in Meiji Japan: God's Work Gone Awry', *Journal of World History* 6, no. 1 (1995): 107–25.
57. Cf. Albert L. Park, *Building a Heaven on Earth: Religion, Activism, and Protest in Japanese-Occupied Korea* (Honolulu: University of Hawai'i Press, 2015); Koen de

Ceuster, 'Wholesome Education and Sound Leisure: The YMCA Sports Programme in Colonial Korea', *European Journal of East Asian Studies* 2, no. 1 (2003): 53–88; Koen de Ceuster, 'The YMCA's Rural Development Program in Colonial Korea, 1925–35: Doctrine and Objectives', *The Review of Korean Studies* 3, no. 1 (2000): 5–33.

58. As the literature on the history of the American YMCA is so extraordinarily rich, I limit myself to a small selection of 'classic' works that are closely related to the thematic foci of the following five chapters of this book: Paula Rachel Lupkin, *Manhood Factories: YMCA Architecture and the Making of Modern Urban Culture* (Minneapolis: University of Minnesota Press, 2010); David P. Setran, *The College 'Y': Student Religion in the Era of Secularization* (New York: Palgrave Macmillan, 2007); Clifford Putney, *Muscular Christianity: Manhood and Sports in Protestant America, 1880–1920* (Cambridge, MA: Harvard University Press, 2003); Thomas Winter, *Making Men, Making Class: The YMCA and Workingmen, 1877–1920* (Chicago, IL: University of Chicago Press, 2002); John DonaldGustav-Wrathall, *Take the Young Stranger by the Hand: Same-Sex Relations and the YMCA* (Chicago, IL: University of Chicago Press, 1999); Nina Mjagkij and Margaret Spratt, eds, *Men and Women Adrift: The YMCA and the YWCA in the City* (New York: New York University Press, 1997).

59. William T. Stead, *The Americanization of the World: Or the Trend of the Twentieth Century* (New York: Horace Markley, 1902).

60. Cf., for instance, Robert W. Rydell and Rob Kroes, *Buffalo Bill in Bologna: The Americanization of the World, 1869–1922* (Chicago: University of Chicago Press, 2005); Jessica C. E. Gienow-Hecht, 'Always Blame the Americans: Anti-Americanism in Europe in the Twentieth Century', *The American Historical Review* 111, no. 4 (2006): 1067–91; Alexander Stephan, ed., *The Americanization of Europe: Culture, Diplomacy, and Anti-Americanism after 1945* (New York: Berghahn Books, 2006); de Grazia, *Irresistible Empire*.

61. Ludovic Tournès, *Américanisation: une histoire mondiale (XVIIIe-XXIe siècle)*, *L'épreuve de l'histoire* (Paris: Fayard, 2020), 134.

62. The concept of American 'soft power' has been popularized in Joseph S. Nye, *Soft Power: The Means to Success in World Politics* (New York: PublicAffairs, 2004). It has since been further elaborated. Cf., for instance, in Inderjeet Paramar and Michael Cox, eds, *Soft Power and US Foreign Policy: Theoretical, Historical and Contemporary Perspectives* (London: Routledge, 2010).

63. Joseph S. Nye, 'Soft Power: The Evolution of a Concept', *Journal of Political Power* 14, no. 1 (2021): 196–208.

64. On the partial overlap between Nye and Gramsci, cf. Geraldo Zahran and Leonardo Ramos, 'From Hegemony to Soft Power: Implications of a Conceptual Change', in *Soft Power and US Foreign Policy: Theoretical, Historical and Contemporary Perspectives*, ed. Inderjeet Paramar and Michael Cox (London: Routledge, 2010), 12–31.

65. Patrick Harries and David Maxwell, *The Spiritual in the Secular: Missionaries and Knowledge about Africa*, ed. Patrick Harries and David Maxwell (Grand Rapids, MI: W. B. Eerdmans, 2012).

66. Cf. also the brief discussion in the section 'Shaping the Future Citizen' of Chapter 1.

67. This at least holds true for Ceylon, which was under the administration of the colonial office. Burma, on the other hand, was officially part of British India from 1885 to 1937.

68. Other facets of the Indian YMCA's philanthropic engagement are not covered here, partly for the sake of narrative coherence and partly because they have already been

dealt with by recent research. The latter holds particularly true for the organization's early and rather sporadic involvement in famine relief, and its 'industrial work scheme' for Indian mill hands working in the textile industry. Cf. Priyanka Srivastava, *The Well-Being of the Labour Force in Colonial Bombay: Discourses and Practices* (Cham: Palgrave Macmillan, 2018), 133–41.

1 'A mission to modernize': Colonial administrators, nationalists and religious bodies in South Asia (1870s–1930s)

1. Cf. Stephen Legg, 'Dyarchy: Democracy, Autocracy, and the Scalar Sovereignty of Interwar India', *Comparative Studies of South Asia, Africa and the Middle East* 36, no. 1 (1 May 2016): 44–65.
2. Tan Tai Yong, *The Garrison State: Military, Government and Society in Colonial Punjab, 1849-1947* (New Delhi: Sage, 2005), 49.
3. Manu Goswami, *Producing India: From Colonial Economy to National Space* (Chicago, IL: University of Chicago Press, 2004), 31–72.
4. For an overview of the growth colonial cities in India, cf. Jim Masselos, 'Empire and City: The Imperial Presence in Urban India', in *The Routledge History of Western Empires*, ed. Robert Aldrich and Kirsten Mackenzie (Abingdon: Routledge, 2014), 330–45.
5. For a concise but illuminating discussion of the 'forever rising and forever new' middle class in colonial India, cf. Sumit Sarkar, *Modern Times: India 1880s–1950s. Environment, Economy, Culture* (Ranikhet: Permanent Black, 2014), 310–26, the quotation is on p. 310. Cf. also Sutapa Dutta, 'Packing a Punch at the Bengali Babu', *South Asia: Journal of South Asian Studies* 44, no. 3 (2021): 437–58; Tithi Bhattacharya, *The Sentinels of Culture: Class, Education, and the Colonial Intellectual in Bengal (1848-85)* (New Delhi: Oxford University Press, 2005).
6. Cf., for instance, Douglas Haynes, ed., *Toward a History of Consumption in South Asia* (Delhi: Oxford University Press, 2010); Utsa Ray, 'Cosmopolitan Consumption: Domesticity, Cooking, and the Middle Class in Colonial India', in *The Global Bourgeoisie: The Rise of the Middle Classes in the Age of Empire*, ed. Christof Dejung, David Motadel and Jürgen Osterhammel (Princeton, NJ: Princeton University Press, 2019), 123–42.
7. Michael Brunner, 'Schooling the Subcontinent: State, Space, Society, and the Dynamics of Education in Colonial South Asia', in *The Routledge Handbook of the History of Colonialism in South Asia*, ed. Harald Fischer-Tiné and Maria Framke (Abingdon: Routledge, 2021), 252–65; Sanjay Seth, *Subject Lessons: The Western Education of Colonial India* (Durham, NC: Duke University Press, 2007).
8. Nile Green, *Terrains of Exchange: Religious Economies of Global Islam* (Oxford: Oxford University Press, 2014).
9. Peter Van Veer, *The Modern Spirit of Asia: The Spiritual and the Secular in India and China* (Princeton, NJ: Princeton University Press, 2014), 45–54 and 95–100. Cf. also Kenneth W. Jones, *Religious Controversy in British India: Dialogues in South Asian Languages* (Albany: State University of New York Press, 1992).
10. Cf., for instance, Niall Ferguson, *Empire: How Britain Made the Modern World* (London: Penguin Books, 2004), 216–18.

11. Thomas Metcalf, *The New Cambridge History of India III, 4. Ideologies of the Raj* (Cambridge: Cambridge University Press, 1994), 39.
12. Using the example of Imperial Germany's colonial regimes in Africa, sociologist Trutz von Trotha defines basic legitimacy (*Basislegitimität*) as a combination of a state's monopoly on violence with its capacity to order and organize, thus providing a certain level of security and stability to the colonized population. Trutz von Trotha, 'Gewalt, Staat und Basislegitimität. Notizen zum Problem der Macht in Afrika (und anderswo)', in *Macht der Identität – Identität der Macht. Politische Prozesse und kultureller Wandel in Afrika*, ed. H. Willer, T. Förster and C. Ortner-Buchberger (Münster: LIT Verlag, 1995), 1–16.
13. Sabyasachi Bhattacharya, *The Colonial State: Theory and Practice* (Delhi: Primus Books, 2016); cf. Hayden J. Bellenoit, *The Formation of the Colonial State in India* (Abingdon: Routledge, 2017).
14. Bhattacharya, *The Colonial State: Theory and Practice*, 46–54, the quote is on p. 53. For a succinct analysis of the function of Imperial Durbars and similar assemblages, cf. Alan Trevithick, 'Some Structural and Sequential Aspects of the British Imperial Assemblages at Delhi, 1877–1911', *Modern Asian Studies* 24, no. 3 (1990): 561–78.
15. James Fitzjames Stephen, 'Foundations of the Government of India', *Nineteenth Century* 14, no. 80 (October 1883): 542. Cf. Karuna Mantena, *Alibis of Empire: Henry Maine and the Ends of Liberal Imperialism* (Princeton, NJ: Princeton University Press, 2010.
16. David A. Washbrook, 'India, 1818–1860: The Two Faces of Colonialism', in *The Oxford History of the British Empire*, ed. Andrew Porter, vol. III: *The Nineteenth Century* (Oxford: Oxford University Press, 1999), 412–15. Cf. Douglas Peers, 'State, Power and Colonialism', in *India and the British Empire*, ed. Douglas Peers and Nandini Gooptu (Oxford: Oxford University Press, 2012), 16–43.
17. Cf. Ravi Ahuja, '"The Bridge-Builders": Some Notes on Railways, Pilgrimage and the British "Civilizing Mission" in Colonial India', in *Colonialism as Civilizing Mission: Cultural Ideology in British India*, ed. Harald Fischer-Tiné and Michael Mann (London: Anthem Press, 2004), 95–116.
18. David Hardiman, 'The Politics of Water in Colonial India', *South Asia: Journal of South Asian Studies* 25, no. 2 (2002): 111–20, quote is on p. 117. Cf. also Neeladri Bhattacharya, *The Great Agrarian Conquest: The Colonial Reshaping of a Rural World* (New York: State University of New York Press, 2019), 385–441; David Gilmartin, *Blood and Water: The Indus River Basin in Modern History* (Oakland: University of California Press, 2015.
19. Mike Davis, *Late Victorian Holocausts: El Niño Famines and the Making of the Third World* (London: Verso, 2007), 7. Cf. also Sarkar, *Modern Times*, 151–60.
20. David Arnold, 'Vagrant India: Famine, Poverty, and Welfare under Colonial Rule', in *Cast Out: Vagrancy and Homelessness in Global and Historical Perspective* (Athens: Ohio University Press, 2008), 117–39.
21. Allan OctavianHume, *Agricultural Reform in India* (London: W. H. Allen, 1879).
22. Prakash Kumar, '"Modernization" and Agrarian Development in India, 1912–52', *Journal of Asian Studies* 79, no. 3 (2020): 633–58; Deepak Kumar, 'Science in Agriculture: A Study in Victorian India', in *Tilling the Land: Agricultural Knowledge and Practices in Colonial India*, ed. Deepak Kumar and Bipasha Raha (Delhi: Primus Books, 2016), 20–48.
23. Atyab Sultan, 'Malcolm Darling and Developmentalism in Colonial Punjab', *Modern Asian Studies* 51, no. 6 (2017): 1891–1921.

24. Surinder S. Jodhka, 'Introduction', in *Village Society*, ed. Surinder S. Jodhka (Delhi: Orient Blackswan, 2012), 1–22; Mantena, *Alibis of Empire*; Ronald Inden, *Imagining India* (Oxford: Basil Blackwell, 1990), 131–61; Clive J. Dewey, 'Images of the Village Community: A Study in Anglo-Indian Ideology', *Modern Asian Studies* 6, no. 3 (1972): 291–328.
25. Metcalf, *Ideologies of the Raj*, 69–72.
26. Bhattacharya, *The Great Agrarian Conquest*, 108.
27. Sultan, 'Malcolm Darling and Developmentalism in Colonial Punjab'; Clive Dewey, *Anglo-Indian Attitudes: The Mind of the Indian Civil Service* (London: Hambledon, 1993).
28. For a concise summary of the various positions in this debate, cf. Jana Tschurenev, *Empire, Civil Society and the Beginnings of Colonial Education in India* (Cambridge: Cambridge University Press, 2019), 20–5.
29. A very early example of this popular argument is found in Bruce T. McCully, *English Education and the Origins of Indian Nationalism* (New York: Columbia University Press, 1940). Tim Allender, *Ruling Through Education: The Politics of Schooling in the Colonial Punjab* (Elgin: New Dawn Press, 2006); Vijaya Ramadas Mandala, 'Colonialism, Education, and the Spatial Dimension of Play – the Creation of Middle Class Space at Schools and Colleges in Modern India (1790–1910)', *The Historian* 80, no. 1 (2018): 34–85 are more recent instances of this line of thought.
30. Parimala V. Rao, 'Myth and Reality in the History of Indian Education', *Espacio, Tiempo y Educación* 6, no. 2 (2019): 217–34.
31. Cf., for instance, I. K. Chaudhary, 'Sanskrit Learning in Colonial Mithila: Continuity and Change', in *Education in Colonial India: Historical Insights*, ed. Deepak Kumar, Joseph Bara, Nandita Khadria and Ch. Radha Gayathri (New Delhi: Manohar, 2013), 125–44; Margrit Pernau, ed., *The Delhi College: Traditional Elites, the Colonial State, and Education before 1857* (New Delhi: Oxford University Press, 2006).
32. Sabyasachi Bhattacharya, 'Introduction: The Contested Terrain of Education', in *The Contested Terrain: Perspectives on Education in India*, ed. Sabyasachi Bhattacharya (Hyderabad: Orient Longman, 1998), 1–29.
33. For the following, cf. also Hans Harder, 'Languages, Literatures and the Public Sphere', in *The Routledge Handbook of the History of Colonialism in South Asia*, ed. Harald Fischer-Tiné and Maria Framke (Abingdon: Routledge, 2022), 412–23.
34. The most thorough discussion of the controversy is provided in Lynn Zastoupil and Martin Moir, 'Introduction', in *The Great Indian Education Debate: Documents Relating to the Orientalist-Anglicist Controversy, 1781–1843*, ed. Lynn Zastoupil and Martin Moir (Richmond, VA: Curzon, 1999), 1–72.
35. *General Report on the Census of India, 1891* (London: Her Majesty's Stationery Office, 1893), 210.
36. Ibid., 224.
37. D. Natarajan, *Census of India 1971: Extracts from the All India Census Reports on Literacy* (New Delhi: Office of the Registrar General, India, Ministry of Home Affairs, 1972), ii.
38. Michael Mann, *Wiring the Nation: Telecommunication, Newspaper Reportage and Nation Building in British India, 1850–1930* (New Delhi: Oxford University Press, 2017), 105–51.
39. Veena Naregal, *Language Politics, Elites and Public Spheres: Western India under Colonialism* (London: Anthem Press, 2002); Francesca Orsini, *The Hindi Public Sphere (1920–1940). Language and Literature in the Age of Nationalism* (New Delhi Oxford

University Press, 2002); Rama Sundari Mantena, 'Vernacular Publics and Political Modernity: Language and Progress in Colonial South India', *Modern Asian Studies* 47, no. 5 (2013): 1678–1705.
40. Francesca Orsini, *Between Print and Pleasure: Popular Literature and Entertaining Fictions in Colonial North India* (New Delhi: Permanent Black, 2009).
41. Cf., for instance, Akshaya Mukul, *Gita Press and the Making of Hindu India* (Noida: HarperCollins, 2015); Francis Robinson, 'Technology and Religious Change: Islam and the Impact of Print', *Modern Asian Studies* 27, no. 1 (1993): 229–51; Richard S. Weiss, 'Religion and the Emergence of Print in Colonial India: Arumuga Navalars Publishing Project', *Indian Economic & Social History Review* 53, no. 4 (2016): 473–500. For a helpful account of colonial surveillance and censorship measures, see Robert Darnton, 'Literary Surveillance in the British Raj: The Contradictions of Liberal Imperialism', *Book History* 4 (2001): 133–76.
42. Robin Jeffery, 'Communications and Capitalism in India, 1750–2000', *South Asia: Journal of South Asian Studies* 25, no. 2 (2002): 69.
43. Niraja Gopal Jayal, *Citizenship and Its Discontents: An Indian History* (Cambridge, MA: Harvard University Press, 2013), 50. A similar interpretation is articulated in Sukanya Banerjee, *Becoming Imperial Citizens: Indians in the Late-Victorian Empire* (Durham, NC: Duke University Press, 2010).
44. Cf. also C. A. Bayly, *Recovering Liberties: Indian Thought in the Age of Liberalism and Empire* (Cambridge: Cambridge University Press, 2012), 188–275; Sudhir Chandra, 'Subject's Citizenship Dream: Notes on the Nineteenth Century?', in *Civil Society, Public Sphere and Citizenship: Dialogues and Perspectives*, ed. Helmut Reifeld and Rajeev Bhargava (New Delhi: Sage, 2005), 106–29.
45. For the role of 'imperial citizenship' in South Asia, see also Mark R. Frost, 'Imperial Citizenship or Else: Liberal Ideals and the India Unmaking of Empire, 1890–1919', *The Journal of Imperial and Commonwealth History* 46, no. 5 (2018): 845–73.
46. Bayly, *Recovering Liberties*, 247–73.
47. David Washbrook, 'The Rhetoric of Democracy and Development in Late Colonial India', in *Nationalism, Democracy and Development: State and Politics in India*, ed. Sugata Bose and Ayesha Jalal (New Delhi: Oxford University Press, 1998), 36–49.
48. Hayden Bellenoit, *Missionary Education and Empire in Late Colonial India, 1860–1920* (London: Pickering and Chatto, 2007); Sanjay Seth, 'Secular Enlightenment and Christian Conversion: Missionaries and Education in Colonial India', in *Education and Social Change in South Asia*, ed. Krishna Kumar and Joachim Oesterheld (New Delhi: Orient Longman, 2007), 27–43.
49. Robert Eric Frykenberg, 'Christian Missions and the Raj', in *Missions and Empires*, ed. Norman Etherington (Oxford: Oxford University Press, 2005), 26–28.
50. Tschurenev, *Empire, Civil Society and the Beginnings of Colonial Education in India*, 203–29 and 245–74.
51. Bhattacharya, 'Introduction: The Contested Terrain of Education'.
52. For a slightly outdated but still valuable overview of Indian social and religious reform organizations, cf. Kenneth W. Jones, *Socio-Religious Reform Movements in British India*, vol. 2, The New Cambridge History of India, III (Cambridge: Cambridge University Press, 1989). A helpful analysis focusing on Hindu reform movement is provided by Amiya P. Sen's 'Introduction', in *Social and Religious Reform: The Hindus of British India*, ed. Amiya P. Sen (New Delhi: Oxford University Press, 2003), 3–63.
53. For the hidden religious agenda in the allegedly 'secular' educational institutions of British India, cf. also Parna Sengupta, *Pedagogy for Religion: Missionary Education and*

the *Fashioning of Hindus and Muslims in Bengal* (Berkeley: University of California Press, 2011); Gauri Viswanathan, *Masks of Conquest: Literary Study and British Rule in India* (New York: Columbia University Press, 1989).

54. NAI, 'Sat Dharm Parcharak', 11 August 1899, in *Selections from the Vernacular Newspapers Published in the Punjab*, 1899, 459. That this trope was still popular in Hindu circles three decades later is evident from Monika Freier, 'Cultivating Emotions: The Gita Press and Its Agenda of Social and Spiritual Reform', *South Asian History and Culture* 3, no. 3 (2012): 402–3.
55. Bipin Chandra Pal, *Swadeshi and Swaraj*, 1 [1907] (Calcutta: Yuganyanti Prakashak, 1954), 257.
56. Sabyasachi Bhattacharya, Joseph Bara and Chinna Rao Yagati, eds, *Educating the Nation: Documents on the Discourse of National Education in India 1880–1920* (New Delhi: Kanishka Publishers, 2003).
57. Joachim Oesterheld, 'Education, Cultural Diversity and Citizenship in Late Colonial India', *EMIGRA Working Papers* 58 (2007). Available online: https://ddd.uab.cat/pub/emigrawp/emigrawp_a2007n58/emigrawp_a2007n58p1.pdf (accessed 23 April 2021).
58. Cf. Brunner, 'Schooling the Subcontinent'.
59. Cf., for instance, Preeti, 'The Transformation of Schooling in Colonial Punjab, 1854–1900', in *New Perspectives in the History of Indian Education*, ed. Parimala V. Rao (New Delhi: Orient Blackswan, 2014), 288–90.
60. On the MA-O College, cf. David Lelyveld, *Aligarh's First Generation: Muslim Solidarity in British India* (Princeton, NJ: Princeton University Press, 1979); for a short overview of DA-V-College and its branches, cf. Vicki Langohr, 'Colonial Education Systems and the Spread of Local Religious Movements: The Cases of British Egypt and Punjab', *Comparative Studies in Society and History* 47, no. 1 (2005): 175–81; the Gurukul system is discussed in Harald Fischer-Tiné, '"The Only Hope for Fallen India": The Gurukul Kangri as an Experiment in National Education', in *Explorations in the History of South Asia: A Volume in Honour of Dietmar Rothermund*, ed. Georg Berkemer, Tilman Frasch, Hermann Kulke and Jürgen Lütt (New Delhi: Manohar, 2001), 277–99; the Khalsa College is analysed in Michael Brunner, *Education and Modernity in Colonial Punjab: Khalsa College, the Sikh Tradition and the Webs of Knowledge, 1880–1947* (Cham: Palgrave Macmillan, 2020); the BHU is addressed in Leah Renold, *A Hindu Education: Early Years of the Banaras Hindu University* (New Delhi: Oxford University Press, 2005).
61. See also Chapter 4.
62. On the Young Men's Buddhist Association in Ceylon, cf. Mark R. Frost, '"Wider Opportunities": Religious Revival, Nationalist Awakening and the Global Dimension in Colombo, 1870–1920', *Modern Asian Studies* 36, no. 4 (2002): 953–60. For the role of the YMBA Burma, cf., for instance, Juliane Schober, *Modern Buddhist Conjunctures in Myanmar: Cultural Narratives, Colonial Legacies, and Civil Society* (Honolulu: University of Hawai'i Press, 2010), 66–75.
63. Cf., for example, J. N. Farquhar, *Modern Religious Movements in India* (New York: Macmillan, 1915), 125 and 444; Harjot Oberoi, *The Construction of Religious Boundaries: Culture, Identity, and Diversity in the Sikh Tradition* (New Delhi: Oxford University Press, 1997), 412–13.
64. D. S. Savardekar, ed., *Directory of Social Work in the City and Island of Bombay* (Bombay: Vaibhav Press, 1926), 98.
65. The Social Service League Bombay, ed., *Directory of Social Work in India (Excepting the City and Island of Bombay)* (Bombay: Vaibhav Press, 1923), 5, 16, 25, and 62–63; Savardekar, *Directory of Social Work*, 98–100.

66. Cf., for instance, 'Report of the Bombay Gymnastic Institute for the Years 1927–28, 1928–29, 1929–30' (Bombay, s.a. [1930]).
67. For an overview, cf. also Filippo Osella, 'Charity and Philanthropy in South Asia: An Introduction', *Modern Asian Studies* 52, no. 1 (2018): 14–18.
68. Jones, *Socio-Religious Reform Movements in British India*.
69. Gwilym Beckerlegge, *Swami Vivekananda's Legacy of Service: A Study of the Ramakrishna Math and Mission* (New Delhi: Oxford University Press, 2006); Maruti T. Kamble, 'Bengal in Karnataka's Reform Movement: A Case Study of the Ramakrishna Math and Mission, 1890–1947', in *Colonialism Modernity and Religious Identities: Religious Reform Movements in South Asia*, ed. Gwilym Beckerlegge (New Delhi: Oxford University Press, 2008), 126–43.
70. P. Seshadri, 'The Spirit of Service', in *Dayananda Commemoration Volume: An Homage to Maharshi Dayananda Saraswati from India and the World in Celebration of the Dayanand Nirvana Ardh Shatabdi*, ed. Har Bilas Sarda (Ajmer: Vedic Yantralay, 1933), 41–5.
71. Soni Soni, 'Famine Orphan "Rescue" Missions: Childhood, Colonialism and Nationalism in Colonial India, 1860s–1920s', unpublished PhD dissertation, ETH-Zurich, 2020, 194–210.
72. Malavika Kasturi, '"All Gifting Is Sacred": The Sanatana Dharma Sabha Movement, the Reform of Dana and Civil Society in Late Colonial India', *The Indian Economic & Social History Review* 47, no. 1 (2010): 107–39; D. E. Haynes, 'From Tribute to Philanthropy: The Politics of Gift Giving in a Western Indian City', *Journal of Asian Studies* 46, no. 2 (1987): 339–60. For an extensive discussion, see also Osella, 'Charity and Philanthropy in South Asia: An Introduction'.
73. The concept of bourgeois Hinduism is elucidated in Brian A. Hatcher, *Bourgeois Hinduism or the Faith of the Modern Vedantists: Rare Discourses from Colonial Bengal* (Oxford: Oxford University Press, 2008), 65–101. Cf. also Sanjay Joshi, *Fractured Modernity: Making of a Middle Class in Colonial North India* (New Delhi: Oxford University Press, 2001), 98–131.
74. Anne Murphy, 'The Formation of the Ethical Sikh Subject in the Era of British Colonial Reform', *Sikh Formations* 11, no. 1–2 (2015): 149–59.
75. Cf., for instance, Maria-Magdalena Fuchs, 'Islamic Modernism in Colonial Punjab: The Anjuman-i Himayat-i Islam, 1884–1923', unpublished PhD dissertation, Princeton University, 2019; Margrit Pernau, 'Love and Compassion for the Community: Emotions and Practices among North Indian Muslims, c. 1870–1930', *The Indian Economic & Social History Review* 54, no. 1 (2017): 21–42; Masood Akhtar Zahid, 'Islamia Anjumans and Educational Development: Perspectives on the 19th Century British Punjab', *Pakistan Journal of History and Culture* 34, no. 2 (2013): 1–23; Ulrike Stark, 'Associational Culture and Civic Engagement in Colonial Lucknow: The Jalsah-e Tahzib', *The Indian Economic & Social History Review* 48, no. 1 (2011): 1–33.
76. The Social Service League Bombay, *Directory of Social Work in India*; Savardekar, *Directory of Social Work*. For a discussion of Bombay as a hotbed of social service activities, see also Prashant Kidambi, 'From "Social Reform" to "Social Service"', in *Civilizing Missions in Colonial and Postcolonial South Asia: From Improvement to Development*, ed. Carey A. Watt and Michael Mann (London: Anthem Press, 2011), 217–40.
77. A. R.Desai, *Social Background of Indian Nationalism* (Bombay: Popular Prakashan, 1966), 241–2.

78. Carey A. Watt, *Serving the Nation: Cultures of Service, Association and Citizenship in Colonial India* (New Delhi: Oxford University Press, 2005), 13–16 and 65–129. Cf. also Osella, 'Charity and Philanthropy in South Asia: An Introduction', 19–25; Malavika Kasturi, 'Gurus and Gifting: Dana, the Math Reform Campaign, and Competing Visions of Hindu Sangathan in Twentieth-Century India', *Modern Asian Studies* 52, no. 1 (2018): 99–131; Georgina Brewis, '"Fill Full the Mouth of Famine": Voluntary Action in Famine Relief in India, 1896–1901', *Modern Asian Studies* 44, no. 4 (2010): 901–12.
79. Gwilym Beckerlegge, 'Iconographic Representations of Renunciation and Activism in the Ramakrishna Math and Mission and the Rashtriya Swayamsevak Sangh', *Journal of Contemporary Religion* 19, no. 1 (2004): 47–66. Cf. also Prathama Banerjee, 'Between the Political and the Non-Political: The Vivekananda Moment and a Critique of the Social in Colonial Bengal, 1890s–1910s', *Social History* 39, no. 3 (2014): 323–39.
80. Watt, *Serving the Nation*, 107.
81. C. A. Bayly, *Origins of Nationality in South Asia: Patriotism and Ethical Government in the Making of Modern India* (Cambridge: Cambridge University Press, 1998).
82. Cf., for example, C. S. Adcock, 'Debating Conversion, Silencing Caste: The Limited Scope of Religious Freedom', *Journal of Law and Religion* 29, no. 3 (2014): 363–77; Susan Bayly, *Caste, Society and Politics in India from the Eighteenth Century to the Modern Age* (Cambridge: Cambridge University Press, 1999), 144–86; R. Srivatsan, *Seva, Saviour and State: Caste Politics, Tribal Welfare and Capitalist Development* (Abingdon: Routledge, 2015), 163–81.
83. For a succinct account of the Servants of India, cf. B. R. Nanda, *Gokhale: The Indian Moderates and the British Raj* (New Delhi: Oxford University Press, 1977), 169–76.
84. Georgina Brewis, 'Education for Service: Social Service and Higher Education in India and Britain, 1905–1919', *History of Education Review* 42, no. 2 (2013): 125.
85. Farquhar, *Modern Religious Movements in India*, 379.
86. Cited in Heimsath, *Indian Nationalism and Hindu Social Reform* (Princeton, NJ: Princeton University Press,1964), 241–2.
87. Joana Simonow, 'After the "Late Victorian Holocausts": Transnational Responses to Famines and Malnutrition in India, c. 1900–1955', Unpublished PhD Thesis, ETH-Zurich, 2019, 43–9.
88. Cf. the useful discussion on social service and citizenship in Elena Valdameri, *Indian Liberalism between Nation and Empire. The Political Life of Gopal Krishna Gokhale* (Abingdon: Routledge, 2022), Chapter 4.
89. For the divide between the 'lettered' public and the 'urban poor' in Bombay, see Manishita Dass, *Outside the Lettered City: Cinema, Modernity and the Public Sphere in Late Colonial India* (Oxford: Oxford University Press, 2015); Prashant Kidambi, *The Making of an Indian Metropolis: Colonial Governance and Public Culture in Bombay, 1890–1920* (Aldershot: Ashgate, 2007), 210–8. For the broader phenomenon, cf. also Nandini Gooptu, *The Politics of the Urban Poor in Early-Twentieth Century India* (Cambridge: Cambridge University Press, 2001).
90. Carey A. Watt, 'Philanthropy and Civilizing Missions in India c. 1820–1960: States, NGOs and Development', in *Civilizing Missions in Colonial and Postcolonial South Asia: From Improvement to Development*, ed. Carey A. Watt and Michael Mann (London: Anthem Press, 2011), 271–316.
91. For a definition of humanitarianism as a border-crossing, transregional form of active compassion that was based on a vision of the unity of humankind, see Michael Barnett, *Empire of Humanity: A History of Humanitarianism* (Ithaca, NY: Cornell University Press, 2011), 15–16.

92. Adrian Ruprecht, 'De-Centering Humanitarianism: The Red Cross and India, c. 1877–1939', unpublished PhD dissertation, University of Cambridge, 2017, 114–28, quote on p. 123.
93. Adrian Ruprecht, 'The Great Eastern Crisis (1875–1878) as a Global Humanitarian Moment', *Journal of Global History* 16, no. 2 (2021): 159–84.
94. Brief accounts on the role of these and other humanitarian organizations during the Great War will be provided in Chapter 2.
95. Cf. Sarah Ansari, 'The Bombay Presidency's "Home Front", 1914–1918', in *India and World War I: A Centennial Assessment*, ed. Roger D. Long and Ian Talbot (London: Routledge, 2018); Sharmishtha Roy Chowdhury, *The First World War, Anti-Colonialism and Imperial Authority in British India, 1914–1924* (London: Routledge, 2019), Chapter 2.
96. On the relief activities of the HMS, cf. also Maria Framke, 'The Politics of Gender and Community: Non-Governmental Relief in Late Colonial and Early Postcolonial India', in *Gendering Humanitarianism: Politics, Practice, and Empowerment during the Twentieth Century*, ed. Esther Möller, Johannes Paulmann and Katharina Stornig (Cham: Palgrave MacMillan, 2020), 143–66.
97. For a concise analysis of the latter two organizations, cf. Ali Raza and Franziska Roy, 'Paramilitary Organizations in Interwar India', *South Asia: Journal of South Asian Studies* 38, no. 4 (2015): 671–89.
98. Franziska Roy, 'International Utopia and National Discipline: Youth and Volunteer Movements in Interwar South Asia', in *The Internationalist Moment: South Asia, Worlds, and World Views, 1917–39*, ed. Ali Raza, Franziska Roy and Benjamin Zachariah (New Delhi: Sage, 2015), 183.
99. Due to constraints of space, I will have to restrict myself to a rather broad-brush account with a focus on some of the more intriguing facets of YMCA work that cannot be discussed in the following chapters. For a comprehensive narrative of the institutional history of the Indian YMCA that is extremely rich in factual detail, cf. David, *The YMCA and the Making*; David, *The YMCA and the Making of Modern India: A Saga of Selfless Sacrifice, Vol. II. 1991–2016*.
100. Geoffrey D. Spurr, 'The London YMCA: A Haven of Masculine Self-Improvement and Socialization for the Late Victorian and Edwardian Clerk', *Canadian Journal of History* 37, no. 2 (2002): 275–301.
101. Kenneth Scott Latourette, *World Service: A History of the Foreign Work and World Service of the Young Men's Christian Associations of the United States and Canada* (New York: Association Press, 1957), 22; Clarence P. Shedd, *History of the World Alliance of the Young Men's Christian Association* (London: Society for Promoting Christian Knowledge, 1955), 84–6; Kjetil Fretheim, 'Whose Kingdom? Which Context? Ecumenical and Contextual Theology in the World Alliance of YMCAs', *International Review of Mission* 97, no. 384/385 (2008): 119–20.
102. For a concise overview of the proliferation of YMCAs around the globe from the 1880s to the 1940s, cf. Harald Fischer-Tiné, Stefan Huebner and Ian Tyrell, 'Introduction. The Rise and Growth of a Global "Moral Empire": The YMCA and YWCA during the Late Nineteenth and Early Twentieth Centuries', in *Spreading Protestant Modernity. Global Perspectives on the Work of the YMCA and the YWCA, 1889–1970*, ed. Harald Fischer-Tiné, Stefan Huebner and Ian Tyrell (Honolulu: University of Hawaii Press, 2020), 10–23.

103. Nina Mjagkij and Margaret Spratt, 'Introduction', in *Men and Women Adrift: The YMCA and the YWCA in the City*, ed. Nina Mjagkij and Margaret Spratt (New York: New York University Press, 1997), 3.
104. C. Howard Hopkins, 'The Kansas-Sudan Missionary Movement in the Y.M.C.A., 1889–1891', Church History 21, no. 4 (1952): 314.
105. Nancy Boyd, *Emissaries: The Overseas Work of the American YWCA 1895–1970* (New York: The Woman's Press, 1986), 29–32.
106. On the 'social gospel' in the United States generally, cf. Christopher A. Evans, *The Social Gospel in American Religion: A History* (New York: New York University Press, 2017); Susan Curtis, *A Consuming Faith: The Social Gospel and Modern American Culture* (Baltimore, MD: Johns Hopkins University Press, 1991).
107. Walter Rauschenbusch, *Christianity and the Present Crisis* (New York: Macmillan, 1907), 208–10. Cf. also Walter Rauschenbusch, *A Theology for the Social Gospel* (New York: Macmillan, 1917).
108. Raghavan, *Fierce Enigmas*, 69.
109. Winter, *Making Men, Making Class*, passim; Mjagkij and Spratt, eds, *Men and Women Adrift*; Nina Mjagkij, *Light in the Darkness: African Americans and the YMCA, 1852–1946* (Lexington, KY: University Press of Kentucky, 1994).
110. C. A. Bayly, *The Birth of the Modern World, 1780–1914: Global Connections and Comparisons* (Oxford: Blackwell, 2004), 330.
111. For a typical contemporary YMCA manifesto for an intensification of its egalitarian approach to social work, cf. Sherwood Eddy, *Religion and Social Justice* (New York: George H. Doran, 1927).
112. William J. Baker, 'To Pray or to Play? The YMCA Question in the United Kingdom and the United States, 1850–1900', International Journal of the History of Sport 11, no. 1 (1994): 42.
113. Roberta J. Park, 'Science, Service, and the Professionalization of Physical Education: 1885–1905', International Journal of the History of Sport 24, no. 12 (2007): 1674–700; Johnson, *The History of YMCA Physical Education*, 153–60.
114. Dominic Erdozain, *The Problem of Pleasure: Sport, Recreation and the Crisis of Victorian Religion* (Woodbridge: Boydell Press, 2010), 124.
115. KFYA, IWI, Box 2, Folder 'India; Calcutta Annual Reports 1859–1860'.
116. Dunderdale, *The YMCA in India*, 5.
117. This southern bias remains a problem for the YMCA until today. Cf. D. S. Sanal Dhas, 'Organization and Services of YMCA in Tamil Nadu with Special Reference to Kanyakumari District since 1956', unpublished PhD dissertation, Tirunelveli, Manonmaniam Sundarar University, 2017, 46–48.
118. Shedd, *History of the World Alliance*, 363; KFYA, IWC, Box 8, L. D. Wishard, 'The Beginning of the Association in India and Ceylon', s.a. [1890].
119. Dunderdale, *The YMCA in India*, 13.
120. Ibid., 12.
121. In colonial South Asia, the term 'Europeans' was used in its broadest sense to denote white-skinned persons. 'Eurasian' was the term usually used to denote persons of mixed descent until about 1910. Later, they were mostly referred to as 'Anglo-Indians'.
122. *Young Men of India*, 34 (1923): 18. There were exceptions to this general policy. Some of the southern branches, like the one in Trivandrum, catered to a 'native Christian' clientele right from the outset.
123. Rosenberg, *Transnational Currents in a Shrinking World*, 68.

124. C. Howard Hopkins, *History of the Y.M.C.A. in North America* (New York: Association Press, 1951), 331–3.
125. Although US capital and staff were dominant, the Canadian and American National YMCAs were technically united until 1912, when a separate Canadian national association was established. Their entanglement continued for years after this split as far as international work and particularly programmes in South Asia were concerned.
126. KFYA, IWC, Box 8, Folder 'Ceylon No. 1885-December 1895', File 'L. D. Wishard, Beginning of the Association in India and Ceylon'.
127. George Sherwood Eddy, *Pathfinders of the World Missionary Crusade* (New York: Abingdon-Cokebury Press, 1945), 44.
128. Cited in KFYA, IWI, Box 89, Folder 'A Brief History 1854–1900', E. C. Worman, *A Brief History of the Young Men's Christian Association in India Burma and Ceylon 1854–1900*, unpublished manuscript, s.a. 12.
129. On the politics of whiteness in British India, cf. Harald Fischer-Tiné, 'The Making of a "Ruling Race": Defining and Defending Whiteness in Colonial India', in *Racism in the Modern World: Historical Perspectives on Cultural Transfer and Adaptation*, ed. Manfred Berg and Simon Wendt (New York: Berghahn, 2011), 211–35.
130. Tyrrell, *Reforming the World*, 89–91; Ankit Prasad, *Social Welfare and Social Action: YMCA at Work* (New Delhi: Mittal Publications, 2005), 7.
131. KFYA, IWI, Box 89, Folder 'A Brief History 1854–1900', Typescript 'The Genesis of the Foreign Work of the Young Men's Christian Associat'n' [*sic*], 4.
132. Tyrrell, *Reforming the World*, 88.
133. Edward C. Carter, *The Men of India and Ceylon* (New York: Foreign Department, International Committee Young Men's Christian Association, 1908), 20–1.
134. Latourette, *World Service*, 119; Tyrrell, *Reforming the World*, 90–1.
135. A. E. Holt, *A Study of the Y.M.C.A. of India, Burma & Ceylon. Made as an Integral Part of the International Survey* (Calcutta: National Council Y.M.C.A., 1933), 6.
136. Prasad, *Social Welfare and Social Action*, 12.
137. Latourette, *World Service*, 117 and 119.
138. KFYA, IWI, Box 51, Folder 'India World Service 1943', E. C. Worman, *Post-War Policy Study: India, Burma and Ceylon*, 5.
139. Latourette, *World Service*, 119.
140. Harper, *In the Shadow of the Mahatma*, 49–53.
141. David, *The YMCA and the Making*, 62–3.
142. Latourette, *World Service*, 119.
143. The Indian YMCA continued as a pan-South Asian organization throughout the 1940s. Burma was the first to break away and form its own national Association in 1951. Pakistan and Ceylon followed in 1955 and 1962, respectively. David, *The YMCA and the Making*, 367.
144. Ibid, 61.
145. Dunderdale, *The YMCA in India*, 89.
146. The following section draws on Harald Fischer-Tiné, 'Third-Stream Orientalism: J. N. Farquhar, the Indian YMCA's Literature Department, and the Representation of South Asian Cultures and Religions (ca. 1910–1940)', *Journal of Asian Studies* 79, no. 3 (2020): 659–83.
147. Holt, *A Study of the Y.M.C.A.*, 143.
148. During the peak year of 1918–19, the Association Press supplied almost 330,000 books, pamphlets and periodicals in English as well as in regional languages to

imperial army centres in India and overseas. *Report of the National Council of Young Men's Christian Associations of India and Ceylon to the Tenth National Convention at Calcutta November 23–27, 1920* (Cuttack: Orissa Mission Press, 1920), 86.
149. Eric J. Sharpe, *Not to Destroy but to Fulfill, the Contribution to J. N. Farquhar to Protestant Missionary Thought in India before 1914* (Uppsala: Gleerup, 1965), 234.
150. C. Howard Hopkins, *John R. Mott (1865–1955): A Biography* (Grand Rapids, MI: William B. Eerdmans, 1979), 672.
151. Hopkins, *History of the Y.M.C.A. in North America*, 1951, 660.
152. Sharpe, *Not to Destroy but to Fulfill*, 252 and 298.
153. Denis Vidal, 'Max Müller and the Theosophists or the Other Half of Victorian Orientalism', in *Orientalism and Anthropology: From Max Müller to Louis Dumont*, ed. Jackie Assayag, Roland Lardinois and Denis Vidal (Pondichery: Institut Français de Pondichéry, 1997), 17–29.
154. Fischer-Tiné, 'Third-Stream Orientalism', 677–8.
155. See, for instance, E. W. Thompson, 'The Arya Samaj and Christian Missions in Bengal', *The Harvest Field* 12, no. 10 (1901): 361–68; KFYA, IWI, Box 2, Folder 'Correspondence, Report Letters 1892–1912', File 'George Sherwood Eddy to YMCA International Committee NY, 15 Jan. 1913'.
156. 'Noted Scholar's Death: Aberdeen Native Dr J.N. Farquhar's Work for India', *Aberdeen Press and Journal*, 18 July 1929, 8.
157. Rimi B. Chatterjee, *A History of Oxford University Press under the Raj* (New Delhi: Oxford University Press, 2006), 198–200.
158. David, *The YMCA and the Making*, 159.
159. *Melā*: Hindi term for a fair or festival.
160. Anonymous, 'Book Island at the People's Fair', *The Times of India*, 26 November 1921, 11.
161. *Report of the National Council*, 83.
162. KFYA, IWI, Box 1, Folder 'Misc Print 1912–1964', L. A. Hogg, Interpreting India: Sixteen Years of a Literary Enterprise [undated typescript, 1928].
163. *Report of the National Council 1921*, 80.
164. Holt, *A Study of the Y.M.C.A.*, 143.
165. Cf. Janet Lydon, *Imperial Emotion: The Politics of Empathy across the British Empire* (Cambridge: Cambridge University Press, 2019), 143–63; Donald Simpson, 'Missions and the Magic Lantern', *International Bulletin of Mission Research* 21, no. 1 (1997): 13–15.
166. David, *The YMCA and the Making*, 237.
167. KFYA, IWI, Box 11, Folder 'India Correspondence and Reports Jan–March 1915', File 'The Evangelistic Forward Movement in India 1915–16'.
168. Cf. Chapter 4.
169. 'Report of the National Council, Y.M.C.A.: Lecture Department', *Young Men of India*, 31, no. 3 (March 1921): 154.
170. YDSPC, Rec. Gr. 115, Series I, Waldo Huntley Heinrichs Papers, Box 7, Folder 61, Diaries 1916, Waldo H. Heinrichs, Diaries, entries for 10 January, 6 June, 15, 25, and 26 August 1916.
171. 'Report of the National Council, Y.M.C.A.: Lecture Department', *Young Men of India* 31, no. 3 (March 1921): 156.
172. 'Report of the National Council, Y.M.C.A.: Lecture Department', 155.
173. V. M. Ilahibaksh, 'Lecture Department', in *Report of National Council to the Twelfth National Convention 1924–1926*, ed. Young Men's Christian Associations of India and Ceylon (Cuttack: Orissa Mission Press, 1926), 61.

174. Cf. for example KFYA, IWI, Box 19, Folder 'Lantern Slide Lecture Guides', File 'Boys India, 1924'.
175. 'Report of the National Council, Y.M.C.A., 1924–6: Lecture Department', 159.
176. KFYA, IWI, Box 47, Folder 'India 1929–1934', Letter from B. L. Rallia Ram, Acting General Secretary, Lahore, to Frank Slack, 2 May 1929.
177. Ilahibaksh, 'Lecture Department', 62.
178. The Malabar Central Relief Committee, *Report of Work, October 1921 to November 1922* (Madras: The Servants of India Society, 1923), 26.
179. KFYA, IWI, Box 47, Folder 'India 1929–1934', Letter from B. L. Rallia Ram, Acting General Secretary, Lahore, to Frank Slack, 2 May 1929.
180. H. H. Peterson, 'Adult Education through Wireless Broadcasting in India', *Young Men of India* 43, no. 10 (October 1931): 573.
181. KFYA, IWI, Box 47, Folder 'India 1929–1934', Letter from B. L. Rallia Ram, Acting General Secretary, Lahore, to Frank Slack, 24 April 1933.
182. The *Amos 'n' Andy* show was originally created and voiced by Freeman Gosden and Charles Correll, two white entertainers in 1926. The programme drew heavily on the racial stereotypes and the kind of humour established by the minstrel tradition established in the first half of the nineteenth century. It was tremendously popular from the outset and was broadcast nightly from coast to coast between 1929 and 1943. For details cf. Susan J. Douglas, *Listening In: Radio and the American Imagination, from Amos 'n' Andy and Edward R. Murrow to Wolfman Jack and Howard Stern* (New York: Random House, 1999), 101–10.
183. Paula Lupkin, 'Manhood Factories: Architecture, Business, and the Evolving Urban Role of the YMCA, 1865–1925', in *Men and Women Adrift*, ed. Mjagkij and Spratt, 40–64.
184. Lupkin, *Manhood Factories: YMCA Architecture and the Making of Modern Urban Culture*, 137–79.
185. Tyrrell, *Reforming the World*, 88.
186. Charles A. Keller, 'The Christian Student Movement, YMCAs, and Transnationalism in Republican China', *The Journal of American-East Asian Relations* 13, Special Volume – Christianity as an Issue in the History of U.S.-China Relations (2004): 61.
187. Wanamaker was one of the most potent sponsors of international Y work. Between 1900 and 1921 he financed YMCA buildings in Madras, Calcutta, Seoul, Kyoto, Peking and Moscow. *Northern Daily Mail*, 15 October 1921, 1.
188. KFYA, IWI, Box 1, Folder 'McConaughy Misc. Print 1890', File 'Prospectus. A Building for the Young Men's Christian Association in Madras, India', 3.
189. *Association News* (Philadelphia), 17 (15), 1896, 2.
190. Ibid., 3.
191. Gilles Tillotson, 'George S. T. Harris: An Architect in Gwalior', *South Asian Studies* 20, no. 1 (2004): 9–24.
192. KFYA, IWI, Box 1, Folder 'McConaughy Misc. Print 1890', File 'Prospectus. A Building for the Young Men's Christian Association in Madras, India, 3'. 6.
193. Yoshino Sugawara, 'Toward the Opposite Site of "Vulgarity": The Birth of Cinema as a "Healthful Entertainment" and the Shanghai YMCA', in Emilie Yueh-yu Yeh (ed.), *Early Film Culture in Hong Kong, Taiwan and Republican China: Kaleidoskopic Histories* (Ann Arbor: University of Michigan Press, 2018), 184.
194. Michael Windover, 'Exchanging Looks: "Art Dekho" Movie Theatres in Bombay', *Architectural History* 52 (2009): 208–10. For the emergence of a cosmopolitan current among urban Indian youth, cf. also Kaushik Bhaumik, 'At Home in the

World: Cinema and the Cultures of the Young in Bombay in the 1920s', in *Towards a History of Consumption in South Asia*, ed. Douglas Haynes, Abigail McGowan, Tirthankar Roy and Harukar Yanagisawa (New Delhi: Oxford University Press, 2010), 136–54.
195. Dunderdale, *The YMCA in India*, 28.
196. Cf., for instance, Farquhar, *Modern Religious Movements in India*, 1915, 278.
197. KFYA, IWI, Box 20, Folder 'Annual and Quarterly Reports 1893–1901', File 'The Young Men's Christian Association of Madras – Report for the Year 1900, by Geo. Benton-Smith, Ag. Gen'l. Secy., Madras 30 August 1900'.
198. David, *The YMCA and the Making*, 205–6.
199. For facts on Henry Schaetti and his work, see KFYA, BF, Box 183, Folder 'Biographical Data, Henry Schaetti'.
200. *The Foreign Mail Annual*, 1916, 56.
201. The phrase is taken from a self-portrayal of the Indian YMCA in one of their pamphlets. Cf. The National Council of the Y.M.C.As of India, Burma and Ceylon, *Youth in Harness: The All India Service of the Y.M.C.A.* (Calcutta: Baptist Mission Press, s.a. [1930]).
202. George Sherwood Eddy, 'Seeking to Reach the Educated Hindus', *The Missionary Review of the World*, New Series, 16, no. 12 (1903): 922–7.
203. Raghavan, *Fierce Enigmas*, 65–9; Dwarka Prasad Singh, *American Attitude towards Indian Nationalist Movement* (New Delhi: Munshiram Manoharlal, 1974), 83–4.
204. Sherwood Eddy, *India Awakening* (New York: Missionary Education Movement of the United States and Canada, 1911), 80.
205. For a detailed analysis, cf. Chapter 2.
206. Gerald Studdert-Kennedy, *British Christians, Indian Nationalists and the Raj* (New Delhi: Oxford University Press, 1991), 145–54.
207. David, *The YMCA and the Making*, 261. Cf. also E. C. Dewick, 'The Y.M.C.A. as an Effective Factor in the Development of the Country', *The Young Men of India* 42, no. 1 (January 1930): 53–9.
208. KFYA, IWC, Box 8, Folder 'Ceylon, Apr 1919 – Oct 1922', E. M. Robinson, 'Report on India and Ceylon for Drs. Mott, Jenkins, Lyon etc., 12 March 1921'.
209. Mayer N. Zald and Patricia Denton, 'From Evangelism to General Services: The Transformation of the YMCA', *Administrative Science Quarterly* viii, no. 2 (1963): 218–21.
210. For Paul's and Swamidoss's much-acclaimed initiatives and the Indian Y's rural work, more generally, cf. Chapter 5 and Tyrrell, 'Vectors of Practicality', 45–52. On the Y's industrial work cf. Srivastava, *The Well-Being of the Labour Force*, 133–41; KFYA, IWI, Box 14, *Annual Report for 1922 of the Empress Mills Welfare Work*, Calcutta: Nagpur, s.a. [1923]; and KFYA, IWI, Box 83, Folder 'National Council Misc. Reports', *Second Quinquennial Report of the Welfare Work of Messrs. Begg, Sutherland & Co., Ltd.*, Cawnpore: s.a. [1939].
211. Dewick, 'The Y.M.C.A. as an Effective Factor', 56.
212. KFYA, IWC, Box 8, Folder 'Ceylon, Apr 1919 – Oct 1922', E. M. Robinson 'Report on India and Ceylon for Drs. Mott, Jenkins, Lyon etc., 12 March 1921'.
213. The most comprehensive study is provided by K. N. Panikkar, *Against Lord and State: Religion and Peasant Uprisings in Malabar, 1836–1921* (New Delhi: Oxford University Press, 1989).
214. The rebellion, which started in late August 1921, was finally quelled by the Indian Army by the beginning of December in the same year.

215. Harald Fischer-Tiné, '"Kindly Elders of the Hindu Biradri": The Arya Samaj's Struggle for Influence and Its Effect on Hindu-Muslim Relations', in *Gurus and Their Followers. Studies in New Religious Movements in Late Colonial India*, ed. A. Copley (New Delhi: Oxford University Press, 2000), 116–18.
216. Prabhu Bapu, *Hindu Mahasabha in Colonial North India, 1915–1930: Constructing Nation and History* (Abingdon: Routledge, 2013), 49–59; Franziska Roy, 'The Torchbearers of Progress: Youth Volunteer Organizations and National Discipline in India, c. 1918-1947', unpublished PhD dissertation, University of Warwick, 2013, 210-1; John Zavos, *The Emergence of Hindu Nationalism in India* (Delhi: Oxford University Press, 2000), 144–9.
217. The Malabar Central Relief Committee, *Report of Work, October 1921 to November 1922*.
218. A. N. Sudarisanam, 'Malabar Relief Work', *Young Men of India* 33, no. 2 (February 1922): 79.
219. I. M. Jacobi, 'Y.M.C.A. Work in Connection with the Malabar Central Relief Committee, Calicut, Malabar', *Young Men of India* 33, no. 9 (September 1922): 519.
220. The Malabar Central Relief Committee, *Report of Work, October 1921 to November 1922*, 14–24.
221. The Malabar Central Relief Committee, 26.
222. On the activities of the 'Ariakode Social Centre' cf. also A. Kanakaraj, *Lighthouses of Rural Reconstruction: The History of the Y.M.C.A's Integrated Rural Development in South India* (Delhi: ISPCK, 2000), 93–8.
223. H. A. Popley, 'Reconstructing Life in a Rebel Area', *Young Men of India* 34, no. 6 (June 1922): 271.
224. Holt, *A Study of the Y.M.C.A.*
225. Ibid., 153.
226. Ibid., 148–55.
227. KFYA, IWI, Box 99, Folder 'Misc. Print', Kanakaraya T. Paul, 'The Handwriting on the Wall', undated pamphlet [c. 1921].
228. S. K. Datta, 'India and Racial Relationships', *Young Men of India* 35 (August 1914): 499–508, 2021.
229. Mrinalini Sinha, *Specters of Mother India: The Global Restructuring of an Empire* (Durham: Duke University Press, 2006), 33. For a comprehensive account, cf. Harold A. Gould, *Sikhs, Swamis, and Spies: The India Lobby in the United States 1900–1946* (New Delhi: Sage, 2006).
230. In a book published in 1931, Sherwood Eddy lengthily quotes pro-Gandhian articles in the US Press. Sherwood Eddy, *The Challenge of the East* (New York: Farrar & Rinehart, 1931), 7–11.
231. *Chicago Defender*, 17 October 1931, 13; quoted in Nico Slate, *Lord Cornwallis Is Dead: The Struggle for Democracy in the United States and India* (Cambridge, MA: Harvard University Press, 2019), 150.
232. David, *The YMCA and the Making*, 213.
233. Ibid., 261.
234. *The Times of India*, 1 February 1928, 9. Harry Hobbs, *Indian Y.M.C.A. and Politics* (Calcutta: H. Hobbs, 1927), 14.
235. Ibid.
236. Raghavan, *Fierce Enigmas*, 96.
237. Cf. also Michael G. Thompson, *For God and Globe: Christian Internationalism in the United States between the Great War and the Cold War* (Ithaca, NY: Cornell

University Press, 2015); Rick L. Nutt, 'G. Sherwood Eddy and the Attitudes of Protestants in the United States toward Global Mission', *Church History* 66, no. 3 (1997): 502–21.
238. Cf. also Anonymous, 'Hostility to British: Dr Sherwood Eddy's Laudation of Russia', *The Englishman*, 24 February 1927, 9.
239. Ibid.
240. S. K. Datta, 'Charges against the Y.M.C.A.: Red Propaganda Accusations Answered by General Secretary', *The Englishman*, 24 February 1927, 16.
241. *The Times*, 21 January 1927, 6. Cf. also *Belfast Newsletter*, 27 January 1927, 9.
242. Priyamvada Gopal, *Insurgent Empire: Anticolonial Resistance and British Dissent* (London: Verso, 2019), 245–60; Michel Louro, '"Where National Revolutionary Ends and Communist Begins": The League against Imperialism and the Meerut Conspiracy Case', *Comparative Studies of South Asia, Africa and the Middle East* 33, no. 3 (2013): 331–44; Franziska Roy and Benjamin Zachariah, 'Meerut and a Hanging: "Young India," Popular Socialism, and the Dynamics of Imperialism', *Comparative Studies of South Asia, Africa and the Middle East* 33, no. 3 (2013): 360–77.
243. Nicholas Owen, 'Alliances from above and below: The Failures and Successes of Communist Anti-Imperialism in India, 1920–34', in *Workers of the Empire Unite: Radical and Popular Challenges to British Imperialism, 1910s to 1960s*, ed. Yann Béliard and Neville Kirk (Liverpool: Liverpool University Press, 2021), 97–101.
244. *Western Daily Press* (Bristol), 16 Sept. 1927, 10.
245. K. T. Paul, ed., *Young Men's Christian Associations of India, Burma and Ceylon and the European Association (Central Association): Report of Committee of Enquiry Appointed by the National Council Y.M.C.A. Together with the Allegations and Correspondence* (Calcutta: Baptist Mission Press, 1927), 10.
246. WAYAG, Box 'India National Work/Minutes of Board Meetings & National Conferences', E. C. Dewick, *Some Notes on the Present Situation in India*, 1932. For a similar 'anti-British stance', cf. also George Sherwood Eddy, 'British Will Lose India Unless They Grant It Dominion Status', *The New York American*, 13 July 1930, 2-E.
247. Charles Merz, 'Blue Sky in India', *Association Men*, 1923, 6.
248. KFYA, IWI, Box 47, Folder 'India 1929–1934', O. O. Stanchfield, Observations growing out of India, Burma and Ceylon visit 4 November 1930–25 February 1931.
249. Ibid.
250. Cf. also the discussion in Chapter 3.
251. KFYA, IWI, Box 51, Folder 'India World Service 1943', Pamphlet 'Post-War Policy Study. India Burma and Ceylon'.

2 'Make them pure, fit and brotherly!': The Indian YMCA's welfare work for railwaymen and soldiers (*c*. 1904–1945)

1. *Young Men of India*, 41, no. 6 (1929): 313.
2. Hobbs, *Indian Y.M.C.A. and Politics*, 11. Cf. also BL/APAC/IOR/L/PJ/6/1936 'Political Activities of the YMCA in India: Reply to Criticism etc.', File 425.
3. Holt, *A Study of the Y.M.C.A. of India, Burma & Ceylon*, 8.

4. Sepoy (from Urdu/Persian *sipāhī* = soldier) was the term used in imperial military nomenclature for South Asian infantry soldiers (cavalry soldiers were sometimes also referred to as 'Sowar', i.e. *savār* = horsemen). From the last third of the nineteenth century, these soldiers were mostly recruited on the basis of the so-called martial race theory from among selected communities such as the Sikhs, Pathans, Rajputs, Dogras as well as Gurkhas from Nepal. Cf. Kaushik Roy, 'Race and Recruitment in the Indian Army: 1880–1918', *Modern Asian Studies* 47, no. 4 (2013): 1310–47; Heather Streets, *Martial Races: The Military, Race and Masculinity in British Imperial Culture, 1857–1914* (Manchester: Manchester University Press, 2004).

5. Noteworthy recent efforts to come up with less Eurocentric histories of the Great War include Thierry Di Costanzo, 'Memory and History of the Great(er) War and India: From a National-Imperial to a More Global Perspective', *E-Rea. Revue Électronique d'études Sur Le Monde Anglophone* 14, no. 2 (2017): 1–18; Michael S. Neiberg, *Fighting the Great War: A Global History* (Cambridge, MA: Harvard University Press, 2006); Hew Strachan, 'The First World War as a Global War', *First World War Studies* 1, no. 1 (2010): 3–14; William Kelleher Storey, *The First World War: A Concise Global History* (New York: Rowman & Littlefield, 2010); Heike Liebau, Katrin Bromber, Katharina Lange, Dyala Hamzah and Ravi Ahuja, eds, *The World in World Wars: Experiences, Perceptions and Perspectives from Africa and Asia* (Leiden: Brill, 2010); Santanu Das, ed., *Race, Empire and First World War Writing* (Cambridge: Cambridge University Press, 2011); Robert Gerwarth Erez Manela, eds, *Empires at War, 1911–1923: The Greater War* (Oxford: Oxford University Press, 2014); Heather Streets-Salter, *World War One in Southeast Asia: Colonialism and Anti-Colonialism in an Era of Global Conflict* (Cambridge: Cambridge University Press, 2017).

6. Abigail Greene, 'Humanitarianism in Its Nineteenth Century Context: Religious, Gendered, National', *The Historical Journal* 57, no. 4 (2014): 1157–75.

7. This topic has garnered a lot of scholarly interest in the past decade. Cf. Bruno Cabanes, *The Great War and the Origins of Humanitarianism, 1918–1924* (Cambridge: Cambridge University Press, 2014); Heather Jones, 'International or Transnational? Humanitarian Action during the First World War', *European Review of History* 16, no. 5 (2009): 697–713; Barnett, *Empire of Humanity*; Davide Rodogno, *Against Massacre: Humanitarian Interventions in the Ottoman Empire, 1815–1914* (Princeton: Princeton University Press, 2012); Paulmann, 'Conjunctures in the History of International Humanitarianism Aid during the Twentieth Century'; Johannes Paulmann, ed., *Dilemmas of Humanitarian Aid in the Twentieth Century* (Oxford: Oxford University Press, 2016).

8. There is by now copious literature on the long-neglected group of such 'marginal whites' in British India. Cf., for instance, Satoshi Mizutani, *The Meaning of White: Race, Class, and the Domiciled Community in British India, 1858–1930* (Oxford: Oxford University Press, 2011); Harald Fischer-Tiné, *Low and Licentious Europeans: Race, Class, and 'White Subalternity' in Colonial India* (New Delhi: Orient BlackSwan, 2009); Fischer-Tiné, 'The Making of a "Ruling Race": Defining and Defending Whiteness in Colonial India'; Sarmistha De, *Marginal Europeans in Colonial India, 1860–1920* (Kolkata: Thema, 2008); Laura Bear, *Lines of the Nation: Indian Railway Workers, Bureaucracy and the Intimate Historical Self* (New York: Columbia University Press, 2007); David Arnold, 'White Colonization and Labour in Colonial India', *Journal of Imperial and Commonwealth*

History 11, no. 2 (1983): 133–58; Erica Wald, 'Health, Discipline and Appropriate Behaviour: The Body of the Soldier and Space of the Cantonment', *Modern Asian Studies* 46, no. 4 (2012): 815–56; Sam Goodman, 'Spaces of Intemperance & the British Raj 1860–1920', *The Journal of Imperial and Commonwealth History* 48, no. 4 (2020): 591–618.

9. Harald Fischer-Tiné, 'Englands interne Zivilisationsmission: Arbeitshäuser für Europäer im kolonialen Indien (ca. 1860–1914)', in *Zivilisierungsmissionen: Imperiale Weltverbesserung seit dem 18. Jahrhundert*, ed. Boris Barth and Jürgen Osterhammel (Konstanz: UVK, 2005), 169–99.
10. We will return to this trope in Chapter 4, in our discussion of the Indian YMCA's boys work.
11. B. R. Barber, *The Second City of the British Empire* (New York: Foreign Department International Committee, s.a. [1912]), 5.
12. Y.M.C.A., Indian National Council, *A Study of the Conditions and Needs of European Railway Men in India: Being the Report to the Indian National Council of the Railway Department Secretary's Investigations Preliminary to Inauguration of the Railway Y.M.C.A Work, Etc.* (Calcutta: Baptist Mission Press, s.a. [1905]), 1.
13. A related programme also brought up very similar arguments: the so-called Eurasian work that exclusively targeted the Anglo-Indian mixed-race community in Bombay, Madras and Calcutta. Cf. David, *The YMCA and the Making*, 234–6.
14. Y.M.C.A., Indian National Council, *A Study of the Conditions and Needs of European Railway Men in India*, 9.
15. KFYA, IWI, Box 89, Folder 'Railroad Work, Annual Reports 1906–1910', *Railway Young Men's Christian Association, Jamalpur. Annual Report 1910*, s.l. s.a. [1910], 4.
16. Y.M.C.A., Indian National Council, *A Study of the Conditions and Needs of European Railway Men*, 24–5.
17. Y.M.C.A., Indian National Council, *A Year's Progress in the Inauguration of the Work of the Railway Young Men's Christian Association in India Etc.* (Calcutta: Baptist Mission Press, 1907).
18. Ian Kerr, *Engines of Change: The Railroads That Made India* (New Delhi: Orient Blackswan, 2007), 90.
19. For a helpful overview of the social history of Jamalpur during the colonial period cf. Nitin Sinha, 'Entering the Black Hole: Between "Mini-England" and "Smell-Like Rotten Potato", the Railway Workshop Town of Jamalpur, 1860s–1940s', *Journal of South Asian History and Culture* 3, no. 3 (2012): 317–47.
20. Tomyns R. Browne, 'Locomotive Superintendent of the East Indian Railway, "An Appreciation"', in *A Year's Progress in the Inauguration of the Work of the Railway Young Men's Christian Association in India Etc.*, ed. Y.M.C.A., Indian National Council (Calcutta: Baptist Mission Press, 1907), 33.
21. Nitin Sinha, 'Railway Imperialism: A Small Town Perspective on Global History, Jamalpur, 1860s–1940s', *Comparativ* 25, no. 4 (2015): 23.
22. Ibid.
23. Dunderdale, *The YMCA in India*, 59.
24. The US secretaries working for the Indian YMCA could draw on the experience of the American Association, whose army work scheme commenced in 1895 and gained traction a few years later during the US brief war with Spain in 1898. Cf. Hopkins, *History of the YMCA in North America*, 452–3.
25. Latourette, *World Service*, 22.
26. David, *The YMCA and the Making*, 132; Eddy, *With Our Soldiers in France*, 23–4.

27. 'Report of the National Council of Young Men's Christian Associations of India and Ceylon to the Tenth National Convention at Calcutta, November 23–7, 1920' (Cuttack: Association Press, 1921), 25–6.
28. BL/APAC/IOR, Special Materials, Photo, 592/4(41).
29. 'Letters from the Front', *The Young Men of India* 27, no. 6 (1916): 2.
30. David, *The YMCA and the Making*, 137–8; cf. also BL/APAC/IOR/L/MIL/71/8577: 1915–21, Brochure: *The Y.M.C.A. with the British Army in India*, n.p., s.a. [1920]: 2.
31. 'Report of the National Council to the Tenth National Convention at Calcutta', 49.
32. Substantial aid was coming from the Australian YMCA that among other things fully financed three secretaries. Cf. Y.M.C.A., *National Budget 1917* (Calcutta: W. Newman, 1918), 2.
33. David, *The YMCA and the Making*, 104.
34. *The Statesman*, 13 April 1917.
35. Robert E. Upton, '"It Gives Us a Power and Strength Which We Do Not Possess": Martiality, Manliness, and India's Great War Enlistment Drive', *Modern Asian Studies* 52, no. 6 (2018): 1977–2012; Santanu Das, *India, Empire, and First World War Culture. Writings, Images, and Songs* (Cambridge: Cambridge University Press, 2018), 39–72.
36. BL/APAC/IOR/Mss Eur F178/11, S. K. Datta Papers, (B) YMCA1914–15, Bulletin No. 1, by E. C. Carter, 31 October 1914.
37. KFYA, IWI, Box 17, Folder 'India Correspondence and Reports Jan-March 1915', Letter from S. S. Day to the Army YMCA, Delhi, 13 January 1915.
38. Young Men's Christian Associations of India and Ceylon, *The Annual Report of the Ceylon Sub-Committee of the National Council for India and Ceylon 1914* (Colombo: Ceylon Observer Press, 1915), 2. For a similar argument cf. also George J. Fisher, 'The Influence of War upon Physical Training in the Young Men's Christian Association', *Physical Training* 15, no. 8 (1918): 340–3. The author claims that due to the physical programmes launched by the Y during the war in India, sports and play had 'broken down caste and introduced virility into a people whose religion opposed physical Development'. Fisher, 340.
39. KFYA, IWI, Box 8, Folder 'Annual and Quarterly Reports 1917 [Mc-Mil]', Report by D. F. McClelland for the Year ending 30 September 1917. For similar statements, cf. also D. F. McClelland 'Two Views of Y.M.C.A. Army Work', *The Young Men of India*, 28, no. 1 (1916): 27; 'Army Department: With the Expeditionary Forces', *The Young Men of India*, 28, no. 3 (1918): 167.
40. KFYA, IWI, Box 8, Folder 'Annual and Quarterly Reports 1917 [W]', Report by W. E. D. Ward for the Year ending 30 September 1917.
41. Cf. BL/APAC/IOR/L/MIL/71/8577: 1915–21, Collection 425, 'Grants to YMCA and Indian Soldier's Fund Committee for Provision of Huts, Furniture, etc. for Troops in France and Mesopotamia'.
42. 'Work in Hospitals and Convalescent Depots in India', *The Young Men of India* 27, no. 1 (1917): 12–13.
43. 'Work in Hospitals and Convalescent Depots in India'; and 'Army Department: In India', *The Young Men of India* 27, no. 6 (1917): 365–7.
44. SSCWH, YWCA of the U.S.A. Records, Box 321, Record Group 5/International Work/Newsletters F-N, 'News from the Foreign Field', October 1914 and January 1917; SSCWH, YWCA of the U.S.A. Records, 'Annual Report of the Foreign Department for the Year Ending 7 Feb 1917', Box 308, Minutes & Reports/Foreign Department 1907–17.

45. For the background, cf. Mahon Murphy, 'Prisoners of War and Civilian Internees Captured by British and Dominion Forces from the German Colonies during the First World War', unpublished PhD dissertation, London School of Economics, 2014.
46. KFYA, IWI, Box 11, Folder 'Annual and Quarterly Reports 1915 [B-G]', Annual Report ending September 1915 from H. Glunkler, YMCA Architect, at present Ahmednagar, prisoner of war camp, India. Ironically, there was also a YMCA worker among the prisoners. The German architect Hermann Glunkler had been a member of the *Christlicher Verein Junger Männer* in his home country before joining the Indian Y in 1913. Apparently, he continued to cooperate with British and American YMCA volunteers on the other side of the barbed wire fence, much to the annoyance of his more patriotically inclined fellow prisoners.
47. For background information from a military history perspective, cf. William Mitchinson, *The Territorials at War, 1914–16* (Houndmills: Palgrave Macmillan, 2014).
48. CRLSC, YMCA/K/2/7, Folder 'Reports', 'Work of the Y.M.C.A. for British and Indian Troops in India'; cf. also KFYA, IWI, Box 99, Young Men's Christian Association, *Territorials: The Bombay Y.M.C.A. Welcomes You to India*, Bombay, s.a. [1915?].
49. SCASC, Armed Forces Collection, typescript by Montagu F. Modder, 'In France, Egypt and India with the Red Triangle', 6.
50. J. Callan, 'Educational Work for British Soldiers', in *Young Men of India* 25, no. 9 (1914): 556–7.
51. BL/APAC/IOR/Mss Eur F178/11, S. K. Datta Papers, (B) YMCA 1914–15, Bulletin No. 9, Gardiner to E. C. Carter, 12 November 1914.
52. R. D. Whitehorn, 'Army Y.M.C.A. Work in India', *The Young Men of India* 27, no. 6 (1916): 327.
53. KFYA, IWI, Box 8, Folder 'Annual and Quarterly Reports 1917 [Mc-Mil]', Report by D. F. McClelland for the Year ending 30 September 1917.
54. 'The Association and the War', *The Young Men of India* 26, no. 1 (1915): 2.
55. Cf. also Paul Davenport, 'Doctrine, Practice and Masculinity: Physical Training in the British Army, 1939–1945', *Journal of War & Culture Studies* 12, no. 2 (2019): 158–9.
56. O. O. Stanchfield, 'Serving the Territorials in India', *The Foreign Mail Annual*, 1916, 5.
57. KFYA, IWI, Box 8, Folder 'India: Annual and Quarterly Reports', Report by W. E. D. Ward, September 1917.
58. E. C. Carter, ed., *In the Camps, Trenches & Prisons of Asia, Africa & Europe* (Oxford: Frederick Hall, 1916), 40; Whitehorn, 'Army Y.M.C.A. Work in India', 329; 'Army Department: In India', 165.
59. Eddy, *With Our Soldiers in France*, 78.
60. BL/APAC/IOR/Mss Eur F178/11, S. K. Datta Papers, (B) YMCA 1914–15, Bulletin No. 11, O. O. Stanchfield to E. C. Carter, 24 November 1914.
61. Ibid.
62. 'The Association and the War', 5.
63. K. T. Paul, *The British Connection with India* (London: Student Christian Movement, 1927), 111–12.
64. Carter, *In the Camps, Trenches & Prisons of Asia, Etc.*, 40; Stanchfield, 'Serving the Territorials in India', 6; Young Men's Christian Association Madras, *Twenty-Fifth Years' Service in Madras, 1914, Annual Report* (Madras: Methodist Publishing House, 1915), 21.
65. R. D. Whitehorn, 'With the Army in India', *The Young Men of India* 28, no. 2 (1917): 83. That religious propaganda, albeit in oblique and indirect ways, was

occasionally also directed at Indian sepoys is evident, cf. S. Perkask Singha, 'And We Break Caste Forever', *Association Men*, February 1918, 130–1.
66. Carter, *In the Camps, Trenches & Prisons of Asia, Etc.*, 42.
67. Ibid.
68. KFYA, IWI, Box 8, Folder 'India: Annual and Quarterly Reports', Report by A. L. Miller, September 1917.
69. As both Palestine and East Africa were less numerically significant and were not the main areas for the YMCA's war work, I will restrict the following analysis to the two main destinations for Indian troops: France and Mesopotamia. I also limit my discussion due to constraints of space.
70. Santanu Das, 'Introduction', in *Race, Empire and First World War Writing*, ed. Santanu Das (Cambridge: Cambridge University Press, 2011), 4–5.
71. Cf. Jeffrey C. Copeland and Yan Xu, eds, *The YMCA at War: Collaboration and Conflict during the World Wars* (Lanham, MD: Lexington Books, 2018). Cf. also Steven W. Pope, 'An Army of Athletes: Playing Fields, Battlefields, and the American Military Sporting Experience, 1890–1920', *Journal of Military History* 59, no. 3 (1995): 435–56; Jeffrey S. Reznick, *Healing the Nation: Soldiers and the Culture of Caregiving in Britain during the Great War* (Manchester: Manchester University Press, 2004), 17–41; Kenneth A. Steuer, *The American YMCA and Prisoner of War Diplomacy with the Central Powers during the First World War* (New York: Columbia University Press, 2009); Michael Snape, *God and the British Soldier: Religion and the British Army in the First and Second World Wars* (Abingdon: Routledge, 2005), 205–40; Mathew Lee Miller, *The American YMCA and Russian Culture: The Preservation and Expansion of Orthodox Christianity* (Lanham, MD: Lexington Books, 2013), 113–29; Tomáš Tlusty, 'The YMCA Organization and Its Physical Education and Sports Activities in Europe during the First World War', *Prace Naukowe Akademii Im. Jana Dlugosza w Czestochowie. Kultura Fizyczna* 14, no. 1 (2015): 27–44; T. Terret, 'American Sammys and French Poilus in the Great War: Sport, Masculinities and Vulnerability', *The International Journal of the History of Sport* 28, no. 3–4 (2011).
72. Copeland and Xu (eds), *The YMCA at War*. Indian soldiers are only very briefly mentioned in one chapter.
73. David, *The YMCA and the Making*, 135.
74. Cf. also BL/APAC/IOR/Mss Eur F178/11, S. K. Datta Papers, 'Y.M.C.A. War Work: correspondence, memoranda and printed material, including: Y.M.C.A. work with the Indian Army in France, 1914–15 etc.'.
75. KFYA, SF, Box 12, Folder 'Training 1898–1922', E. C. Carter to J. Mott, 26 September 1914.
76. Dunderdale, *The YMCA in India*, 59; Katherine Mayo, *'That Damn Y': A Record of Overseas Service* (Boston, MA: Houghton Mifflin, 1920), 9–12.
77. KFYA, IWI, Box 89, Folder 'India Reports 1912–1938', Extract of letter from France from J. Callan to E. C. Carter, 2 December 1914. Callan was soon replaced by S. K. Datta, one of the most distinguished Indian Christian leaders who would later become General Secretary of the Association (1919–27).
78. Eddy, *With Our Soldiers in France*, 92–3. Cf. also BL/APAC/IOR/L/MIL/71/8577: 1915–21, 'Outline of the Work of the Indian Y.M.C.A. in France from November 1914 to April 1920', [typescript, 15 pp]: 2. The fear that the Y's activities might create rumours of a planned mass conversion led the military authorities prohibit the use of notepaper headed with the red triangle. Cf. David Omissi,

'Introduction', in *Indian Voices of the Great War: Soldiers' Letters 1914–18*, ed. David Omissi (Gurgaon: Penguin Books, 2014), 14.
79. KFYA, SF, Box 12, Folder 'Training 1898–1922', Beauchamp Duff, General, C-in-C India, to J. Callan, 16 September 1914.
80. KFYA, SF, Box 12, Folder 'Training 1898–1922', J. Callan to E. C. Carter, 9 December 1914.
81. A few months after the armistice, similar 'leave clubs' were opened in Brussels and Cologne for Indian Officers serving in the Rhine Army.
82. David, *The YMCA and the Making*, 135.
83. KFYA, IWI, Box 89, Folder 'India Reports 1912–1938', Extract of letter from France from J. Callan to E. C. Carter, 2 December 1914.
84. Eddy, *With Our Soldiers in France*, 124.
85. KFYA, SF, Box 12, Folder 'Training, 1898–1922', Typescript by K. J. Saunders, 5 November 1915, 'A Year's Work of the Y.M.C.A., Indian Expeditionary Force', 5–6.
86. CRSC, YMCA/K/2/7, K. J. Saunders, *With the Indians in France: Being an Account of the Work of the Army Y.M.C.A of India with Indian Expedition Force A*.
87. The Indian YMCA's only service to British regiments in France consisted in furnishing Hindustani teachers to British officers for improving communication with their rank-and-file soldiers. Cf. National Council of the Young Men's Christian Associations of India and Ceylon, *The Red Triangle in the East* (Calcutta: B.M.P, s.a. [1910]), 28.
88. For an account of the operational history of the Indian expeditionary forces on the Western front, see Morton-Jack, *Indian Army on the Western Front*. There is also a growing literature on the South Asian soldiers' lived experience of the Great War in Europe. Cf., for instance, Shrabani Basu, 'Turbans in the Trenches: Indian Sepoys and Sowars on the Western Front during the Great War', in *Indian Soldiers in the First World War: Re-Visiting a Global Conflict*, ed. Ashutosh Kumar and Claude Markovits (Abingdon: Routledge, 2021), 11–40; Claude Markovits, *De l'Indus à La Somme: Les Indiens en France Pendant La Grande Guerre* (Paris: Éditions de la Maison des Sciences de l'Homme, 2019); Das, *India, Empire, and First World War Culture*; Shrabani Basu, *For King and Another Country: Indian Soldiers on the Western Front 1914–1918* (London: Bloomsbury, 2015); Gajendra Singh, 'Throwing Snowballs in France: Muslim Sipahis of the Indian Army and Sheikh Ahmad's Dream, 1915–1918', *Modern Asian Studies* 48, no. 4 (2014): 1024–67; David Omissi, 'Europe through Indian Eyes: Indian Soldiers Encounter England and France, 1914–1918', *The English Historical Review* 122, no. 496 (2007): 371–96.
89. BL/APAC/IOR/L/MIL/71/8577: 1915–21, 'Outline of the Work of the Indian Y.M.C.A. in France', 6. On the Indian Labour Corps in France cf. also Radhika Singha, *The Coolie's Great War: Indian Labour in a Global Conflict* (London: Hurst, 2020); Radhika Singha, 'The Short Career of the Indian Labour Corps in France, 1917–1919', *International Labor and Working-Class History* 87, no. 2 (2015): 27–62; Radhika Singha, 'The Recruiter's Eye on "the Primitive": To France – and Back – in the Indian Labour Corps, 1917–19', in *Other Combatants, Other Fronts: Competing Histories of the First World War*, ed. James E. Kitchen, Alisia Miller and Laura Rowe (Newcastle upon Tyne: Cambridge Scholars, 2011), 199–224.
90. *The Red Triangle in the East*, 30.
91. Dwight H. Ingram, 'Army Department: With the Expeditionary Forces', *The Young Men of India* 27, no. 7 (1917): 427.
92. Ibid.
93. 'Report of the National Council to the Tenth National Convention at Calcutta', 32.

94. Ingram, 'Army Department: With the Expeditionary Forces', 168.
95. For concise overviews of the Indian forces deployment in Mesopotamia, cf. Ross Anderson, 'Logistics of the Indian Expeditionary Force D in Mesopotamia: 1914–18', in *The Indian Army in the Two World Wars*, ed. Kaushik Roy (Leiden: Brill, 2012), 105–44; Kristian Coates-Ulrichsen, 'Learning the Hard Way: The Indian Army in Mesopotamia, 1914–1918', in *The British Army in India: Virtues and Necessity*, ed. Rob Jonson (Newcastle: Cambridge Scholars, 2014), 51–64.
96. Kenneth J. Saunders, *Impressions of Mesopotamia* (London: The Red Triangle Press, s.a.), 4.
97. National Council of the Young Men's Christian Associations of India and Ceylon, *The Red Triangle in the East*, 28.
98. [Carter], *In the Camps, Trenches & Prisons of Asia, etc.*, 31.
99. Conrad Hoffmann, 'Indians in the Prisoner-of-War Camps of Germany', *Young Men of India* 41, no. 3 (1929): 151–2.
100. Nadja Durbach, 'The Politics of Provisioning: Feeding South Asian Prisoners During the First World War', *War & Society* 37, no. 2 (2018): 81.
101. BL/APAC/IOR/L/PJ/6/8 1441, File 3230/16, Letter by E. C. Carter, National Secretary of the Indian Y.M.C.A., to the Under Secretary of State for India, 29 November 1916.
102. On this point, cf. Siddharta Dasgupta, 'From Victory to Defeat: The Indian Army in Mesopotamia, 1914–1916', in *Indian Soldiers in the First World War*, ed. Ashutosh Kumar and Claude Markovits (Abingdon: Routledge, 2021), 104–23; Roy, *Indian Army and the First World War*, 242–303; Nikolas Gardner, 'British Prestige and the Mesopotamia Campaign, 1914–1916', *The Historian* 77, no. 2 (2015): 269–89.
103. KFYA, IWI, Box 8, Folder 'India: Annual and Quarterly Reports', Report by W.E.D. Ward, September 1917.
104. BL/APAC/IOR/L/PJ/6/8 1441, File 5130/16, 'Y.M.C.A. Workers for Mesopotamia and India: Proposed Special Form of Application.'
105. Ibid.
106. The distrust authorities felt about potential German connections was so deep-seated that YMCA director K. T. Paul did not dare to employ YMCA secretary Waldo H. Heinrichs any longer in India because of his German name and ancestry. He was subsequently transferred to Europe. Cf. YDSP, Rec. Gr. 115, Series I, Waldo Huntley Heinrichs Papers, Box 7, Folder 61, Diaries 1916, entry for 4 July 1916.
107. BL/APAC/IOR/L/PJ/6/8 1441, File 3230/16, Letter by E. C. Carter, National Secretary of the I.Y.M.C.A., to the Under Secretary of State for India, 29 November 1916.
108. BL/APAC/IOR/L/PJ/6/1475, 'US Missionaries: Applications to proceed to India; suspicion regarding the pacifist tendencies of Mr H. A. Walter, engaged in YMCA work at Lahore', January–November 1917. Walter, however, did not engage in pacifist agitation but in the study of the local Islamic Ahmadiyya sect, on which he published a book in the YMCA's 'The Religious Life of India' series shortly before his death during the influenza epidemic of 1918. Howard Arnold Walter, *The Ahmadiya Movement* (Calcutta: Association Press, 1918). Cf. also Fischer-Tiné, 'Third-Stream Orientalism', 664.
109. Duane Spencer Hatch, 'Working with D. Spencer "Chick" Hatch, Part I – India: Along the Afghan Frontier', *The Quill and Scroll* 68, no. 4 (1962): 15.
110. According to the official history of the Association, it was thus named because it was run by a 'unit of Princeton men who, with Harvard units, had volunteered for Mesopotamia long before America entered the war'. William Howard Taft

and Frederick Morgan Harris, eds, *Service with Fighting Men: An Account of the Work of the American Young Men's Christian Associations in the World War*, vol. 2 (New York: Association Press, 1922), 403–4. Cf. also YDSP, Rec. Gr. 115, Series I, Waldo Huntley Heinrichs Papers, Box 7, Folder 61, Diaries 1916, entry for 11 September 1916.
111. National Council of the Young Men's Christian Associations of India and Ceylon, *The Red Triangle in the East*, 28; cf. also Leonard A. Dixon, 'The Red Triangle in Mesopotamia, 1916', *The Young Men of India* 28, no. 2 (1917): 65–6.
112. Kaushik Roy, *The Army in British India: From Colonial Warfare to Total War 1857–1947* (London: Bloomsbury, 2012), 86.
113. Cf., for instance, Leonard A. Dixon, '1918 in Mesopotamia', *The Young Men of India* 29, no. 2 (1919): 84.
114. The reference here is to Indian author Mulk Raj Anand's celebrated war novel; Mulk Raj Anand, *Across the Black Waters* (London: Jonathan Cape, 1940). The title alludes to the fact that service overseas was regarded as ritually polluting by many upper-caste Hindu soldiers.
115. KFYA, IWI, Box 13, Folder 'India: Printed Matters', J. G. H., A Night in Camp with the Indian Expeditionary Force, s.a. Calcutta: The Army Y.M.C.A., 5. [8 p., brochure probably published in [1916].
116. '10,000,000 Feet of Films for Army Camps', *Association Men*, November 1917, 202.
117. Emma Hanna, 'Putting the Moral into Morale: YMCA Cinemas on the Western Front, 1914–1918', *Historical Journal of Film, Radio and Television* 35, no. 4 (2015): 615–30.
118. According to Indian historian Kaushik Roy, it was a conscious British recruitment strategy to focus on illiterate agricultural groups for military service, as it was assumed that simple Indian villagers were docile and free of political ambitions. Cf. Roy, 'Race and Recruitment'.
119. The history of everyday technology in South Asia has recently attracted the interest of historians; cf., for instance, David Arnold, *Everyday Technology: Machines and the Making of India's Modernity* (Chicago, IL: University of Chicago Press, 2013). Specifically, on the history of the gramophone in India, cf. Bradley Shope, *American Popular Music and Britain's Raj* (Rochester: Rochester University Press, 2016), 10–3; Christina Lubinski, 'Die nationalistische Note. Westliche Grammophone und indischer Nationalismus vor dem ersten Weltkrieg', *Historische Anthropologie* 26, no. 1 (2016): 27–49. The transformation of film from an elite to a mass medium is touched upon in Sudhir Mahadevan, *A Very Old Machine: The Many Origins of Cinema in India* (Albany: State University of New York Press, 2015); Dass, *Outside the Lettered City*.
120. Lisa Trivedi, 'Visually Mapping the "Nation": Swadeshi Politics in Nationalist India, 1920–1930', *Journal of Asian Studies* 62, no. 1 (2003): 11–41.
121. Cf. also Das, *India, Empire, and First World War Culture*, 206–15.
122. Eddy, *With Our Soldiers in France*, 95.
123. BL/APAC/IOR/L/MIL/71/8577: 1915–21, 'Outline of the Work of the Indian Y.M.C.A. in France', 12; 'Report of the National Council to the Tenth National Convention at Calcutta', 31.
124. BL/APAC/IOR/L/MIL/71/8577: 1915–21, 'Outline of the Work of the Indian Y.M.C.A. in France', 12–13.
125. For the popularity of French classes cf. the brochure CRSC, YMCA/K/2/7, 'The Army YMCA of India with the Indian Expeditionary Force'.

126. Eddy, *With Our Soldiers in France*, 100–1.
127. Gajendra Singh, 'Mirrors of Violence: Interracial Sex, Colonial Anxieties and Disciplining the Body of the Indian Soldier during the First World War', in *Anxieties, Fear and Panic in Colonial Settings: Empires on the Verge of a Nervous Breakdown*, ed. Harald Fischer-Tiné (Basingstoke: Palgrave Macmillan, 2016), 170–97; Gajendra Singh, *The Testimonies of Indian Soldiers and the Two World Wars: Between Self and Sepoy* (London: Bloomsbury, 2014), 46–9, 98 and 116; David Omissi, ed., *Indian Voices of the Great War: Soldiers Letters 1914–18* (Gurgaon: Penguin Books, 2014), 113–14, 118–19 and 225–6. Cf. also Santanu Das, *Touch and Intimacy in First World War Literature* (Cambridge: Cambridge University Press, 2006).
128. KFYA, SF, Box 12, Folder 'Training 1898–1922', J. Callan to E. C. Carter, 9 December 1914.
129. CRLSC, YMCA/K/2/7, Joseph Callan, to A. K. Yapp, 17 November 1914.
130. BL/APAC/IOR/Mss Eur F178/11, S. K. Datta Papers (B) YMCA, 1914–15, Bulletin No. 11, J. Callan to E. C. Carter, 13 November 1914.
131. Dixon, '1918 in Mesopotamia', 84; National Council of the Young Men's Christian Associations of India and Ceylon, *The Red Triangle in the East*, 8–9.
132. Cf. Nico Slate, *Colored Cosmopolitanism: The Shared Struggle for Freedom in the United States and India* (Cambridge, MA: Harvard University Press, 2012), 21–5.
133. 'Report of the National Council to the Tenth National Convention at Calcutta', 38.
134. Cf., for instance, Alaka Atreva Chudal, 'Story-Telling in Prison: Oral Performance of a Gorkha Prisoner of World War I', *European Bulletin of Himalaya Research*, no. 54 (2020): 17.
135. Saunders, *Impressions of Mesopotamia*, 5.
136. Dixon, '1918 in Mesopotamia', 84.
137. Ibid. Similar literacy campaigns were successfully undertaken by YMCA workers targeting the Chinese Labour Corps in France. Cf. Yurou Zhong, 'Script Crisis and Literary Modernity in China, 1916–1958', unpublished PhD dissertation, New York, Columbia University, 2014, 25–74.
138. Eddy, *With Our Soldiers in France*, 91.
139. Ibid.
140. Whitehorn, 'With the Army in India', 82.
141. Ibid.
142. Dixon, '1918 in Mesopotamia', 84.
143. CRSC, YMCA/K/2/7, W. H. Moore, 'The Indian Y.M.C.A. Army Work' (=Y.M.C.A. Campaign Leaflet 13 b).
144. S. P. Singha, 'Among Indian Troops', *The Young Men of India* 29, no. 2 (1919): 91.
145. Tammy Proctor, *Civilians in a World War, 1914–1918* (New York: New York University Press, 2010).
146. As discussed in the introduction, Karen Phoenix has coined the interesting concept of the 'Y-space', as a social space that was 'in line with progressive US viewpoints and cultural standards' and hence could constitute an 'alternative to empire' in certain constellations. Cf. Phoenix, 'A Social Gospel for India', 2014, 203–4.
147. YDSP, Rec. Gr. 115, Series I, Waldo Huntley Heinrichs Papers, Box 7, Folder 61, 'Diaries 1916', entry for 14 January 1916.
148. KFYA, IWI, Box 17, Folder 'India: Correspondence and Reports, Jan–March 1915', Letter from E. C. Carter to John R. Mott, 18 February 1915.

149. Michael G. Thompson, *For God and Globe: Christian Internationalism in the United States between the Great War and the Cold War* (Ithaca, NY: Cornell University Press, 2015), 27–46.
150. J. N. Farquhar, 'Impressions of War Time India', *Foreign Mail* 25, no. 4 (July–August 1918): 25.
151. BL/APAC/IOR/L/PJ/6/8 1441, File 3230/16, Letter by E. C. Carter, National Secy. of the Indian Y.M.C.A., to the Under Secretary of State for India', 29 November 1916.
152. David Henry Anthony III, *Max Yergan: Race Man, Internationalist, Cold Warrior* (New York: New York University Press, 2006), 22.
153. Taft and Harris, *Service with Fighting Men*, 2:405.
154. Eddy, *With Our Soldiers in France*, 78.
155. L. C. Haworth, 'When Tommy Atkins Lands in India', in *Camps, Trenches & Prisons of Asia*, February 1918, 430; [Carter], *In the Camps, Trenches & Prisons of Asia, Etc.*, 46–7.
156. KFYA, IWI, Box 99, Young Men's Christian Association, Bombay, Territorials: The Bombay Y.M.C.A. Welcomes you to India, Bombay s.a. [1915?].
157. KFYA, IWI, Box 8, Folder 'Annual and Quarterly Reports 1917 [Mc-Mil]', Report by D. F. McClelland for the Year ending 30 September 1917.
158. KFYA, IWI, Box 99, Young Men's Christian Association, Bombay, Territorials: The Bombay Y.M.C.A. Welcomes you to India, Bombay s.a. [1915?]: 16.
159. Cf., for instance, Wald, *Vice in the Barracks*; Douglas Peers, 'Privates Off Parade: Regimenting Sexuality in the Nineteenth-Century Indian Empire', *The International History Review* 20, no. 4 (1998): 824–54; Douglas Peers, 'State, Power and Colonialism', in *India and the British Empire*, eds, Douglas Peers and Nandini Gooptu (Oxford: Oxford University Press, 2012), 16–43.; Harald Fischer-Tiné, 'Liquid Boundaries: Race, Class and Alcohol in Colonial India', in *A History of Alcohol and Drugs in Modern South Asia: Intoxicating Affairs*, ed. Harald Fischer-Tiné (Abingdon: Routledge, 2014), 89–115. When it comes to the First World War, the bulk of the literature focuses not on European troops but on parallel anxieties regarding the colonial soldiery deployed in Europe. Cf., for instance, Singh, 'Mirrors of Violence'; Christian Koller, 'The Recruitment of Colonial Troops in Africa and Asia and Their Deployment in Europe during the First World War', *Immigrants and Minorities* 26, no. 1–2 (2008): 111–33; Philippa Levine, 'Battle Colors: Race, Sex, and Colonial Soldiery in World War I', *Journal of Women's History* 9, no. 4 (1998): 104–30.
160. KFYA, IWI, Box 99, Young Men's Christian Association, Territorials: The Bombay Y.M.C.A. Welcomes You to India, Bombay, undated [1915?]: 16.
161. Ibid., 12.
162. Ibid.
163. Ibid., 14.
164. Ibid. Ella Wilcox's poem was widely used for similar purposes during the war on the fronts. Thus, for example, it was shown in the Canadian anti-vice film *Whatever a Man Soweth* (1917). In this film, cf. also Laura Doan, 'Sex, Education and the Great War Soldier: A Queer Analysis of the Practice of "Hetero" Sex', *Journal of British Studies* 51, no. 3 (2012): 641–63.
165. KFYA, IWI, Box 99, Young Men's Christian Association, Territorials: The Bombay Y.M.C.A. Welcomes You to India, Bombay undated [1915?]: 13.
166. Arthur K. Yapp, *The Romance of the Red Triangle: The Story of the Coming of the Red Triangle and the Service Rendered by the Y.M.C.A. to the Sailors and Soldiers of the British Empire* (London: Hodder and Stoughton, 1918), 164–5.

167. Singha, 'The Recruiter's Eye on "the Primitive"', 213.
168. For the role of racialism in the American YMCA, cf. Mjagkij, *Light in the Darkness: African Americans and the YMCA, 1852–1946*. For racism targeted at Afro-American soldiers in the US military during the First World War, cf. Mjagkij, 86–100; Chad Williams, *Torchbearers of Democracy: African American Soldiers in the World War I Era* (Chapel Hill: University of North Carolina Press, 2010), 115–16.
169. On Hatch cf. Chapter 5, and Harald Fischer-Tiné, 'The YMCA and Low-Modernist Rural Development in South Asia, c. 1922–1957', *Past & Present* 240, no. 1 (2018): 193–234.
170. Hatch, 'Working with D. Spencer "Chick" Hatch, Part I', 20.
171. Hatch, 15.
172. The Anglo-Indian term 'pucca sahib' was used to refer to a colonizer living up to the ideal of a 'real master', one who embodied imperial authority.
173. Pith helmet.
174. Hatch, 'Beyond the Ends of the Roads', 113.
175. Hindi/Urdu sentence. It would roughly translate as 'Go fetch some water, quick!'
176. Cf. Hatch, 'Working with D. Spencer "Chick" Hatch, Part I', 14–15 and 18.
177. UATSHC, Box 3, unpublished Typescript, Hatch, 'Beyond the End of the Road: Legs for Knowledge', s.a. [c. 1962].
178. Akbar S. Ahmed, *Resistance and Control in Pakistan*, Revised (London: Routledge, 2004), 33–4.
179. Henry Schwarz, *Constructing the Criminal Tribe in India: Acting Like a Thief* (Malden, MA: Wiley-Blackwell, 2010); Mark Brown, *Penal Power and Colonial Rule* (Abingdon: Routledge, 2014), 126–90. On British perceptions of North-West-Frontier tribes, cf. Kate Imy, 'Kidnapping and a "Confirmed Sodomite": An Intimate Enemy on the Northwest Frontier of India, 1915–1925', *Twentieth Century British History* 28, no. 1 (2016): 29–56. Especially on the Mahsuds, cf., for instance, R. B. J. Bruce, *Notes on the Dera Ghazi Khan District and Its Border Tribes* (Lahore: Government Printing Press, 1870).
180. Hatch, 'Working with D. Spencer "Chick" Hatch, Part I', 20.
181. Ibid., 18.
182. 'Beyond the Ends of the Roads', 92.
183. Cf., for instance, S. J. Harrison, 'Skulls and Scientific Collecting in the Victorian Military: Keeping the Enemy Dead in British Frontier Warfare', *Comparative Studies in Societies and History* 50, no. 1 (2008): 285–303. Cf. also Kim Wagner, *The Skull of Alum Bheg: The Life and Death of a Rebel of 1857* (New York: Oxford University Press, 2018), 191–224.
184. For a brief discussion of the historical trajectories of such prejudices, cf. Valerie Anderson, *Race and Power in British India: Anglo-Indians, Class and Identity in the Nineteenth Century* (London: Bloomsbury Academic, 2020), 152–4; Lionel Caplan, 'Iconographies of Anglo-Indian Women: Gender Constructs and Contrasts in a Changing Society', *Modern Asian Studies* 34, no. 4 (2000): 863–92.
185. 'Half-caste' was a widespread pejorative term used by the British in India to denote the mixed-race community of British India that was also popularized by contemporary fiction. Cf. Kiran Mascarenhas, 'The Half-Caste: A Half-Told Tale', *Women's Writing* 20, no. 3 (2013): 344–57.
186. YDSP, Rec. Gr. 115, Series I, Waldo Huntley Heinrichs Papers, Box 7, Folder 61, Diaries 1916, entry for 14 February 1916.

187. Eddy, *With Our Soldiers in France*, 95–6. The locus classicus for the articulation of such stereotypes is George MacMunn, *The Martial Races of India* (London: Sampson Low, 1933). Cf. also David Omissi, 'Martial Races: Ethnicity and Security in Colonial India 1858–1939', *War & Society* 9, no. 1 (1999): 1–27. For an exemplary in-depth analysis of the popular colonial clichés regarding the Gurkhas, cf. Lionel Caplan, *Warrior Gentlemen: Gurkhas in the Western Imagination* (Providence: Berghahn Books, 1995). On the construction of the Sikhs as 'belligerent', cf. the classic Richard Fox, *Lions of the Punjab: Culture in the Making* (Berkeley: University of California Press, 1985).
188. KFYA, IWI, Box 8, Folder 'India: Annual and Quarterly Reports', Report by A. L. Miller, September 1917.
189. BL/APAC/IOR/L/MIL/71/8577: 1915–1921, Collection 425, 'Grants to YMCA and Indian Soldier's Fund Committee for provision of huts, furniture, etc. for troops in France and Mesopotamia'.
190. 'Twelfth National Convention of Young Men's Christian Associations of India, Burma and Ceylon and Report of National Council, 1924–26' (Calcutta, 1927), 9–10.
191. 'Twelfth National Convention Report 1924–26', 50. The Y's remaining army centres were Nowshera, Risalpur, Jubbulpore, Trimulgherry and the Wellington and Ronaldshay Huts in Calcutta. The centre in Bangalore still existed in 1926 but was closed down soon afterwards.
192. Peter Grant, *Philanthropy and Voluntary Action in the First World War* (Abingdon: Routledge, 2014), 168–72.
193. Eric Shepherd, 'Service Institutes and Philanthropic Bodies', *Royal United Services Institution Journal* 73, no. 489 (1928): 135–37; Donald Anderson, 'Navy, Army, and Air Force Institutes in War and Peace', *Royal United Services Institution Journal* 85, no. 537 (1940): 64–72.
194. 'Twelfth National Convention Report 1924–26', 50.
195. Ibid., 51.
196. If not indicated otherwise, the following is based on National Council of the KFYA, IWI, Box 72, YMCA, India, Burma and Ceylon, 'Report on the War Emergency Service', and David, *The YMCA and the Making*, 327–38.
197. 'Report on the War Emergency Service', 25.
198. Ibid.
199. D. F. McClelland, 'Report of the National General Secretary', *Young Men of India* 57, no. 5–6 (1945): 74.
200. Dunderdale, *The YMCA in India*, 77–8.
201. KFYA, IWI, Box 96, 'The Recreation Hut for Allied Forces at the Y.M.C.A. College of Physical Education Saidapet'.
202. KFYA, IWI, Box 63, File 'P. M. Joseph, A Short Report on the Y.M.C.A. College of Physical Education at Saidapet, s.a. [1947/48]'.
203. Roy, *Indian Army and the First World War*, 359.
204. National Council of the Young Men's Christian Associations of India and Ceylon, *The Red Triangle in the East*, 25.
205. KFYA, IWI, Box 17, Folder 'India: Correspondence and Reports, Jan–March 1915', Letter from E. C. Carter to John R. Mott, 18 February 1915.
206. Eddy, *With Our Soldiers in France*, 92.
207. KFYA, SF, Box 12, Folder 'Training 1898–1922', J. Callan to E. C. Carter, 9 December 1914.
208. Singha, 'Among Indian Troops', 90.

209. KFYA, SF, Box 12, Folder 'Training, 1898–1922', 'A Year's Work of the Y.M.C.A., Indian Expeditionary Force'. Typescript by K. J. Saunders, 5 November 1915, 5.

3 'Physical ministry': The Indian YMCA's sports and physical education programmes (*c.* 1900–1950)

1. The concept of 'sportization' or 'sportification' goes back to the work of Norbert Elias, who used it to describe the process through which popular games and other physical contests were transformed by the development of rules and norms, and by changing the definitions of the tolerable limits of violence. Cf. Norbert Elias and Eric Dunning, *Quest for Excitement: Sport and Leisure in the Civilising Process* (Dublin: Dublin University Press, 2008).
2. Cf. Laurent Dubois, 'Diffusion and Empire', in *The Oxford Handbook of Sport History*, ed. Robert Edelman and Wayne Wilson (New York: Oxford University Press, 2017), 171–9; Allen Guttman, *Games and Empires: Modern Sports and Cultural Imperialism* (New York: Columbia University Press, 1994); Brian Stoddart, 'Sport, Cultural Imperialism and Colonial Response in the British Empire', *Comparative Studies in Society and History* 30, no. 4 (1988): 649–73.
3. For an overview of the main arguments and literature, cf. Chris Valiotis, 'South Asia' in S. W. Pope and John Nauright (eds), *Routledge Companion to Sport History* (Abingdon: Routledge, 2010); see especially pp. 572–8.
4. Roy, 'International Utopia and National Discipline: Youth and Volunteer Movements in Interwar South Asia'; Arafaat Valiani, *Militant Publics in India: Physical Culture and Violence in the Making of a Modern Polity* (New York: Palgrave Macmillan, 2011), 35–48.
5. The work of Joseph Alter was path-breaking in this respect, as it pointed to the complex transnational processes at work in the reconfiguration of Yoga and various other physical activities. Cf. Joseph S. Alter, 'Yoga at the Fin de Siècle: Muscular Christianity with a Hindu Twist', in *Muscular Christianity in Colonial and Post-Colonial Worlds*, ed. John Mac Aloon (London: Routledge, 2008), 59–76; Joseph S. Alter, 'Physical Education, Sport and the Intersection and Articulation of "Modernities": The Hanuman Vyayam Prasarak Mandal', *Journal of the History of Sport* 24 (2007): 1156–71; Joseph S. Alter, 'Indian Clubs and Colonialism: Hindu Masculinity and Muscular Christianity', *Comparative Studies in Society and History* 46 no. 3 (2004): 497–534. Very recently, Canadian historian Patricia Vertinsky and her student Aishwarya Ramachandran have started working on the role of the YMCA. Cf. Patricia Vertinsky and Aishwarya Ramachandran, 'Imperial Benevolence and Emancipatory Discourses: Harry Crowe Buck and Charles Harold McCloy Take the "Y" to India and China in the Early Decades of the Twentieth Century', in *Critical Reflections on Physical Culture on the Edges of Empire*, ed. F. J. Cleophas (Cape Town: Sun Press, 2021), 101–11.
6. Cf. for example, Mandala, 'Colonialism, Education, and the Spatial Dimension of Play'; Basudhita Basu, 'Sports Education in Colonial Bengal: A Double-Edged Sword', *South Asia Research* 38, no. 3 (2018): 268–86; Sudipa Topdar, 'The Corporeal Empire: Physical Education and Politicising Children's Bodies in Late Colonial Bengal', *Gender & History* 29, no. 1 (2017): 176–97; James A. Mangan, *The Games Ethic and Imperialism: Aspects of the Diffusion of an Ideal* (London: Frank Cass, 1998). Cf. especially 121–41.

7. See, for instance, the special issue of *The International Journal of the History of Sport* 28 (2011) devoted to American imperialism in the realm of sports.
8. Mark Dyreson, 'Prologue – the Paradoxes of Imitation and Resistance: The Origins of an American Empire of Sports', *The International Journal of the History of Sport* 28 (2011): 2415–20.
9. Sebastian Conrad, *What Is Global History?* (Princeton, NJ: Princeton University Press, 2017), 97. Cf. also Bayly, *The Birth of the Modern World*.
10. Cf. Babli Sinha, 'Empire Films and the Dissemination of Americanism in Colonial India', *South Asian History and Culture* 2 (2011): 140–56; Bradley Shope, 'The Public Consumption of Western Music in Colonial India: From Imperialist Exclusivity to Global Receptivity', *South Asia Journal of South Asian Studies* 31 (2008): 271–89; Arnold, *Everyday Technology: Machines and the Making of India's Modernity*, 152–3. For a systematic articulation of this argument, cf. also Arnold, 'Globalization and Contingent Colonialism'.
11. James Burns, 'Excessive Americanisms: Hollywood in the British Empire, 1918–1930', *Britain in the World* 7, no. 2 (2014): 196–211.
12. A. G. Noehren, 'Official Report of the Director of Physical Education to the Educational Department, Government of Bombay 1927–28' (Bombay: Tutorial Press, 1928), 21.
13. John H. Gray, 'India's Physical Education: What Shall It Be?', *Vyayam*, 1930, 7. Cf. also Carey A. Watt, 'Cultural Exchange, Appropriation and Physical Culture: Strongman Eugen Sandow in Colonial India, 1904–1905', *The International Journal of the History of Sport* 33, no. 16 (2016): 1921–42; Carey A. Watt, '"No Showy Muscles": The Scouting Frontiers: The Boy Scouts and The Global Dimension of Physical Culture and Bodily Health in Britain and Colonial India', in *Youth and the Scout Movement's First Century*, ed. Nelson R. Block and Tammy M. Proctor (Newcastle: Cambridge Scholars, 1999), 139–41; ;Mark Singleton, 'Transnational Exchange and the Genesis of Modern Postural Yoga', in *Yoga Traveling: Bodily Practice in Transcultural Perspective*, ed. Beatrix Hauser (Heidelberg: Springer, 2013), 42–44 and 47.
14. Cf., for instance, Tournès, *Américanisation: Une Histoire Mondiale*, 191–5; Gerald R. Gems, *The Athletic Crusade: Sport and American Cultural Imperialism* (Lincoln: University of Nebraska Press, 2006), 16–66; Stefan Huebner, 'The YMCA's Message, Public Health and Masculinity 1910s–1920s: Transnational Impacts of the Physical Education Programs in China, the Philippines, and Japan?', in *Spreading Protestant Modernity*, ed. Harald Fischer-Tiné, Stefan Huebner and Ian R. Tyrrell, 99–118; Guoqui Xu, 'Networking through the Y. The Role of the YMCA in China's Search for New National Identity and Internationalization', in *Networking the International System: Global Histories of International Organizations*, ed. Madeleine Herren (Cham: Springer, 2014), 133–47; Ceuster, 'Wholesome Education and Sound Leisure: The YMCA Sports Programme in Colonial Korea'; Chun Hsing, *Baptized in the Fire of Revolution: The American Social Gospel and the YMCA in China, 1919–1937* (Bethlehem, PA: Lehigh University Press, 1996).
15. William J. Baker, *Playing with God: Religion and Modern Sport* (Cambridge, MA: Harvard University Press, 2007), 42.
16. John Rosselli, 'The Self-Image of Effeteness: Physical Education and Nationalism in Nineteenth-Century Bengal', *Past and Present* 86 (1980): 221–48.
17. For a succinct discussion of colonial *clichés* on the Indian body, cf. Paul Dimeo, 'A Parcel of Dummies? Sport and the Body in Indian History', in *Confronting the*

Body: The Politics of Physicality in Colonial and Post-Colonial India, ed. James H. Mills and Satadru Sen (London: Anthem Press, 2004), 42–45.

18. There is a copious scholarship on nationalist (re-)masculinization programmes. Cf., for example, Conor Heffernan, 'What's Wrong with a Little Swinging? Indian Clubs as a Tool of Suppression and Rebellion in Post-Rebellion India', *The International Journal of History of Sport* 34, no. 7–8 (2017): 566–70; Arafaat Valiani, 'Recuperating Indian Masculinity: Mohandas Gandhi, War and the Indian Diaspora in South Africa (1899–1914)', *South Asian History and Culture* 5, no. 4 (2014): 505–20; Sikata Banerjee, *Make Me a Man!: Masculinity, Hinduism, and Nationalism in India* (New York: State University of New York Press, 2005), 43–74; Fischer-Tiné, 'Character Building and Manly Games', 432–55; Indira Chowdhury-Sengupta, *The Frail Hero and Virile History: Gender and the Politics of Culture in Colonial Bengal* (New Delhi: Oxford University Press, 1998); Mrinalini Sinha, *Colonial Masculinity: The 'Manly Englishman' and the 'Effeminate Bengali' in the Late Nineteenth Century* (Manchester: Manchester University Press, 1995).

19. Mark Singleton, *Yoga Body: The Origins of Modern Posture Practice* (Oxford: Oxford University Press, 2010); Mark Singleton, 'Yoga, Eugenics, and Spiritual Darwinism in the Early Twentieth Century', *International Journal of Hindu Studies* 11, no. 82 (2007): 125–46; Joseph S. Alter, 'Wrestling with the History of Yoga as Sport in Modern India', *India International Centre Quarterly* 44, no. 3–4 (2018): 252–65; Joseph S. Alter, 'Yoga at the Fin-de-Siècle: Muscular Christianity with a "Hindu" Twist', *The International Journal of the History of Sport* 23, no. 5 (2006): 759–76.

20. Cf. Namrata Ganneri, '"Pahalwan" Portraits: Manly Consumers of Physical Culture in Western India', *Tasveer Ghar – A Digital Archive of South Asian Popular Culture*. Available online: http://www.tasveergharindia.net/essay/pahalwan-portraits.html (accessed 11 August 2021); Joseph S. Alter, Moral Materialism: Sex and Masculinity in Modern India (Gurgaon: Penguin Books India, 2011), 87–117; Joseph S. Alter, 'Somatic Nationalism: Indian Wrestling and Militant Hinduism', *Modern Asian Studies* 28, no. 3 (1994): 557–88.

21. H. N. Wanchoo, *Studies in Indian Education* (Allahabad: Allahabad Law Journal Press, 1934), 116–18. [I am grateful to Carey A. Watt for sharing this source with me!]. Cf. also Ronojoy Sen, *A Nation at Play: A History of Sport in India* (New York: Columbia University Press, 2015), 94–9; Arafaat Valiani, 'Physical Training, Ethical Discipline, and Creative Violence: Zones of Self-Mastery in the Hindu Nationalist Movement', *Cultural Anthropology* 25, no. 1 (2010): 73–99.

22. Aishwarya Ramachandran and Conor Heffernan, 'A Distinctly Indian Body? K. V. Iyer and Physical Culture in 1930s India', *The International Journal of the History of Sport* 36, no. 12 (2019): 1054. Cf. also Carey A. Watt, 'Physical Culture and the Body in Colonial India, c. 1800–1947', in *The Routledge Handbook of the History of Colonialism in South Asia*, ed. Harald Fischer-Tiné and Maria Framke (Abingdon: Routledge, 2022), 345–58.

23. Cf., for instance, Ramachandra Guha, *A Corner of a Foreign Field: The Indian History of a British Sport* (London: Picador, 2003); Kausik Bandyopadhyay, *Scoring off the Field: Football Culture in Bengal, 1911–1980* (New Delhi: Routledge, 2011).

24. Souvik Naha, 'The Rise of Modern Sport and the Olympic Movement in India', in *The Routledge Handbook of Sport in Asia*, ed. Fan Hong and Lu Zhouxiang (Abingdon: Routledge, 2021), 127. This concept is prominent in the influential Allen Guttman, *Modern Sport and Cultural Imperialism* (New York: Columbia University Press, 1994). Cf. also Boria Majumdar, 'Tom Brown Goes Global: The "Brown"

Ethic in Colonial and Post-Colonial India', in *Muscular Christianity in Colonial and Post-Colonial Worlds*, ed. John Mac Aloon, Boria Majumdar and James A. Mangan (London: Routledge, 2008), 105–20.
25. Sebastian Conrad, 'Globalizing the Beautiful Body: Eugen Sandow, Bodybuilding, and the Ideal of Muscular Manliness at the Turn of the Twentieth Century', *Journal of World History* 32, no. 1 (2021): 95–125.
26. The term is borrowed from Conor Heffernan, 'Strength Peddlers: Eddie O'Callaghan and the Selling of Irish Strength', *Sport in History* 38, no. 1 (2018): 23–45.
27. On workout equipment, cf. Michael Anton Budd, *The Sculpture Machine: Physical Culture and Body Politics in the Age of Empire* (New York: New York University Press, 1997), 107. Prominent among the bestsellers of physical culture and fitness manuals that enjoyed a global circulation were, inter alia, Eugen Sandow, *Strength and How to Obtain It. With Anatomical Chart Illustrating the Exercises for Physical Development Etc.* (London: Gale & Polden, 1897); Bernarr MacFadden, *Macfadden's Physical Training: An Illustrated System of Exercise for the Development of Health, Strength and Beauty* (New York: MacFadden, 1900); J. P. Müller, *My System: 15 Minutes Work a Day for Health's Sake!* (London: Ewart, Seymour, 1905).
28. Watt, 'Cultural Exchange', 1926. On Eugen Sandow's global influence and his tour through India, cf. also Carey A. Watt, 'Physical Culture as "Natural Healing": Eugen Sandow's Campaign Against the Vices of Civilization c. 1890-1920', in *Global Anti-Vice Activism, 1890-1950: Fighting Drinks, Drugs, and 'Immorality'*, ed. Jessica Pliley, Harald Fischer-Tiné and Robert Kramm-Masaoka (Cambridge: Cambridge University Press, 2016), 74–99; David Waller, *The Perfect Man: The Muscular Life and Times of Eugen Sandow, Victorian Strongman* (London: Victorian Secrets, 2011), 196–203.
29. Shohei Sato, 'The Sportification of Judo: Global Convergence and Evolution', *Journal of Global History* 8, no. 2 (2013): 299–317.
30. Raúl Sánchez García, 'The Long-Term Development of Japanese Martial Arts', in *The Routledge Handbook of Sport in Asia*, ed. Fan Hong and Lu Zhouxiang (Abingdon: Routledge, 2021), 59.
31. John H. Gray cited in George F. Andrews, 'Physical Education in India', *The Journal of Health and Physical Education* 4, no. 2 (1933): 11. Cf. also P. R. Nisha, *Jumbos and Jumping Devils: A Social History of Indian Circus* (New Delhi: Oxford University Press, 2020), 59–79.
32. Lala Lajpat Rai, *The Problem of National Education in India* (London: Allen and Unwin, 1920), 153.
33. Ibid., 169.
34. In his monograph on national education, Lala Lajpat Rai quotes passages from the American bulletin *verbatim* over fifteen pages! Cf. Rai, 154–68.
35. Rai, 154. On Rai's activities in the United States, cf. Babli Sinha, 'Dissensus, Education and Lala Lajpat Rai's Encounter with W. E. B. DuBois', *South Asian History and Culture* 6, no. 4 (2015): 463–76.
36. Ray, 'Cosmopolitan Consumption: Domesticity, Cooking, and the Middle Class in Colonial India'; Kaushik Bhaumik, 'At Home in the World: Cinema and Cultures of the Young in Bombay in the 1920s', in *Towards a History of Consumption in South Asia*, ed. Douglas E. Haynes, Abigail McGowan, Tirthankar Roy and Haruka Yanagisawa (New Delhi: Oxford University Press, 2010), 136–54.
37. William J. Baker, 'Religion', in *The Routledge Companion to Sports History*, ed. S. W. Pope (London: Routledge, 2010), 217.
38. Baker, *Playing with God*, 50–5; Hopkins, *History of the YMCA*, 246–51.

39. Neal Garnham, 'Both Praying and Playing: "Muscular Christianity" and the YMCA in North-East County Durham.' *Journal of Social History* 35, no. 2 (2001): 397–407.
40. Cf. also Baker, 'To Pray or to Play?'; Erdozain, *The Problem of Pleasure*, 119–25 and 211–21.
41. Johnson, *History of YMCA Physical Education*, 52–5.
42. Steven J. Overmann, *The Protestant Ethic and the Spirit of Sport* (Macon, GA: Mercer University Press, 2011), 155–6. On Gulick's work at Springfield, cf. Clifford Putney, 'Luther Gulick: His Contributions to Springfield College, the YMCA, and "Muscular Christianity"', *Historical Journal of Massachusetts* 39, no. 1–2 (2011): 144–69.
43. David G. McComb, *Sports in World History* (New York: Routledge, 2004), 51–2; Putney, *Muscular Christianity*, 69–72; Keith Myerscough, 'The Game with no Name: The Invention of Basketball', *The International Journal of the History of Sport* 12, no. 1 (1995): 137–52.
44. Luther Halsey Gulick, 'The Efficient Life', *Physical Training* 13, (1913): 12.
45. Putney, *Muscular Christianity*, 71.
46. Luther H. Gulick, *A Philosophy of Play* (New York: Charles Scribner's & Sons, 1920), xiv.
47. Steven A. Riess, *City Games: The Evolution of American Urban Society and the Rise of Sports* (Urbana: University of Illinois Press, 1989); Cf. also Luther Halsey Gulick, 'Women's Program. Camp Fire Girls', *The Journal of Education* 78 (1913): 6–7. For the Indian YMCA's engagement with various Scouts and Guides groups, cf. also Chapter 4.
48. Putney, *Muscular Christianity*, 71; Tony Ladd and James A. Mathisen, *Muscular Christianity Evangelical Protestants and the Development of American Sport* (Grand Rapids, MI: Baker Books, 1999), 61–2.
49. Cf., for instance, Joseph Callan, 'Physical Illiteracy', *Young Men of India* 49 (1937): 179. On the philosophy of 'developing the whole man' through physical education as developed by Gulick and others in the 1880s and 1890s, cf. Gustav-Wrathall, *Take the Young Stranger by the Hand*, 22–30. The quote is on p. 24.
50. H. C. Buck, 'An Interpretation of Physical Education', *Young Men of India* 45, no. 10 (1933): 383–4.
51. David P. Setran, '"From Moral Aristocracy to Christian Social Democracy": The Transformation of Character Education in the Hi-Y, 1910–1940', *History of Education Quarterly* 45, no. 2 (2005): 217.
52. J. H. Gray, 'India's Physical Renaissance', *The Young Men of India* 25 (1914): 345.
53. Luther H. Gulick, 'Physical Education: A New Profession', in *Proceedings of the American Association for the Advancement of Physical Education at Its Fifth Annual Meeting Held in Cambridge and Boston, Mass. 4 and 5 April 1890* (Ithaca, NY: Andrus and Church, 1890), 65. Cf. also Roberta J. Park, 'Science, Service and the Professionalization of Physical Education, 1885–1905', *The International Journal of the History of Sport* 24 (2007): 1676–8.
54. Gulick, 'Physical Education: A New Profession', 65–6.
55. Gustav-Wrathall, *Take the Young Stranger by the Hand*, 5.
56. Putney, *Muscular Christianity*, 127.
57. Patricia Vertinsky and Aishwarya Ramachandran, eds, 'The "Y" Goes to India: Springfield College, Muscular Missionaries, and the Transnational Circulation of Physical Culture Practices', *Journal of Sport History* 46, no. 3 (2019): 364; Putney, *Muscular Christianity*, 131–2.

58. Aishwarya Ramachandran, 'Counterflows of Knowledge: The Transnational Circulation of Physical Culture Practices between India and the West during the Early 20th Century', unpublished MA thesis, Vancouver, University of British Columbia, 2019, 23. Cf. also M. D. David, 'The Missionary Muscular Culture in Modern India', in *Discoveries, Missionary Expansion, and Asian Cultures*, ed. T. R. De Souza (New Delhi: Concept Publishing, 1994), 195–209.
59. Laurence L. Doggett, 'The Training School and the Foreign Field', *The Association Seminar & Springfield Student* 17, no. 4 (1909): 131–43.
60. SCASC, 'A College for Leaders: A Springfield Institution serving the Youth of the World', promotional pamphlet, not paginated, s.a. [1935]. Cf. also Stefan Huebner, 'Muscular Christian Exchanges: Asian Sports Experts and the International YMCA Training School (1910s to 1930s)', in *Global Exchanges: Scholarships and Transnational Circulations in the Modern World*, ed. Ludovic Tournès and Giles Scott-Smith (New York: Berghahn, 2018), 97–112.
61. Laurence L. Doggett, *Man and a School: Pioneering in Higher Education* (New York: Association Press, 1943), 285.
62. 'An Athletic Club', *The Young Men of India* 1, no. 2 (1890): 65.
63. O. Kandaswamy Chetty, *50 Years with the Youth of Madras: The History of the Madras Y.M.C.A., 1890–1940* (Madras: Diocesan Press, 1940), 4.
64. KFYA, IWI, Box 1, Prospectus, 'A Building for the YMCA Madras', s.a. [c. 1896].
65. Gems, *The Athletic Crusade*, 20.
66. KFYA, IWI, Box 14, Folder 'Madras, MISC Reports 1893–1931', The Madras Young Men's Christian Association Quarterly Meeting [reprint of an article in the *Christian Patriot*, 2 October 1897].
67. Chetty, *50 Years with the Youth of Madras*, 9.
68. Baker, *Playing with God*, 50–5; Antonio Sotomayor, 'The Triangle of Empire: Sport, Religion, and Imperialism in Puerto Rico's YMCA, 1898–1926', *The Americas: A Quarterly Review of Latin American History* 74, no. 4 (2017): 481–512; Roberta J. Park, 'From La "bomba" to "Béisbol": Sport and the Americanisation of Puerto Rico, 1898–1950', *The International Journal of the History of Sport* 28, no. 17 (2011): 2575–93; Patricia Vertinsky, Aishwarya Ramachandran and Bo Wang, 'How about Some Muscle? Charles H. McCloy's Contributions to Physical Education in China between 1913 and 1926', *The International Journal of the History of Sport* 36, no. 15–16 (2019): 1372–89; Claudia Guedes, 'Changing the Cultural Landscape. English Engineers, American Missionaries, and the YMCA, bring Sports to Brazil, the 1870s to the 1930s', *International Journal of the History of Sport* 28 (2011): 2594–608.
69. SCASC, Harry L. Kingman, 'Physical Education in China, India, Japan, Latin America and the Philippine Islands', unpublished graduation thesis, Springfield, MA, International Young Men's Christian Association College, 1916), 46.
70. KFYA, IWI, Box 14, Folder 'Madras, MISC Reports 1893–1931', 'The Madras Young Men's Christian Association Quarterly Meeting' [reprint of an article in the *Christian Patriot*, 2 October 1897].
71. 'Report of the National Council to the Tenth National Convention at Calcutta', 142. To put this development into perspective, however, it needs to be emphasized that the same trend was observable in the North American YMCA too. Cf., for instance, David MacLeod, *Building Character in the American Boy* (Madison: University of Wisconsin Press, 1983), 81–2.
72. J. H. Gray, 'Physical Department. Its Place and Opportunities in India [Pt. I]', *The Young Men of India* 21 (1910): 56.

73. Paul R. Danner, 'India and Ceylon', *The Foreign Mail Annual*, 1917, 19.
74. Gray, 'India's Physical Education: What Shall It Be?', 7.
75. H. C. Buck, 'Physical Education in India', *Physical Training* 20, no. 1 (1922): 24.
76. KFYA, BF, Box 73, File 'Biographical Data. Gray, John Henry', Letter by J. H. Gray to Wuh Chi Tang, 22 August 1952.
77. KFYA, BF, Box 73, File 'Biographical Data. Gray, John Henry', typewritten biodata sheet.
78. SCASC, Cody S. Moffat, 'The Western Influence of [*sic*!] Physical Education in India', unpublished Master of Physical Education thesis, Springfield, MA, Springfield College, 1950, 42.
79. Andrew D. Morris, *Marrow of the Nation: A History of Sport and Physical Culture in Republican China* (Berkeley: University of California Press, 2004), 59 and 77–9. Gray returned to India in 1928 to serve another five years as National Physical Director, before ending his long career in Burma (1933–9). From KFYA, BF, Box 73, File 'Biographical Data. Gray, John Henry'.
80. Gray, 'Physical Department. Its Place and Opportunities in India [Pt. I]', 76–7. This iconoclastic strategy reminds us of the methods developed by British 'imperial' missionaries such as C. E. Tyndale-Biscoe. Cf. Sen, *A Nation at Play*, 62–8; C. E. Tyndale-Biscoe, *Character Building in Kashmir* (London: C.M.S., 1920).
81. Gray, 'Physical Department. Its Place and Opportunities in India [Pt. I]', 76–7.
82. Ibid., 78; J. H. Gray, 'More than Record Making: What Physical Education Means in India', *Association Men* (August 1916): 610.
83. Gray, 'India's Physical Renaissance', 341.
84. Gray, 'More than Record Making', 611. The link between sport and democracy that was articulated here for the first time by the National Physical Director would become a running trope in the YMCA's fitness discourse in South Asia over the next decades. In all likelihood, it was also influenced by the teachings of his Springfield professor Luther Gulick. Even as early as the late 1880s, Gulick had argued that team games in particular would be a perfect tool to prepare young men 'for wider loyalty and a more discerning self-devotion on which democracy rests' by offering 'freedom conditioned by rules and by the desires of other'. Gulick, *A Philosophy of Play*, 262–3.
85. KFYA, BF, Box 73, Folder 'Biographical Data – Gray, John Henry', Dr. John Henry Gray, typewritten manuscript, s.a. [1919].
86. Kingman, 'Physical Education in China, India, Etc.', 52.
87. Johnson, *The History of the YMCA Physical Education*, 54.
88. Gray, 'More than Record Making', 611.
89. C.P. Segard, *Annual Report of the Director of Physical Education to the Department of Public Instruction, Bengal for the Year 1918–1919* (Calcutta: Bengal Secretariat Book Depot, 1919), 1; C. P. Segard, *Quinquennial Report on Physical Education in the Province of Bengal for the Years 1911–12 to 1916–17* (Calcutta: Bengal Secretariat Book Depot, 1917), 1; Government of Bengal, *Report of the Committee of Enquiry into School and College Hygiene* (Calcutta: Bengal Secretariat Book Depot, 1915).
90. I. H. Nish, *Calcutta Y.M.C.A.: A History 1857–1957* (Calcutta: Y.M.C.A. Publishing House, 1957), 37–40; Dunderdale, *The YMCA in India*, 103.
91. J. H. Gray, *Major Games: Games Handbook* [=Triangle Athletic Series] (Calcutta: Association Press, 1918).
92. NAI, Educational Proceedings, June 1914, 43-A, statement by H. Butler, 15 April 1914.

93. 'Extract from a Letter by John H. Gray', *The Association Seminar* 22, no. 10 (July 1914): 401.
94. KFYA, IWI, Box 62, Folder 'Madras, Physical Training School, 1924–27', National Physical Training School Madras [undated typescript, *c.* 1927].
95. KFYA, BF, Box 154, Folder 'Biographical Data, Noehren, Arthur G.'; typescript by F. V. Slack, dated 17 February 1928.
96. KFYA, BF, Box 154, Folder 'Biographical Data, Noehren, Arthur G.'; Typescript 'Biography of Arthur G. Noehren, M.D., Physical Director Young Men's Christian Association, Madras India', September 1925, 1–2.
97. Johnson, *The History of the YMCA Physical Education*, 157.
98. KFYA, BF, Box 28, Folder 'Biographical Data, Cammack, Robert Walter'; KFYA, IWC, Box 8, Folder 'Ceylon, Jan 1923–Apr 1923', R. W. Cammack 'Y.M.C.A. Physical Department work in Ceylon – Report for 1922'. Cammack submitted a thesis at Springfield in 1920 in which he painstakingly documented his early activities in Ceylon. Cf. SCASC, R. Walter Cammack, 'Physical Education in Ceylon', unpublished graduation thesis, Springfield, MA, International Young Men's Christian Association College, 1920).
99. For an insight into the YMCA's cooperation with princely states, cf. KFYA, IWI, Box 10, H. Beall, Chief Inspector Physical Education to the Office of the Chief Inspector of Secondary Schools, H. E. H. the Nizam's Government, 15 January 1921.
100. KFYA, IWI, Box 1, John Henry Gray, 'The Pros and Cons of the Development of Modern Physical Education in India through the Indian National Council and local Y.M.C.A.s', s.a., 4.
101. *Times of India*, 5 August 1913, 4.
102. UPSAL, Education Proceedings 58 of 1916, Files 1–3, April 1916, Appendix B 'Tentative Plan of Physical Education for Nagpur University, submitted by the National Council of Young Men's Christian Associations', 12. I am grateful to my former student Soni Soni for making me aware of this particular source.
103. D. F. McClelland, 'H.C. Buck', in *Three Y.M.C.A. Pioneers*, ed. S. P. Appasamy (Calcutta, 1958), 12–8.
104. KFYA, IWI, Box 35, Folder 'India Correspondence, June-Sept. 1923', letter by A. G. Noehren to Frank V. Slack, 24 May 1923.
105. *Times of India*, 10 July 1923, 9; *Times of India*, 7 October 1925, 12. Cf. also A. G. Noehren, 'Indian Athletes at the Olympic Games', *Young Men of India* 25 (1924): 598–609; Naha, 'The Rise of Modern Sport and the Olympic Movement in India', 129–30; Boria Majumdar and Nalin Mehta, *India and the Olympics* (London: Routledge, 2009), 17–24.
106. P. M. Joseph, 'The Y.M.C.A. College of Physical Education', *Young Men of India* 45, no. 10 (1933): 387.
107. Gray, 'More than Record Making', 611.
108. Segard, 'Annual Report of the Director of Physical Education', 1.
109. KFYA, IWI, Box 1, John Henry Gray, 'The Pros and Cons of the Development of Modern Physical Education in India through the Indian National Council and local Y.M.C.A.s', s.a.
110. Ibid.
111. *North Adams Evening Transcript*, 22 April 1938, 8–9.
112. YDSPC, Rec. Gr. 115, Series I, Waldo Huntley Heinrichs Papers, Box 7, Folder 61, *Diaries 1916*, entry for 14 January 1916.
113. Mark Dyreson, 'Imperial "Deep Play": Reading Sport and Visions of the Five Empires of the "New World", 1919–1941', *The International History of Sport*

28 (2011): 2431. Cf. also Barbara J. Keys, *Globalizing Sport: National Rivalry and International Community* (Cambridge, MA: Harvard University Press, 2006), 64–9.
114. KFYA, BF, Box 73, Folder 'Biographical Data. Gray, John Henry', Letter by J.H. Gray to Wuh Chi Tang, 22 August 1952.
115. Holt, *A Study of the Y.M.C.A. of India, etc.*, 210–1.
116. David, *The YMCA and the Making*, 168.
117. 'Pioneer of Physical Education', *The Hindu*, 17 April 2003. Available online: https://www.thehindu.com/todays-paper/tp-features/tp-metroplus/pioneer-of-physical-education/article28405626.ece (accessed 16 February 2017). Cf. also Ambi Harsha, *Development of Physical Education in Madras, 1918–1948* (Madras: Christian Literature Society, 1982), 16–22.
118. I borrow the term 'somatic engineering' from Denise Gimpel, 'Civilizing Bodies. Somatic Engineering in China', in *Sport across Asia: Politics, Cultures, and Identities*, ed. Katrin Bromber, Birgit Krawietz and Joseph Maguire (New York: Routledge, 2011), 32–58.
119. H. C. Buck, 'The Physical Department of the Y.M.C.A.', *The Young Men of India* 32 (1921): 340.
120. H. C. Buck, 'Ourselves', *The Annual of the Y.M.C.A. School of Physical Education* (Madras: Diocesan Press, 1928), 3.
121. KFYA, IWI, Box 62, Folder 'Madras School of Physical Education, 1919–1923', Letter by G. S. Eddy to M. G. Goldsmith 22 July 1919 and Letter by D. F. McClelland to G.S. Eddy, 7 January 1920.
122. *The Young Men of India*, 65, no. 9 (1943): 125.
123. KFYA, IWI, Box 62, Folder 'Madras Physical Training School, 1932', Letter H. C. Buck to F. V. Slack, 14 October 1932; typescript introduction to the 'Y.M.C.A. College of Physical Education Project'.
124. NAI, Government of India, Educational Proceedings, D 27, June 1930.
125. Y.M.C.A. College of Physical Education Saidapet, Madras, *Prospectus 1940–41* (Madras: Methodist Publishing House, 1941), 3; KFYA, IWI, Box 80, Folder 'Blue Prints of the Physical Education College Madras'.
126. Johnson, *The History of the YMCA Physical Education*, 255.
127. KFYA, IWI, Box 1, Buck Report 1930.
128. David, *The YMCA and the Making*, 176.
129. KFYA, BF, Box 25, Folder 'Biographical Data Harry Crowe Buck', typescript, Physical and Health Education as Means toward Abundant Living, s.a. [1939].
130. Until 1949, the women's section remained under the direct control of the Madras educational authorities. KFYA, IWI, Box 63, File 'Note by the General Secretary on the Y.M.C.A. College of Physical Education at Saidapet, s.a., s.l.'.
131. Johnson, *History of YMCA Physical Education*, 256.
132. Moffat, 'The Western Influence of [*sic*!] Physical Education in India', 52.
133. KFYA, IWI, Box 63, File 'P. M. Joseph, A short report on the Y.M.C.A. College of Physical Education at Saidapet, s.a. [1947/48]'.
134. KFYA, BF, Box 25, Folder 'Biographical Data Harry Crowe Buck', typescript, Mr H. C. Buck (Excerpts from a Tribute by C. A. Abraham), s.a. [1943].
135. KFYA, IWI, Box 62, Folder 'Madras Physical Training School, 1932', typescript, Y.M.C.A. College of Physical Project, 1; KFYA, IWI, Box 1, Folder 'Physical Education College 1922–1939', Inauguration of the Y.M.C.A. Physical Education College at Saidapet, Madras.

136. KFYA, IWI, Box 62, Folder 'Madras Physical Training School, 1932', typescript, Y.M.C.A. College of Physical Project, 1.
137. H. C. Buck, 'Looking Forward in Physical Education (Presidential Address Delivered to the Eighth Provincial Physical Education Conference of Madras)', in *Buck Commemoration Volume: Being A Memorial Dedicated to Harry Crowe Buck*, ed. L. K. Govindarajulu (Chennai: Buck Commemoration Volume Committee, 1949), 238–9.
138. Cf., for instance, WAYAG, Box 'India Boys' Work', Lahore Young Men's Christian Association, 'School for Democracy', in Sixty-Fifth Annual Report (Report and Audited Statement of Accounts for the Year 1940), Lahore: 1941.
139. Madras College of Physical Education, *Prospectus 1940–41*, 21.
140. Sumathi Ramaswamy, *The Goddess and the Nation* (Durham: Duke University Press, 2010).
141. Cf. Vertinsky et al., 'How about Some Muscle?'; Stefan Huebner, *Pan Asian Sports and the Emergence of Modern Asia, 1913–1974* (Singapore: NUS Press, 2016), 30–5.
142. J. H. Gray, 'The Development of Physical Education in India', *Young Men of India* 45 (1933): 385–6.; KFYA, IWI, Box 1, Folder 'Physical Education College 1922–1939', H. C. Buck, *Report on the National Y.M.C.A. School of Physical Education*, April 1922; Buck, 'The Physical Department of the Y.M.C.A.', 340.
143. 'Directory of Students', *Vyayam*, April 1930, 38–43.
144. The information on Singh is gathered from the Khalsa College's monthly journal *Durbar*. I am grateful to my former doctoral student Michael Brunner for sharing this source with me. Cf. *Durbar*, April/May 1932, 44; *Durbar*, November 1932, 45; *Durbar*, October 1934, 27; *Durbar*, April 1936, 72; and *Durbar*, March 1939, 67. Cf. also Brunner, *Education and Modernity in Colonial Punjab*, 218–23.
145. *Durbar*, December 1946, 3.
146. NAI, Proceedings of the Law (Education) Department, Government of Madras, Government Order No 111, dated 15 January 1929. 'Report of the Committee on Physical Education in Secondary Schools, Government of Madras Appendix G, 13–16.
147. Buck, 'The Physical Department of the Y.M.C.A.', 341.
148. F. Weber, 'Physical Education in the Association Programme', *The Young Men of India* 45 (1933): 390.
149. 'Play That Opens Doors', *The Young Men of India* 50 (1938): 251–3.
150. Joseph Alter, 'Gandhi's Body, Gandhi's Truth. Nonviolence and the Biomoral Imperative of Public Health', *Journal of Asian Studies* 55, no. 2 (1996): 301–22.
151. Legg, 'Dyarchy: Democracy, Autocracy'.
152. *Svadeśī* (Hindi) literally means 'coming from one's own country'.
153. KFYA, BF, Box 73, File 'Biographical Data. Gray, John Henry', Letter by J. H. Gray to Wuh Chi Tang, 22 August 1952.
154. There is a significant body of literature on the growth of the Eugenic movement in late colonial India. Cf., for instance, Sarah Hodges, 'South Asia's Eugenic Pasts', in *The Oxford Handbook of the History of Eugenics*, ed. Philippa Levine and Alison Bashford (New York: Oxford University Press, 2010), 228–42; Sanjam Ahluwalia, *Reproductive Restraints: Birth Control in India, 1877–1947* (Urbana: University of Illinois Press, 2008); Harald Fischer-Tiné, 'From Brahmacharya to "Conscious Race Culture": Indian Nationalism, Hindu Tradition and Victorian Discourses of Science', in *Beyond Representation: The Construction of Identity in Colonial India*, ed. Crispin Bates (New Delhi: Oxford University Press, 2006), 230–59.

155. Joseph Alter, 'Yoga and Physical Education: Swami Kuvalayananda's Nationalist Project', *Asian Medicine: Tradition and Modernity* 3 (2007): 20–36.
156. Government of Bombay, *Report of the Physical Education Committee* (Bombay: Government Central Press, 1947), 2.
157. KFYA, IWI, Box 62, Folder 'Madras (Physical Training School), 1938–1954'; Clipping of articles from the *Madras Mail* and *The Hindu*, 1 July 1939.
158. KFYA, IWI, Box 63, File 'Proceedings of the Director of Public Instruction Madras R.C. No. 83-E/46, 4 Nov. 1947', 'Physical Education: Y.M.C.A. College of Physical Education, Saidapet, Management of'.
159. KFYA, IWI, Box 63, Letter of D. F. McClelland to J. H. Gray, 27 May 1946.
160. KFYA, IWI, Box 63, Memorandum presented by the Deputation from the Council of the YMCA College of Physical Education, Saidapet, Madras, on the Tuesday 1 March, 1949 to the Hon'ble Shri Avinashilingam, Minister for Education, Government of Madras, Fort St George.
161. 'Government Not to Take over YMCA College of Physical Education: Management Agree to Conditions', *The Indian Express*, 2 March 1949, 1.
162. David, *The YMCA and the Making*, 255.
163. Noehren, 'Official Report', 1.
164. Eddy, *The Challenge of the East*, 56.
165. This concept is inspired by Joseph Alter's term 'somatic nationalism'. Cf. Alter, 'Somatic Nationalism'.
166. Sherwood Eddy, *The New Era in Asia* (New York: Missionary Education Movement of the United States and Canada, 1913), 56.
167. The National Council of the Y.M.C.A.s of India, Burma and Ceylon, *Youth in Harness: The All India Service of the Y.M.C.A.* s.a. [1930].
168. Buck, 'The Physical Department of the Y.M.C.A.', 345.
169. The concept of *Eigensinn* was famously introduced by German historian Alf Lüdtke in the 1980s to render acts of subversion and resistance of subaltern groups in asymmetrical power relations visible. In thus doing, he restored their agency and subjectivity, which had almost completely got lost under the combined influence of Marxist inspired social history and the linguistic turn. Cf. Alf Lüdtke, 'Cash, Coffee-Breaks, Horseplay. Eigensinn and Politics among Factory Workers in Germany circa 1900', in *Confrontation. Class Consciousness, and the Labor Process: Studies in Proletarian Class Formation*, ed. Michael Hanagan and Charles Stephenson (New York: Greenwood, 1986), 65–95.
170. Cf. Maarten van Bottenburg, 'Beyond Diffusion: Sport and Its Remaking in Cross-Cultural Contexts', *Journal of Sport History* 37 (2010): 401–12; Katrin Bromber, Birgit Krawietz and Joseph Maguire, 'Introduction: From Asian Sports to Sport in Asia', in *Sport across Asia: Politics, Cultures, and Identities*, ed. Katrin Bromber, Birgit Krawietz and Joseph Maguire (New York: Routledge, 2011), 1–10.
171. KFYA, IWI, Box 20, Biennial Report of George Sherwood Eddy, November 1898.
172. KFYA, IWI, Box 11, Folder: 'India Annual and Quarterly Reports 1926', *Annual Report 1926 by Harvey E. Becknell*. For the classic treatment of the British stereotype of the educated Bengali, cf. Sinha, *Colonial Masculinity*.
173. KFYA, IWI, Box 8, Folder 'India Annual and Quarterly Reports 1917 [Mc - Mil]', Annual Report by W.E. Elliott for the Year ending 30 September 1917.
174. Danner, 'India and Ceylon', 19.
175. Gray, 'The Development of Physical Education', 385.

176. J. H. Gray, 'Physical Education in India', *American Physical Education Review* 24, no. 7 (1919): 375.
177. Ibid.
178. Arthur G. Noehren, 'Meeting a Tremendous Need for Physical Reform', *Foreign Mail* 23 (1916): 19.
179. KFYA, BF, Box 154, Folder 'Biographical Data, Noehren, Arthur G.'; Typescript 'Biography of Arthur G. Noehren, M.D., Physical Director Young Men's Christian Association, Madras India', September 1925, 1–2. For Noehren's assessment of Indian boyhood, cf. also Chapter 4.
180. Buck, 'The Physical Department of the Y.M.C.A.', 345.
181. KFYA, IWI, Box 19, Folder 'Eddy, G. Sherwood, Report Letters 1896–1898', Report Letter No. 5, May 1897, The Scourges of India.
182. KFYA, IWI, Box 74, Folder 'National Council India, Burma, Ceylon 1931', Letter W. Healy to Frank [V. Slack], Rangoon, 7 July 1931.
183. Jagannath, 'The Aims of Physical Education', *The Annual of the Y.M.C.A. School of Physical Education, 1928–1929*, Madras 1929, 23.
184. Ibid.
185. George Mosse, *The Image of Man: The Creation of Modern Masculinity* (New York: Oxford University Press, 1996), 5–6. Cf. also Ina Zweininger-Bargielowska, *Managing the Body: Beauty, Health and Fitness in Britain, 1880–1939* (Oxford: Oxford University Press, 2010), 17–20.
186. Such an interpretation also provides some historical depth to similar arguments that twenty-first century Bollywood stars' fancy for bleaching creams can be read as complicity with Euro-American capitalist ideals of modernity and whiteness. Cf., for instance, Goldie Osuri, 'Ash-Coloured Whiteness: The Transfiguration of Aishwarya Rai', *South Asian Popular Culture* 6, no. 2 (2008): 109–23.
187. Benoy Kumar Sarkar, *The Futurism of Young Asia, and Other Essays on the Relations between the East and the West* (Leipzig: Markert & Petters, 1922), III. That the production of fair-skinned offspring was one of the main goals in a particular current of Indian 'vernacular' medical advisory literature has recently been discussed in Luzia Savary, '"Vernacular Eugenics"?: Santati-Śāstra in Popular Hindi Advisory Literature (1900–1940)', *South Asia: Journal of South Asian Studies* 37 (2014): 381–97. Cf. also the same author's recent monograph: Luzia Savary, *Evolution, Race and Public Spheres in India: Vernacular Concepts and Sciences (1860–1930)* (Abingdon: Routledge, 2019).
188. Huebner, 'Uplifting the Weak and Degenerated Races of East Asia'.
189. J. Howell Atwood, Arthur W. Hardy and Owen E. Pence, *The Racial Factor in Y.M.C.A.'s: A Report on Negro-White Relationships in Twenty-Four Cities* (New York: Association Press for Bureau of Records, Studies and Trends, National Board of Y.M.C.A.'s, 1946). Cf. also Mark Robert Schneider, *African Americans in the Jazz Age: A Decade of Struggle and Promise* (Lanham, MD: Rowman & Littlefield, 2006), 40–1; Mjagkij, *Light in the Darkness*.
190. Gray, 'The Development of Physical Education in India', 385.
191. Foreign Division of the Young Men's Christian Association of the United States and Canada, *The Y.M.C.A. in India* (New York, n.d.), not paginated.
192. *Second Quinquennial Report of the Welfare Work of Messrs. Begg* (Cawnpore: Sutherland, s.a. [1939]).
193. Namrata R. Ganneri, 'The Debate on "Revival" and the Physical Culture Movement in Western India (1900–1950)', in *Sport across Asia: Politics, Cultures, and Identities*,

ed. Katrin Bromber, Birgit Krawietz and Joseph Maguire (New York: Routledge, 2011), 121–43. The seminal study on Indian wrestling still is Joseph S. Alter, *The Wrestler's Body: Identity and Ideology in North India* (Berkeley: University of California Press, 1992).
194. Patricia Vertinsky, 'Yoga Comes to American Physical Education: Josephine Rathbone and Corrective Physical Education', *Journal of Sports History* 41, no. 2 (2014): 287–311.
195. A list of the more important representatives of this Indian competition would include, amongst others, the Deshpande brothers who founded Hanuman Vyayam Prasarak Mandal in Amravati; the Ghose brothers and Yogoda in Ranchi; under the inspired leadership of Yogananda and his younger brother, Bishnu Charan Ghose, Shri Yogendra in Bombay; and Raj Ratan Manikrao in Baroda. For more details, cf. Ganneri, 'The Debate on "Revival"'.
196. Noehren, 'Official Report', 13–14.
197. *Report of the Conference on Physical Education Held at Madras on the 14th and 15th October 1927 under the Presidency of the Hon, Dr. P. Subbaroyan, M.A., C.C.L., LL.D., Chief Minister to the Government of Madras* (Madras: Superintendent, Government Press, 1928), 3–7.
198. H. C. Buck, 'The Place of Indigenous Activities in the Physical Education Programme', in *Buck Commemoration Volume*, 247.
199. Vertinsky and Ramachandran, 'The "Y" Goes to India', 367.
200. *Buck's Book of Rules of Games and Sports*, revised by the Staff of the Y.M.C.A. College, Saidapet, Madras,12th ed. (Calcutta: Y.M.C.A. Publication House, 1950), 192–227.
201. Noehren, 'Official Report', 14–15.
202. Ibid., 14; Weber, 'Physical Education in the Association Programme', 390.
203. Singleton, *Yoga Body*, 91.
204. Ibid., 93.
205. Cf. also Ramachandran, 'Counterflows of Knowledge', 37–41; Vertinsky, 'Yoga Comes to American Physical Education'; Patricia Vertinsky, ' "Building the Body Beautiful": The Women's League of Health and Beauty: Yoga and Female Agency in 1930s Britain', *Rethinking History: The Journal of Theory and Practice* 16 (2012): 517–42.

4 'One-fifth of the world's boyhood': American 'boyology' and the Indian YMCA's work with early adolescents (*c.* 1900–1950)

1. I will focus solely on the 'secular' dimensions of the programme in what follows. As one might expect from a Christian Association, religious schemes played an important but variable role that depended on the target group (i.e. European, 'Eurasian' or South Asian boys). This extreme variation would require extensive contextualization that is beyond the scope of this chapter. The same caveat needs to be made about the exclusive focus on boys at the expense of female adolescents. There were special programmes for girls too, carried out by the YWCA and on a drastically smaller scale. However, not only did the discourse on girls and young women differ considerably from the one on boys, the two Young Christian groups were also largely independent of each other. This makes it difficult for a single study to do justice to the work done in South Asia by both groups.

2. I have borrowed the phrase from Harry Hendrick, *Children, Childhood and English Society, 1880–1990* (Cambridge: Cambridge University Press, 1997), 81.
3. The term 'boyology' was first coined in a YMCA publication published in the United States during the First World War: Henry W. Gibson, *Boyology or Boy Analysis* (New York: Association Press, 1916). For a brief contextualization, cf. also Kenneth Kidd, 'Boyology in the Twentieth Century', *Children's Literature* 28 (2000): 44–72.
4. Anson T. Leary, 'America's Greatest Problem – Its Youth', unpublished graduation thesis, Springfield, MA, International Young Men's Christian Association College, 1917, 67.
5. The phrase is borrowed from Tournès, *Américanisation: une histoire mondiale*, 134. Cf. also ibid., 134–50 and 191–5.
6. For a succinct definition and discussion of informal education and its role in helping children and adolescents in 'the acquisition of the "correct" emotional toolbox', cf. Stephanie Olsen, *Juvenile Nation: Youth, Emotions and the Making of the Modern British Citizen, 1880–1914* (London: Bloomsbury, 2014), 7–11.
7. David, *The YMCA and the Making*, 231–2.
8. This topic has been studied mostly by British historians from the 1970s onwards. The 'classic' survey study remains John Springhall, *Youth, Empire and Society: British Youth Movements, 1883–1940* (Hamden, CT: Archon Books, 1977). For programmes specifically targeting adolescent migration to build imperial citizenship, cf. also Rebecca J. Bates, 'Building Imperial Youth? Reflections on Labour and the Construction of Working-Class Childhood in Late Victorian England', *Paedagogica Historica* 45, no. 1–2 (2009): 143–56; Geoffrey Sherington, '"A Better Class of Boy" the Big Brother Movement, Youth Migration and Citizenship of Empire', *Australian Historical Studies* 33, no. 120 (2002): 267–85.
9. The literature on the scout/guide movement is extraordinarily rich. Cf., for instance, Kristine Alexander, *Guiding Modern Girls: Girlhood, Empire, and Internationalism in the 1920s and 1930s* (Vancouver: UBC Press, 2017); Benjamin René Jordan, *Modern Manhood and the Boy Scouts of America: Citizenship, Race, and the Environment, 1910–1930* (Chapel Hill: University of North Carolina Press, 2016); Nelson R. Block Tammy M. Proctor, eds., *Scouting Frontiers: Youth and the Scout Movement's First Century* (Cambridge: Cambridge Scholars Press, 2009); Sam Pryke, 'The Popularity of Nationalism in the Early British Boy Scout Movement', *Social History* 23, no. 3 (October 1998): 309–24; Sarah Mills, 'Scouting for Girls? Gender and the Scout Movement in Britain', *Gender, Place & Culture* 18, no. 4 (August 2011): 537–56.
10. The most recent study on the brigade is an unpublished PhD thesis: Christopher J. Speckman, 'The Boys' Brigade and Urban Cultures, 1883–1933: A Relationship Examined', unpublished PhD dissertation, University of Portsmouth, 2016. Cf. also the slightly outdated John Springhall, Brian Fraser and Michael Hoare, eds, *Sure and Steadfast: A History of the Boys' Brigade, 1883 to 1983* (London: Collins, 1983).
11. Harry Hendrick, *Images of Youth: Age, Class, and the Male Youth Problem, 1880–1920* (Oxford: Oxford University Press, 1990), 161.
12. David I. MacLeod, *Building Character in the American Boy: The Boy Scouts, YMCA and Their Forerunners, 1870–1920* (Madison: University of Wisconsin Press, 1983), 87–93.
13. Hopkins, *American Empire*, 266. Cf. also Mischa Honeck, *Our Frontier Is the World: The Boy Scouts in the Age of American Ascendancy* (Ithaca, NY: Cornell University Press, 2018); Jordan, *Modern Manhood and the Boy Scouts*.

14. On the shifting conceptions of childhood in the long nineteenth century, cf. Peter Stearns, *Childhood in World History* (New York: Routledge, 2011), 71–83; Hendrick, *Children, Childhood and English Society*, 9–15.
15. Julia Grant, *The Boy Problem: Educating Boys in Urban America* (Baltimore, MD: Johns Hopkins University Press, 2014), 5.
16. Robert Snape, 'Juvenile Organizations Committees and the State Regulation of Youth Leisure in Britain, 1916-1939', *The Journal of the History of Childhood and Youth* 13, no. 2 (2020): 248–49; Roberta J. Park, 'Boys' Clubs Are Better than Policemen's Clubs: Endeavours by Philanthropists, Social Reformers, and Others to Prevent Juvenile Crime, the Late 1800s to 1917', *The International Journal of the History of Sport* 24, no. 6 (2007): 749–75.
17. Cf., especially, E. J. Urwick, *Studies of Boy Life in Our Cities* (London: Dent, 1904). For an analysis of the strongly class-flavoured boy problem discourse in the United Kingdom, cf. Hendrick, *Images of Youth*.
18. Cf. P. Setran, 'Developing the "Christian Gentleman": The Medieval Impulse in Protestant Ministry to Adolescent Boys, 1890–1920', *Religion and American Culture: A Journal of Interpretation* 20, no. 2 (2010): 165–204; Angela M. Hornsby, '"The Boy Problem": North Carolina Race Men Groom the Next Generation, 1900–1930', *Journal of Negro History* 86, no. 4 (2001): 280.
19. Hornsby, '"The Boy Problem"', 281.
20. Kenneth B. Kidd, *Making American Boys: Boyology and the Feral Tale* (Minneapolis: University of Minnesota Press, 2004), 2.
21. Ian Tyrrell, *Crisis of the Wasteful Nation: Empire and Conservation in Theodore Roosevelt's America* (Chicago, IL: University of Chicago Press, 2015), 4; Jill Lepore, *These Truths: A History of the United States* (New York: W. W. Norton, 2018), 374.
22. Theodore Roosevelt, 'The Strenuous Life', in *The Strenuous Life: Essays and Addresses* (New York: Charles Scribner, 1906), 1 and 9. Cf. also Arnaldi Testi, 'The Gender of Reform Politics: Theodore Roosevelt and the Culture of Masculinity', *The Journal of American History* 81, no. 4 (1995): 1509–33.
23. G. Stanley Hall, *Adolescence: Its Psychology and Its Relations to Physiology, Anthropology, Sociology, Sex, Crime, Religion, and Education*, Vol. I and II (New York: D. Appleton, 1904). On the influence of social Darwinism on his work cf. Lester F. Goodchild, 'G. Stanley Hall and an American Social Darwinist Pedagogy: His Progressive Educational Ideas on Gender and Race', *History of Education Quarterly* 52, no. 1 (2012): 62–98.
24. Gulick, *A Philosophy of Play*. For a concise contextualization of Gulick's work and audience, cf. also Howard P. Chudacoff, *Children at Play: An American History* (New York: New York University Press, 2001), 72–3.
25. George Walter Fiske, *Boy Life and Self-Government* (New York: Young Men's Christian Association Press, 1910), 45. Cf. also Alonzo R. Pixley, 'Religious Education and the Boy Problem', unpublished thesis, Springfield, MA, International Young Men's Christian Association College, 1911; Paul E. Hitchcock, 'The Boy Problem – and How It Is Dealt with in the Elementary School', unpublished BA thesis, Springfield, MA, International Young Men's Christian Association College, 1917.
26. Kidd, *Making American Boys*. Cf. also Leslie Paris, *Children's Nature: The Rise of the American Summer Camp* (New York: New York University Press, 2008), 189–225.
27. Gibson, *Boyology or Boy Analysis*, 70.
28. Ibid., 72–3.

29. Luther H. Gulick, 'The Alleged Effemination of Our American Boys', *American Physical Education Review* 10, no. 3 (1905): 213–20. Cf. Putney, 'Luther Gulick: His Contributions'.
30. Hanford M. Burr, 'Dr Luther Gulick, 1865–1918: A Symposium', *American Physical Education Review* 23, no. 7 (1918): 414.
31. Hopkins, *History of the Y.M.C.A.*, 462.
32. On the role of Springfield graduates in spreading the YMCA gospel in South Asia and elsewhere, cf. Doggett, 'The Training School and the Foreign Field'; SCASC, promotional pamphlet 1926, 'A College for Leaders: A Springfield Institution Serving the Youth of the World', s.a. [1935]. Doggett, *Man and a School*; Vertinsky and Ramachandran, 'The "Y" Goes to India'; Huebner, 'Muscular Christian Exchanges'.
33. SCASC, 'Training for Work with Boys: International YMCA College', Promotional Pamphlet, 1926.
34. Cody S. Moffat, 'The Western Influence of Physical Education on India', unpublished MEd thesis, Springfield College, 1950, 42; cf. also, SCASC, 'International YMCA College: A Worldwide Influence in Religious-Social Leadership', promotional pamphlet, 1923.
35. Doggett, 'The Training School and the Foreign Field', 135–8.
36. SCASC, George F. Andrews, 'History of the Playground Movement and Organization and Administration of Playgrounds', unpublished MEd thesis, Springfield, MA, International Young Men's Christian Association College, 1932, 104–6; SCASC, Lester H. Libby, 'The Leader's Handbook', unpublished thesis-cum-textbook, Springfield, MA, International Young Men's Christian Association College Springfield, s.a. [1917].
37. SCASC, Letter from Laurence L. Doggett to Granville Stanley Hall, May 15, 1918.
38. Satadru Sen, *Colonial Childhoods: The Juvenile Periphery of India, 1850–1945* (London: Anthem Press, 2005); Satadru Sen, 'A Separate Punishment: Juvenile Offenders in Colonial India', *The Journal of Asian Studies* 63, no. 1 (2004): 81–104.
39. There were several girls' schools and high schools, too, but compared to the overall number of educational institutions in the region, these remained almost a *quantité négligeable* well into the twentieth century.
40. Nita Kumar, 'India's Trial with Citizenship, Modernisation and Nationhood', in *Mass Education and the Limits of State Building, c.1870–1930*, ed. Laurence Brocklin and Nicola Sheldon (Basingstoke: Palgrave Macmillan, 2012), 297.
41. Sinha, *Colonial Masculinity*; Satadru Sen, 'Schools, Athletes and Confrontation: The Student Body in Colonial India', in *Confronting the Body* ed. James H. Mills and Satadru Sen (London: Anthem Press, 2012), 58–79; Topdar, 'The Corporeal Empire'.
42. For a succinct overview of the protracted struggle carried out by Indian intellectuals and political activists to come to grips with 'the West', cf. Dipesh Chakrabarty, 'From Civilization to Globalization: The "West" as a Shifting Signifier in Indian Modernity', *Inter-Asia Cultural Studies* 13, no. 1 (2012): 138–52.
43. Cf., for instance, Sripadrao Satavlekar, 'Mahāśay gurukul aur mistar kālej kī bāt cīt', *Saddharm Pracārak* [A conversation between Mahashay Gurukul and Mister College], 12 April 1911, 7–8.
44. Cf., for instance, Pal, *Swadeshi and Swaraj*, 257.
45. Brunner, 'Schooling the Subcontinent'. See also Krishna Kumar, 'Colonial Citizen as an Educational Ideal.' *Economic and Political Weekly* 24, no. 4 (1989): PE45–51.
46. Lala Lajpat Rai, 'Exhortation to the Youth to Develop Grit and Determination', in *The Collected Works of Lala Lajpat Rai*, ed. B. R. Nanda, Vol. IV (New Delhi: Manohar Publishers, 2004), 401.

47. Ibid., 403–5.
48. Watt, 'Philanthropy and Civilizing Missions', 283.
49. Roy, 'The Torchbearers of Progress', 2.
50. On the distribution of edifying literature and temperance propaganda targeted at adolescents by Christian missionaries in colonial South Asia, cf. Olsen, *Juvenile Nation*, 123–9.
51. Cf. Jayal, *Citizenship and Its Discontents: An Indian History*, 109–35; Mohinder Singh, 'Spectres of the West: Negotiating a Civilizational Figure in Hindi', in *Civilizing Emotions: Concepts in Nineteenth Century Asia and Europe*, ed. Margrit Pernau and Helge Jordheim (Cambridge: Cambridge University Press, 2015), 193.
52. For the 'middle-class character of civilizing missions', see, for instance, Michael Adas, 'Contested Hegemony: The Great War and the Afro-Asian Assault on the Civilizing Mission Ideology', *Journal of World History* 15, no. 1 (2004): 31–63.
53. Roy, 'The Torchbearers of Progress', 43–4.
54. National Council, *Youth in Harness*.
55. David, *The YMCA and the Making*, 231; WAYAG, Young Men's Christian Association Madras, *Twenty-Fifth Years' Service in Madras, 1914, Annual Report*, 19.
56. KFYA, IWB, Box 4, Folder 'Rangoon Annual Reports 1902–1915'. A Year's Retrospect: Being the Annual Report of the Rangoon Young Men's Christian Association, from 1 December 1901 to 30 November 1902, 3.
57. *Report of the National Council to the Tenth National Convention at Calcutta*, 57–8.
58. Hopkins, *History of the Y.M.C.A.*, 660.
59. *Y.M.C.A. Year Book and Official Rosters. 1903–1904* (New York: National Councils of the Young Men's Christian Associations of Canada and the United States of America, 1904), 27.
60. Nish, *Flaming Milestones*, 18.
61. Latourette, *World Service*, 1957, 117.
62. 'Annual Report of the Young Men's Christian Association of Calcutta for 1907' (Calcutta, 1908), 16; 'Young Men's Christian Association of Calcutta: Annual Report 1915' (Calcutta: Edinburgh Press, 1916), 25; 'Young Men's Christian Association of Calcutta: Annual Report 1926' (Calcutta: Edinburgh Press, 1916), 13.
63. UTCAB, Young Men's Christian Association, 'Report of the Indian National Council, Proceedings of the Seventh National Council, Bangalore Dec 29th 1904–Jan 2nd 1905', 4.
64. KFYA, IWI, Box 5, Folder: 'Annual and Quarterly Reports 1912', File 'C.S. Paterson, Secretary, Calcutta, India, Report for Quarter Ending 31 March'.
65. WAYAG, Box India, Boys' Work 1922–1949, W. B. Hilton, 'Report on Y.M.C.A. Work with early adolescents in India' [18 August 1922].
66. KFYA, SF, Box 9, Folder 'Boys' Work on Foreign Field', F. V. Slack, 'Facts about Boys' Work in India' [May 1920], 10–24.
67. Ibid., 23.
68. Dunderdale, *The YMCA in India*, 81.
69. WAYAG, Box India. Boys' Work 1922–1949, Tracy Strong, 'The Y.M.C.A. and One Fifth of the World's Boyhood: A Report on the Boys' Work of the Y.M.C.A. in India' [May 1933].
70. KFYA, SF, Box 9, Folder 'Boys' Work on Foreign Field' [May 1920], 3.
71. Henri Johannot, 'The Field of Action', in *History of the World Alliance of Christian Associations*, ed. Clarence Prouty Shedd (London: SPCK, 1955), 615.
72. WAYAG, T1, Box 42, 'Report of the First Conference of YMCA Workers among Boys', 3–4.

73. *Year Book of the Young Men's Christian Associations of North America for the Year May 1, 1923 to April 30, 1924* (New York: Association Press, 1924), 18.
74. For a succinct account of Protestant Christian Internationalism after 1918, cf. Robert, 'The First Globalization: The Internationalization of the Protestant Missionary Movement between the World Wars'. On interwar internationalism more generally, cf., for instance, Glenda Sluga, 'Remembering 1919: International Organizations and the Future of International Order', *International Affairs* 95, no. 1 (2019): 25–43; Daniel Gorman, *The Emergence of International Society in the 1920s* (Cambridge: Cambridge University Press, 2012); Daniel Laqua, ed., *Internationalism Reconfigured: Transnational Ideas and Movements between the World Wars* (London: I. B. Tauris, 2011).
75. Charles E. Heald, ed., *The Place of Boyhood in the Nations of the World: Being the Report of the Second World Conference of Y.M.C.A. Workers among Boys, Held at Pörtschach Am Zee (sic), Austria, 30th May to 10th June, 1923* (Geneva: World's Committee Young Men's Christian Associations, Boys' Division, 1923).
76. Ibid., 351; Eddy Sherwood, *A Century with Youth: A History of the YMCA from 1844 to 1944* (New York: Association Press, 1944), 107.
77. John R. Mott, 'Boyhood, the Greatest Asset of Any Nation', in *The Place of Boyhood*, ed. C. E. Heald, 259.
78. KFYA, SF, Box 9, Folder "Boys' Work on Foreign Field" [May 1920], 2 and 8.
79. M. S. Cherian, 'Boys Work in Villages', *Young Men of India* 49, no. 8 (1937): 209–10; cf. also Kanakaraj, *Lighthouses of Rural Reconstruction*, 96 and 110.
80. Paul, *Young Men's Christian Associations of India, Burma and Ceylon and the European Association (Central Association)*, 45–46.
81. Johannot, 'The Field of Action', 656.
82. Dunderdale, *The YMCA in India*, 85.
83. Latourette, *World Service*, 141–4.
84. 'Boys Division, National Council of Y.M.C.A.s India, Burma and Ceylon' (Travancore: London Mission Press, 1941), 6.
85. Nish, *Flaming Milestones*, 18.
86. KFYA, IWI, Box 86, Folder 'Rough Report of the Secretaries' Conference, Lanauli, January 10–15, 1907', P. E. Curtis, Work among European Boys, 45.
87. Mizutani, *The Meaning of White*.
88. David Washbrook, 'Avatars of Identity: The British Community in India', in *Settlers and Expatriates: Britons over the Seas*, ed. Robert Bickers (Oxford: Oxford University Press, 2010), 180; Elizabeth Buettner, *Empire Families: Britons and Late Imperial India* (New York: Oxford University Press, 2004), 146–87.
89. Fischer-Tiné, *Low and Licentious Europeans*.
90. Most outspoken in this regard is a BA thesis submitted at Springfield during the First World War, on the temptations that young Europeans faced in India. The author devotes an entire chapter to the corrupting influence of Indian *nautch* (dancing) girls. Cf. SCASC, Thomas B. Hill, 'The Problems of European Young Men in India', unpublished graduation thesis, Springfield, MA, International YMCA College, 1917.
91. Carter, *The Men of India and Ceylon*, 8.
92. David M. Pomfret, *Youth and Empire: Transcolonial Childhoods in British and French Asia* (Stanford, CA: Stanford University Press, 2015), 25. Specifically for the South Asian context, cf. also Satoshi Mizutani, '"Degenerate Whites" and Their Spaces of Disorder: Disciplining Racial and Class Ambiguities in Colonial Calcutta (*c.* 1880–1930)', ed. A. Tambe and Harald Fischer-Tiné (Abingdon: Routledge, 2009), 155–91.

93. Curtis, Work among European Boys, 46.
94. Ibid., 46–7.
95. Dane Kennedy, 'The Perils of the Midday Sun: Climatic Anxieties in the Colonial Tropics', in *Imperialism and the Natural World*, ed. John Mckenzie (Manchester: Manchester University Press, 1990), 118–40.
96. For the boom of boys' clubs in the United States, cf. also Grant, *The Boy Problem*, 49–57.
97. KFYA, IWI, Box 86, Folder 'Rough Report of the Secretaries' Conference, Lanauli, January 10–15, 1907', H. G. Banurji, Boys' Work: Amongst Indian High School Boys, 48–52.
98. Ibid., 49.
99. Rosselli, 'The Self-Image of Effeteness'; Chowdhury-Sengupta, *The Frail Hero and Virile History*.
100. Banurji, Boys' Work: Amongst Indian High School Boys, 49.
101. Ibid., 50.
102. Ibid., 48. While Banurji's account may have been somewhat exaggerated, there is strong evidence that several Indian cities, including Calcutta, faced a growing cocaine problem in the first two decades of the twentieth century. Cf. R. N. Chopra and G. S. Chopra, 'Cocaine Habit in India', *The Indian Journal of Medical Research* 18, no. 3 (1931): 1016–24. Cf. also James H. Mills, 'Decolonising Drugs in Asia: The Case of Cocaine in Colonial India', *Third World Quarterly* 39, no. 2 (2018): 218–31.
103. For accounts of moral panics about the 'cocaine craze' in early twentieth-century America, cf., for example, Joseph Spillane, *Cocaine: From Medical Marvel to Modern Menace in the United States* (Baltimore, MD: Johns Hopkins University Press, 2000), 105–22; Jill Jonnes, *Hep-Cats, Narcs and Pipe Dreams: A History of America's Romance with Illegal Drugs* (New York: Scribner's Sons, 1995), 31–6.
104. Banurji, Boys' Work: Amongst Indian High School Boys, 52.
105. Sumit Sarkar, *Swadeshi Movement in Bengal 1903–1908*, 2nd revised ed. (Ranikhet: Orient Blackswan, 2010).
106. KFYA, SF, Box 9, Folder 'Boys' Work on Foreign Field', C. S. Paterson, Memorandum on Boys Work in the Foreign Field (from its inception to 1918) [1919], 5.
107. WAYAG, Young Men's Christian Association, Madras, *Twenty-Fifth Year's Service in Madras, 1914* (Madras: Methodist Publishing House, 1914), 19.
108. KFYA, BF, Box 54, Fruits of Service: Young Men's Christian Association, Madras, Annual Report, 1947', 43; cf. also the brochure 'The Boys Branch of the Y.M.C.A. Calcutta' [1928]; WAYAG, Box INDIA Boys Work.
109. KFYA, BF, Box 153, Folder 'Charles S. Paterson', s.a. [1936], Leaflet titled 'Help Wanted: Men'.
110. WAYAG, Box 'India. Boys' Work, 1922–1949', Tracy Strong, 'The Y.M.C.A. and One Fifth of the World's Boyhood: A Report on the Boys' Work of the Y.M.C.A. in India' [May 1933], 12–13.
111. Emmot Dedmon, *Great Enterprises: 100 Years of the YMCA of Metropolitan Chicago* (New York: Rand McNally, 1957), 93; Kidd, *Making American Boys*, 44–47; cf. also Gustav-Wrathall, *Take the Young Stranger by the Hand*, 160–5; George Chauncey, Jr., 'Christian Brotherhood or Sexual Perversion? Homosexual Identities and the Construction of Sexual Boundaries in the World War One Era', *Journal of Social History* 19, no. 2 (1985): 189–211.
112. Gustav-Wrathall, *Take the Young Stranger by the Hand*, 165–6.

113. WAYAG, Box 'INDIA Management, Mission, National Reports 1891–1950', Folder 'Report of the General Board of Young Men's Christian Associations of India, Burma & Ceylon 1938–1947, to the Fifteenth National Convention at Matheran, February 26–28, 1947, with Proceedings of the Convention, Calcutta 1947', 18.
114. Antoinette Burton, 'The Body in/as World History', in *A Companion to World History*, ed. Douglas Northrop (Malden, MA: Wiley–Blackwell, 2012), 279.
115. KFYA, SF, Box 9, Folder "Boys' Work on Foreign Field", File 'Donald I. Dutcher, Boys' Work in the Foreign Field [1920]', 1.
116. A prominent exception was Arthur G. Noehren, who had studied in Princeton and at the University of Virginia. KFYA, BF, Box 162, Folder 'Biographical Data Arthur G. Noehren', File 'Biography of Arthur G. Noehren, Physical Director, Young Men's Christian Association, Madras, India'.
117. KFYA, SF, Box 9, Folder 'Boys' Work on Foreign Field', File 'C. S. Paterson, Memorandum on Boys Work in the Foreign Field (from Its Inception to 1918) [1919]', 5.
118. 'The World at Play', *The Playground* 10, no. 8 (1916): 270. For a concise summary of the Playground movement in the United States, cf. Grant, *The Boy Problem*, 58–66.
119. A. G. Noehren, 'Physical Department', in *Twelfth National Convention Young Men's Christian Associations India Burma, and Ceylon and Report of National Council 1924–26* (Calcutta: Baptist Mission Press, 1927), 68.
120. Ibid., 68.
121. Government of Bombay, 'Report of the Physical Education Committee', 94.
122. KFYA, SF, Box 9, Folder 'Boys' Work on Foreign Field', File 'C. S. Paterson, Memorandum on Boys Work in the Foreign Field (from Its Inception to 1918) [1919]', 5 and 15.
123. Luther H. Gulick, *Manual for Physical Measurements in Connection with the Association Gymnasium Records* (New York: The International Committee of Young Men's Christian Associations, 1892).
124. Baker, *Playing with God*, 56. For a detailed account of the methods taught and practised at the Springfield College in the post Gulick era, cf. SCASC, Byron G. Sherman, 'Medical and Physical Examination of Y.M.C.A. Boys', unpublished post-graduation minor thesis, Springfield, MA, Y.M.C.A. College, 1916.
125. C. S. Paterson, Memorandum on Boys Work in the Foreign Field, 20. On the CSET in Canada, cf. Patricia Dirks, 'Canada's Boys – An Imperial or National Asset? Responses to Baden-Powell's Boy Scout Movement in Pre-War Canada', in *Canada and the British World: Culture, Migration, and Identity*, ed. P. Buckner and R. R. Francis (Vancouver: UBC Press, 2006), 121–5.
126. KFYA, BF, Box 162, Folder 'Biographical data Arthur G. Noehren', File 'Biography of Arthur G. Noehren, Physical Director, Young Men's Christian Association, Madras, India'.
127. RYND, A. G. Noehren, 'The YMCA and Health Education' (Report of National Council, 1924–1926, n.d.), 172.
128. Ibid.
129. H. G. Beall, 'The "Lloyd Adams Fitness Shield" – A Graded Physical Efficiency Test for Indian Boys', *American Physical Education Review* 26, no. 7 (1921): 319.
130. KFYA, SF, Box 9, Folder 'Boys' Work on Foreign Field', File 'Suggestions for Group Leaders: Bulletin No. 4 (Issued by Boys' Division, National Council Y.M.C.A.s India, Burma & Ceylon)'.

131. As early as 1914, the Madras boys' branch, for instance, reported the existence two football clubs with seventy members. WAYAG, YMCA, Madras, *Twenty-Fifth Year's Service*, 19.
132. Frank Crane, 'A Philosopher's Viewpoint of the Foreign Work', *Physical Training* 21, no. 3 (1924): 94.
133. KFYA, IS, Box 9, Folder 'Boys' Work on Foreign Field', File 'C. S. Paterson, Memorandum on Boys Work in the Foreign Field (from Its Inception to 1918) [1919]', 5.
134. Banerjee, *Make Me a Man!*, Chapters 2 and 3. Cf. also Valiani, *Militant Publics in India*.
135. Shoran Singha, 'North India', in Heald (ed.), *The Place of Boyhood*, 292.
136. Ibid.
137. KFYA, SF, Box 9, Folder 'Boys' Work on Foreign Field', File 'C. S. Paterson, Memorandum on Boys Work in the Foreign Field (from Its Inception to 1918) [1919]', 7.
138. KFYA, SF, Box 9, Folder 'Boys' Work on Foreign Field', File 'F. V. Slack, "Facts about Boys' Work in India" [May 1920]', 10.
139. 'Springfield Men Leaders in the Camping Movement', *The Springfield Student* 30, no. 7 (1939): 1.
140. WAYAG, Box 'India. Boys' Work, 1922–1949', File 'Tracy Strong', 'The Y.M.C.A. and One Fifth of the World's Boyhood: A Report on the Boys' Work of the Y.M.C.A. in India' [May 1933].
141. Ibid., 10–11.
142. Ibid., 15.
143. Ibid., 10. For a persuasive analysis of such intercultural complexities in a similar context, cf. also Jialin Christina Wu, 'A Life of Make Believe: Being Boy Scouts and "Playing Indian" in British Malaya (1910–1942)', *Gender & History* 26, no. 3 (2014): 589–619.
144. Cf., for instance, WAYAG. Box 'INDIA Boys' Work, 1922–49', *A Decade of Progress, 1928-1937. The Madras Boys' and Girls' Exhibition* (Madras: Boys' Division, National Council Y.M.C.A., India, Burma and Ceylon, 1937).
145. J. H. Dunderdale, *Why Bother with Boys* (Nagercoil: London Mission Press, 1941), 21.
146. Government of Bombay, 'Report of the Physical Education Committee', 105.
147. Ibid., 60.
148. Carey A. Watt, 'The Promise of "Character" and the Spectre of Sedition: The Boy Scout Movement and Colonial Consternation in India, 1908–1921', *South Asia* 22, no. 2 (1999): 38.
149. Ibid., 41–2.
150. Roy, 'The Torchbearers of Progress', 53–6.
151. Cf. Joseph McQuade, *A Genealogy of Terrorism: Colonial Law and the Origins of an Idea* (Cambridge: Cambridge University Press, 2021), Chapters 2–4; Michael Silvestri, *Policing 'Bengali Terrorism' in India and the World: Imperial Intelligence and Revolutionary Nationalism, 1905–1939* (Cham: Palgrave Macmillan, 2019), 25–73; Durba Ghosh, *Gentlemanly Terrorists: Political Violence and the Colonial State in India, 1919–1947* (Cambridge: Cambridge University Press, 2017); Kama MacLean, *A Revolutionary History of Interwar India: Violence, Image, Voice and Text* (C. Hurst, 2015).
152. Satadru Sen, 'Anarchies of Youth: The Oaten Affair and Colonial Bengal', in *Disciplined Natives: Race, Freedom and Confinement in Colonial India*, ed. Satadru Sen (Delhi: Primus Books, 2012), 13–41; Kama MacLean, 'On the Art of Panicking

Quietly: British Expatriate Responses to "Terrorist Outrages" in India, 1912–33', in *Anxieties, Fear and Panic in Colonial Settings Empires on the Verge of a Nervous Breakdown*, ed. Harald Fischer-Tiné (Cham: Springer, 2016), 135–66.
153. Watt, 'The Promise of "Character" and the Spectre of Sedition', 54.
154. WAYAG, Box 'India. Boys' Work, 1922–1949', File 'Tracy Strong', 'The Y.M.C.A. and One Fifth of the World's Boyhood: A Report on the Boys' Work of the Y.M.C.A. in India' [May 1933], 15.
155. J. C. L. Nasir, 'Boys Work at the Lahore YMCA', *The Young Men of India* 49, no. 8 (1937): 208.
156. D. Swamidoss, 'India', in *The Place of Boyhood*, ed. C. E. Heald, 288.
157. Ibid., 289–90.
158. RYND, Young Men's Christian Association, Lahore, Annual Report for 1926, 7.
159. 'Boys' Camp in Madras', *Young Men of India* 40, no. 5 (May 1928): 303.
160. E. C. Worman, 'Report on Boys Work, 1924–1926' (Young Men's Christian Associations India, Burma, and Ceylon, Report of the National Council, 1924–26, n.d.), 160.
161. YDSPC, Rec. Gr. 115, Series I, Waldo Huntley Heinrichs Papers, Box 7, Folder 63, Diaries 1922–1929, Waldo H. Heinrichs, Diaries, entry for 20 September1929.
162. For facts on Waldo H. Heinrichs of Lahore and his work, cf. KFYA, BF, Box 89, Folder 'Biographical Data, Waldo Huntley Heinrichs'.
163. Cf. also Brunner, *Education and Modernity in Colonial Punjab*, 213–15.
164. YDSPC, Heinrichs, Diaries, entry for 13 July 1916.
165. YDSPC, Heinrichs, Diaries, entry for 14 January 1916.
166. KFYA, ISF, Box 9, Folder 'Boys' Work on Foreign Field', File 'C. S. Paterson, Memorandum on Boys Work in the Foreign Field (from its inception to 1918) [1919]', 7.
167. Fischer-Tiné, Huebner, and Tyrrell, 'The Rise and Growth of a Global "Moral Empire', 15.
168. *Bustee* (an English corruption of the Hindi word बस्ती/*bastī*) refers to an overcrowded area where many people live in poverty.
169. P. K. Chowdhury, 'A Short Report of Boys' Work in Calcutta', *Young Men of India* 49, no. 8 (May 1937): 207.
170. KFYA, IWI, Box 34, Folder 'Annual Reports', *Citizens in the Making: Y.M.C.A. Calcutta 1931* (Calcutta G. P. Press, 1932), 8; KFYA, IWI, Box 5, Folder 'Annual & Quarterly Reports', *Building Morale: Y.M.C.A. Calcutta 1941* (Calcutta G. P. Press, 1942), 14.
171. H. J. Payne, 'Work among Boys in 1931', *Rangoon Men* 6, no. 2 (1932): 27.
172. Muriel Wasi, 'School for Citizens: Bangalore Boys' Clubs Train Urchins for Responsiblity', *The Illustrated Weekly of India*, 14 March 1948.
173. Gerald Horne, *The End of Empires: African Americans and India* (Philadelphia: Temple University Press, 2009), 186–92. On the original Boys Town in Omaha, cf. Hugh Reilly and Kevin Warneke, *Father Flanagan of Boys Town: A Man of Vision* (Boys Town, NE: Boys Town Press, 2008), 111–33.
174. KFYA, IWI, Box 60, Folder 'Madras (Boys Town)', File 'Madras Boys Town: Haven for Homeless Boys'.
175. KFYA, IWI, Box 60, 'Folder 'Boys' Town, Madras, 1949–52', File 'Youth World Service and Restoration Project No. 4: India's Model Youth Project – $ 8,000'.
176. 'YMCA Secretary at Madras Speaks on All India Radio Network', *Indianapolis Recorder*, 10 May 1947, 13.
177. 'India Boys' Town Founder Speaks to Y', *The Covina Argus-Citizen*, 17 October 1952, 1.

178. The International Division of the YMCA in New York also produced a short documentary titled *Assignment India*, celebrating Burr's pioneering work in the Madras Boys' Town. The film is available online under https://umedia.lib.umn.edu/item/p16022coll225:31.
179. Robert Turnbull, 'Boys Town in India Saves Many Waifs', *The New York Times*, 9 April 1952, 7. Available online: https://www.nytimes.com/1952/04/09/archives/boys-town-in-india-saves-many-waifs-institution-opened-in-madras-by.html?searchResultPosition=1 (accessed 25 May 2022).
180. V. G. Williams, 'Under-Privileged Boys at Work', *Young Men of India* 49, no. 8 (August 1937): 210–11.
181. Ibid., 210.
182. 'Annual Report of the Young Men's Christian Association of Calcutta for 1907', 15.
183. Banurji, Boys' Work: Amongst Indian High School Boys, 50.
184. Ibid, 51.
185. 'Annual Report of the Young Men's Christian Association of Calcutta for 1907' (Calcutta, 1908) 9; 'Young Men's Christian Association of Calcutta, Annual Report 1918' (Calcutta, 1919), 24.
186. KFYA, IWI, Box 34, Folder 'Annual Reports', *Citizens in the Making: Y.M.C.A. Calcutta 1931* (Calcutta G. P. Press, 1932), 14.
187. Ibid.
188. For an analysis of the WCTU's transnational work, cf. Ian Tyrell, *Woman's World/Woman's Empire: The Woman's Christian Temperance Union in International Perspective 1880–1930* (Chapel Hill: The University of Carolina Press, 1991).
189. 'Sixteenth Annual Report of the Young Men's Christian Association of Calcutta for 1909' (Calcutta, 1910), 14.
190. 'Annual Report of the Young Men's Christian Association of Calcutta for 1908' (Calcutta, 1909), 7–8.
191. Paul A. Kramer, 'Empires, Exceptions, and Anglo-Saxons: Race and Rule between the British and United States Empires, 1880–1910', *The Journal of American History* 88, no. 4 (March 2002): 1341–42.
192. K. T. Paul, 'Citizenship in Modern India', *Young Men of India* 31, no. 1 (1921): 34.
193. I borrow this phrase from Satadru Sen, *Traces of Empire: India, America and Postcolonial Cultures. Essays and Criticism* (New Delhi: Primus Books, 2014).
194. KFYA, IWI, Box 60, Folder 'Boys' Town, Madras, 1949–52', File Youth World Service and Restoration Project No. 4: India's Model Youth Project – $ 8,000.
195. Cited in David, *The YMCA and the Making*, 365. For an analysis for disciplinary varieties of citizen training in Nehruvian India, cf. also Watt, 'Philanthropy and Civilizing Missions', 293–302; Ganesh Kudaisya, *A Republic in the Making: India in the 1950s* (New Delhi: Oxford University Press, 2017), 113–70.

5 'The gospel of rural reconstruction': The YMCA's rural development programmes in South Asia (*c.* 1916–1955)

1. UATSHC, Box 3, Folder 6, Duane Spencer Hatch, typewritten report (Trivandrum 25 April 1933).
2. Ekbladh, *The Great American Mission*, 2. Cf. also Nick Cullather, *The Hungry World: America's Cold War Battle against Poverty in Asia* (Cambridge, MA: Harvard

University Press, 2010); Akhil Gupta, *Postcolonial Developments: Agriculture in the Making of Modern India* (Durham, NC: Duke University Press, 1998), 52–62.
3. Nicole Sackley, 'Foundation in the Field: The Ford Foundation New Delhi Office and the Construction of Development Knowledge, 1951–1970', in *American Foundations and the Coproduction of World Order in the Twentieth Century*, ed. John Krige and Helke Rausch (Göttingen: Vandenhoeck & Ruprecht, 2012), 232–60; Inderjeet Parmar, *Foundations of the American Century: The Ford, Carnegie, and Rockefeller Foundations in the Rise of American Power* (New York: Columbia University Press, 2012). On 'high modernism' as an exclusive and inherently authoritarian form of development, cf. James C. Scott, *Seeing Like a State: How Certain Schemes to Improve the Human Condition Have Failed* (New Haven, CT: Yale University Press, 1998).
4. Cf., for instance, Cullather, *The Hungry World*, 84.
5. For the editing out of Christian missionaries from the history of development, cf. also Michael R. Feener and Catherine Scheer, 'Development's Missions', in *The Mission of Development: Religion and Technopolitics in Asia*, ed. Michael R. Feener, Catherine Scheer and Philip Fountain (Leiden: Brill, 2019), 1–27.
6. Sackley, 'The Village as Cold War Site'; Nicole Sackley, 'Village Models: Etawah, India, and the Making and Remaking of Development in the Early Cold War', *Diplomatic History* xxxvii, no. 4 (2013): 755–6. An illuminating perspective on the League of Nations as another key site for the emergence of a transnational epistemic community of development experts in the interwar years is provided by Margherita Zanasi, 'Exporting Development: The League of Nations and Republican China', *Comparative Studies in Society and History* 49, no. 1 (2007).
7. Benjamin Siegel, 'Modernizing Peasants and 'Master Farmers': All-India Crop Competitions and the Politics of Progressive Agriculture in Early Independent India', *Comparative Studies of South Asia, Africa and the Middle East* 37, no. 1 (2017): 64–85. Cf. also Daniel Immerwahr's book, which refers to the pre-independence pioneers of rural reconstruction in a single endnote: Immerwahr, *Thinking Small: The United States and the Lure of Community Development*, 210, endnote 26. Albert Mayer's Etawah Pilot Project, by contrast, has recently received a great deal of scholarly attention: cf. Sackley, 'Village Models', 77–94; Jack Loveridge, 'Between Hunger and Growth: Pursuing Rural Development in Partition's Aftermath, 1947–1957', *Contemporary South Asia* xxv, no. 1 (2017).
8. Cf. especially Prakash Kumar, 'American Modernisers and the Cow Question in Colonial and Nationalist India', *South Asia Journal of South Asian Studies* 44, no. 1 (2021): 185–200; Prakash Kumar, "Modernization' and Agrarian Development in India, 1912–52', *Journal of Asian Studies* 79, no. 3 (2020): 633–58; Rajsekhar Basu, 'Missionaries as Agricultural Pioneers: Protestant Missionaries and Agricultural Improvement in Twentieth-Century India', in *Tilling the Land: Agricultural Knowledge and Practices in Colonial India*, ed. Deepak Kumar and Bipasha Raha (Delhi: 2016); Subir Sinha, 'Lineages of the Developmentalist State: Transnationality and Village India, 1900–1965', *Comparative Studies in Society and History* 1, no. 1 (2008); Chatterjee, *The Making of Indian Secularism*, Chapter 5.
9. The 'Indian beginnings' of the YMCA's rural reconstruction programme in South Asia have recently been briefly touched upon in Tyrrell, 'Vectors of Practicality'.
10. Under this title, popular *Reader's Digest* author Jerome Beatty included a portrait of Hatch in his book on great American expats: Jerome Beatty, *Americans All Over* (New York: John Day, 1940), 302–13.

11. In post-1950s maps and literature, the name of the village is mostly given (linguistically more correctly) as Marthandam. In order to avoid confusion, however, I will use the older version Martandam, which is consistently used in the majority of my sources.
12. Albert Mayer et al., *Pilot Project, India: The Story of Rural Development at Etawah, Uttar Pradesh* (Berkeley: University of California Press, 1958), 34.
13. Cf., for instance, Park, *Building a Heaven on Earth*, 120–30; Chang Liu, *Peasants and Revolution in Rural China: Rural Political Change in the North China Plain and the Yangzi Delta* (London: Routledge, 2007), 137–40; Charles W. Hayford, *To the People: James Yen and Village China* (New York: Columbia University Press, 1990).
14. The only book-length study that exists on the Y's rural regeneration experiments in South Asia is the rather descriptive Kanakaraj, *Light Houses of Rural Reconstruction*. Besides this, the major in-house histories of the Indian YMCA devote short chapters to its 'rural work'. Cf., for example, David, *The YMCA and the Making*, 309–22; Dunderdale, *The YMCA in India*, 113–24. The only critical engagement with the YMCA's rural work has been rather broad. Cf. Tyrrell, 'Vectors of Practicality', 39–60; Raghavan, *Fierce Enigmas*, 73–80.
15. For instance, Sara Lorenzini, in her recent monograph on the global history of development, devotes a mere nine pages to the pre–Second World War era. Sara Lorenzini, *Global Development: A Cold War History* (Princeton, NJ: Princeton University Press, 2017), 9–18. However, for recent examples of studies that more fully acknowledge the importance of interwar developments, cf. Stephen J. Macekura and Erez Manela, eds, *The Development Century: A Global History* (Cambridge: Cambridge University Press, 2019); Corinna R. Unger, *International Development: A Postwar History* (London: Bloomsbury, 2018).
16. A similar point has most recently been made by Amalia Ribi Forclaz, 'Agriculture, American Expertise, and the Quest for Global Data: Leon Estabrook and the First World Agricultural Census of 1930', *Journal of Global History* 11, no. 1 (2016).
17. On the importance of the idiom and practice of development in late colonialism, cf. Miguel Bandeira Jerónimo, 'Repressive Developmentalism: Idioms, Repertoires and Trajectories in late Colonialism', in *The Oxford Handbook of the Ends of Empire*, ed. Martin Thomas and Andrew S. Thompson (Oxford: Oxford University Press, 2018), 537–54; Frederick Cooper, 'Development, Modernization, and the Social Sciences in the Era of Decolonization: The Examples of British and French Africa', in *The Ends of European Colonial Empires: Cases and Comparisons*, ed. Miguel Bandeira Jerónimo and António Costa Pinto (Basingstoke: Palgrave Macmillan, 2015); Helen Tilley, *Africa as a Living Laboratory: Empire, Development and the Problem of Scientific Knowledge, 1870–1950* (Chicago, IL: University of Chicago Press, 2011), 115–68; Joseph Morgan Hodge, *Triumph of the Expert: Agrarian Doctrines of Development and the Legacies of British Colonialism* (Athens: Ohio University Press, 2007).
18. Cf., for example, the otherwise excellent study by Corinna R. Unger, *Entwicklungspfade in Indien: Eine Internationale Geschichte, 1947–1980* (Göttingen: Wallstein Verlag, 2015); Corinna Unger, 'Towards Global Equilibrium: American Foundations and Indian Modernization, 1950s to 1970s', *Journal of Global History* 6, no. 1 (2011).
19. Nathan Citino has recently articulated the need for more 'regional emphasis in the study of international development' as a 'much-needed complement to the prevailing globalism' and Western-centrism of existing research. Nathan J. Citino,

Envisioning the Arab Future: Modernization in U.S.–Arab Relations, 1945–1967 (Cambridge: Cambridge University Press, 2017), 2.

20. Ekbladh, *The Great American Mission*. The concept of techno-politics is defined in Timothy Mitchell, *Rule of Experts: Egypt, Techno-Politics, Modernity* (Berkeley: University of California Press, 2002), 41–2. For a critical discussion, cf. also Feener and Scheer, 'Development's Missions', 15–20.
21. For the early transnational export of such schemes to other world regions, cf., for instance, Andrew Zimmermann, *Alabama in Africa: Booker T. Washington the German Empire and the Globalization of the New South* (Princeton, NJ: Princeton University Press, 2010); Tore C. Olsson, *Agrarian Crossings: Reformers and the Remaking of the US and Mexican Countryside* (Princeton, NJ: Princeton University Press, 2017). One of the rare existing studies of a similar 'grass-roots movement of community development, practical education, and moral reawakening' in South Asia is Aaron D. Purcell, 'Collaboration and the Small Community: Arthur Morgan and the Mitraniketan Project in Kerala', *The Historian* 65, no. 3 (2003): 643–64.
22. Fischer-Tiné, *Pidgin-Knowledge*.
23. On epistemic communities, cf. Peter M. Haas, 'Introduction: Epistemic Communities and International Policy Coordination', *International Organization* 46, no. 1 (1992): 1–35. For an analysis of development experts as an 'epistemic community', cf. Hans Dieter Evers, Markus Kaiser and Christine Müller, 'Knowledge in Development: Epistemic Machineries in a Global Context', *International Social Science Journal* 60, no. 195 (2009), 55–68.
24. UATSHC, Box 3, Duane Spencer Hatch, 'Beyond the Ends of the Roads: Legs for Knowledge', unpublished Mss, s.a. [c. 1962].
25. Cyrus Schayegh, 'The Interwar Germination of Development and Modernization Theory and Practice: Politics, Institution Building, and Knowledge Production between the Rockefeller Foundation and the American University of Beirut', *Geschichte und Gesellschaft* 41, no. 4 (2015): 649.
26. Corinna Unger, on the contrary, posits that the Cold War can be seen as a watershed that accelerated globalization processes and enabled a new global consciousness among rural development experts: Unger, 'Towards Global Equilibrium', 125–6.
27. Thomas Davies, *NGOs: A New History of Transnational Civil Society* (London: Hurst Publishers, 2013), 35–6.
28. John Augustus Voelcker, *Report on the Improvement of Indian Agriculture* (London: Eyre and Spottiswoode, 1893).
29. For the aims and methods of the Pusa Institute, cf. *Prospectus of the Agricultural Research Institute and College, Pusa* (Calcutta: Superintendent Government Printing, India, 1909).
30. Frank L. Brayne, *The Remaking of Village India (Being the Second Edition of 'Village Uplift in India')* (London: H. Milford, Oxford University Press, 1929); Frank L. Brayne, *Better Villages* (London: H. Milford, Oxford University Press, 1937). Cf. also Sultan, 'Malcolm Darling and Developmentalism in Colonial Punjab'; Clive Dewey, *Anglo-Indian Attitudes: Mind of the Indian Civil Service* (London: Hambledon, 1993), 61–101.
31. Rupa Viswanath, *The Pariah Problem: Caste, Religion and the Social in Modern India* (New York: Columbia University Press, 2014); cf. especially 71–90.
32. Christian Harding, 'The Christian Village Experiment in Punjab: Social and Religious Reformation', *South Asia: Journal of South Asian Studies* 31, no. 3 (2008): 397–418.
33. Christopher Harding, *Religious Transformation in South Asia: The Meaning of Conversion in Colonial Punjab* (Oxford: Oxford University Press, 2008), 234–7.

34. Kumar, "'Modernization' and Agrarian Development'; Chatterjee, *The Making of Indian Secularism*, 147–50.
35. Sandipan Baksi, 'Modernizing Agriculture in the Colonial Era: A View from Some Hindi Periodicals 1880–1940', in *Tilling the Land Agricultural Knowledge and Practices in Colonial India*, ed. Deepak Kumar and Bipasha Raha (Delhi: Primus Books, 2016); cf. especially 75–85.
36. Cf., for instance, Fischer-Tiné, *Der Gurukul Kangri*, 98; Michael P. Brunner, 'Teaching Development: Debates on 'Scientific Agriculture' and 'Rural Reconstruction' at Khalsa College, Amritsar, c. 1915–1947', *The Indian Economic & Social History Review* 55, no. 1 (2018): 77–132.
37. Prem Chand Lal, *Reconstruction and Education in Rural India: In the Light of the Programme Carried on at Sriniketan the Institute of Rural Reconstruction Founded by Rabindranath Tagore* (London: G. Allen & Unwin Limited, 1932); Leonard K. Elmhirst, *Poet and Plowman* (Calcutta: Visva-Bharati, 1975).
38. Darren C. Zook, 'Developing the Rural Citizen: Southern India, 1900–47', *South Asia: Journal of South Asian Studies* 23, no. 1 (2000): 79.
39. Aaron Windel, *Cooperative Rule: Community Development in Britain's Late Empire*. Oakland: University of California Press, 2021, 19–37; Nikolay Kamenov, 'The Place of the 'Cooperative Agrarian History of India, c. 1900–1970'', *Journal of Asian Studies* 79, no. 1 (2020): 104–10; Corinna R. Unger, 'The Decolonization of Development: Rural Development in India before and after 1947', in *Internationalism, Imperialism and the Formation of the Contemporary World*, ed. Bandeira Jerónimo, 254–60.
40. Rochana Bajpai and Carlo Bonura, 'South Asian and Southeast Asian Ideologies', in *The Oxford Handbook of Political Ideologies*, ed. Michael Freeden, Layman T. Sargent and Marc Stears (Oxford: Oxford University Press, 2013), quote on 667.
41. Surinder S. Jodhka, 'Nation and Village: Images of Rural India in Gandhi, Nehru and Ambedkar', *Economic and Political Weekly* 37, no. 32 (2002): 3343–53.
42. Jawaharlal Nehru, *A Bunch of Old Letters: Written Mostly to Jawaharlal Nehru and Some Written by Him* (Bombay: Asia Publishing House, 1958), 506.
43. Cf., for instance, S. G. Beri and G. B. Jathar, *Some Aspects of Rural Reconstruction in India (A Paper Submitted to the Indian Economic Conference in Lucknow, 1928)* (Bombay: Oxford University Press, s.a. [1929]); Sugata Dasgupta, *A Poet and a Plan: Tagore's Experiments in Rural Reconstruction* (Calcutta: Thacker, Spink, 1933); G. Rudrappa, *The Work of Rural Reconstruction in the Mysore State and British India: Further Reflections and Thoughts* (Bangalore, 1935).
44. K. T. Paul, 'Agriculture and Christianity in India: Development of Co-operative Societies', *Rural Manhood* 4, no. 10 (1913): 363–5.
45. Sherwood Eddy, 'Famine Stricken India', *Rural Manhood* 10, no. 6 (1919): 245.
46. Ibid., 246.
47. *Peace Programme of the YMCA Simla–Delhi and the Indian National Council* (Delhi, 1921), 3–6.
48. For a succinct discussion, cf. Enya Hu, 'The Gospel of Intellectuality: Indoctrinating Yenching Educational Missionaries in the Progressive Era', in *The Mission of Development: Religion and Technopolitics in Asia*, ed. Michael R. Feener, Catherine Scheer and Philip Fountain (Leiden: Brill, 2019), 36–51. On the 'social gospel' in the United States generally, cf. Evans, *The Social Gospel in American Religion: A History*; Curtis, *A Consuming Faith*.

49. Chatterjee, *The Making of Indian Secularism*, 137–8. Cf. also D. Swamidoss, 'The Message of the Indian Villager to the Y.M.C.A.', *Young Men of India* 29, no. 4 (1918): 199–204.
50. KFYA, BF, Box 73, 'Biographical Data. Duane Spencer Hatch', *The Troy Record*, 27 September 1934, and 'Notes on Spencer Hatch', s.a.
51. Hatch, 'Working with D. Spencer 'Chick' Hatch, Part I', 15.
52. For details on the YMCA's 'army work' during the First World War and Spencer Hatch's involvement therein, cf. Chapter 2.
53. J. T. Marten, *Census of India, 1921. Part II – Tables*, Vol. 1 (Calcutta: Superintendent Government Printing, India, 1923) 340.
54. Fischer-Tiné, 'The Making of a 'Ruling Race''.
55. Hatch, 'Working with D. Spencer 'Chick' Hatch, Part I', 20.
56. Ibid.
57. Duane Spencer Hatch, 'Working with D. Spencer 'Chick' Hatch, Part II – the Troops in Mesopotamia', *The Quill and Scroll* 69, no. 1 (1963): 27; Duane Spencer Hatch, 'Working with D. Spencer 'Chick' Hatch, Part III – India: The First 18 Years', *The Quill and Scroll* 69, no. 3 (1963): 13.
58. Travancore is largely but not entirely identical to today's state of Kerala. During the realignment of Indian states according to linguistic criteria, Travancore was united with the district of Malabar and the former princely state of Cochin to form the Malayalam-speaking state of Kerala. Martandam, on the other hand, was part of the Kanyakumari district where Tamil was the predominant language and was therefore incorporated into the state of Tamil Nadu in 1956.
59. Alfred Charles True, *A History of Agricultural Education in the United States 1785–1925* (Washington, DC: U.S. Government Printing Office, 1929), 276–7; Roy V. Scott, *The Reluctant Farmer: The Rise of Agricultural Extension to 1914* (Urbana: University of Illinois Press, 1970), 245–8.
60. Hatch, 'Beyond the Ends of the Roads', 149.
61. Duane Spencer Hatch, *Up from Poverty in Rural India* (Bombay: Oxford University Press, 1932), 61–2.
62. Herbert A. Popley, *K. T. Paul, Christian Leader* (Calcutta: Y.M.C.A. Publishing House, 1938), 70.
63. Hatch, 'Beyond the Ends of the Roads', 149.
64. Popley, *K. T. Paul*, 75.
65. Cf. for instance Duane Spencer Hatch, 'My Job Is Village Reconstruction', *Christian Rural Fellowship Bulletin* xcviii (1944): 8.
66. Hatch, 'Beyond the Ends of the Roads', 150.
67. Duane Spencer Hatch, *Toward Freedom from Want from India to Mexico* (Bombay: Oxford University Press, 1949), 35.
68. Dipesh Chakrabarty, *Provincializing Europe: Postcolonial Thought and Historical Difference* (Princeton, NJ: Princeton University Press, 2000), 9.
69. *The Cornell Daily Sun*, 21 October 1941, 7.
70. Hatch, 'Beyond the Ends of the Roads', 157.
71. Ibid., 214. This investment in local knowledge significantly differentiates the Hatches from a later generation of more detached and technocratic rural development experts, including Albert Mayer, the architect of the famous Etawah Pilot Project in northern India. Sackley, 'Village Models', 762.
72. Emily Gilchriest Hatch, 'The Kathakali: The Indigenous Drama of Malabar' (PhD thesis, Cornell University, 1934).

73. Duane Spencer Hatch, 'Poverty and Self-Help in Rural India' (unpublished PhD dissertation, Cornell University, 1928).
74. Hatch, 'Beyond the Ends of the Roads', 153.
75. UATSHC, Box 3, 9, Duane Spencer Hatch, 'Too Big to Measure', unpublished book Mss., s.a. [1955].
76. Beatty, *Americans All Over*, 308–9.
77. Ibid.
78. KFYA, IWI, Box 10, Folder 'Annual and Quarterly Reports, 1919–1924', Duane Spencer Hatch, 'Annual Report of 1924', 15 June 1925, 1.
79. Popley, *K. T. Paul*, 60–2.
80. *Young Men of India* 44, no. 8 (1932): 426.
81. For the pioneering rural work done by Indian Y workers, cf. also Daniel Swamidoss, 'The Y.M.C.A. in the Villages of South India', *Young Men of India* 28, no. 8 (1917): 454–7; Kanakaraj, *Light Houses of Rural Reconstruction*, 47–117.
82. Beatty, *Americans All Over*, 305.
83. Hatch, *Up from Poverty in Rural India*, xii and 6.
84. Ibid., 5.
85. Hatch, 'Poverty and Self-Help in Rural India', 306.
86. Hatch, *Up from Poverty in Rural India*, 4.
87. Hatch, 'Poverty and Self-Help in Rural India', 277.
88. David Arnold, 'Agriculture and "Improvement" in Early Colonial India: A Pre-History of Development', *Journal of Agrarian Change* v, no. 4 (2005): 508–11; Arturo Escobar, *Encountering Development: The Making and Unmaking of the Third World* (Princeton, NJ: Princeton University Press, 1995), 8.
89. Hatch, 'Poverty and Self-Help in Rural India', 269 and 271.
90. Ibid., 388–95; Hatch, *Toward Freedom from Want*, 33–4. On Knapp's discovery of the agricultural demonstration technique, cf. Joseph Cannon Bailey, *Seaman A. Knapp, Schoolmaster of American Agriculture* (New York: Columbia University Press, 1945); on its spread to Asia, cf. Bret Wallach, *Losing Asia: Modernization and the Culture of Development* (Baltimore, MD: Johns Hopkins University Press, 1996), chapter 7.
91. Hatch, 'Poverty and Self-Help in Rural India', 396–8; Hatch, *Toward Freedom from Want*, 35. In the bibliography to his first book, Hatch lists several titles relating to 'extension work among negroes', Hatch, *Up from Poverty in Rural India*, 58.
92. Booker T. Washington, *Up from Slavery: An Autobiography* (New York: Doubleday, Page, 1901).
93. Hatch, *Up from Poverty in Rural India*, 70; Duane Spencer Hatch, *Rural Reconstruction and Evangelicalism or Evangelism and Christian Service. From an Address Delivered at a Special Session of Tambaram World Conference Etc.* (Trivandrum: Y.M.C.A. District Office, 1940), 19.
94. Scott, *Seeing Like a State*.
95. Jess Gilbert, 'Low Modernism and the Agrarian New Deal: A Different Kind of State', in *Fighting for the Farm: Rural America Transformed*, ed. Jane Adams (Philadelphia: University of Pennsylvania Press, 2003), 129–46; Jess Gilbert, *Planning Democracy: Agrarian Intellectuals and the Intended New Deal* (New Haven, CT: Yale University Press, 2015).
96. Olsson, *Agrarian Crossings*.
97. Duane Spencer Hatch, *Further Upward in Rural India* (Bombay: Oxford University Press, 1938), 31–3. The respect was at least partly mutual, as the Mahatma sent a telegram in 1940 congratulating Hatch on the celebration of a 'national honey week'

held at Martandam. KFYA, IWI, Box 51, Folder 'General, 1940', 'National Honey Week: Mr. Gandhi Sends Message', 22 April 1940.
98. E. S. Sunda, 'Rural Reconstruction: Some First Steps', *Young Men of India* 42, no. 9 (1931): 652.
99. Hatch, *Toward Freedom from Want*, 35. To make this last point, Hatch quoted from a speech by the Republican US president Herbert Hoover.
100. On the Green Revolution in India, cf. Gupta, *Postcolonial Developments*; B. H. Farmer, 'Perspectives on the Green Revolution in South Asia', *Modern Asian Studies* 20, no. 1 (1986), 175–99.
101. Hatch, 'Beyond the Ends of the Roads', 192–3.
102. UATSHC, Box 2, Duane Spencer Hatch, 'Early Times at the Martandam Project', Mss., s.a. [*c*. 1960], 13.
103. Hatch, *Up from Poverty in Rural India*, 71–2; KFYA, IWI, Box 47, Folder 'India 1920–28', Duane Spencer Hatch, 'The YMCA in South Travancore, 1923', 4.
104. Hatch, 'Working with D. Spencer 'Chick' Hatch, Part III', 15; 'Report on the YMCA in South Travancore, 1923' by D. Spencer Hatch, 4.
105. Beatty, *Americans All Over*, 308–9.
106. L. A. Hogg, *Hope for the Villager: Youth to the Rescue in South India. Being an Account of the Rural Reconstruction Work of the YMCA* (Bombay: D. B. Taporevala, 1931), 5; Hatch, 'Working with D. Spencer 'Chick' Hatch, Part III', 15.
107. Hatch, 'YMCA in South Travancore', 4.
108. Hatch, 'Poverty and Self-Help in Rural India', 359–88.
109. Hatch, *Toward Freedom from Want*, 81–7.
110. Unger, *Entwicklungspfade in Indien*, 33. For a typical argument presenting co-operatives as instruments not only of material but also of moral improvement, cf. S. Manuel, 'How Country Work Operates in India', *Association Men*, December 1921, 118–19.
111. Hatch, 'Poverty and Self-Help in Rural India', 448.
112. Hogg, *Hope for the Villager*, 6; Hatch, *Toward Freedom from Want*, 38–9.
113. On the origins and chequered history of agricultural cooperatives in late colonial South Asia, cf. Kamenov, 'The Place of the "Cooperative"'; Peter Robb, 'Bihar, the Colonial State and Agricultural Development in India, 1880–1920', *Indian Economic & Social History Review* 25, no. 2 (1988): 207–16.
114. Hatch, 'Beyond the Ends of the Roads', 157.
115. Ibid.
116. Hatch, *Toward Freedom from Want*, 55.
117. UATSHC, Box 2, Folder 'Booklets and Pamphlets, 1931–1972'; WAYAG, Box 2/2, 'Rural Work', Emily Gilchriest Hatch, *Mar-Tan-Dam: Not on the Map?*, s.a. [1933].
118. Hatch, *Rural Reconstruction and Evangelism*, 15.
119. F. L. W. Richardson, 'Thirty Years of Rural Reconstruction', *Applied Anthropology* 2, no. 3 (1943): 51. For details of the sanitation scheme, cf. Hatch, *Further Upward in Rural India*, 116–23.
120. Harald Fischer-Tiné, 'Eradicating the "Scourge of Drink" and the "Un-pardonable Sin of Illegitimate Sexual Enjoyment": M. K. Gandhi as Anti-Vice Crusader', *Interdisziplinäre Zeitschrift für Südasienforschung* ii, no. 1 (2017); David M. Fahey and Padma Manian, 'Poverty and Purification: The Politics of Gandhi's Campaign for Prohibition', *The Historian* 67, no. 3 (2005).
121. 'Twelfth National Convention Report 1924–26', 81.

122. Hatch, 'Beyond the Ends of the Roads', 230–1. Cf. also KFYA, IWI, Box 10, Folder 'Annual and Quarterly Reports, 1919–1924', Duane Spencer Hatch, 'Annual Report of 1924',15 June 1925, 3.
123. Gary R. Hess, 'American Agricultural Missionaries and Efforts at Economic Improvement in India', *Agricultural History* 42, no. 1 (1968): 31.
124. C. H. Schopmeyer, *Extension Projects in Rural Community Organization* (Washington, DC: U.S. Extension Service Circulars, 1927).
125. K. T. Paul was also an ardent advocate of the drama as a perfect medium to educate (illiterate) adults. Cf. K. T. Paul, 'Adult Education in Regard to Rural Reconstruction', *Young Men of India* 42, no. 6 (1931): 426–7.
126. Hatch, 'Poverty and Self-Help in Rural India', 494.
127. Emily Gilchriest Hatch, *Little Plays* (Madras: Hogarth Press, 1932); Emily Gilchriest Hatch, *Out of the Pot into the World: A Temperance Play* (Howrah: s.n., 1926).
128. Hatch, 'Early Times at the Martandam Project', 21.
129. Hatch, 'Beyond the Ends of the Roads', 222. It is revealing that this type of didactic plays continue to be used in development programmes in the twenty-first century. For the discussion of a case from Nigeria, cf. Liwhu Betiang, 'Theatre of Rural Empowerment: The Example of Living Earth Nigeria Foundation's Community Theatre Initiative in Cross River State, Nigeria', *Research in Drama Education: The Journal of Applied Theatre and Performance* 15, no. 1 (2010): 59–78. I am grateful to Joanna Simonow for making me aware of this article.
130. Hatch, 'YMCA in South Travancore', 2.
131. Cf. also Harald Fischer-Tiné, Julia Hauser and Ashok Malhotra, 'Introduction: Feeding Bodies, Nurturing Identities: The Politics of Diet in Late Colonial and Early Post-Colonial India', *South Asia Journal of South Asian Studies* 44, no. 1 (2021): 107–16.
132. Government of India, 'Royal Commission on Agriculture in India: Report' (Bombay: Government of India Press, 1928), 493–7. Cf. also Catriona Ellis, "'If You Cannot Feed the Body of a Child You Cannot Feed the Brain': Education and Nutrition in Late Colonial Madras', *South Asia Journal of South Asian Studies* 44, no. 1 (2021): 135–51; Sunil S. Amrith, 'Food and Welfare in India, *c*. 1900–1950', *Comparative Studies in Society and History* 1, no. 4 (2008): 1016–21. David Arnold, 'The 'Discovery' of Malnutrition and Diet in Colonial India', *Indian Economic and Social History Review* 31, no. 1 (1994).
133. Gilchriest Hatch, *Little Plays*, 33–88. It ought to be stressed that temperance was a core element of the YMCA's general programme and not limited to rural populations. American YMCA secretaries were also very much involved in urban anti-alcohol campaigns. Cf. Nikhil Menon, 'Battling the Bottle: Experiments in Regulating Drink in Late Colonial Madras', *Indian Economic & Social History Review* lii, no. 1 (2015): 44 and 47.
134. UATSHC, Box 9, Reel 1, 'Extra Martandam Footage' (DVD).
135. Gilchriest Hatch, *Little Plays*, 50.
136. UATSHC, Box 9, Reel 1, 'Extra Martandam Footage' (DVD).
137. Gilchriest Hatch, *Little Plays,* 19–20.
138. Brayne, *Better Villages*, 140–1; cf. also F. L. Brayne, 'The Indian Village', *Journal of the Central Asian Society* 19, no. 4 (1932).
139. M. K. Gandhi, 'Village Insanitation', in *M. K. Gandhi: Social Service, Work and Reform*, Vol. 1, ed. V. B. Kher (Ahmedabad: Navajivan Publishing House, 1976), 94.

140. Studdert-Kennedy, *British Christians, Indian Nationalists and the Raj*, 135.
141. Hatch, *Toward Freedom from Want*, 156.
142. Ibid., 5.
143. Beatty, *Americans All Over*, 306.
144. Cf. Taylor C. Sherman, 'Education in Early Postcolonial India: Expansion, Experimentation and Planned Self-Help', *History of Education* 47, no. 4 (2018): 504–20; Benjamin Siegel, *Hungry Nation: Food, Famine, and the Making of Modern India* (Cambridge: Cambridge University Press, 2018); Benjamin Siegel, "Self-Help Which Ennobles a Nation': Development, Citizenship, and the Obligations of Eating in India's Austerity Years', *Modern Asian Studies* 50, no. 3 (2016): 975–1018.
145. For an excellent overview of the *longue durée* history of the concept, cf. Hubertus Büschel, *Hilfe zur Selbsthilfe: Deutsche Entwicklungsarbeit in Afrika 1960–1975* (Frankfurt: Campus, 2014), 51–181.
146. Hubertus Büschel, 'Eine Brücke am Mount Meru: Zur Globalgeschichte von Hilfe zur Selbsthilfe und Gewalt in Tanganjika', in *Entwicklungswelten: Globalgeschichte der Entwicklungszusammenarbeit*, ed. Hubertus Büschel and Daniel Speich (Frankfurt: Campus, 2009), 180.
147. Büschel, *Hilfe zur Selbsthilfe*, 179–81.
148. KFYA, IWI, Box 10, Folder 'Annual and Quarterly Reports, 1919–1924', Duane Spencer Hatch, 'Annual Report of 1924', 15 June 1925, 1.
149. Ibid. To some extent, Hatch's excitement about the Indian tendency to imitate American ways seems to foreshadow the agenda of the American Peace Corps founded under John F. Kennedy in the early 1960s. Cf. Fritz Fischer, *Making Them Like Us: Peace Corps Volunteers in the 1960s* (Washington, DC: Smithsonian Institution Press, 1998).
150. UATSHC, Box 2, Folder 8, 'Address by Spencer D. Hatch', s.a. [1944], 18.
151. Cf. Kevin M. Lowe, *Baptized with the Soil: Christian Agrarians and the Crusade for Rural America* (Oxford: Oxford University Press, 2016), 16–17.
152. Peter van der Veer, ed., *Conversion to Modernities: The Globalization of Christianity* (London: Routledge, 1996), 1–21.
153. Feener and Scheer, 'Development's Missions', 21. Cf. also Barnett, *Empire of Humanity: A History of Humanitarianism*. Cf. also Harris and Maxwell, *The Spiritual in the Secular*.
154. KFYA, IWI, Box 10, Folder 'Annual and Quarterly Reports, 1919–1924', Duane Spencer Hatch, 'Annual Report of 1924', 15 June 1925, 3.
155. Sam Higginbottom, *The Gospel and the Plow, or, The Old Gospel and Modern Farming in Ancient India* (New York: Macmillan, 1921); Sam Higginbottom, 'The Future of Agriculture in India', *Young Men of India* 28, no. 8 (1917): 449–53. Cf. also Kumar, 'American Modernisers and the Cow Question', 187–8.
156. Hatch, *Rural Reconstruction and Evangelism*, 9 and 4.
157. Ibid., 9 and 11.
158. Basil Joseph Mathews, *Flaming Milestone: Being an Interpretation and the Official Report of the Twenty-First World's Conference of the World's Alliance of Y.M.C.A.s Held in January 1937, in Mysore, South India* (Geneva: World's Committee of the Y.M.C.A.'s, 1938), 141–7.
159. KFYA, IWI, box 10, 'India 1929–1934', digest of journal by the agricultural expert Kenyon L. Butterfield.
160. Kenyon L. Butterfield, *The Christian Enterprise among Rural People* (Nashville, TN: Cokesbury Press, 1933), 67. Cf. also Kenyon L. Butterfield, *The Christian Mission*

in Rural India; Report and Recommendations by Kenyon L. Butterfield, Counsellor on Rural Work, International Missionary Council, with a Foreword by Dr. John R. Mott (New York: International Missionary Council, 1930).

161. There is an ongoing debate in development literature about the role of 'FBO's. A detailed engagement with this controversy is beyond the scope of this book. Cf. Ben Jones and Marie Juul Petersen, 'Instrumental, Narrow, Normative? Reviewing Recent Work on Religion and Development', *Third World Quarterly* 32, no. 7 (2011); Gerard Clarke and Michael Jennings, eds, *Development, Civil Society and Faith-Based Organizations: Bridging the Sacred and the Secular* (Basingstoke: Palgrave Macmillan, 2008).

162. For biographical details on Ouwerkerk, see the introduction to her posthumously published book: Louise Ouwerkerk, *No Elephants for the Maharaja: Social and Political Change in the Princely State of Travancore, 1921–1947* (New Delhi: Manohar Publishers, 1994).

163. Miss [sic] Ouwerkerk, 'The Lessons of Marthandam', in *Developing Village India: Studies in Village Problems*, ed. M. S. Randhawa, revised (Bombay: Orient Longmans, 1951), 39.

164. Beatty, *Americans All Over*, 310.

165. Cf. for instance Duane Spencer Hatch, 'Summer School, Travancore and Cochin', *Young Men of India* 37, no. 6 (1930): 429–30; Duane Spencer Hatch, 'The First Travancore Poultry Exhibition', *Young Men of India* 39, no. 2 (1932): 68–9; Hatch, 'Poverty and Self-Help in Rural India', 493–506; Hatch, *Toward Freedom from Want*, 77–80 and 136–44.

166. Gilchriest Hatch, *Mar-Tan-Dam: Not on the Map?*, 8–9.

167. Ibid., 1. Cf. also T. K. Velu Pillai, *The Travancore State Manual*, vol. 3 (Trivandrum: Government of Travancore, 1940), 75–9.

168. Emily Gilchriest Hatch, *Travancore: A Guide Book for the Visitor*, 2nd ed. (London: Oxford University Press, 1939), 186.

169. KFYA, IWI, Box 13, 'Printed Material, 1939–1967', Martandam Practical Training School in Rural Reconstruction, 'Accomplishment Bulletin: News from Old Boys and Girls and What They Have Done', April 1940.

170. Martandam Practical Training School in Rural Reconstruction, 'Accomplishment Bulletin', 2 and 4.

171. UATSHC, Box 2, Folder 8, 'Address by Spencer D. Hatch', s.a. [1944], 18–19. This legacy appears to have lasted several years, as Hatch's books continued to appear on reading lists for rural experts training in Egypt in the mid-1950s; UATSHC, Box 3, Folder 6/3, 'Written Works, Reports, Programmes and Memorandums, 1952–1954', File 'Arab States Fundamental Education Centre, Sirs-el-Layyan, Menoufia, Egypt: Programme of Training for the Period between Dec 1952 and October 1954'. For the background of rural reconstruction schemes in Egypt, cf. Mitchell, *Rule of Experts*; Omnia El Shakry, *The Great Social Laboratory: Subjects of Knowledge in Colonial and Postcolonial Egypt* (Stanford, CA: Stanford University Press, 2007), 113–44.

172. The most obvious example is provided by V. T. Krishnamachari (1881–1964). Though not a student of the Martandam College, he was initiated by Hatch into the art of rural reconstruction during the 1930s in Baroda. Krishnamachari went on to become 'Nehru's right hand man on the all-important Planning Commission'; Wallach, *Losing Asia*, 135.

173. Hatch, 'Beyond the Ends of the Roads', 284.

174. Cf., for example, the book review by J. L. Hypes, 'Further Upward in Rural India, by D. Spencer Hatch', *American Sociological Review* iv, no. 1 (1939): 132–3. The reviewer praised Hatch's programme, particularly for 'exemplifying democracy and a form of cooperation that includes both public and private agencies'.
175. Richardson, 'Thirty Years of Rural Reconstruction'.
176. Sinha, 'Lineages of the Developmentalist State', 66–71. Cf. also Raghavan, *Fierce Enigmas*, 78–80.
177. Hatch, 'Beyond the Ends of the Roads', 192; Hatch, *Up from Poverty in Rural India*, 33.
178. Hatch, *Toward Freedom from Want*, 36–7.
179. Gilchriest Hatch, *Travancore*, 186.
180. C. F. Strickland, *Rural Welfare in India* (London: Oxford University Press, 1936), 40.
181. Ouwerkerk, *No Elephants*, 175; RAC, Davison Fund Records, IV 3 B 5.2, Series ii, Box 21, Folder 164, Letter by Frank Slack to F. S. Harmon, 12 November 1936. I am grateful to Stefan Hübner for making me aware of this source.
182. Hatch, *Further Upward in Rural India*, 166–9. Sir Don Baron Jayatileka, the Ceylonese Chief Minister, later even spent a few days in Martandam to get a first-hand impression of the Y's rural work. Cf. Hatch, *Toward Freedom from Want*, 280–1.
183. Hatch, 'Beyond the Ends of the Roads', 257.
184. Iris Borowy, *Coming to Terms with World Health: The League of Nations Health Organization 1921–1946* (Frankfurt: Peter Lang, 2009), 349.
185. Sunil S. Amrith and Patricia Clavin, 'Feeding the World: Connecting Europe and Asia, 1930–1945', *Past and Present* 218, Supplement no. 8 (2013): 29–50; Socrates Litsios, 'Revisiting Bandoeng', *Social Medicine* viii, no. 3 (2014); Sunil S. Amrith, 'The Internationalization of Health in South East Asia', in *Histories of Health in Southeast Asia: Perspectives on the Long Twentieth Century*, ed. Tim Harper and Sunil S. Amrith (Bloomington: Indiana University Press, 2014), 171–4.
186. 'Report of the Intergovernmental Conference of Far-Eastern Countries on Rural Hygiene, Held at Bandoeng (Java), August 3rd to 13th, 1937' (Geneva, 1937), 23–4.
187. Lion Murard, 'Designs within Disorder: International Conferences on Rural Health Care and the Art of the Local, 1931–39', in *Shifting Boundaries of Public Health: Europe in the Twentieth Century*, ed. Susan Gross Solomon, Lion Murard and Patrick Zylberman (Rochester, NY: University of Rochester Press, 2008), 152.
188. Hatch, 'Beyond the Ends of the Roads', 170–6.
189. Hatch, 'Early Times at the Martandam Project', 17.
190. RAC, Davison Fund Records, IV 3 B 5.2, Series ii, Box 21, Folder 167, 'Martandam Rural Center', 20 December 1935.
191. Hatch, *Toward Freedom from Want*, 268–80.
192. UATSHC, Box 2, Folder 8, 'Address by Spencer D. Hatch', s.a. [1944], 18.
193. Hatch, 'My Job Is Village Reconstruction', 8.
194. Olsson, *Agrarian Crossings*; Gupta, *Postcolonial Developments*, 53–4. For a more detailed discussion, cf. also Cullather, *The Hungry World*, 43–71; Jonathan Harwood, 'Peasant Friendly Plant Breeding and the Early Years of the Green Revolution in Mexico', *Agricultural History* 83, no. 3 (2009); Raj Patel, 'The Long Green Revolution', *Journal of Peasant Studies* 40, no. 1 (2013): 5–10.
195. For details of the YMCA's rural reconstruction activities in Mexico, cf. Hatch, *Toward Freedom from Want*, 285–96; 'Y Field Activities in Mexico', *Mexican-American Review*, 1952, 40 and 90; Emily Gilchriest Hatch, 'In Mexico: Part IV of the Duane Spencer Hatch Story', *The Quill and Scroll* 69, no. 4 (1963): 11–17.

196. Hatch, 'My Job Is Village Reconstruction', 8.
197. J. P. McEvoy, 'Hatch Helps Those Who Help Themselves', *The Reader's Digest* 47 (1945): 45–8.
198. That the American YMCA also played a pioneering role in the use of the new medium for 'pastoral exhibitions' of various kinds is evident from Ronald Walter Greene, 'Pastoral Exhibitions: The YMCA Motion Picture Bureau and the Transition to 16 mm, 1928–39', in *Useful Cinema*, ed. Charles R. Acland and Haidee Wasson (Durham, NC: Duke University Press, 2011), 205–29.
199. On the founding of the FAO, cf. Ruth Jachertz, ' "Keep Food out of Politics": The UN Food and Agriculture Organization, 1945–1965', in *International Organizations and Development, 1945–1990*, ed. Marc Frey, Sönke Kunkel and Corinna R. Unger (Basingstoke: Palgrave Macmillan, 2014), 75–100; Amy L. S. Staples, *The Birth of Development: How the World Bank, Food and Agriculture Organization, and World Health Organization Changed the World, 1945–1965* (Kent, OH: The Kent State University Press, 2006), 78–81; Sergio Marchisio and Antonietta Di Blase, *The Food and Agriculture Organization (FAO)* (Dordrecht: Martinus Nijhoff, 1991), 9–15.
200. Gilchriest Hatch, 'In Mexico', 17.
201. L. S. Rowe, 'Inter-American Institute of Agricultural Sciences', *The Scientific Monthly* 56, no. 2 (1943).
202. 'Annual Report of the Inter-American Institute of Agricultural Sciences for the Year 1950' (Turrialba, 1951), 135.
203. UATSHC, Box 3, Folder 14/3, 'Photographs, Albums Delhi State (1) 1950–1952'.
204. Emily Gilchriest Hatch, 'Working with D. Spencer 'Chick' Hatch, Conclusion: Ceylon and the Colorado River Indian Tribes', *The Quill and Scroll* 67, no. 2 (1964): 24.
205. Hatch, 'Early Times at the Martandam Project', 9.
206. Cf. also Duane Spencer Hatch, 'What Are We up to in Minneriya?', *Free World* 1, no. 3 (1951): 28–31.
207. Frank Ninkovich, *The Global Republic: America's Inadvertent Rise to World Power* (Chicago, IL: University of Chicago Press, 2014), 173.
208. Gilchriest Hatch, 'Working with D. Spencer 'Chick' Hatch, Conclusion', 26–9.
209. Wade Davies, 'Cornell's Field Seminar in Applied Anthropology: Social Scientists and American Indians in the Postwar Southwest', *Journal of the Southwest* 43, no. 3 (2001): quote in 317.
210. Jacob Tropp, 'Transnational Development Training and Native American 'Laboratories' in the Early Cold War', *Journal of Global History* 13, no. 3 (2018): 474.
211. Frederick Cooper, 'Writing the History of Development', *Journal of Modern European History* 8, no. 1 (2010): 7.
212. Cf. also my discussion of the methodological aspects of the present case study in Fischer-Tiné, 'Marrying Global History'.
213. Chatterjee, *The Making of Indian Secularism*, 151.

Conclusion: Modernization without modernity

1. Sarkar, *Modern Times*, 50.
2. Kramer, 'Power and Connection?', 1387.
3. Cf., for instance, UATSC, Box 8 Folder 9, 'Fundamental Education around the World–UNESCO Radio Talk in Paris, 1950 [CD]; Box 9, Item 8, *The Jungle and the Plough*, documentary film, 1963 [DVD].

4. For a more exhaustive discussion, see also my article Fischer-Tiné, 'Marrying Global History', on which the next paragraphs partly draw.
5. The concept of the *jeux d'échelles* ('playing with the scales') was introduced shortly before the global turn by the French historian Jacques Revel. J. Revel, *Jeux d'échelles: la micro-analyse à l'expérience* (Paris, 1996).
6. As already suggested in Chapter 2, it would nevertheless be worthwhile to explore the letters of South Asian soldiers. Even if they were dictated to a YMCA secretary and later censored by military authorities, they might open up new perspectives.
7. Cf., for instance, Sven Beckert and Dominic Sachsenmaier, eds, *Global History Globally: Research and Practice around the World* (London: Bloomsbury, 2018); G. Balachandran, 'History after the Global Turn: Perspectives from Rim and Region', *History Australia* 14, no. 1 (2017): 6–12.
8. For an exhaustive engagement with the critics of global history, see also Richard Drayton and David Motadel, 'Discussion: The Futures of Global History', *Journal of Global History* 13, no. 1 (2018): 1–21; Sebastian Conrad, *Globalgeschichte: eine Einführung* (München: C. H. Beck, 2013), 87–111.
9. If not indicated otherwise, the following section is based on the information provided in David, *The YMCA and the Making*, 375–463.
10. Government of Madhya Pradesh, Report of the Christian Missionary Activities Enquiry Committee, 2 vols. (Nagpur: Government Printing, 1956); cf. also Frykenberg, *Christianity in India*, 475–6; Sebastian C. H. Kim, *In Search of Identity: Debates on Religious Conversion in India* (Delhi: Oxford University Press, 2003), 66.
11. Christophe Jaffrelot, *The Hindu Nationalist Movement in India* (London: Hurst, 1996), 164; Frampton F. Fox, 'Foreign Money for India: Antidependency and Anticonversion Perspectives', *International Bulletin of Missionary Research* 30, no. 3 (2006):140.
12. Bipan Chandra, Mridula Mukherjee and Aditya Mukherjee, *India since Independence* (Gurgaon: Penguin Books, 2008), 106–12.
13. Dunderdale, *The Y.M.C.A. in India*, 137.
14. David, *The YMCA and the Making*, 378–80.
15. On the occasion of the 100th anniversary of the Universal Alliance of YMCA's in 1955, the International Committee of the North American Y announced a massive fundraising campaign to finance new Association buildings all over the world. Money started flowing in 1958, and the building activities continued until the mid-1960s. Cf. also https://umedia.lib.umn.edu/item/p16022coll225:23.
16. *Y.M.C.A. Rural Demonstration Centre Martandam, Golden Jubilee Souvenir 1916–1966* (Nagercoil: The Diocesan Press, s.a. [1967]), 22.
17. David, *The YMCA and the Making*, 390–2.
18. Ibid., 417.

Bibliography

Archives and main series of records

British Library Asia, Pacific and Africa Collection — BL, APAC
    India Office Records — IOR
    European Manuscript Section — Mss Eur
Cadbury Research Library, Special Collections University of Birmingham, UK — CRLSC
Duane Spencer Hatch Collection at the University of Arizona, Tucson, AZ — UATSHC
Kautz Family YMCA Archives, University of Minnesota, Minneapolis, MN — KFYA
    Biographical Files — BF
    International Work in Burma — IWB
    International Work in Ceylon/Sri Lanka — IWC
    International Work India — IWI
    Subject Files — SF
Library and Archives of the United Theological College at Bangalore — UTCAB
National Archives of India, New Delhi — NAI
Research Collection of the YMCA, New Delhi, Jai Singh Marg (YMCA New Delhi headquarter) — RYND
Rockefeller Archive Center, Davison Fund Records, Sleepy Hollow, NY — RAC
Sophia Smith Collection of Women's History at Smith College, Northampton, MA — SSCWH
Springfield College Archives and Special Collections — SCASC
Uttar Pradesh State Archives, Lucknow — UPSAL
World Alliance of Young Men's Christian Associations Archive, Geneva — WAYAG
Yale University, Divinity School, Special Collections in New Haven, CT — YDSPC

Journal and newspaper titles

Aberdeen Press and Journal
American Physical Education Review
American Sociological Review
Applied Anthropology
Association Men
The Association Seminar
The Association Seminar & Springfield Student
Christian Rural Fellowship Bulletin
Church History
The Cornell Daily Sun
The Covina Argus-Citizen

Durbar
The Englishman
Foreign Mail
The Foreign Mail Annual
Free World
The Harvest Field
History of Education
The Hindu
The Illustrated Weekly of India
The Indian Express
The Indian Journal of Medical Research
Indianapolis Recorder
The International Journal of the History of Sport
Journal of the Central Asian Society
The Journal of Education
The Journal of Health and Physical Education
Mexican-American Review
The Missionary Review of the World
The Morning News
The New York American
The New York Times
Nineteenth Century
North Adams Evening Transcript
Physical Training
The Playground
The Quill and Scroll
Rangoon Men
The Reader's Digest
Royal United Services Institution Journal
Rural Manhood
Saddharm Pracārak
The Scientific Monthly
The Springfield Student
The Times of India
Vyayam
The Young Men of India

Published sources and literature pre-1960

Anand, Mulk Raj. *Across the Black Waters*. London: Jonathan Cape, 1940.
Andrews, George F. 'History of the Playground Movement and Organization and Administration of Playgrounds'. Unpublished MEd thesis, International Young Men's Christian Association College, Springfield, MA, 1932.
'Annual Report of the Inter-American Institute of Agricultural Sciences for the Year 1950'. Turrialba, 1951.

'Annual Report of the Young Men's Christian Association of Calcutta for 1907'. Calcutta, 1908.
'Annual Report of the Young Men's Christian Association of Calcutta for 1908'. Calcutta, 1909.
Atwood, J. Howell, Arthur W. Hardy and Owen E. Pence. *The Racial Factor in Y.M.C.A.s: A Report on Negro-White Relationships in Twenty-Four Cities*. New York: Association Press for Bureau of Records, Studies and Trends, National Board of YMCAs, 1946.
Bailey, Joseph Cannon. *Seaman A. Knapp, Schoolmaster of American Agriculture*. New York: Columbia University Press, 1945.
Barber, B. R. *The Second City of the British Empire*. New York: Foreign Department International Committee, 1912.
Beatty, Jerome. *Americans All Over*. New York: John Day, 1940.
Beri, S. G., and G. B. Jathar. *Some Aspects of Rural Reconstruction in India (A Paper Submitted to the Indian Economic Conference in Lucknow, 1928)*. Bombay: Oxford University Press, s.a. [1929].
Boys Division, National Council of Y.M.C.A.s India, Burma and Ceylon. Travancore: London Mission Press, 1941.
Brayne, Frank L. *Better Villages*. London: H. Milford, Oxford University Press, 1937.
Brayne, Frank L. *The Remaking of Village India (Being the Second Edition of 'Village Uplift in India')*. London: H. Milford, Oxford University Press, 1929.
Browne, Tomyns R. 'Locomotive Superintendent of the East Indian Railway: "An Appreciation"'. In *A Year's Progress in the Inauguration of the Work of the Railway Young Men's Christian Association in India Etc.*, edited by Y.M.C.A., Indian National Council, 31–4. Calcutta: Baptist Mission Press, 1907.
Bruce, R. B. J. *Notes on the Dera Ghazi Khan District and Its Border Tribes*. Lahore: Government Printing Press, 1870.
Buck, H. C. 'Looking Forward in Physical Education (Presidential Address Delivered to the Eighth Provincial Physical Education Conference of Madras)'. In *Buck Commemoration Volume: Being a Memorial Dedicated to Harry Crowe Buck*, edited by L. K. Govindarajulu, 237–45. Madras: Buck Commemoration Volume Committee, 1949.
Buck, H. C. 'Ourselves'. *The Annual of the Y.M.C.A. School of Physical Education*. Madras: Diocesan Press, 1928.
Buck, H. C. 'The Place of Indigenous Activities in the Physical Education Programme'. In *Buck Commemoration Volume: Being a Memorial Dedicated to Harry Crowe Buck*, edited by L. K. Govindarajulu, 247–51. Chennai: Buck Commemoration Volume Committee, 1949.
Buck's Book of Rules of Games and Sports. 12th edition. Calcutta: Y.M.C.A. Publication House, 1950.
Burr, Hanford M. 'Dr Luther Gulick, 1865–1918: A Symposium'. *American Physical Education Review* 23, no. 7 (1918): 413–26.
Butterfield, Kenyon L. *The Christian Enterprise among Rural People*. Nashville, TN: Cokesbury Press, 1933.
Butterfield, Kenyon L. *The Christian Mission in Rural India; Report and Recommendations by Kenyon L. Butterfield, Counsellor on Rural Work, International Missionary Council, with a Foreword by Dr. John R. Mott*. New York: International Missionary Council, 1930.
Cammack, R. Walter. 'A Normal Course in Physical Training for Grade School Teachers'. Unpublished Master of Physical Education thesis, Springfield College, Springfield, MA, 1917.

Cammack, R. Walter. 'Physical Education in Ceylon'. Unpublished Graduation thesis, International Young Men's Christian Association College, Springfield MA, 1920.
Carter, E. C., ed. *In the Camps, Trenches & Prisons of Asia, Africa & Europe*. Oxford: Frederick Hall, 1916.
Carter, Edward C. *The Men of India and Ceylon*. New York: Foreign Department, International Committee Young Men's Christian Association, 1908.
Chetty, O. Kandaswamy. *50 Years with the Youth of Madras: The History of the Madras Y.M.C.A., 1890–1940*. Madras: s.n. 1940.
Dasgupta, Sugata. *A Poet and a Plan: Tagore's Experiments in Rural Reconstruction*. Calcutta: Thacker, Spink, 1933.
Dedmon, Emmot. *Great Enterprises: 100 Years of the YMCA of Metropolitan Chicago*. New York: Rand McNally, 1957.
Doggett, Laurence L. *Man and a School: Pioneering in Higher Education*. New York: Association Press, 1943.
Dunderdale, J. H. *Why Bother with Boys*. Nagercoil: London Mission Press, 1941.
Dunderdale, J. H. *The YMCA in India: 100 Years of Service with Youth*. New Delhi: YMCA Publishing House, 1962.
Eddy, George Sherwood. *Pathfinders of the World Missionary Crusade*. New York: Abingdon-Cokebury Press, 1945.
Eddy, Sherwood. *A Century with Youth: A History of the YMCA from 1844 to 1944*. New York: Association Press, 1944.
Eddy, Sherwood. *The Challenge of the East*. New York: Farrar & Rinehart, 1931.
Eddy, Sherwood. *Eighty Adventurous Years: An Autobiography*. New York: Harpers & Brothers, 1955.
Eddy, Sherwood. *India Awakening*. New York: Missionary Education Movement of the United States and Canada, 1911.
Eddy, Sherwood. *The New Era in Asia*. New York: Missionary Education Movement of the United States and Canada, 1913.
Eddy, Sherwood. *Religion and Social Justice*. New York: George H. Doran, 1927.
Eddy, Sherwood. *With Our Soldiers in France*. New York: Association Press, 1917.
Farquhar, J. N. *Modern Religious Movements in India*. New York: Macmillan, 1915.
Fiske, George Walter. *Boy Life and Self-Government*. New York: Young Men's Christian Association Press, 1910.
Foreign Division of the Young Men's Christian Association of the United States and Canada. *The Y.M.C.A. in India*. New York, s.a. [1924].
Gandhi, M. K. 'Village Insanitation'. In *M.K. Gandhi: Social Service, Work and Reform*, Vol. 1, edited by V. B. Kher. Ahmedabad: Navajivan Publishing House, 1976.
General Report on the Census of India, 1891. London: Her Majesty's Stationery Office, 1893.
Gibson, Henry W. *Boyology or Boy Analysis*. New York: Association Press, 1916.
Gilchriest Hatch, Emily. *Little Plays*. Madras: Hogarth Press, 1932.
Gilchriest Hatch, Emily. *Out of the Pot into the World: A Temperance Play*. Howrah, 1926.
Gilchriest Hatch, Emily. 'The Kathakali: The Indigenous Drama of Malabar'. PhD thesis, Cornell University, 1934.
Gilchriest Hatch, Emily. *Travancore: A Guide Book for the Visitor*. 2nd edition. London: Oxford University Press, 1939.
Government of Bengal. *Report of the Committee of Enquiry into School and College Hygiene*. Calcutta: Bengal Secretariat Book Depot, 1915.
Government of Bombay. *Report of the Physical Education Committee*. Bombay: Government Central Press, 1947.

Government of India. *Royal Commission on Agriculture in India: Report.* Bombay: Government of India Press, 1928.

Gray, J. H. *Major Games: Games Handbook* [=Triangle Athletic Series] (Calcutta: Association Press, 1918).

Gulick, Luther H. *Manual for Physical Measurements in Connection with the Association Gymnasium Records.* New York: The International Committee of Young Men's Christian Associations, 1892.

Gulick, Luther H. *A Philosophy of Play.* New York: Charles Scribner's Sons, 1920.

Gulick, Luther H. 'Physical Education: A New Profession'. In *Proceedings of the American Association for the Advancement of Physical Education at Its Fifth Annual Meeting Held in Cambridge and Boston, Mass. 4 and 5 April 1890*, 59–66. Ithaca, NY: Andrus and Church, 1890.

Hall, G. Stanley. *Adolescence: Its Psychology and Its Relations to Physiology, Anthropology, Sociology, Sex, Crime, Religion, and Education.* Vol. I and II. New York: D. Appleton, 1904.

Hatch, Duane Spencer. 'Beyond the Ends of the Roads: Legs for Knowledge', unpublished manuscript, s.a. [*c.* 1962].

Hatch, Duane Spencer. *Further Upward in Rural India.* Bombay: Oxford University Press, 1938.

Hatch, Duane Spencer. 'Poverty and Self-Help in Rural India'. Unpublished PhD dissertation, Cornell University, 1928.

Hatch, Duane Spencer. *Rural Reconstruction and Evangelicalism or Evangelism and Christian Service. From an Address Delivered at a Special Session of Tambaram World Conference Etc.* Trivandrum: Y.M.C.A. District Office, 1940.

Hatch, Duane Spencer. *Toward Freedom from Want from India to Mexico.* Bombay: Oxford University Press, 1949.

Hatch, Duane Spencer. *Up from Poverty in Rural India.* Bombay: Oxford University Press, 1932.

Heald, Charles E., ed. *The Place of Boyhood in the Nations of the World: Being the Report of the Second World Conference of Y.M.C.A. Workers among Boys, Held at Pörtschach Am Zee [Sic], Austria, 30th May to 10th June, 1923.* Geneva: World's Committee Young Men's Christian Associations, Boys' Division, 1923.

Higginbottom, Sam. *The Gospel and the Plow, or, the Old Gospel and Modern Farming in Ancient India.* New York: Macmillan, 1921.

Hill, Thomas B. 'The Problems of European Young Men in India', unpublished Thesis, International YMCA College, Springfield, MA, 1917.

Hitchcock, Paul E. 'The Boy Problem – and How It Is Dealt with in the Elementary School'. Unpublished BA Thesis, International Young Men's Christian Association College, 1917.

Hobbs, Harry. *Indian Y.M.C.A and Politics.* Calcutta: H. Hobbs, 1927.

Hogg, L. A. *Hope for the Villager: Youth to the Rescue in South India. Being an Account of the Rural Reconstruction Work of the YMCA.* Bombay: D. B. Taporevala, 1931.

Holt, A. E. *A Study of the Y.M.C.A. of India, Burma & Ceylon. Made as an Integral Part of the International Survey.* Calcutta: National Council of Y.M.C.A.s of India, Burma and Ceylon, 1933.

Hopkins, C. Howard. *History of the Y.M.C.A. in North America.* New York: Association Press, 1951.

Hume, Allan Octavian. *Agricultural Reform in India.* London: W. H. Allen, 1879.

Ilahibaksh, V. M. 'Lecture Department'. In *Report of National Council to the Twelfth National Convention 1924–1926*, edited by Young Men's Christian Associations of India and Ceylon, 59–62. Cuttack: Orissa Mission Press, 1926.

Jagannath. 'The Aims of Physical Education'. *The Annual of the Y.M.C.A. School of Physical Education, 1928–1929*, Madras: s.n., 1929, 21–3.

Johannot, Henri. 'The Field of Action'. In *History of the World Alliance of Christian Associations*, edited by Clarence Prouty Shedd, 613–61. London: SPCK, 1955.

Kingman, Harry L. 'Physical Education in China, India, Japan, Latin America and the Philippine Islands'. Unpublished graduation thesis, International Young Men's Christian Association College, 1916.

Lal, Prem Chand. *Reconstruction and Education in Rural India: In the Light of the Programme Carried on at Sriniketan, the Institute of Rural Reconstruction Founded by Rabindranath Tagore*. London: G. Allen & Unwin, 1932.

Latourette, Kenneth Scott. *World Service: A History of the Foreign Work and World Service of the Young Men's Christian Associations of the United States and Canada*. New York: Association Press, 1957.

Leary, Anson T. 'America's Greatest Problem – Its Youth'. Unpublished graduation thesis, International Young Men's Christian Association College, 1917.

Libby, Lester H. 'The Leader's Handbook'. Unpublished thesis-cum-textbook, Springfield, MA, International Young Men's Christian Association College Springfield, s.a. [1917].

MacFadden, Bernarr. *Macfadden's Physical Training: An Illustrated System of Exercise for the Development of Health, Strength and Beauty*. New York: MacFadden, 1900.

MacMunn, George. *The Martial Races of India*. London: Sampson Low, 1933.

The Malabar Central Relief Committee. *Report of Work, October 1921 to November 1922*. Madras: The Servants of India Society, 1923.

Marten, J. T. *Census of India, 1921. Part II – Tables*. Vol. 1. Calcutta: Superintendent Government Printing, India, 1923.

Mathews, Basil Joseph. *Flaming Milestone: Being an Interpretation and the Official Report of the Twenty-First World's Conference of the World's Alliance of Y.M.C.A.s Held in January 1937, in Mysore, South India*. Geneva: World's Committee of the Y.M.C.A.s, 1938.

Mayer, Albert, McKim Marriott and Richard L. Park. *Pilot Project, India: The Story of Rural Development at Etawah, Uttar Pradesh*. Berkeley: University of California Press, 1958.

Mayo, Katherine. *That Damn Y': A Record of Overseas Service*. Boston, MA: Houghton Mifflin, 1920.

McClelland, D. F. 'H. C. Buck'. In *Three Y.M.C.A. Pioneers*, edited by S. P. Appasamy, 12–18. Calcutta: YMCA Publishing House, 1958.

McClelland, D. F. 'Report of the National General Secretary', *Young Men of India, Burma, and Ceylon* 57, no. 5–6 (1945): 68–86.

McCully, Bruce T. *English Education and the Origins of Indian Nationalism*. New York: Columbia University Press, 1940.

Moffat, Cody S. 'The Western Influence of [sic!] Physical Education in India'. Unpublished Master of Physical Education thesis, Springfield College, 1950.

Mott, John R. 'Boyhood, the Greatest Asset of Any Nation'. In *The Place of Boyhood in the Nations of the World: Being the Report of the Second World Conference of Y.M.C.A. Workers among Boys, Held at Pörtschach Am Zee [sic], Austria, 30th May to 10th June, 1923*, edited by Charles E. Heald, 249–59. Geneva: World's Committee Young Men's Christian Associations, Boys' Division, 1923.

Mukherjee, Haridas, and Uma Mukherjee. *A Phase of the Swadeshi Movement: National Education, 1905–1910*. Calcutta: Chuckervertty Chatterjee, 1953.

Müller, J. P. *My System: 15 Minutes Work a Day for Health's Sake!* London: Ewart, Seymour, 1905.

The National Council of the Y.M.C.A.s of India, Burma and Ceylon. *Youth in Harness: The All India Service of the Y.M.C.A.* Calcutta: Baptist Mission Press, s.a. [1930].

National Council of the Young Men's Christian Associations of India and Ceylon. *The Red Triangle in the East*. Calcutta: B.M.P., s.a. [1910].

Nehru, Jawaharlal. *A Bunch of Old Letters: Written Mostly to Jawaharlal Nehru and Some Written by Him*. Bombay: Asia Publishing House, 1958.

Nish, I. H. *Calcutta Y.M.C.A.: A History 1857–1957*. Calcutta: Y.M.C.A. Publishing House, 1957.

Noehren, A. G. *Official Report of the Director of Physical Education to the Educational Department, Government of Bombay 1927–28*. Bombay: Tutorial Press, 1928.

Noehren, A. G. 'Physical Department'. In *Twelfth National Convention Young Men's Christian Associations of India Burma, and Ceylon and Report of National Council 1924–26*, 68–71. Calcutta: Baptist Mission Press, 1927.

Noehren, A. G. 'The YMCA and Health Education'. Report of National Council, 1924–1926, s.a.

Ouwerkerk, Miss [sic]. 'The Lessons of Marthandam'. In *Developing Village India: Studies in Village Problems*, edited by M. S. Randhawa, Revised edition. Bombay: The Indian Council of Agriculture Research, 1951.

Pal, Bipin Chandra. *Swadeshi and Swaraj*. 1 [1907]. Calcutta: Yuganyanti Prakashak, 1954.

Paul, K. T. *The British Connection with India*. London: Student Christian Movement, 1927.

Paul, K. T., ed. *Young Men's Christian Associations of India, Burma and Ceylon and the European Association (Central Association): Report of Committee of Enquiry Appointed by the National Council Y.M.C.A. Together with the Allegations and Correspondence*. Calcutta: Baptist Mission Press, 1927.

Peace Programme of the YMCA Simla–Delhi and the Indian National Council. Delhi: s.n., 1921.

Pillai, T. K. Velu. *The Travancore State Manual*. Vol. 3. Trivandrum: Government of Travancore, 1940.

Pixley, Alonzo R. 'Religious Education and the Boy Problem'. Unpublished thesis, International Young Men's Christian Association College, 1911.

Popley, Herbert A. *K. T. Paul, Christian Leader*. Calcutta: Y.M.C.A. Publishing House, 1938.

Prospectus of the Agricultural Research Institute and College, Pusa. Calcutta: Superintendent Government Printing, India, 1909.

Rai, Lala Lajpat. 'Exhortation to the Youth to Develop Grit and Determination'. In *The Collected Works of Lala Lajpat Rai*, edited by B. R. Nanda, Vol. IV, 401–5. New Delhi: Manohar Publishers, 2004.

Rai, Lala Lajpat. *The Problem of National Education in India*. London: Allen and Unwin, 1920.

Rauschenbusch, Walter. *Christianity and the Present Crisis*. New York: Macmillan, 1907.

Rauschenbusch, Walter. *A Theology for the Social Gospel*. New York: Macmillan, 1917.

'Report of the Bombay Gymnastic Institute for the Years 1927–28, 1928–29, 1929–30'. Bombay, s.a. [1930].

Report of the Conference on Physical Education Held at Madras on the 14th and 15th October 1927 under the Presidency of the Hon, Dr. P. Subbaroyan, M. A., C.C.L.,

LL.D., *Chief Minister to the Government of Madras*. Madras: Superintendent Madras Government Press, 1928.

Report of the Intergovernmental Conference of Far-Eastern Countries on Rural Hygiene, Held at Bandoeng (Java), August 3rd to 13th, 1937. Geneva, 1937.

Report of the National Council of Young Men's Christian Associations of India and Ceylon to the Tenth National Convention at Calcutta, November 23–27, 1920. Cuttack: Association Press, 1921.

Roosevelt, Theodore. 'The Strenuous Life'. In *The Strenuous Life: Essays and Addresses*, 1–22. New York: Charles Scribner's Sons, 1906.

Rudrappa, G. *The Work of Rural Reconstruction in the Mysore State and British India: Further Reflections and Thoughts*. Bangalore: The Bangalore Press, 1935.

Sandow, Eugen. *Strength and How to Obtain It. With Anatomical Chart Illustrating the Exercises for Physical Development Etc*. London: Gale & Polden, 1897.

Sarkar, Benoy Kumar. *The Futurism of Young Asia, and Other Essays on the Relations between the East and the West*. Leipzig: Markert & Petters, 1922.

Satavlekar, Sripadrao. 'Mahāśay gurukul aur mistar kālej kī bāt cīt'. *Saddharm Pracārak* A Conversation between Mahashay Gurukul and Mister College], 12 April 1911, 7–8.

Saunders, Kenneth J. *Impressions of Mesopotamia*. London: The Red Triangle Press, s.a.

Savardekar, D. S., ed. *Directory of Social Work in the City and Island of Bombay*. Bombay: Vaibhav Press, 1926.

Schopmeyer, C. H. *Extension Projects in Rural Community Organization*. Washington, DC: US Extension Service Circulars, 1927.

Second Quinquennial Report of the Welfare Work of Messrs. Begg. Cawnpore: Sutherland [1939].

Segard, C. P. *Annual Report of the Director of Physical Education to the Department of Public Instruction, Bengal for the Year 1918–1919*. Calcutta: Bengal Secretariat Book Depot, 1919.

Segard, C. P. *Quinquennial Report on Physical Education in the Province of Bengal for the Years 1911–12 to 1916–17*. Calcutta: Bengal Secretariat Book Depot, 1917.

Seshadri, P. 'The Spirit of Service'. In *Dayananda Commemoration Volume. An Homage to Maharshi Dayananda Saraswati from India and the World in Celebration of the Dayanand Nirvana Ardh Shatabdi*, edited by Har Bilas Sarda, 41–5. Ajmer: Vedic Yantralay, 1933.

Shedd, Clarence P. *History of the World Alliance of the Young Men's Christian Association*. London: SPCK, 1955.

Sherman, Byron G. 'Medical and Physical Examination of Y.M.C.A. Boys'. Unpublished post-graduation minor thesis, Y.M.C.A. College, 1916.

Singha, Shoran. 'North India'. In *The Place of Boyhood in the Nations of the World: Being the Report of the Second World Conference of Y.M.C.A. Workers among Boys, Held at Pörtschach Am Zee [sic], Austria, 30th May to 10th June, 1923*, edited by Charles E. Heald, 290–2. Geneva: World's Committee Young Men's Christian Associations, Boys' Division, 1923.

'Sixteenth Annual Report of the Young Men's Christian Association of Calcutta for 1909'. Calcutta, 1910.

The Social Service League Bombay, ed. *Directory of Social Work in India (Excepting the City and Island of Bombay)*. Bombay: Vaibhav Press, 1923.

Stead, William T. *The Americanization of the World: Or the Trend of the Twentieth Century*. New York: Horace Markley, 1902.

Strickland, C. F. *Rural Welfare in India*. London: Oxford University Press, 1936.
Swamidoss, D. 'India'. In *The Place of Boyhood in the Nations of the World: Being the Report of the Second World Conference of Y.M.C.A. Workers among Boys, Held at Pörtschach Am Zee [sic], Austria, 30th May to 10th June, 1923*, edited by Charles E. Heald, 287–90. Geneva: World's Committee Young Men's Christian Associations, Boys' Division, 1923.
Taft, William Howard, and Frederick Morgan Harris, eds. *Service with Fighting Men: An Account of the Work of the American Young Men's Christian Associations in the World War*. Vol. 2. New York: Association Press, 1922.
True, Alfred Charles. *A History of Agricultural Education in the United States 1785–1925*. Washington, DC: US Government Printing Office, 1929.
Twelfth National Convention of Young Men's Christian Associations of India, Burma and Ceylon and Report of National Council, 1924–26. Calcutta: Baptist Mission Press, 1927.
Tyndale-Biscoe, C. E. *Character Building in Kashmir*. London: C.M.S., 1920.
Urwick, E. J. *Studies of Boy Life in Our Cities*. London: Dent, 1904.
US National Commission for UNESCO, *Newsletter*, No. 17, 25 February 1953.
Voelcker, John Augustus. *Report on the Improvement of Indian Agriculture*. London: Eyre and Spottiswoode, 1893.
Walter, Howard Arnold. *The Ahmadiya Movement*. Calcutta: Association Press, 1918.
Wanchoo, H. N. *Studies in Indian Education*. Allahabad: Allahabad Law Journal Press, 1934.
Washington, Booker T. *Up from Slavery: An Autobiography*. New York: Doubleday, Page, 1901.
Worman, E. C. 'Report on Boys Work, 1924–1926'. Young Men's Christian Associations India, Burma, and Ceylon, Report of the National Council, 1924–6, n.d.
Yapp, Arthur K. *The Romance of the Red Triangle: The Story of the Coming of the Red Triangle and the Service Rendered by the Y.M.C.A. to the Sailors and Soldiers of the British Empire*. London: Hodder and Stoughton, 1918.
Year Book of the Young Men's Christian Associations of North America for the Year May 1, 1923 to April 30, 1924. New York: Association Press, 1924.
Y.M.C.A. College of Physical Education Saidapet, Madras. *Prospectus 1940–41*. Madras: Methodist Publishing House, 1941.
Y.M.C.A., Indian National Council. *A Study of the Conditions and Needs of European Railway Men in India: Being the Report to the Indian National Council of the Railway Department Secretary's Investigations Preliminary to Inauguration of the Railway Y.M.C.A Work, Etc*. Calcutta: Baptist Mission Press, 1905.
Y.M.C.A. *National Budget 1917*. Calcutta: W. Newman, 1918.
Y.M.C.A. *A Year's Progress in the Inauguration of the Work of the Railway Young Men's Christian Association in India Etc*. Calcutta: Baptist Mission Press, 1907.
Y.M.C.A. *Year Book and Official Rosters. 1903–1904*. New York: National Councils of the Young Men's Christian Associations of Canada and the United States of America, 1904.
'Young Men's Christian Association of Calcutta: Annual Report 1915'. Calcutta: Edinburgh Press, 1916.
'Young Men's Christian Association of Calcutta, Annual Report 1918'. Calcutta: Edinburgh Press, 1919.
'Young Men's Christian Association of Calcutta: Annual Report 1926'. Calcutta: Edinburgh Press, 1926.
Young Men's Christian Association of Madras. *Twenty-Fifth Years' Service in Madras, 1914, Annual Report*. Madras: Methodist Publishing House, 1915.

Young Men's Christian Associations of India and Ceylon. *The Annual Report of the Ceylon Sub-Committee of the National Council for India and Ceylon 1914*. Colombo: Ceylon Observer Press, 1915.

Literature

Adas, Michael. 'Contested Hegemony: The Great War and the Afro-Asian Assault on the Civilizing Mission Ideology.' *Journal of World History* 15, no. 1 (2004): 31–63.

Adcock, C. S. 'Debating Conversion, Silencing Caste: The Limited Scope of Religious Freedom'. *Journal of Law and Religion* 29, no. 3 (2014): 363–77.

Ahluwalia, Sanjam. *Reproductive Restraints: Birth Control in India, 1877–1947*. Urbana: University of Illinois Press, 2008.

Ahmed, Akbar S. *Resistance and Control in Pakistan*. Revised. London: Routledge, 2004.

Ahuja, Ravi. '"The Bridge-Builders": Some Notes on Railways, Pilgrimage and the British "Civilizing Mission" in Colonial India'. In *Colonialism as Civilizing Mission. Cultural Ideology in British India*, edited by Harald Fischer-Tiné and Michael Mann, 95–116. London: Anthem Press, 2004.

Alexander, Kristine. *Guiding Modern Girls: Girlhood, Empire, and Internationalism in the 1920s and 1930s*. Vancouver: UBC Press, 2017.

Allender, Tim. *Ruling through Education: The Politics of Schooling in the Colonial Punjab*. Elgin: New Dawn Press, 2006.

Alter, Joseph S. 'Gandhi's Body, Gandhi's Truth. Nonviolence and the Biomoral Imperative of Public Health'. *Journal of Asian Studies* 55 (1996): 301–22.

Alter, Joseph S. 'Indian Clubs and Colonialism: Hindu Masculinity and Muscular Christianity'. *Comparative Studies in Society and History* 46 (2004): 497–534.

Alter, Joseph S. *Moral Materialism: Sex and Masculinity in Modern India*. Gurgaon: Penguin Books India, 2011.

Alter, Joseph S. 'Physical Education, Sport and the Intersection and Articulation of "Modernities": The Hanuman Vyayam Prasarak Mandal'. *Journal of the History of Sport* 24 (2007): 1156–71.

Alter, Joseph S. 'Somatic Nationalism: Indian Wrestling and Militant Hinduism'. *Modern Asian Studies* 28, no. 3 (1994): 557–88.

Alter, Joseph S. *The Wrestler's Body: Identity and Ideology in North India*. Berkeley: University of California Press, 1992.

Alter, Joseph S. 'Wrestling with the History of Yoga as Sport in Modern India'. *India International Centre Quarterly* 44, no. 3–4 (2018): 252–65.

Alter, Joseph S. 'Yoga and Physical Education: Swami Kuvalayananda's Nationalist Project'. *Asian Medicine: Tradition and Modernity* 3 (2007): 20–36.

Alter, Joseph S. 'Yoga at the Fin de Siècle: Muscular Christianity with a Hindu Twist'. In *Muscular Christianity in Colonial and Post-Colonial Worlds*, edited by John Mac Aloon, 59–76. London: Routledge, 2008.

Alter, Joseph S. 'Yoga at the Fin-de-Siècle: Muscular Christianity with a "Hindu" Twist'. *The International Journal of the History of Sport* 23, no. 5 (2006): 759–76.

Amrith, Sunil S. 'Food and Welfare in India, c.1900–1950'. *Comparative Studies in Society and History* 50, no. 4 (2008): 1016–21.

Amrith, Sunil S. 'The Internationalization of Health in South East Asia'. In *Histories of Health in Southeast Asia: Perspectives on the Long Twentieth Century*, edited by Tim Harper and Sunil S. Amrith, 171–4. Bloomington: Indiana University Press, 2014.

Amrith, Sunil S., and Patricia Clavin, 'Feeding the World: Connecting Europe and Asia, 1930–1945', *Past & Present* 218, no. 8 suppl. (2013): 29–50.

Anderson, Ross. 'Logistics of the Indian Expeditionary Force D in Mesopotamia: 1914–18'. In *The Indian Army in the Two World Wars*, edited by Kaushik Roy, 105–44. Leiden: Brill, 2012.

Anderson, Valerie. *Race and Power in British India: Anglo-Indians, Class and Identity in the Nineteenth Century*. London: Bloomsbury Academic, 2020.

Ansari, Sarah. 'The Bombay Presidency's "Home Front", 1914–1918'. In *India and World War I: A Centennial Assessment*, edited by Roger D. Long and Ian Talbot. London: Routledge, 2018.

Anthony, David Henry, III. *Max Yergan: Race Man, Internationalist, Cold Warrior*. New York: New York University Press, 2006.

Arnold, David. 'Agriculture and "Improvement" in Early Colonial India: A Pre-History of Development'. *Journal of Agrarian Change* v, no. 4 (2005): 508–11.

Arnold, David. 'The "Discovery" of Malnutrition and Diet in Colonial India'. *Indian Economic and Social History Review* 31, no. 1 (1994): 1–26

Arnold, David. *Everyday Technology: Machines and the Making of India's Modernity*. Chicago: University of Chicago Press, 2013.

Arnold, David. 'Globalization and Contingent Colonialism: Towards a Transnational History of "British" India'. *Journal of Colonialism and Colonial History* 16, no. 2 (2015), DOI: 10.1353/cch.2015.0019.

Arnold, David. 'Vagrant India: Famine, Poverty, and Welfare under Colonial Rule'. In *Cast Out: Vagrancy and Homelessness in Global and Historical Perspective*, 117–39. Athens: Ohio University Press, 2008.

Arnold, David. 'White Colonisation and Labour in Colonial India'. *Journal of Imperial and Commonwealth History* 11, no. 2 (1983): 133–58.

Asad, Talal. *Formation of the Secular: Christianity, Islam, Modernity*. Stanford, CA: Stanford University Press, 2003.

Bajpai, Rochana, and Carlo Bonura. 'South Asian and Southeast Asian Ideologies'. In *The Oxford Handbook of Political Ideologies*, edited by Michael Freeden, Layman T. Sargent and Marc Stears, 661–81. Oxford: Oxford University Press, 2013.

Baker, William J. *Playing with God: Religion and Modern Sport*. Cambridge, MA: Harvard University Press, 2007.

Baker, William J. 'To Pray or to Play? The YMCA Question in the United Kingdom and the United States, 1850–1900'. *The International Journal of the History of Sport* 11, no. 1 (1994): 42–62.

Baker, William J. 'Religion'. In *The Routledge Companion to Sports History*, edited by S. W. Pope, 216–28. London: Routledge, 2010.

Baksi, Sandipan. 'Modernizing Agriculture in the Colonial Era: A View from Some Hindi Periodicals 1880–1940'. In *Tilling the Land Agricultural Knowledge and Practices in Colonial India*, edited by Deepak Kumar and Bipasha Raha, 71–98. Delhi: Primus Books, 2016.

Balachandran, G. 'Claiming Histories beyond Nations: Situating Global History'. *Indian Economic & Social History Review* 49, no. 2 (2012): 247–72.

Balachandran, G. 'History after the Global Turn: Perspectives from Rim and Region'. *History Australia* 14 (2017): 6–12.

Bandeira Jerónimo, Miguel. 'Repressive Developmentalism: Idioms, Repertoires and Trajectories in late Colonialism', in *The Oxford Handbook of the Ends of Empire*, ed. Martin Thomas and Andrew S. Thompson, 537–54. Oxford: Oxford University Press, 2018.

Bandyopadhyay, Kausik. *Scoring off the Field: Football Culture in Bengal, 1911–1980*. New Delhi: Routledge, 2011.

Banerjee, Prathama. 'Between the Political and the Non-Political: The Vivekananda Moment and a Critique of the Social in Colonial Bengal, 1890s–1910s'. *Social History* 39, no. 3 (2014): 323–39.

Banerjee, Sikata. *Make Me a Man! Masculinity, Hinduism, and Nationalism in India*. New York: State University of New York Press, 2005.

Banerjee, Sukanya. *Becoming Imperial Citizens: Indians in the Late-Victorian Empire*. Durham, NC: Duke University Press, 2010.

Bapu, Prabhu. *Hindu Mahasabha in Colonial North India, 1915–1930: Constructing Nation and History*. Abingdon: Routledge, 2013.

Barnett, Michael. *Empire of Humanity: A History of Humanitarianism*. Ithaca, NY: Cornell University Press, 2011.

Basu, Basudhita. 'Sports Education in Colonial Bengal: A Double-Edged Sword'. *South Asia Research* 38, no. 3 (2018): 268–86.

Basu, Rajsekhar. 'Missionaries as Agricultural Pioneers: Protestant Missionaries and Agricultural Improvement in Twentieth-Century India'. In *Tilling the Land: Agricultural Knowledge and Practices in Colonial India*, edited by Deepak Kumar and Bipasha Raha, 99–121. Delhi: Primus Books, 2016.

Basu, Shrabani. *For King and Another Country: Indian Soldiers on the Western Front 1914–1918*. London: Bloomsbury, 2015.

Basu, Shrabani. 'Turbans in the Trenches: Indian Sepoys and Sowars on the Western Front during the Great War'. In *Indian Soldiers in the First World War: Re-Visiting a Global Conflict*, edited by Ashutosh Kumar and Claude Markovits, 11–40. Abingdon: Routledge, 2021.

Bates, Rebecca J. 'Building Imperial Youth? Reflections on Labour and the Construction of Working-Class Childhood in Late Victorian England'. *Paedagogica Historica* 45, no. 1–2 (2009): 143–56.

Bayly, C. A. *The Birth of the Modern World, 1780–1914: Global Connections and Comparisons*. Oxford: Blackwell, 2004.

Bayly, C. A. *Origins of Nationality in South Asia: Patriotism and Ethical Government in the Making of Modern India*. Cambridge: Cambridge University Press, 1998.

Bayly, C. A. *Recovering Liberties: Indian Thought in the Age of Liberalism and Empire*. Cambridge: Cambridge University Press, 2012.

Bayly, Susan. *Caste, Society and Politics in India from the Eighteenth Century to the Modern Age*. Cambridge: Cambridge University Press, 1999.

Bear, Laura. *Lines of the Nation: Indian Railway Workers, Bureaucracy and the Intimate Historical Self*. New York: Columbia University Press, 2007.

Beckerlegge, Gwilym. 'Iconographic Representations of Renunciation and Activism in the Ramakrishna Math and Mission and the Rashtriya Swayamsevak Sangh'. *Journal of Contemporary Religion* 19, no. 1 (2004): 47–66.

Beckerlegge, Gwilym. *Swami Vivekananda's Legacy of Service: A Study of the Ramakrishna Math and Mission*. New Delhi: Oxford University Press, 2006.

Bellenoit, Hayden J. *The Formation of the Colonial State in India*. Abingdon: Routledge, 2017.

Bellenoit, Hayden. *Missionary Education and Empire in Late Colonial India, 1860–1920*. London: Pickering and Chatto, 2007.

Betiang, Liwhu. 'Theatre of Rural Empowerment: The Example of Living Earth Nigeria Foundation's Community Theatre Initiative in Cross River State, Nigeria'. *Research in Drama Education: The Journal of Applied Theatre and Performance* 15, no. 1 (2010): 59–78.

Bhattacharya, Neeladri. *The Great Agrarian Conquest: The Colonial Reshaping of a Rural World*. New York: State University of New York Press, 2019.

Bhattacharya, Sabyasachi. 'Introduction: The Contested Terrain of Education'. In *The Contested Terrain: Perspectives on Education in India*, edited by Sabyasachi Bhattacharya, 1–29. Hyderabad: Orient Longman, 1998.

Bhattacharya, Sabyasachi. *The Colonial State: Theory and Practice*. Delhi: Primus Books, 2016.

Bhattacharya, Sabyasachi, Joseph Bara and Chinna Rao Yagati, eds. *Educating the Nation: Documents on the Discourse of National Education in India 1880–1920*. New Delhi: Kanishka Publishers, 2003.

Bhattacharya, Tithi. *The Sentinels of Culture: Class, Education, and the Colonial Intellectual in Bengal (1848–85)*. New Delhi: Oxford University Press, 2005.

Bhaumik, Kaushik. 'At Home in the World: Cinema and Cultures of the Young in Bombay in the 1920s'. In *Towards a History of Consumption in South Asia*, edited by Douglas E. Haynes, Abigail McGowan, Tirthankar Roy and Haruka Yanagisawa, 136–54. New Delhi: Oxford University Press, 2010.

Block, Nelson R., and Tammy M. Proctor, eds. *Scouting Frontiers: Youth and the Scout Movement's First Century*. Cambridge: Cambridge Scholars Press, 2009.

Boli, John, and Gerald Thomas. *Constructing World Culture: International Nongovernmental Organisations since 1875*. Stanford, CA: Stanford University Press, 1999.

Borowy, Iris. *Coming to Terms with World Health: The League of Nations Health Organization 1921–1946*. Frankfurt: Peter Lang, 2009.

Bottenburg, Maarten van. 'Beyond Diffusion: Sport and Its Remaking in Cross-Cultural Contexts'. *Journal of Sport History* 37 (2010): 401–12.

Boyd, Nancy. *Emissaries: The Overseas Work of the American YWCA 1895–1970*. New York: The Woman's Press, 1986.

Brewis, Georgina. 'Education for Service: Social Service and Higher Education in India and Britain, 1905–1919'. *History of Education Review* 42, no. 2 (2013): 119–36.

Brewis, Georgina. '"Fill Full the Mouth of Famine": Voluntary Action in Famine Relief in India, 1896–1901'. *Modern Asian Studies* 44, no. 4 (2010): 887–918.

Bromber, Katrin, Birgit Krawietz and Joseph Maguire. 'Introduction: From Asian Sports to Sport in Asia'. In *Sport across Asia: Politics, Cultures, and Identities*, edited by Katrin Bromber, Birgit Krawietz and Joseph Maguire, 1–10. New York: Routledge, 2011.

Brown, Mark. *Penal Power and Colonial Rule*. Abingdon: Routledge, 2014.

Brown, Theodore M., and Elizabeth Fee. 'The Bandoeng Conference of 1937: A Milestone in Health and Development'. *American Journal of Public Health* 98, no. 1 (2008): 42–3.

Brunner, Michael. *Education and Modernity in Colonial Punjab: Khalsa College, the Sikh Tradition and the Webs of Knowledge, 1880–1947*. Cham: Palgrave Macmillan, 2020.

Brunner, Michael. 'Schooling the Subcontinent: State, Space, Society, and the Dynamics of Education in Colonial South Asia'. In *The Routledge Handbook of the History of*

Colonialism in South Asia, edited by Harald Fischer-Tiné and Maria Framke, 252–65. Abingdon: Routledge, 2021.

Brunner, Michael P. 'Teaching Development: Debates on "Scientific Agriculture" and "Rural Reconstruction" at Khalsa College, Amritsar, c. 1915–1947'. *The Indian Economic & Social History Review* 55, no. 1 (2018): 77–132.

Budd, Michael Anton. *The Sculpture Machine: Physical Culture and Body Politics in the Age of Empire*. New York: New York University Press, 1997.

Buettner, Elizabeth. *Empire Families: Britons and Late Imperial India*. New York: Oxford University Press, 2004.

Burbank, Jane, and Frederick Cooper. *Empires in World History: Power and Politics of Difference*. Princeton, NJ: Princeton University Press, 2010.

Burns, James. 'Excessive Americanisms: Hollywood in the British Empire, 1918–1930'. *Britain in the World* 7, no. 2 (2014): 196–211.

Burton, Antoinette. 'The Body in/as World History', in: *A Companion to World History*, edited by Douglas Northrop, 272–85. Malden, MA: Wiley–Blackwell, 2012.

Büschel, Hubertus. 'Eine Brücke am Mount Meru: Zur Globalgeschichte von Hilfe zur Selbsthilfe und Gewalt in Tanganjika'. In *Entwicklungswelten: Globalgeschichte der Entwicklungszusammenarbeit*, edited by Hubertus Büschel and Daniel Speich, 175–206. Frankfurt: Campus, 2009.

Büschel, Hubertus. *Hilfe zur Selbsthilfe: Deutsche Entwicklungsarbeit in Afrika 1960–1975*. Frankfurt: Campus, 2014.

Cabanes, Bruno. *The Great War and the Origins of Humanitarianism, 1918–1924*. Cambridge: Cambridge University Press, 2014.

Caplan, Lionel. 'Iconographies of Anglo-Indian Women: Gender Constructs and Contrasts in a Changing Society'. *Modern Asian Studies* 34, no. 4 (2000): 863–92.

Caplan, Lionel. *Warrior Gentlemen: Gurkhas in the Western Imagination*. Providence: Berghahn Books, 1995.

Cavallo, Dominick. *Muscles and Morals. Organised Playgrounds and Urban Reform. 1880–1920*. Philadelphia: University of Pennsylvania Press, 1981.

Ceuster, Koen de. 'Wholesome Education and Sound Leisure: The YMCA Sports Programme in Colonial Korea'. *European Journal of East Asian Studies* 2, no. 1 (2003): 53–88.

Ceuster, Koen de. 'The YMCA's Rural Development Program in Colonial Korea, 1925–35: Doctrine and Objectives'. *The Review of Korean Studies* 3, no. 1 (2000): 5–33.

Chakrabarty, Dipesh. 'From Civilization to Globalization: The "West" as a Shifting Signifier in Indian Modernity'. *Inter-Asia Cultural Studies* 13, no. 1 (2012): 138–52.

Chakrabarty, Dipesh. 'The Muddle of Modernity'. *American Historical Review* 116, no. 3 (2011): 663–75.

Chakrabarty, Dipesh. *Provincializing Europe: Postcolonial Thought and Historical Difference*. Princeton, NJ: Princeton University Press, 2000.

Chakravorty-Spivak, Gayatri. 'The Rani of Sirmur: An Essay in Reading the Archives'. *History and Theory* 24, no. 3 (1985): 247–72.

Chandra, Sudhir. 'Subject's Citizenship Dream: Notes on the Nineteenth Century?' In *Civil Society, Public Sphere and Citizenship: Dialogues and Perspectives*, edited by Helmut Reifeld and Rajeev Bhargava, 106–29. New Delhi: Sage, 2005.

Chatterjee, Nandini. *The Making of Indian Secularism: Empire Law and Christianity, 1830–1960*. Basingstoke: Palgrave Macmillan, 2011.

Chatterjee, Partha. *The Nation and Its Fragments: Colonial and Postcolonial Histories*. Princeton, NJ: Princeton University Press, 1993.

Chatterjee, Rimi B. *A History of Oxford University Press under the Raj*. New Delhi: Oxford University Press, 2006.

Chaudhary, I. K. 'Sanskrit Learning in Colonial Mithila: Continuity and Change'. In *Education in Colonial India: Historical Insights*, edited by Deepak Kumar, Joseph Bara, Nandita Khadria and Ch. Radha Gayathri, 125–44. New Delhi: Manohar, 2013.

Chauncey, George. 'Christian Brotherhood or Sexual Perversion? Homosexual Identities and the Construction of Sexual Boundaries in the World War One Era'. *Journal of Social History* 19, no. 2 (1985): 189–211.

Chowdhury, Indira, ed. *The Frail Hero and Virile History: Gender and the Politics of Culture in Colonial Bengal*. New Delhi: Oxford University Press, 1998.

Chowdhury, Sharmishtha Roy. *The First World War, Anti-Colonialism and Imperial Authority in British India, 1914–1924*. London: Routledge, 2019.

Chowdhury-Sengupta, Indira. *The Frail Hero and Virile History: Gender and the Politics of Culture in Colonial Bengal*. New Delhi: Oxford University Press, 1998.

Chudacoff, Howard P. *Children at Play: An American History*. New York: New York University Press, 2001.

Chudal, Alaka Atreva. 'Story-Telling in Prison: Oral Performance of a Gorkha Prisoner of World War I'. *European Bulletin of Himalaya Research*, no. 54 (2020): 5–35.

Citino, Nathan J. *Envisioning the Arab Future: Modernization in U.S.–Arab Relations, 1945–1967*. Cambridge: Cambridge University Press, 2017.

Clark, Christopher, and Michael Ledger-Lomas. 'The Protestant International'. In *Religious Internationals in the Modern World: Globalization and Faith Communities since 1750*, edited by Abigail Greene and Vincent Viaene, 23–52. Basingstoke: Palgrave Macmillan, 2012.

Clarke, Gerard, and Michael Jennings, eds. *Development, Civil Society and Faith-Based Organizations: Bridging the Sacred and the Secular*. Basingstoke: Palgrave Macmillan, 2008.

Coates-Ulrichsen, Kristian. 'Learning the Hard Way: The Indian Army in Mesopotamia, 1914–1918'. In *The British Army in India: Virtues and Necessity*, edited by Rob Jonson, 51–64. Newcastle: Cambridge Scholars, 2014.

Conrad, Sebastian. 'Globalizing the Beautiful Body: Eugen Sandow, Bodybuilding, and the Ideal of Muscular Manliness at the Turn of the Twentieth Century'. *Journal of World History* 32, no. 1 (2021): 95–125.

Conrad, Sebastian. *Globalgeschichte: eine Einführung*. München: C. H. Beck, 2013.

Conrad, Sebastian. *What Is Global History?* Princeton, NJ: Princeton University Press, 2017.

Cooper, Frederick. 'Development, Modernization, and the Social Sciences in the Era of Decolonization: The Examples of British and French Africa'. In *The Ends of European Colonial Empires: Cases and Comparisons*, edited by Miguel Bandeira Jerónimo and António Costa Pinto, 15–50. Basingstoke: Palgrave Macmillan, 2015.

Cooper, Frederick. 'Writing the History of Development'. *Journal of Modern European History* viii, no. 1 (2010): 7.

Copeland, Jeffrey C., and Yan Xu, eds. *The YMCA at War: Collaboration and Conflict during the World Wars*. Lanham, MD: Lexington Books, 2018.

Cotesta, Vittorio. 'Three Critics of Weber's Thesis of the Uniqueness of the West: Jack Goody, Kenneth Pomeranz, and S. N. Eisenstadt. Strengths and Weaknesses'. *Max Weber Studies* 14, no. 2 (2014): 147–67.

Cullather, Nick. *The Hungry World: America's Cold War Battle against Poverty in Asia*. Cambridge, MA: Harvard University Press, 2010.

Curtis, Susan. *A Consuming Faith: The Social Gospel and Modern American Culture*. Baltimore, MD: Johns Hopkins University Press, 1991.

Darnton, Robert. 'Literary Surveillance in the British Raj: The Contradictions of Liberal Imperialism'. *Book History* 4 (2001): 133–76.

Das, Santanu. *India, Empire, and First World War Culture. Writings, Images, and Songs*. Cambridge: Cambridge University Press, 2018.

Das, Santanu. 'Introduction'. In *Race, Empire and First World War Writing*, edited by Santanu Das, 1–32. Cambridge: Cambridge University Press, 2011.

Das, Santanu, ed. *Race, Empire and First World War Writing*. Cambridge: Cambridge University Press, 2011.

Das, Santanu. *Touch and Intimacy in First World War Literature*. Cambridge: Cambridge University Press, 2006.

Dasgupta, Siddharta. 'From Victory to Defeat: The Indian Army in Mesopotamia, 1914–1916'. In *Indian Soldiers in the First World War: Re-visiting a Global Conflict*, edited by Ashutosh Kumar and Claude Markovits, 104–23. Abingdon: Routledge, 2021.

Dass, Manishita. *Outside the Lettered City: Cinema, Modernity and the Public Sphere in Late Colonial India*. Oxford: Oxford University Press, 2015.

Davenport, Paul. 'Doctrine, Practice and Masculinity: Physical Training in the British Army, 1939–1945'. *Journal of War & Culture Studies* 12, no. 2 (2019): 156–75.

David, M. D. 'The Missionary Muscular Culture in Modern India'. In *Discoveries, Missionary Expansion, and Asian Cultures*, 195–209. New Delhi: Concept Publishing, 1994.

David, M. D. *The YMCA and the Making of Modern India (A Centenary History)*. New Delhi: National Council of YMCAs of India, 1991.

David, M. D. *The YMCA and the Making of Modern India: A Saga of Selfless Sacrifice, Vol. II. 1991–2016*. New Delhi: National Council of YMCAs of India, 2017.

Davidann, Jon Thares. 'The American YMCA in Meiji Japan: God's Work Gone Awry'. *Journal of World History* 6, no. 1 (1995): 107–25.

Davidann, Jon Thares. *A World of Crisis and Progress: The American YMCA in Japan, 1890–1930*. Bethlehem, PA: Lehigh University Press, 1998.

Davies, Thomas. *NGOs: A New History of Transnational Civil Society*. London: Hurst Publishers, 2013.

Davies, Wade. 'Cornell's Field Seminar in Applied Anthropology: Social Scientists and American Indians in the Postwar Southwest'. *Journal of the Southwest* 43, no. 3 (2001): 317–41.

Davis, Mike. *Late Victorian Holocausts: El Niño Famines and the Making of the Third World*. London: Verso, 2007.

De, Sarmistha. *Marginal Europeans in Colonial India, 1860–1920*. Kolkata: Thema, 2008.

Desai, A. R. *Social Background of Indian Nationalism*. Bombay: Popular Prakashan, 1966.

Dewey, Clive. *Anglo-Indian Attitudes: Mind of the Indian Civil Service*. London: Hambledon, 1993.

Dewey, Clive J. 'Images of the Village Community: A Study in Anglo-Indian Ideology'. *Modern Asian Studies* 6, no. 3 (1972): 291–328.

Dhas, D. S. Sanal. 'Organisation and Services of YMCA in Tamil Nadu with Special Reference to Kanyakumari District since 1956'. Unpublished PhD dissertation, Manonmaniam Sundaranar University, 2017.

Di Costanzo, Thierry. 'Memory and History of the Great(er) War and India: From a National-Imperial to a More Global Perspective'. *E-Rea. Revue Électronique d'études Sur Le Monde Anglophone* 14, no. 2 (2017): 1–18.

Dimeo, Paul. 'A Parcel of Dummies? Sport and the Body in Indian History'. In *Confronting the Body: The Politics of Physicality in Colonial and Post-Colonial India*, edited by James H. Mills and Satadru Sen, 39–57. London: Anthem Press, 2004.

Dirks, Patricia. 'Canada's Boys – An Imperial or National Asset? Responses to Baden-Powell's Boy Scout Movement in Pre-war Canada'. In *Canada and the British World: Culture, Migration, and Identity*, edited by P. Buckner and R. R.Francis, 111–28. Vancouver: UBC Press, 2006.

Doan, Laura. 'Sex, Education and the Great War Soldier: A Queer Analysis of the Practice of "Hetero" Sex'. *Journal of British Studies* 51, no. 3 (2012): 641–63.

Douglas, Susan J. *Listening In: Radio and the American Imagination, from Amos 'n' Andy and Edward R. Murrow to Wolfman Jack and Howard Stern*. New York: Random House, 1999.

Dube, Saurabh. 'Makeovers of Modernity: An Introduction'. In *Handbook of Modernity in South Asia: Modern Makeovers*, edited by Saurabh Dube, 1–25. New Delhi: Oxford University Press, 2011.

Dube, Saurabh, and Ishita Banerjee-Dube, eds. *Unbecoming Modern: Colonialism, Modernity, Colonial Modernities*. New Delhi: Social Science Press, 2006.

Dubois, Laurent. 'Diffusion and Empire'. In *The Oxford Handbook of Sport History*, edited by Robert Edelman and Wayne Wilson, 171–82. New York: Oxford University Press, 2017.

Durbach, Nadja. 'The Politics of Provisioning: Feeding South Asian Prisoners during the First World War'. *War & Society* 37, no. 2 (2018): 75–90.

Dutta, Sutapa. 'Packing a Punch at the Bengali Babu'. *South Asia: Journal of South Asian Studies* 44, no. 3 (2021): 437–58.

Dyreson, Mark. 'Imperial "Deep Play": Reading Sport and Visions of the Five Empires of the "New World", 1919–1941'. *The International Journal of the History of Sport* 2, no. 17 (2011): 2421–47.

Dyreson, Mark. 'Prologue – The Paradoxes of Imitation and Resistance: The Origins of an American Empire of Sports'. *The International Journal of the History of Sport* 28, (2011): 2415–20.

Ekbladh, David. *The Great American Mission: Modernization and the Construction of an American World Order*. Princeton, NJ: Princeton University Press, 2010.

El Shakry, Omnia. *The Great Social Laboratory: Subjects of Knowledge in Colonial and Postcolonial Egypt*. Stanford, CA: Stanford University Press, 2007.

Elias, Norbert, and Eric Dunning. *Quest for Excitement: Sport and Leisure in the Civilising Process*. Collected Works of Norbert Elias 7. Dublin: Dublin University Press, 2008.

Ellis, Catriona. '"If You Cannot Feed the Body of a Child You Cannot Feed the Brain": Education and Nutrition in Late Colonial Madras'. *South Asia Journal of South Asian Studies* 44, no. 1 (2021): 135–51.

Elmhirst, Leonard K. *Poet and Plowman*. Calcutta: Visva-Bharati, 1975.

Erdozain, Dominic. *The Problem of Pleasure: Sport, Recreation and the Crisis of Victorian Religion*. Woodbridge: Boydell Press, 2010.

Escobar, Arturo. *Encountering Development: The Making and Unmaking of the Third World*. Princeton, NJ: Princeton University Press, 1995.

Evans, Christopher A. *The Social Gospel in American Religion: A History*. New York: New York University Press, 2017.

Evers, Hans Dieter, Markus Kaiser and Christine Müller. 'Knowledge in Development: Epistemic Machineries in a Global Context'. *International Social Science Journal* 60, no. 195 (2009): 55–68.

Fahey, David M., and Padma Manian. 'Poverty and Purification: The Politics of Gandhi's Campaign for Prohibition'. *The Historian* 67, no. 3 (2005): 489–506.
Farmer, B. H. 'Perspectives on the Green Revolution in South Asia'. *Modern Asian Studies* 20, no. 1 (1986): 175–99.
Feener, Michael R., and Catherine Scheer. 'Development's Missions'. In *The Mission of Development: Religion and Technopolitics in Asia*, edited by Michael R. Feener, Catherine Scheer and Philip Fountain, 1–27. Leiden: Brill, 2019.
Ferguson, Niall. *Empire: How Britain Made the Modern World*. London: Penguin Books, 2004.
Fischer, Fritz. *Making Them Like Us: Peace Corps Volunteers in the 1960s*. Washington, DC: Smithsonian Institution Press, 1998.
Fischer-Tiné, Harald. '"Character Building and Manly Games": Viktorianische Konzepte von Männlichkeit und ihre Aneignung im frühen Hindu Nationalismus'. *Historische Anthropologie* 9, no. 3 (2001): 432–55.
Fischer-Tiné, Harald. *Der Gurukul Kangri oder die Erziehung der Arya Nation: Kolonialismus, Hindureform und 'nationale Bildung' in Britisch-Indien (1897–1922)*. Würzburg: Ergon-Verlag, 2003.
Fischer-Tiné, Harald. 'Englands interne Zivilisationsmission: Arbeitshäuser für Europäer im kolonialen Indien (ca. 1860–1914)'. In *Zivilisierungsmissionen: Imperiale Weltverbesserung seit dem 18. Jahrhundert*, edited by Boris Barth and Jürgen Osterhammel, 169–99. Konstanz: UVK, 2005.
Fischer-Tiné, Harald. 'Eradicating the "Scourge of Drink" and the "Un-pardonable Sin of Illegitimate Sexual Enjoyment": M. K. Gandhi as Anti-Vice Crusader'. *Interdisziplinäre Zeitschrift für Südasienforschung* ii, no. 1 (2017): 117–30.
Fischer-Tiné, Harald. 'Fitness for Modernity: The YMCA and Physical Education Schemes in Late Colonial South Asia (c. 1890–1940)'. *Modern Asian Studies* 53, no. 2 (2019): 512–59.
Fischer-Tiné, Harald. 'From Brahmacharya to "Conscious Race Culture": Indian Nationalism, Hindu Tradition and Victorian Discourses of Science'. In *Beyond Representation: The Construction of Identity in Colonial India*, edited by Crispin Bates, 230–59. New Delhi: Oxford University Press, 2006.
Fischer-Tiné, Harald. 'Global Civil Society and the Forces of Empire: The Salvation Army, British Imperialism and the "Pre-History" of NGOs (ca. 1880–1920)'. In *Competing Visions of World Order: Global Moments and Movements, 1880s–1930s*, edited by Sebastian Conrad and Dominic Sachsenmaier, 29–67. New York: Palgrave Macmillan, 2007.
Fischer-Tiné, Harald. '"Kindly Elders of the Hindu Biradri": The Arya Samaj's Struggle for Influence and Its Effect on Hindu-Muslim Relations'. In *Gurus and Their Followers. Studies in New Religious Movements in Late Colonial India*, edited by A. Copley, 107–27. New Delhi: Oxford University Press, 2000.
Fischer-Tiné, Harald. 'Liquid Boundaries: Race, Class and Alcohol in Colonial India'. In *A History of Alcohol and Drugs in Modern South Asia: Intoxicating Affairs*, edited by Harald Fischer-Tiné, 89–115. Abingdon: Routledge, 2014.
Fischer-Tiné, Harald. *Low and Licentious Europeans: Race, Class, and 'White Subalternity' in Colonial India*. New Delhi: Orient BlackSwan, 2009.
Fischer-Tiné, Harald. 'The Making of a "Ruling Race": Defining and Defending Whiteness in Colonial India'. In *Racism in the Modern World: Historical Perspectives on Cultural Transfer and Adaptation*, edited by Manfred Berg and Simon Wendt, 211–35. New York: Berghahn Books, 2011.

Fischer-Tiné, Harald. 'Marrying Global History with South Asian History: Potential and Limits of Global Microhistory in a Regional Inflection'. *Comparativ* 29, no. 2 (2019): 52–77.

Fischer-Tiné, Harald. '"The Only Hope for Fallen India": The Gurukul Kangri as an Experiment in National Education'. In *Explorations in the History of South Asia: A Volume in Honour of Dietmar Rothermund*, edited by Georg Berkemer, Jürgen Lutt, Hermann Kulke and Tilman Frasch, 277–99. New Delhi: Manohar, 2001.

Fischer-Tiné, Harald. *Pidgin-Knowledge: Wissen und Kolonialismus*. Zürich: Diaphanes, 2013.

Fischer-Tiné, Harald. *Shyamji Krishnavarma: Sanskrit, Sociology and Anti-Imperialism*. New Delhi: Routledge India, 2014.

Fischer-Tiné, Harald. 'Third-Stream Orientalism: J. N. Farquhar, the Indian YMCA's Literature Department, and the Representation of South Asian Cultures and Religions (ca. 1910–1940)'. *The Journal of Asian Studies* 79, no. 3 (2020): 659–83.

Fischer-Tiné, Harald. 'Unparalleled Opportunities: The Indian Y.M.C.A.'s Army Work Schemes for Imperial Troops during the Great War (1914–1920)'. *Journal of Imperial and Commonwealth History* 47, no. 1 (2019): 100–137.

Fischer-Tiné, Harald. 'The YMCA and Low-Modernist Rural Development in South Asia, c. 1922–1957'. *Past & Present* 240, no. 1 (2018): 193–234.

Fischer-Tiné, Harald, Julia Hauser and Ashok Malhotra. 'Introduction: Feeding Bodies, Nurturing Identities: The Politics of Diet in Late Colonial and Early Post-Colonial India'. *South Asia Journal of South Asian Studies* 44, no. 1 (2021): 107–16.

Fischer-Tiné, Harald, Stefan Huebner and Ian Tyrell. 'Introduction. The Rise and Growth of a Global "Moral Empire": The YMCA and YWCA during the Late Nineteenth and Early Twentieth Centuries'. In *Spreading Protestant Modernity. Global Perspectives on the Work of the YMCA and the YWCA, 1889–1970*, edited by Harald Fischer-Tiné, Stefan Huebner and Ian Tyrell, 1–35. Honolulu, HI: University of Hawaii Press, 2021.

Forsythe, David P. *The Humanitarians: The International Committee of the Red Cross*. Cambridge: Cambridge University Press, 2005.

Fox, Richard. *Lions of the Punjab: Culture in the Making*. Berkeley: University of California Press, 1985.

Framke, Maria. 'The Politics of Gender and Community: Non-Governmental Relief in Late Colonial and Early Postcolonial India'. In *Gendering Humanitarianism: Politics, Practice, and Empowerment during the Twentieth Century*, edited by Esther Möller, Johannes Paulmann and Katharina Stornig, 143–66. Palgrave MacMillan, 2020.

Freier, Monika. 'Cultivating emotions: The Gita Press and Its Agenda of Social and Spiritual Reform'. *South Asian History and Culture* 3, no. 3 (2012): 397–413.

Fretheim, Kjetil. 'Whose Kingdom? Which Context? Ecumenical and Contextual Theology in the World Alliance of YMCAs'. *International Review of Mission* 97, no. 384/385 (2008): 116–28.

Frost, Mark R. 'Imperial Citizenship or Else: Liberal Ideals and the India Unmaking of Empire, 1890–1919'. *The Journal of Imperial and Commonwealth History* 46, no. 5 (2018): 845–73.

Frost, Mark R. '"Wider Opportunities": Religious Revival, Nationalist Awakening and the Global Dimension in Colombo, 1870–1920?' *Modern Asian Studies* 36, no. 4 (2002): 937–67.

Frykenberg, Robert E. *Christianity in India: From the Beginnings to the Present*. Oxford: Oxford University Press, 2008.

Frykenberg, Robert Eric. 'Christian Missions and the Raj'. In *Missions and Empires*, edited by Norman Etherington, 107–31. Oxford: Oxford University Press, 2005.

Fuchs, Maria-Magdalena. 'Islamic Modernism in Colonial Punjab: The Anjuman-i Himayat-i Islam, 1884–1923'. Unpublished PhD dissertation, Princeton University, 2019.

Ganneri, Namrata R. 'The Debate on "Revival" and the Physical Culture Movement in Western India (1900–1950)'. In *Sport across Asia: Politics, Cultures, and Identities*, edited by Katrin Bromber, Birgit Krawietz and Joseph Maguire, 121–43. New York: Routledge, 2011.

Ganneri, Namrata. '"Pahalwan" Portraits: Manly Consumers of Physical Culture in Western India'. *Tasveer Ghar – A Digital Archive of South Asian Popular Culture*. Accessed 11 August 2021. http://www.tasveergharindia.net/essay/pahalwan-portraits.html.

Gardner, Nikolas. 'British Prestige and the Mesopotamia Campaign, 1914–1916'. *The Historian* 77, no. 2 (2015): 269–89.

Garnham, Neal, 'Both Praying and Playing: 'Muscular Christianity' and the YMCA in North-East County Durham.' *Journal of Social History* 35, no. 2 (2001): 397–407.

Gems, Gerald R. *The Athletic Crusade: Sport and American Cultural Imperialism*. Lincoln: University of Nebraska Press, 2006.

Gerwarth, Robert, and Erez Manela, eds. *Empires at War, 1911–1923: The Greater War*. Oxford: Oxford University Press, 2014.

Geyer, Martin H., and Johannes Paulmann, eds. *The Mechanics of Internationalism: Culture, Society, and Politics from the 1840s to the First World War*. Oxford: Oxford University Press, 2001.

Ghosh, Durba. *Gentlemanly Terrorists: Political Violence and the Colonial State in India, 1919–1947*. Cambridge: Cambridge University Press, 2017.

Gienow-Hecht, Jessica C. E. 'Always Blame the Americans: Anti-Americanism in Europe in the Twentieth Century'. *The American Historical Review* 111, no. 4 (2006): 1067–91.

Gilbert, Jess. 'Low Modernism and the Agrarian New Deal: A Different Kind of State'. In *Fighting for the Farm: Rural America Transformed*, edited by Jane Adams, 129–46. Philadelphia: University of Pennsylvania Press, 2003.

Gilbert, Jess. *Planning Democracy: Agrarian Intellectuals and the Intended New Deal*. New Haven, CT: Yale University Press, 2015.

Gilmartin, David. *Blood and Water: The Indus River Basin in Modern History*. Oakland, CA: University of California Press, 2015.

Gimpel, Denise. 'Civilizing Bodies. Somatic Engineering in China'. In *Sport across Asia: Politics, Cultures, and Identities*, edited by Katrin Bromber, Birgit Krawietz and Joseph Maguire, 32–58. New York: Routledge, 2011.

Goodchild, Lester F. 'G. Stanley Hall and an American Social Darwinist Pedagogy: His Progressive Educational Ideas on Gender and Race'. *History of Education Quarterly* 52, no. 1 (2012): 62–98.

Goodman, Sam. 'Spaces of Intemperance & the British Raj 1860–1920'. *The Journal of Imperial and Commonwealth History* 48, no. 4 (2020): 591–618.

Gooptu, Nandini. *The Politics of the Urban Poor in Early-Twentieth Century India*. Cambridge: Cambridge University Press, 2001.

Gopal, Priyamvada. *Insurgent Empire: Anticolonial Resistance and British Dissent*. London: Verso, 2019.

Gordon, David M. 'Reading Archives as Sources'. *Oxford Research Encyclopedia of African History*, 20 November 2018. https://doi.org/10.1093/acrefore/9780190277734.013.227.

Gorman, Daniel. 'Ecumenical Internationalism: Willoughby Dickinson, the League of Nations and the World Alliance for Promoting International Friendship through the Churches'. *Journal of Contemporary History* 45, no. 1 (2010): 51–73.
Gorman, Daniel. *The Emergence of International Society in the 1920s*. Cambridge: Cambridge University Press, 2012.
Goswami, Manu. *Producing India: From Colonial Economy to National Space*. Chicago, IL: The University of Chicago Press, 2004.
Gould, Harold A. *Sikhs, Swamis, and Spies: The India Lobby in the United States 1900–1946*. New Delhi: Sage, 2006.
Grant, Julia. *The Boy Problem: Educating Boys in Urban America*. Baltimore, MD: Johns Hopkins University Press, 2014.
Grant, Peter. *Philanthropy and Voluntary Action in the First World War*. Abingdon: Routledge, 2014.
Grazia, Victoria de. *Irresistible Empire: America's Advance through 20th Century Europe*. Cambridge, MA: The Belknap Press of Harvard University Press, 2005.
Green, Abigail. 'Religious Internationalism'. In *Internationalisms: A Twentieth-Century History*, edited by Glenda Sluga and Patricia Clavin, 17–37. Cambridge: Cambridge University Press, 2017.
Green, Nile. *Terrains of Exchange: Religious Economies of Global Islam*. Oxford: Oxford University Press, 2014.
Greene, Abigail. 'Humanitarianism in Its Nineteenth Century Context: Religious, Gendered, National'. *The Historical Journal* 57, no. 4 (2014): 1157–75.
Greene, Abigail, and Vincent Viaene, eds. *Religious Internationals in the Modern World: Globalization and Faith Communities since 1750*. Basingstoke: Palgrave Macmillan, 2012.
Greene, Ronald Walter. 'Pastoral Exhibitions: The YMCA Motion Picture Bureau and the Transition to 16 mm, 1928–39'. In *Useful Cinema*, edited by Charles R. Acland and Haidee Wasson, 205–29. Durham, NC: Duke University Press, 2011.
Guedes, Claudia. 'Changing the Cultural Landscape. English Engineers, American Missionaries, and the YMCA, Bring Sports to Brazil, the 1870s to the 1930s'. *International Journal of the History of Sport* 28, no. 17 (2011): 2594–608.
Guha, Ramachandra. *A Corner of a Foreign Field: The Indian History of a British Sport*. London: Picador, 2003.
Gupta, Akhil. *Postcolonial Developments: Agriculture in the Making of Modern India*. Durham, NC: Duke University Press, 1998.
Gustav-Wrathall, John Donald. *Take the Young Stranger by the Hand: Same Sex-Relations and the YMCA*. Chicago, IL: University of Chicago Press, 1999.
Guttman, Allen. *Games and Empires: Modern Sports and Cultural Imperialism*. New York: Columbia University Press, 1994.
Guttman, Allen. *Modern Sport and Cultural Imperialism*. New York: Columbia University Press, 1994.
Haas, Peter M., 'Introduction: Epistemic Communities and International Policy Coordination', *International Organization* 46, no. 1 (1992): 1–35.
Hanna, Emma. 'Putting the Moral into Morale: YMCA Cinemas on the Western Front, 1914–1918'. *Historical Journal of Film, Radio and Television* 35, no. 4 (2015): 615–30.
Harder, Hans. 'Languages, Literatures and the Public Sphere'. In *The Routledge Handbook of the History of Colonialism in South Asia*, edited by Harald Fischer-Tiné and MariaFramke, 412–23. Abingdon: Routledge, 2022.

Hardiman, David. 'The Politics of Water in Colonial India'. *South Asia: Journal of South Asian Studies* 25, no. 2 (2002): 111–20.

Harding, Christopher. 'The Christian Village Experiment in Punjab: Social and Religious Reformation'. *South Asia: Journal of South Asian Studies* 31, no. 3 (2008): 397–418.

Harding, Christopher. *Religious Transformation in South Asia: The Meaning of Conversion in Colonial Punjab*. Oxford: Oxford University Press, 2008.

Harper, Susan Billington. *In the Shadow of the Mahatma: Bishop V. S. Azariah and the Travails of Christianity in British India*. Grand Rapids, MI: W. B. Eerdmans, 2000.

Harries, Patrick, and David Maxwell. 'The Spiritual in the Secular'. In *The Spiritual in the Secular: Missionaries and Knowledge about Africa*, edited by Patrick Harries and David Maxwell, 1–8. Grand Rapids, MI: W. B. Eerdmans, 2012.

Harris, Patrick, and David Maxwell, eds. *The Spiritual in the Secular: Missionaries and Knowledge about Africa*. Grand Rapids, MI: W. B. Eerdmans, 2012.

Harrison, S. J. 'Skulls and Scientific Collecting in the Victorian Military: Keeping the Enemy Dead in British Frontier Warfare'. *Comparative Studies in Societies and History* 50, no. 1 (2008): 285–303.

Harsha, Ambi. *Development of Physical Education in Madras, 1918–1948*. Madras: Christian Literature Society, 1982.

Harwood, Jonathan. 'Peasant Friendly Plant Breeding and the Early Years of the Green Revolution in Mexico'. *Agricultural History* 83, no. 3 (2009): 384–410.

Hatcher, Brian A. *Bourgeois Hinduism or the Faith of the Modern Vedantists: Rare Discourses from Colonial Bengal*. Oxford: Oxford University Press, 2008.

Hayford, Charles W. *To the People: James Yen and Village China*. New York: Columbia University Press, 1990.

Haynes, D. E. 'From Tribute to Philanthropy: The Politics of Gift Giving in a Western Indian City'. *Journal of Asian Studies* 46, no. 2 (1987): 339–60.

Haynes, Douglas, ed. *Toward a History of Consumption in South Asia*. Delhi: Oxford University Press, 2010.

Heavens, John E. 'The International Committee of the North American Young Men's Christian Association and Its Foreign Work in China, 1895–1937'. Unpublished PhD dissertation, University of Cambridge, 2013.

Heffernan, Conor. 'Strength Peddlers: Eddie O'Callaghan and the Selling of Irish Strength'. *Sport in History* 38, no. 1 (2018): 23–45.

Heffernan, Conor. 'What's Wrong with a Little Swinging? Indian Clubs as a Tool of Suppression and Rebellion in in Post-Rebellion India'. *The International Journal of History of Sport* 34, no. 7–8 (2017): 554–77.

Hegde, Sasheej. 'Reassembling Modernity: Thinking at the Limit'. *Social Scientist* 37, no. 9/10 (2009): 66–88.

Heimsath, Charles H. *Indian Nationalism and Hindu Social Reform*. Princeton, NJ: Princeton University Press, 1964.

Hendrick, Harry. *Children, Childhood and English Society, 1880–1990*. Cambridge: Cambridge University Press, 1997.

Hendrick, Harry. *Images of Youth: Age, Class, and the Male Youth Problem, 1880–1920*. Oxford: Oxford University Press, 1990.

Hess, Gary R. 'American Agricultural Missionaries and Efforts at Economic Improvement in India'. *Agricultural History* 42, no. 1 (1968): 23–34.

Hodge, Joseph Morgan. *Triumph of the Expert: Agrarian Doctrines of Development and the Legacies of British Colonialism*. Athens: Ohio University Press, 2007.

Hodges, Sarah. 'South Asia's Eugenic Pasts'. In *The Oxford Handbook of the History of Eugenics*, edited by Philippa Levine and Alison Bashford, 228–42. New York: Oxford University Press, 2010.

Hoganson, Kristin L., and Jay Sexton, eds. *Crossing Empires: Taking U.S. History in Transimperial Terrain*. Durham, NC: Duke University Press, 2020.

Hollinger, David A. 'Christianity and Its American Fate: Where History Interrogates Secularization Theory'. In *The Worlds of American Intellectual History*, edited by Joel Isaac, 280–303. New York: Oxford University Press, 2017.

Honeck, Mischa. *Our Frontier Is the World: The Boy Scouts in the Age of American Ascendancy*. Ithaca, NJ: Cornell University Press, 2018.

Hopkins, A. G. *American Empire: A Global History*. Princeton, NJ: Princeton University Press, 2018.

Hopkins, C. Howard. *John R. Mott (1865–1955): A Biography*. Grand Rapids, MI: W. B. Eerdmans, 1979.

Horne, Gerald. *The End of Empires: African Americans and India*. Philadelphia, PA: Temple University Press, 2009.

Hornsby, Angela M. '"The Boy Problem": North Carolina Race Men Groom the Next Generation, 1900–1930'. *Journal of Negro History* 86, no. 4 (2001): 276–304.

Hsing, Chun. *Baptized in the Fire of Revolution: The American Social Gospel and the YMCA in China, 1919–1937*. Bethlehem, PA: Lehigh University Press, 1996.

Hu, Enya. 'The Gospel of Intellectuality: Indoctrinating Yenching Educational Missionaries in the Progressive Era'. In *The Mission of Development: Religion and Technopolitics in Asia*, edited by Michael R. Feener, Catherine Scheer and Philip Fountain, 28–58. Leiden: Brill, 2019.

Huebner, Stefan. 'Muscular Christian Exchanges: Asian Sports Experts and the International YMCA Training School (1910s to 1930s)'. In *Global Exchanges: Scholarships and Transnational Circulations in the Modern World*, edited by Ludovic Tournès and Giles Scott-Smith, 97–112. New York: Berghahn Books, 2018.

Huebner, Stefan. *Pan-Asian Sports and the Emergence of Modern Asia, 1913–1974*. Singapore: NUS Press, 2016.

Huebner, Stefan. '"Uplifting the Weak and Degenerated Races of East Asia": American and Indigenous Views of Sport and Body in Early Twentieth Century East Asia'. In *Race and Racism in Modern East Asia. Vol. II: Interactions, Nationalism, Gender and Lineage*, edited by Rotem Kowner and Walter Demel, 198–216. Leiden: Brill, 2015.

Huebner, Stefan. 'The YMCA's Message, Public Health and Masculinity 1910s–1920s: Transnational Impacts of the Physical Education Programs in China, the Philippines, and Japan?' In *Spreading Protestant Modernity: Global Perspectives on the Social Work of the YMCA and YWCA, 1889–1970*, edited by Harald Fischer-Tiné, Stefan Huebner and Ian R Tyrrell, 99–118. Honolulu: University of Hawai'i Press, 2021.

Immerwahr, Daniel. *Thinking Small: The United States and the Lure of Community Development*. Cambridge, MA: Harvard University Press, 2015.

Imy, Kate. 'Kidnapping and a "Confirmed Sodomite": An Intimate Enemy on the Northwest Frontier of India, 1915–1925'. *Twentieth Century British History* 28, no. 1 (2016): 29–56.

Inden, Ronald. *Imagining India*. Oxford: Basil Blackwell, 1990.

Iriye, Akira. *Global Community: The Role of International Organizations in the Making of the Contemporary World*. Berkeley: University of California Press, 2002.

Jachertz, Ruth. '"Keep Food Out of Politics": The UN Food and Agriculture Organization, 1945–1965'. In *International Organizations and Development, 1945–1990*, edited

by Marc Frey, Sönke Kunkel and Corinna R. Unger, 75–100. Basingstoke: Palgrave Macmillan, 2014.
Jaffrelot, Christophe. *The Hindu Nationalist Movement in India*. London: Hurst, 1996.
Jayal, Niraja Gopal. *Citizenship and Its Discontents: An Indian History*. Cambridge, MA: Harvard University Press, 2013.
Jeffery, Robin. 'Communications and Capitalism in India, 1750–2000'. *South Asia: Journal of South Asian Studies* 25, no. 2 (2002): 61–75.
Jodhka, Surinder S. 'Introduction'. In *Village Society*, edited by Surinder S. Jodhka, 1–22. Delhi: Orient Blackswan, 2012.
Jodhka, Surinder S. 'Nation and Village: Images of Rural India in Gandhi, Nehru and Ambedkar'. *Economic and Political Weekly* 37, no. 32 (2002): 3343–53.
Johnson, Charles Denton. 'Re-thinking the Emergence of the Struggle for South African Liberation in the United States: Max Yergan and the Council on African Affairs, 1922–1946'. *Journal of Southern African Studies* 39, no. 1 (2013): 171–92.
Johnson, Elmer L. *The History of YMCA Physical Education*. Chicago, IL: Association Press, 1979.
Jones, Ben, and Marie Juul Petersen. 'Instrumental, Narrow, Normative?: Reviewing Recent Work on Religion and Development'. *Third World Quarterly* 32, no. 7 (2011): 1291–1306.
Jones, Heather. 'International or Transnational? Humanitarian Action during the First World War'. *European Review of History* 16, no. 5 (2009): 697–713.
Jones, Kenneth W. *Religious Controversy in British India: Dialogues in South Asian Languages*. Albany: State University of New York Press, 1992.
Jones, Kenneth W. *Socio-religious Reform Movements in British India*. Vol. 2. The New Cambridge History of India, III. Cambridge: Cambridge University Press, 1989.
Jonnes, Jill. *Hep-Cats, Narcs and Pipe Dreams: A History of America's Romance with Illegal Drugs*. New York: Scribner, 1995.
Jordan, Benjamin R. *Modern Manhood and the Boy Scouts of America: Citizenship, Race, and the Environment, 1910–1930*. Chapel Hill: University of North Carolina Press, 2016.
Joshi, Sanjay. *Fractured Modernity: Making of a Middle Class in Colonial North India*. New Delhi: Oxford University Press, 2001.
Kamble, Maruti T. 'Bengal in Karnataka's Reform Movement: A Case Study of the Ramakrishna Math and Mission, 1890–1947'. In *Colonialism Modernity and Religious Identities: Religious Reform Movements in South Asia*, edited by Gwilym Beckerlegge, 126–43. New Delhi: Oxford University Press, 2008.
Kamenov, Nikolay. 'The Place of the "Cooperative Agrarian History of India, c. 1900–1970"'. *Journal of Asian Studies* 79, no. 1 (2020): 103–28.
Kanakaraj, A. *The Light Houses of Rural Reconstruction: The History of the Y.M.C.A.'s Integrated Rural Development in South India*. Delhi: Indian Society for Promoting Christian Knowledge, 2000.
Kasturi, Malavika. '"All Gifting Is Sacred": The Sanatana Dharma Sabha Movement, the Reform of Dana and Civil Society in Late Colonial India'. *The Indian Economic & Social History Review* 47, no. 1 (2010): 107–39.
Kasturi, Malavika. 'Gurus and Gifting: Dana, the Math Reform Campaign, and Competing Visions of Hindu Sangathan in Twentieth-Century India'. *Modern Asian Studies* 52, no. 1 (2018): 99–131.
Keller, Charles A. 'The Christian Student Movement, YMCAs, and Transnationalism in Republican China'. *The Journal of American-East Asian Relations* 13 (2004): 55–80.

Kennedy, Dane. 'The Perils of the Midday Sun: Climatic Anxieties in the Colonial Tropics'. In *Imperialism and the Natural World*, edited by John Mckenzie, 118–40. Manchester: Manchester University Press, 1990.

Kerr, Ian. *Engines of Change: The Railroads That Made India*. New Delhi: Orient Blackswan, 2007.

Keys, Barbara J. *Globalizing Sport: National Rivalry and International Community*. Cambridge, MA: Harvard University Press, 2006.

Kidambi, Prashant. 'From "Social Reform" to "Social Service"'. In *Civilizing Missions in Colonial and Postcolonial South Asia: From Improvement to Development*, edited by Carey A. Watt and Michael Mann, 217–40. London: Anthem Press, 2011.

Kidambi, Prashant. *The Making of an Indian Metropolis: Colonial Governance and Public Culture in Bombay, 1890-1920*. Aldershot: Ashgate, 2007.

Kidd, Kenneth. 'Boyology in the Twentieth Century'. *Children's Literature* 28 (2000): 44–72.

Kidd, Kenneth B. *Making American Boys: Boyology and the Feral Tale*. Minneapolis: University of Minnesota Press, 2004.

Koller, Christian. 'The Recruitment of Colonial Troops in Africa and Asia and Their Deployment in Europe during the First World War'. *Immigrants and Minorities* 26, no. 1–2 (2008): 111–33.

Kramer, Paul A. 'Empires, Exceptions, and Anglo-Saxons: Race and Rule between the British and United States Empires, 1880-1910'. *The Journal of American History* 88, no. 4 (March 2002): 1315–53.

Kramer, Paul A. 'Power and Connection: Imperial Histories of the United States in the World'. *American Historical Review* 116, no. 5 (2011): 1348–91.

Kudaisya, Gyanesh. *A Republic in the Making: India in the 1950s*. New Delhi: Oxford University Press, 2017.

Kumar, Deepak. 'Science in Agriculture: A Study in Victorian India'. In *Tilling the Land Agricultural Knowledge and Practices in Colonial India*, edited by Deepak Kumar and Bipasha Raha, 20–48. Delhi: Primus Books, 2016.

Kumar, Nita. 'India's Trial with Citizenship, Modernisation and Nationhood'. In *Mass Education and the Limits of State Building, c.1870-1930*, edited by Laurence Brocklin and Nicola Sheldon, 283–304. Basingstoke: Palgrave Macmillan, 2012.

Kumar, Prakash. 'American Modernisers and the Cow Question in Colonial and Nationalist India'. *South Asia Journal of South Asian Studies* 44, no. 1 (2021): 185–200.

Kumar, Prakash. '"Modernization" and Agrarian Development in India, 1912–52'. *Journal of Asian Studies* 79, no. 3 (2020): 633–58.

Ladd, Tony, and James A. Mathisen. *Muscular Christianity Evangelical Protestants and the Development of American Sport*. Grand Rapids, MI: Baker Books, 1999.

Langohr, Vicki. 'Colonial Education Systems and the Spread of Local Religious Movements: The Cases of British Egypt and Punjab'. *Comparative Studies in Society and History* 47, no. 1 (2005): 161–89.

Laqua, Daniel, ed. *Internationalism Reconfigured: Transnational Ideas and Movements between the World Wars*. London: I. B. Tauris, 2011.

Legg, Stephen. 'Dyarchy: Democracy, Autocracy, and the Scalar Sovereignty of Interwar India'. *Comparative Studies of South Asia, Africa and the Middle East* 36, no. 1 (2016): 44–65.

Lelyveld, David. *Aligarh's First Generation: Muslim Solidarity in British India*. Princeton, NJ: Princeton University Press, 1979.

Lepore, Jill. *These Truths: A History of the United States*. New York: W. W. Norton, 2018.

Levine, Philippa. 'Battle Colors: Race, Sex, and Colonial Soldiery in World War I'. *Journal of Women's History* 9, no. 4 (1998): 104–30.
Liebau, Heike, Katrin Bromber, Katharina Lange, Dyala Hamzah and Ravi Ahuja, eds. *The World in World Wars: Experiences, Perceptions and Perspectives from Africa and Asia*. Leiden: Brill, 2010.
Litsios, Socrates. 'Revisiting Bandoeng'. *Social Medicine* 8, no. 3 (2014): 113–27.
Liu, Chang. *Peasants and Revolution in Rural China: Rural Political Change in the North China Plain and the Yangzi Delta*. London: Routledge, 2007.
Lorenzini, Sara. *Global Development: A Cold War History*. Princeton, NJ: Princeton University Press, 2017.
Louro, Michel. '"Where National Revolutionary Ends and Communist Begins": The League against Imperialism and the Meerut Conspiracy Case'. *Comparative Studies of South Asia, Africa and the Middle East* 33, no. 3 (2013): 331–44.
Loveridge, Jack. 'Between Hunger and Growth: Pursuing Rural Development in Partition's Aftermath, 1947–1957'. *Contemporary South Asia* 25, no. 1 (2017): 56–69.
Lowe, Kevin M. *Baptized with the Soil: Christian Agrarians and the Crusade for Rural America*. Oxford: Oxford University Press, 2016.
Lubinski, Christina. 'Die nationalistische Note. Westliche Grammophone und indischer Nationalismus vor dem ersten Weltkrieg'. *Historische Anthropologie* 26, no. 1 (2016): 27–49.
Lüdtke, Alf. 'Cash, Coffee-Breaks, Horseplay. Eigensinn and Politics among Factory Workers in Germany circa 1900'. In *Confrontation. Class Consciousness, and the Labor Process: Studies in Proletarian Class Formation*, edited by Michael Hanagan and Charles Stephenson, 65–95. New York: Greenwood, 1986.
Lupkin, Paula. 'Manhood Factories: Architecture, Business, and the Evolving Urban Role of the YMCA, 1865–1925'. In *Men and Women Adrift: The YMCA and the YWCA in the City*, edited by Nina Mjagkij and Margaret Spratt, 40–64. New York: New York University Press, 1997.
Lupkin, Paula Rachel. *Manhood Factories: YMCA Architecture and the Making of Modern Urban Culture*. Minneapolis: University of Minnesota Press, 2010.
Lydon, Janet. *Imperial Emotion: The Politics of Empathy across the British Empire*. Cambridge: Cambridge University Press, 2019.
Mabille, François. *Approches de l'internationalisme Catholique*. Paris: L'Harmattan, 2002.
Macekura, Stephen J., and Erez Manela, eds. *The Development Century: A Global History*. Cambridge: Cambridge University Press, 2019.
MacLean, Kama. 'On the Art of Panicking Quietly: British Expatriate Responses to "Terrorist Outrages" in India, 1912–33'. In *Anxieties, Fear and Panic in Colonial Settings Empires on the Verge of a Nervous Breakdown*, edited by Harald Fischer-Tiné, 135–66. Cham: Palgrave Macmillan, 2016.
MacLean, Kama. *A Revolutionary History of Interwar India: Violence, Image, Voice and Text*. London: C. Hurst, 2015.
MacLeod, David I. *Building Character in the American Boy: The Boy Scouts, YMCA and Their Forerunners, 1870–1920*. Madison: The University of Wisconsin Press, 1983.
Mahadevan, Sudhir. *A Very Old Machine: The Many Origins of Cinema in India*. Albany: State University of New York Press, 2015.
Majumdar, Boria. 'Tom Brown Goes Global: The "Brown" Ethic in Colonial and Post-Colonial India'. In *Muscular Christianity in Colonial and Post-Colonial Worlds*, edited by John Mac Aloon, Boria Majumdar and James A. Mangan, 105–20. London: Routledge, 2008.

Majumdar, Boria, and Nalin Mehta. *India and the Olympics*. London: Routledge, 2009.

Mandala, Vijaya Ramadas. 'Colonialism, Education, and the Spatial Dimension of Play – the Creation of Middle Class Space at Schools and Colleges in Modern India (1790–1910)'. *The Historian* 80, no. 1 (2018): 34–85.

Mangan, James A. *The Games Ethic and Imperialism: Aspects of the Diffusion of an Ideal*. London: Frank Cass, 1998.

Manjapra, Kris K. *Age of Entanglement: German and Indian Intellectuals across Empires*. Cambridge, MA: Harvard University Press, 2014.

Mann, Michael. *Wiring the Nation: Telecommunication, Newspaper-Reportage, and Nation Building in British India*. New Delhi: Oxford University Press, 2017.

Mantena, Karuna. *Alibis of Empire: Henry Maine and the Ends of Liberal Imperialism*. Princeton, NJ: Princeton University Press, 2010.

Mantena, Rama Sundari. 'Vernacular Publics and Political Modernity: Language and Progress in Colonial South India'. *Modern Asian Studies* 47, no. 5 (2013): 1678–705.

Marchisio, Sergio, and Antonietta Di Blase. *The Food and Agriculture Organization (FAO)*. Dordrecht: Martinus Nijhoff, 1991.

Markovits, Claude. *De l'Indus à La Somme: Les Indiens En France Pendant La Grande Guerre*. Paris: Éditions de la Maison des Sciences de l'Homme, 2019.

Markovits, Claude. *India and the World: A History of Connections, 1750–2000*. Cambridge: Cambridge University Press, 2021.

Mascarenhas, Kiran. 'The Half-Caste: A Half-Told Tale'. *Women's Writing* 20, no. 3 (2013): 344–57.

Masselos, Jim. 'Empire and City: The Imperial Presence in Urban India'. In *The Routledge History of Western Empires*, edited by Robert Aldrich and Kirsten Mackenzie, 330–45. Abingdon: Routledge, 2014.

Maul, Daniel Roger. 'The Rise of a Humanitarian Superpower: American NGOs and International Relief'. In *Internationalism, Imperialism and the Formation of the Formation of the Contemporary World*, edited by M. B. Jernimo and J. P. Monteiro, 127–46. Cham: Palgrave Macmillan, 2018.

McComb, David G. *Sports in World History*. New York: Routledge, 2004.

McQuade, Joseph. *A Genealogy of Terrorism: Colonial Law and the Origins of an Idea*. Cambridge: Cambridge University Press, 2021.

Menon, Nikhil. 'Battling the Bottle: Experiments in Regulating Drink in Late Colonial Madras'. *Indian Economic & Social History Review* 52, no. 1 (2015).

Metcalf, Thomas. *The New Cambridge History of India III, 4. Ideologies of the Raj*. Cambridge: Cambridge University Press, 1994.

Miller, Mathew Lee. *The American YMCA and Russian Culture: The Preservation and Expansion of Orthodox Christianity*. Lanham, MD: Lexington Books, 2013.

Mills, James H. 'Decolonising Drugs in Asia: The Case of Cocaine in Colonial India'. *Third World Quarterly* 39, no. 2 (2018): 218–31.

Mills, Sarah. 'Scouting for Girls? Gender and the Scout Movement in Britain'. *Gender, Place & Culture* 18, no. 4 (August 2011): 537–56.

Mitchell, Timothy. *Rule of Experts: Egypt, Techno-Politics, Modernity*. Berkeley: University of California Press, 2002.

Mitchinson, William. *The Territorials at War, 1914–16*. Basingstoke: Palgrave Macmillan, 2014.

Mitter, Rana. 'Modernity'. In *The Palgrave Dictionary of Transnational History*, edited by Akira Iriye and Pierre-Yves Saunier, 720–23. Basingstoke: Palgrave Macmillan, 2009.

Mizutani, Satoshi. '"Degenerate Whites" and Their Spaces of Disorder: Disciplining Racial and Class Ambiguities in Colonial Calcutta (c. 1880–1930)'. In *The Limits of British Colonial Control in South Asia. Spaces of Disorder in the Indian Ocean Region* edited by Ashwini Tambe and Harald Fischer-Tiné, 155–91. Abingdon: Routledge, 2009.

Mizutani, Satoshi. *The Meaning of White: Race, Class, and the Domiciled Community in British India, 1858-1930*. Oxford: Oxford University Press, 2011.

Mjagkij, Nina. *Light in the Darkness: African Americans and the YMCA, 1852-1946*. Lexington: University Press of Kentucky, 1994.

Mjagkij, Nina, and Magaret Spratt, eds. *Men and Women Adrift: The YMCA and the YWCA in the City*. New York: New York University Press, 1997.

Mjagkij, Nina, and Margaret Spratt. 'Introduction'. In *Men and Women Adrift: The YMCA and the YWCA in the City*, edited by Nina Mjagkij and Margaret Spratt, 1–21. New York: New York University Press, 1997.

Morris, Andrew D. *Marrow of the Nation: A History of Sport and Physical Culture in Republican China*. Berkeley: University of California Press, 2004.

Mosse, George. *The Image of Man: The Creation of Modern Masculinity*. New York: Oxford University Press, 1996.

Mukul, Akshaya. *Gita Press and the Making of Hindu India*. Noida: HarperCollins, 2015.

Mulready-Stone, Kristin. 'Character Conservancy in Shanghai's Emergency: The YMCA in Shanghai, 1931–1942'. In *The YMCA at War: Collaboration and Conflict during the World Wars*, edited by Jeffrey C. Copeland and Yan Xu, 143–60. Lanham, MD: Lexington Books, 2018.

Murard, Lion. 'Designs within Disorder: International Conferences on Rural Health Care and the Art of the Local, 1931–39'. In *Shifting Boundaries of Public Health: Europe in the Twentieth Century*, edited by Susan Gross Solomon, Lion Murard and Patrick Zylberman, 141–74. Rochester, NY: University of Rochester Press, 2008.

Murphy, Anne. 'The Formation of the Ethical Sikh Subject in the Era of British Colonial Reform'. *Sikh Formations* 11, no. 1–2 (2015): 149–59.

Murphy, Mahon. 'Prisoners of War and Civilian Internees Captured by British and Dominion Forces from the German Colonies during the First World War'. Unpublished PhD dissertation, London School of Economics, 2014.

Myerscough, Keith. 'The Game with No Name: The Invention of Basketball'. *The International Journal of the History of Sport* 12, no. 1 (1995): 137–52.

Naha, Souvik. 'The Rise of Modern Sport and the Olympic Movement in India'. In *The Routledge Handbook of Sport in Asia*, edited by Fan Hong and Lu Zhouxiang, 126–34. Abingdon: Routledge, 2021.

Nanda, B. R. *Gokhale: The Indian Moderates and the British Raj*. New Delhi: Oxford University Press, 1977.

Naregal, Veena. *Language Politics, Elites and Public Spheres: Western India under Colonialism*. London: Anthem Press, 2002.

Natarajan, D. *Census of India 1971: Extracts from the All India Census Reports on Literacy*. New Delhi: Office of the Registrar General, India, Ministry of Home Affairs, 1972.

Natarajan, Radhika. ' "Village Life and How to Improve It": Textual Routes of Community Development in the Late British Empire'. In *Reading the Postwar Future: Textual Turning Points from 1944* edited by Kirrily Freeman and John Munro, 96–112. London: Bloomsbury Academic, 2019.

Neiberg, Michael S. *Fighting the Great War: A Global History*. Cambridge, MA: Harvard University Press, 2006.

Ninkovich, Frank. *The Global Republic: America's Inadvertent Rise to World Power*. Chicago: University of Chicago Press, 2014.
Ninkovich, Frank. *The United States and Imperialism*. Malden, MA: Blackwell, 2001.
Nish, Ian H. *Flaming Milestones. Calcutta YMCA: A Story, 1857–1982*. Calcutta: Calcutta YMCA, 1983.
Nisha, P. R. *Jumbos and Jumping Devils: A Social History of Indian Circus*. New Delhi: Oxford University Press, 2020.
Nutt, Rick L. 'G. Sherwood Eddy and the Attitudes of Protestants in the United States toward Global Mission'. *Church History* 66, no. 3 (1997): 502–21.
Nye, Joseph S. 'Soft Power: The Evolution of a Concept'. *Journal of Political Power* 14, no. 1 (2021): 196–208.
Nye, Joseph S. *Soft Power: The Means to Success in World Politics*. New York: PublicAffairs, 2004.
Oberoi, Harjot. *The Construction of Religious Boundaries: Culture, Identity, and Diversity in the Sikh Tradition*. New Delhi: Oxford University Press, 1997.
Oesterheld, Joachim. 'Education, Cultural Diversity and Citizenship in Late Colonial India'. *EMIGRA Working Papers* 58 (2007), https://ddd.uab.cat/pub/emigrawp/emigrawp_a2007n58/emigrawp a20 07n58p1.pdf.
Olsen, Stephanie. *Juvenile Nation: Youth, Emotions and the Making of the Modern British Citizen, 1880–1914*. London: Bloomsbury, 2014.
Olsson, Tore C. *Agrarian Crossings: Reformers and the Remaking of the US and Mexican Countryside*. Princeton, NJ: Princeton University Press, 2017.
Omissi, David. 'Europe through Indian Eyes: Indian Soldiers Encounter England and France, 1914–1918'. *The English Historical Review* 122, no. 496 (2007): 371–96.
Omissi, David, ed. *Indian Voices of the Great War: Soldiers Letters 1914–18*. Gurgaon: Penguin Books, 2014.
Omissi, David. 'Introduction'. In *Indian Voices of the Great War: Soldiers Letters 1914–18*, edited by David Omissi, 1–22. Gurgaon: Penguin Books, 2014.
Omissi, David. 'Martial Races: Ethnicity and Security in Colonial India 1858–1939'. *War & Society* 9, no. 1 (1999): 1–27.
Orsini, Francesca. *Between Print and Pleasure: Popular Literature and Entertaining Fictions in Colonial North India*. New Delhi: Permanent Black, 2009.
Orsini, Francesca. *The Hindi Public Sphere (1920–1940). Language and Literature in the Age of Nationalism*. New Delhi: Oxford University Press, 2002.
Osella, Filippo. 'Charity and Philanthropy in South Asia: An Introduction'. *Modern Asian Studies* 52, no. 1 (2018): 4–34.
Osuri, Goldie. 'Ash-Coloured Whiteness: The Transfiguration of Aishwarya Rai'. *South Asian Popular Culture* 6, no. 2 (2008): 109–23.
Ouwerkerk, Louise. *No Elephants for the Maharaja: Social and Political Change in the Princely State of Travancore, 1921–1947*. New Delhi: Manohar, 1994.
Overmann, Steven J. *The Protestant Ethic and the Spirit of Sport*. Macon, GA: Mercer University Press, 2011.
Owen, Nicholas. 'Alliances from Above and Below: The Failures and Successes of Communist Anti-Imperialism in India, 1920–34'. In *Workers of the Empire Unite: Radical and Popular Challenges to British Imperialism, 1910s to 1960s*, edited by Yann Béliard and Neville Kirk, 81–114. Liverpool: Liverpool University Press, 2021.
Panikkar, K. N. *Against Lord and State: Religion and Peasant Uprisings in Malabar, 1836–1921*. New Delhi: Oxford University Press, 1989.

Paramar, Inderjeet, and Michael Cox, eds. *Soft Power and US Foreign Policy: Theoretical, Historical and Contemporary Perspectives*. London: Routledge, 2010.

Paris, Leslie. *Children's Nature: The Rise of the American Summer Camp*. New York: New York University Press, 2008.

Park, Albert L. *Building a Heaven on Earth: Religion, Activism, and Protest in Japanese-Occupied Korea*. Honolulu: University of Hawai'i Press, 2015.

Park, Roberta J. 'Boys' Clubs Are Better than Policemen's Clubs: Endeavours by Philanthropists, Social Reformers, and Others to Prevent Juvenile Crime, the Late 1800s to 1917'. *The International Journal of the History of Sport* 24, no. 6 (2007): 749–75.

Park, Roberta J. 'From La "bomba" to "Béisbol": Sport and the Americanisation of Puerto Rico, 1898–1950'. *The International Journal of the History of Sport* 28, no. 17 (2011): 2575–93.

Park, Roberta J. 'Science, Service, and the Professionalization of Physical Education: 1885–1905'. *The International Journal of the History of Sport* 24, no. 12 (2007): 1674–1700.

Parmar, Inderjeet. *Foundations of the American Century: The Ford, Carnegie, and Rockefeller Foundations in the Rise of American Power*. New York: Columbia University Press, 2012.

Patel, Raj. 'The Long Green Revolution'. *Journal of Peasant Studies* 40, no. 1 (2013): 5–10.

Paulmann, Johannes. 'Conjunctures in the History of International Humanitarianism Aid during the Twentieth Century'. *Humanity* 4, no. 2 (2013): 215–38.

Paulmann, Johannes, ed. *Dilemmas of Humanitarian Aid in the Twentieth Century*. Oxford: Oxford University Press, 2016.

Peers, Douglas. 'Imperial Vice: Sex, Drink and the Health of British Troops in North Indian Cantonments, 1800–1858'. In *Guardians of Empire*, edited by David Killingray and David Omissi, 25–52. Manchester: Manchester University Press, 1999.

Peers, Douglas. 'Privates Off Parade: Regimenting Sexuality in the Nineteenth-Century Indian Empire'. *The International History Review* 20, no. 4 (1998): 824–54.

Peers, Douglas. 'State, Power and Colonialism'. In *India and the British Empire*, edited by Douglas Peers and Nandini Gooptu, 16–43. Oxford: Oxford University Press, 2012.

Pernau, Margrit, ed. *The Delhi College: Traditional Elites, the Colonial State, and Education before 1857*. New Delhi: Oxford University Press, 2006.

Pernau, Margrit. 'Love and Compassion for the Community: Emotions and Practices among North Indian Muslims, c. 1870–1930'. *The Indian Economic & Social History Review* 54, no. 1 (2017): 21–42.

Phoenix, Karen. '"Not by Might, nor by Power, but by Spirit": The Global Reform Efforts of the Young Women's Christian Association of the United States 1895–1939'. Unpublished PhD dissertation, University of Illinois at Urbana-Champaign, 2010.

Phoenix, Karen. 'A Social Gospel for India'. *The Journal of the Gilded Age and Progressive Era* 13, no. 2 (2014): 200–22.

Pomfret, David M. *Youth and Empire: Transcolonial Childhoods in British and French Asia*. Stanford, CA: Stanford University Press, 2015.

Pope, Steven W. 'An Army of Athletes: Playing Fields, Battlefields, and the American Military Sporting Experience, 1890–1920'. *Journal of Military History* 59, no. 3 (1995): 435–56.

Prasad, Ankit. *Social Welfare and Social Action: YMCA at Work*. New Delhi: Mittal Publications, 2005.

Preeti. 'The Transformation of Schooling in Colonial Punjab, 1854–1900'. In *New Perspectives in the History of Indian Education*, edited by Parimala V. Rao, 267–99. New Delhi: Orient Blackswan, 2014.

Preston, Andrew. 'America's Global Imperium'. In *The Oxford World History of Empire*, edited by Peter Fibiger Bang, C. A. Bayly and Walter Scheidel, 1217–48. Oxford: Oxford University Press, 2021.

Preston, Andrew, and Doug Rossinow, eds. 'Outside In: The Transnational Circuitry of US History'. Oxford: Oxford University Press, 2017.

Proctor, Tammy M. *Civilians in a World War, 1914–1918*. New York: New York University Press, 2010.

Pryke, Sam. 'The Popularity of Nationalism in the Early British Boy Scout Movement'. *Social History* 23, no. 3 (October 1998): 309–24.

Purcell, Aaron D. 'Collaboration and the Small Community: Arthur Morgan and the Mitraniketan Project in Kerala'. *The Historian* 65, no. 3 (2003): 643–64.

Putney, Clifford. 'Luther Gulick: His Contributions to Springfield College, the YMCA, and "Muscular Christianity"'. *Historical Journal of Massachusetts* 39, no. 1–2 (2011): 144–69.

Putney, Clifford. *Muscular Christianity: Manhood and Sports in Protestant America, 1880–1920*. Cambridge, MA: Harvard University Press, 2003.

Raghavan, Srinath. *Fierce Enigmas: A History of the United States in South Asia*. New York: Basic Books, 2018.

Ramachandran, Aishwarya. 'Counterflows of Knowledge: The Transnational Circulation of Physical Culture Practices between India and the West during the Early 20th Century'. Unpublished MA thesis, Vancouver: University of British Columbia, 2019.

Ramachandran, Aishwarya, and Conor Heffernan. 'A Distinctly Indian Body? K. V. Iyer and Physical Culture in 1930s India'. *The International Journal of the History of Sport* 36, no. 12 (2019): 1053–75.

Ramaswamy, Sumathi. *The Goddess and the Nation*. Durham, NC: Duke University Press, 2010.

Rao, Parimala V. 'Myth and Reality in the History of Indian Education'. *Espacio, Tiempo y Educación* 6, no. 2 (2019): 217–34.

Ray, Utsa. 'Cosmopolitan Consumption: Domesticity, Cooking, and the Middle Class in Colonial India'. In *The Global Bourgeoisie: The Rise of the Middle Classes in the Age of Empire*, edited by Christof Dejung, David Motadel and Jürgen Osterhammel, 123–42. Princeton, NJ: Princeton University Press, 2019.

Raza, Ali, and Franziska Roy. 'Paramilitary Organisations in Interwar India'. *South Asia: Journal of South Asian Studies* 38, no. 4 (2015): 671–89.

Reeves-Ellington, Barbara, Kathryn Kish and Connie A. Shemo Sklar, eds. *Competing Kingdoms: Women, Mission, Nation, and the American Protestant Empire, 1812–1960*. Durham, NC: Duke University Press, 2010.

Reilly, Hugh, and Kevin Warneke. *Father Flanagan of Boys Town: A Man of Vision*. Boys Town, NE: Boys Town Press, 2008.

Renold, Leah. *A Hindu Education: Early Years of the Banaras Hindu University*. New Delhi: Oxford University Press, 2005.

Reznick, Jeffrey S. *Healing the Nation: Soldiers and the Culture of Caregiving in Britain during the Great War*. Manchester: Manchester University Press, 2004.

Ribi Forclaz, Amalia. ' Agriculture, American Expertise, and the Quest for Global Data: Leon Estabrook and the First World Agricultural Census of 1930 '. *Journal of Global History* 11, no. 1 (2016): 44–65.

Riess, Steven A. *City Games: The Evolution of American Urban Society and the Rise of Sports*. Urbana: University of Illinois Press, 1989.

Robb, Peter. 'Bihar, the Colonial State and Agricultural Development in India, 1880–1920'. *Indian Economic & Social History Review* 25, no. 2 (1988): 205–35.

Robert, Dana L. 'The First Globalization: The Internationalization of the Protestant Missionary Movement between the World Wars'. *International Bulletin of Missionary Research* 26, no. 2 (2002): 50–66.

Robinson, Francis. 'Technology and Religious Change: Islam and the Impact of Print'. *Modern Asian Studies* 27, no. 1 (1993): 229–51.

Rodogno, Davide. *Against Massacre: Humanitarian Interventions in the Ottoman Empire, 1815–1914*. Princeton, NJ: Princeton University Press, 2012.

Rodogno, Davide, Bernhard Struck and Jakob Vogel, eds. *Shaping the Transnational Sphere, Experts, Networks and Issues from the 1840s to the 1930s*. New York: Berghahn Books, 2015.

Rosenberg, Emily S. *Transnational Currents in a Shrinking World*. Cambridge: Belknap Press of Harvard University Press, 2014.

Rosselli, John. 'The Self-Image of Effeteness: Physical Education and Nationalism in Nineteenth-Century Bengal'. *Past and Present* 86 (1980): 221–48.

Roy, Franziska. 'International Utopia and National Discipline: Youth and Volunteer Movements in Interwar South Asia'. In *The Internationalist Moment: South Asia, Worlds, and World Views, 1917–39*, edited by Ali Raza, Franziska Roy and Benjamin Zachariah, 150–87. New Delhi: Sage, 2015.

Roy, Franziska. 'The Torchbearers of Progress: Youth Volunteer Organisations and National Discipline in India, c. 1918–1947'. Unpublished PhD dissertation, University of Warwick, 2013.

Roy, Franziska, and Benjamin Zachariah. 'Meerut and a Hanging: "Young India," Popular Socialism, and the Dynamics of Imperialism'. *Comparative Studies of South Asia, Africa and the Middle East* 33, no. 3 (2013): 360–77.

Roy, Kaushik. *The Army in British India: From Colonial Warfare to Total War 1857–1947*. London: Bloomsbury, 2012.

Roy, Kaushik. 'Race and Recruitment in the Indian Army: 1880–1918'. *Modern Asian Studies* 47, no. 4 (2013): 1310–47.

Ruprecht, Adrian. 'De-Centering Humanitarianism: The Red Cross and India, c. 1877–1939'. Unpublished PhD dissertation, University of Cambridge, 2017.

Ruprecht, Adrian. 'The Great Eastern Crisis (1875–1878) as a Global Humanitarian Moment'. *Journal of Global History* 16, no. 2 (2021): 159–84.

Rydell, Robert W., and Rob Kroes. *Buffalo Bill in Bologna: The Americanization of the World, 1869–1922*. Chicago, IL: University of Chicago Press, 2005.

Sackley, Nicole. 'Foundation in the Field: The Ford Foundation New Delhi Office and the Construction of Development Knowledge, 1951–1970'. In *American Foundations and the Coproduction of World Order in the Twentieth Century*, edited by John Krige and Helke Rausch, 232–60. Göttingen: Vandenhoeck & Ruprecht, 2012.

Sackley, Nicole. 'The Village as Cold War Site: Experts, Development, and the History of Rural Reconstruction'. *Journal of Global History* 6, no. 3 (2011).

Sackley, Nicole. 'Village Models: Etawah, India, and the Making and Remaking of Development in the Early Cold War'. *Diplomatic History* 37, no. 4 (2013): 755–56.

Sánchez García, Raúl. 'The Long-Term Development of Japanese Martial Arts'. In *The Routledge Handbook of Sport in Asia*, edited by Fan Hong and Lu Zhouxiang, 54–63. Abingdon: Routledge, 2021.

Sarkar, Sumit. *Modern Times: India 1880s–1950s. Environment, Economy Culture*. Ranikhet: Permanent Black, 2014.

Sarkar, Sumit. *Swadeshi Movement in Bengal 1903–1908*. 2nd Revised edition. Ranikhet: Orient Blackswan, 2010.

Sato, Shohei. 'The Sportification of Judo: Global Convergence and Evolution'. *Journal of Global History* 8, no. 2 (2013): 299–317.

Savary, Luzia. *Evolution, Race and Public Spheres in India: Vernacular Concepts and Sciences (1860–1930)*. Abingdon: Routledge, 2019.

Savary, Luzia. '"Vernacular Eugenics"? Santati-Śāstra in Popular Hindi Advisory Literature (1900–1940)'. *South Asia: Journal of South Asian Studies* 37, no. 3 (2014): 381–97.

Schayegh, Cyrus. 'The Interwar Germination of Development and Modernization Theory and Practice: Politics, Institution Building, and Knowledge Production between the Rockefeller Foundation and the American University of Beirut'. *Geschichte und Gesellschaft* 41, no. 4 (2015).

Schneider, Mark Robert. *African Americans in the Jazz Age: A Decade of Struggle and Promise*. Lanham, MD: Rowman & Littlefield, 2006.

Schober, Juliane. *Modern Buddhist Conjunctures in Myanmar: Cultural Narratives, Colonial Legacies, and Civil Society*. Honolulu: University of Hawai'i Press, 2010.

Schopmeyer, C. H. *Extension Projects in Rural Community Organization*. Washington, DC: US Extension Service Circulars, 1927.

Schwarz, Henry. *Constructing the Criminal Tribe in India: Acting Like a Thief*. Malden, MA: Wiley-Blackwell, 2010.

Scott, James C. *Seeing Like a State: How Certain Schemes to Improve the Human Condition Have Failed*. New Haven, CT: Yale University Press, 1998.

Scott, Roy V. *The Reluctant Farmer: The Rise of Agricultural Extension to 1914*. Urbana, IL: University of Illinois Press, 1970.

Sen, Amiya P. 'Introduction'. In *Social and Religious Reform: The Hindus of British India*, edited by Amiya P. Sen, 3–63. New Delhi: Oxford University Press, 2003.

Sen, Ronojoy. *A Nation at Play: A History of Sport in India*. New York: Columbia University Press, 2015.

Sen, Satadru. 'Anarchies of Youth: The Oaten Affair and Colonial Bengal'. In *Disciplined Natives: Race, Freedom and Confinement in Colonial India*, edited by Satadru Sen, 13–41. Delhi: Primus Books, 2012.

Sen, Satadru. *Colonial Childhoods: The Juvenile Periphery of India, 1850–1945*. London: Anthem Press, 2005.

Sen, Satadru. 'Schools, Athletes and Confrontation: The Student Body in Colonial India'. In *Confronting the Body: The Politics of Physicality in Colonial and Post-Colonial India*, edited by James H. Mills and Satadru Sen, 58–79. London: Anthem Press, 2004.

Sen, Satadru. 'A Separate Punishment: Juvenile Offenders in Colonial India'. *The Journal of Asian Studies* 63, no. 1 (2004): 81–104.

Sen, Satadru. *Traces of Empire: India, America and Postcolonial Cultures. Essays and Criticism*. New Delhi: Primus Books, 2014.

Sengupta, Nirmal. *Traditional Knowledge in Modern India: Preservation, Promotion, Ethical Access and Benefit Sharing Mechanisms*. New Delhi: Springer Nature India, 2018.

Sengupta, Parna. *Pedagogy for Religion: Missionary Education and the Fashioning of Hindus and Muslims in Bengal*. Berkeley: University of California Press, 2011.

Seth, Sanjay. 'Secular Enlightenment and Christian Conversion: Missionaries and Education in Colonial India'. In *Education and Social Change in South Asia*, edited by Krishna Kumar and Joachim Oesterheld, 27–43. New Delhi: Orient Longman, 2007.

Seth, Sanjay. *Subject Lessons: The Western Education of Colonial India*. Durham, NC: Duke University Press, 2007.

Setran, David P. *The College "Y": Student Religion in the Era of Secularization.* New York: Palgrave Macmillan, 2007.
Setran, David P. 'Developing the "Christian Gentleman": The Medieval Impulse in Protestant Ministry to Adolescent Boys, 1890–1920'. *Religion and American Culture: A Journal of Interpretation* 20, no. 2 (2010): 165–204.
Setran, David P. '"From Moral Aristocracy to Christian Social Democracy": The Transformation of Character Education in the Hi-Y, 1910–1940'. *History of Education Quarterly* 45, no. 2 (2005): 207–46.
Sharpe, Eric J. *Not to Destroy but to Fulfill, the Contribution to J. N. Farquhar to Protestant Missionary Thought in India before 1914.* Uppsala: Gleerup, 1965.
Sherington, Geoffrey. '"A Better Class of Boy" the Big Brother Movement, Youth Migration and Citizenship of Empire'. *Australian Historical Studies* 33, no. 120 (2002): 267–85.
Sherman, Taylor C. 'Education in Early Postcolonial India: Expansion, Experimentation and Planned Self-Help'. *History of Education* 47, no. 4 (2018): 504–20.
Shope, Bradley. *American Popular Music and Britain's Raj.* Rochester: University of Rochester Press, 2016.
Shope, Bradley. 'The Public Consumption of Western Music in Colonial India: From Imperialist Exclusivity to Global Receptivity'. *South Asia Journal of South Asian Studies* 31, no. 2 (2008): 271–89.
Siegel, Benjamin. *Hungry Nation: Food, Famine, and the Making of Modern India.* Cambridge: Cambridge University Press, 2018.
Siegel, Benjamin. 'Modernizing Peasants and "Master Farmers": All-India Crop Competitions and the Politics of Progressive Agriculture in Early Independent India'. *Comparative Studies of South Asia, Africa and the Middle East* 37, no. 1 (2017): 64–85.
Siegel, Benjamin. '"Self-Help Which Ennobles a Nation": Development, Citizenship, and the Obligations of Eating in India's Austerity Years'. *Modern Asian Studies* 50, no. 3 (2016): 975–1018.
Silvestri, Michael. *Policing 'Bengali Terrorism' in India and the World: Imperial Intelligence and Revolutionary Nationalism, 1905–1939.* Cham: Palgrave Macmillan, 2019.
Simonow, Joanna. 'After the "Late Victorian Holocausts": Transnational Responses to Famines and Malnutrition in India, c. 1900–1955'. Unpublished PhD dissertation, ETH-Zürich, 2019.
Simpson, Donald. 'Missions and the Magic Lantern'. *International Bulletin of Mission Research* 21, no. 1 (1997): 13–15.
Singh, Dwarka Prasad. *American Attitude towards Indian Nationalist Movement.* New Delhi: Munshiram Manoharlal, 1974.
Singh, Gajendra. 'Mirrors of Violence: Interracial Sex, Colonial Anxieties and Disciplining the Body of the Indian Soldier during the First World War'. In *Anxieties, Fear and Panic in Colonial Settings: Empires on the Verge of a Nervous Breakdown*, edited by Harald Fischer-Tiné, 170–97. Basingstoke: Palgrave Macmillan, 2017.
Singh, Gajendra. *The Testimonies of Indian Soldiers and the Two World Wars: Between Self and Sepoy.* London: Bloomsbury, 2014.
Singh, Gajendra. 'Throwing Snowballs in France: Muslim Sipahis of the Indian Army and Sheikh Ahmad's Dream, 1915–1918'. *Modern Asian Studies* 48, no. 4 (2014): 1024–67.
Singh, Mohinder. 'Spectres of the West: Negotiating a Civilizational Figure in Hindi'. In *Civilizing Emotions: Concepts in Nineteenth Century Asia and Europe*, edited by Margrit Pernau and Helge Jordheim, 187–206. Cambridge: Cambridge University Press, 2015.
Singha, Radhika. *The Coolie's Great War: Indian Labour in a Global Conflict.* London: Hurst, 2020.

Singha, Radhika. 'The Recruiter's Eye on "the Primitive": To France – and Back – in the Indian Labour Corps, 1917-19'. In *Other Combatants, Other Fronts: Competing Histories of the First World War*, edited by James E. Kitchen, Alisia Miller and Laura Rowe, 199-224. Newcastle upon Tyne: Cambridge Scholars, 2011.

Singha, Radhika. 'The Short Career of the Indian Labour Corps in France, 1917-1919'. *International Labor and Working-Class History* 87, no. 2 (2015): 27-62.

Singleton, Mark. 'Transnational Exchange and the Genesis of Modern Postural Yoga'. In *Yoga Traveling: Bodily Practice in Transcultural Perspective*, edited by Beatrix Hauser, 37-56. Heidelberg: Springer, 2013.

Singleton, Mark. *Yoga Body: The Origins of Modern Posture Practice*. Oxford: Oxford University Press, 2010.

Singleton, Mark. 'Yoga, Eugenics, and Spiritual Darwinism in the Early Twentieth Century'. *International Journal of Hindu Studies* 11, no. 82 (2007): 125-46.

Sinha, Babli. 'Dissensus, Education and Lala Lajpat Rai's Encounter with W. E. B. DuBois'. *South Asian History and Culture* 6, no. 4 (2015): 463-76.

Sinha, Babli. 'Empire Films and the Dissemination of Americanism in Colonial India'. *South Asian History and Culture* 2, no. 4 (2011): 140-56.

Sinha, Babli. *South Asian Transnationalism: Cultural Exchange in the Twentieth Century*. London: Routledge, 2014.

Sinha, Mrinalini. *Colonial Masculinity: The 'Manly Englishman' and the 'Effeminate Bengali' in the Late Nineteenth Century*. Manchester: Manchester University Press, 1995.

Sinha, Mrinalini. *Specters of Mother India: The Global Restructuring of an Empire*. Durham, NC: Duke University Press, 2006.

Sinha, Nitin. 'Entering the Black Hole: Between "Mini-England" and "Smell-Like Rotten Potato", the Railway Workshop Town of Jamalpur, 1860s-1940s'. *Journal of South Asian History and Culture* 3, no. 3 (2012): 317-47.

Sinha, Nitin. 'Railway Imperialism: A Small Town Perspective on Global History, Jamalpur, 1860s-1940s'. *Comparativ* 25, no. 4 (2015): 17-34.

Sinha, Subir. 'Lineages of the Developmentalist State: Transnationality and Village India, 1900-1965'. *Comparative Studies in Society and History* 50, no. 1 (2008): 57-90.

Slate, Nico. *Colored Cosmopolitanism: The Shared Struggle for Freedom in the United States and India*. Cambridge, MA: Harvard University Press, 2012.

Slate, Nico. *Lord Cornwallis Is Dead: The Struggle for Democracy in the United States and India*. Cambridge, MA: Harvard University Press, 2019.

Sluga, Glenda. 'Remembering 1919: International Organizations and the Future of International Order'. *International Affairs* 95, no. 1 (2019): 25-43.

Snape, Michael. *God and the British Soldier: Religion and the British Army in the First and Second World Wars*. Abingdon: Routledge, 2005.

Snape, Robert. 'Juvenile Organizations Committees and the State Regulation of Youth Leisure in Britain, 1916-1939'. *The Journal of the History of Childhood and Youth* 13, no. 2 (2020): 247-67.

Soni, Soni. 'Famine Orphan "Rescue" Missions: Childhood, Colonialism and Nationalism in Colonial India, 1860s-1920s'. Unpublished PhD dissertation, ETH-Zurich, 2020.

Sotomayor, Antonio. 'The Triangle of Empire: Sport, Religion, and Imperialism in Puerto Rico's YMCA, 1898-1926'. *The Americas: A Quarterly Review of Latin American History* 74, no. 4 (2017): 481-512.

Speckman, Christopher J. 'The Boys' Brigade and Urban Cultures, 1883-1933: A Relationship Examined'. Unpublished PhD dissertation, University of Portsmouth, 2016.

Spillane, Joseph. *Cocaine: From Medical Marvel to Modern Menace in the United States*. Baltimore, MD: Johns Hopkins University Press, 2000.

Springhall, John. *Youth, Empire and Society: British Youth Movements, 1883–1940*. Hamden, CT: Archon Books, 1977.

Springhall, John, Brian Fraser and Michael Hoare, eds. *Sure and Steadfast: A History of the Boys' Brigade, 1883 to 1983*. London: Collins, 1983.

Spurr, Geoffrey D. 'The London YMCA: A Haven of Masculine Self-Improvement and Socialization for the Late Victorian and Edwardian Clerk'. *Canadian Journal of History* 37, no. 2 (2002): 275–301.

Srivastava, Priyanka. *The Well-Being of the Labour Force in Colonial Bombay: Discourses and Practices*. Cham: Palgrave Macmillan, 2018.

Srivatsan, R. *Seva, Saviour and State: Caste Politics, Tribal Welfare and Capitalist Development*. Abingdon: Routledge, 2015.

Staples, Amy L. S. *The Birth of Development: How the World Bank, Food and Agriculture Organization, and World Health Organization Changed the World, 1945–1965*. Kent, OH: The Kent State University Press, 2006.

Stark, Ulrike. 'Associational Culture and Civic Engagement in Colonial Lucknow: The Jalsah-e Tahzib'. *The Indian Economic & Social History Review* 48, no. 1 (2011): 1–33.

Stearns, Peter. *Childhood in World History*. New York: Routledge, 2011.

Stephan, Alexander, ed. *The Americanization of Europe: Culture, Diplomacy, and Anti-Americanism after 1945*. New York: Berghahn Books, 2006.

Steuer, Kenneth A. *Pursuit of an "Unparalleled Opportunity": The American YMCA and Prisoner of War Diplomacy with the Central Powers during the First World War*. New York: Columbia University Press, 2009.

Stoddart, Brian. 'Sport, Cultural Imperialism and Colonial Response in the British Empire'. *Comparative Studies in Society and History* 30, no. 4 (1988): 649–73.

Stoler, Ann Laura. *Along the Archival Grain: Epistemic Anxieties and Colonial Common Sense*. Princeton, NJ: Princeton University Press, 2008.

Stolte, Carolien, and Harald Fischer-Tiné. 'Imagining Asia in India: Nationalism and Internationalism (*ca*. 1905–1940)'. *Comparative Studies in Society and History* 54, no. 1 (2012): 65–92.

Storey, William Kelleher. *The First World War: A Concise Global History*. New York: Rowman & Littlefield, 2010.

Strachan, Hew. 'The First World War as a Global War'. *First World War Studies* 1, no. 1 (2010): 3–14.

Streets, Heather. *Martial Races: The Military, Race and Masculinity in British Imperial Culture, 1857–1914*. Manchester: Manchester University Press, 2004.

Streets-Salter, Heather. *World War One in Southeast Asia: Colonialism and Anti-Colonialism in an Era of Global Conflict*. Cambridge: Cambridge University Press, 2017.

Studdert-Kennedy, Gerald. *British Christians, Indian Nationalists and the Raj*. New Delhi: Oxford University Press, 1991.

Subrahmanyam, Sanjay. 'One Asia or Many? Reflections from Connected History'. *Modern Asian Studies* 50, no. 1 (2016): 5–43.

Subrahmanyam, Sanjay. 'Vignettes of Early Modernity in South Asia, 1400–1750'. *Daedalus* 127, no. 3 (1998): 75–104.

Sugawara, Yoshino. 'Toward the Opposite Site of "Vulgarity": The Birth of Cinema as a "Healthful Entertainment" and the Shanghai YMCA'. In *Early Film Culture in Hong*

Kong, Taiwan and Republican China: Kaleidoscopic Histories edited by Emilie Yueh-yu Yeh, 179–201. Ann Arbor: University of Michigan Press, 2018.
Sultan, Atyab. 'Malcolm Darling and Developmentalism in Colonial Punjab'. *Modern Asian Studies* 51, no. 6 (2017): 1891–1921.
Tan, Tai Yong. *The Garrison State: Military, Government and Society in Colonial Punjab, 1849–1947*. New Delhi: Sage, 2005.
Terret, T. 'American Sammys and French Poilus in the Great War: Sport, Masculinities and Vulnerability'. *The International Journal of the History of Sport* 28, no. 3–4 (2011): 351–71.
Testi, Arnaldi. 'The Gender of Reform Politics: Theodore Roosevelt and the Culture of Masculinity'. *The Journal of American History* 81, no. 4 (1995): 1509–33.
Thompson, Michael G. *For God and Globe: Christian Internationalism in the United States between the Great War and the Cold War*. Ithaca, NY: Cornell University Press, 2015.
Thompson, Michael G. 'Sherwood Eddy, the Missionary Enterprise, and the Rise of Christian Internationalism in 1920s America'. *Modern Intellectual History* 12, no. 1 (2015): 65–93.
Tilley, Helen. *Africa as a Living Laboratory: Empire, Development and the Problem of Scientific Knowledge, 1870–1950*. Chicago, IL: University of Chicago Press, 2011.
Tillotson, Gilles. 'George S. T. Harris: An Architect in Gwalior'. *South Asian Studies* 20, no. 1 (2004): 9–24.
Tlusty, Tomáš. 'The YMCA Organisation and Its Physical Education and Sports Activities in Europe during the First World War'. *Prace Naukowe Akademii im. Jana Długosza w Częstochowie. Kultura Fizyczna* 14, no. 1 (2015): 27–44.
Topdar, Sudipa. 'The Corporeal Empire: Physical Education and Politicising Children's Bodies in Late Colonial Bengal'. *Gender & History* 29, no. 1 (2017): 176–97.
Tournès, Ludovic. *Américanisation: Une histoire mondiale (XVIIIe-XXIe siècle)*. Paris: Fayard, 2020.
Trevithick, Alan. 'Some Structural and Sequential Aspects of the British Imperial Assemblages at Delhi, 1877–1911'. *Modern Asian Studies* 24, no. 3 (1990): 561–78.
Trivedi, Lisa. 'Visually Mapping the 'Nation': Swadeshi Politics in Nationalist India, 1920–1930'. *Journal of Asian Studies* 62, no. 1 (2003): 11–41.
Tropp, Jacob. 'Transnational Development Training and Native American "Laboratories" in the Early Cold War'. *Journal of Global History* 13, no. 3 (2018): 469–90.
Trotha, Trutz von. 'Gewalt, Staat und Basislegitimität. Notizen zum Problem der Macht in Afrika (und anderswo)'. In *Macht der Identität – Identität der Macht. Politische Prozesse und kultureller Wandel in Afrika*, edited by H. Willer, T. Förster and C.Ortner-Buchberger, 1–16. Münster: LIT Verlag, 1995.
Trouillot, Michel-Rolph. *Silencing the Past: Power and the Production of History*. Boston, MA: Beacon Press, 1995.
Tschurenev, Jana. *Empire, Civil Society and the Beginnings of Colonial Education in India*. Cambridge: Cambridge University Press, 2019.
Tyrrell, Ian. *Crisis of the Wasteful Nation: Empire and Conservation in Theodore Roosevelt's America*. Chicago, IL: University of Chicago Press, 2015.
Tyrrell, Ian. 'Vectors of Practicality: Social Gospel, the North American YMCA in Asia, and the Global Context'. In *Spreading Protestant Modernity: Global Perspectives on the Social Work of the YMCA and YWCA, 1889–1970*, edited by Harald Fischer-Tiné, Stefan Huebner and Ian Tyrrell, 39–60. Honolulu: University of Hawai'i Press, 2021.

Tyrell, Ian. *Woman's World/Woman's Empire: The Woman's Christian Temperance Union in International Perspective 1880-1930*. Chapel Hill: The University of North Carolina Press, 1991.

Tyrrell, Ian R. 'American Protestant Missionaries, Moral Reformers, and the Reinterpretation of American "Expansion" in the Late Nineteenth Century'. In *Outside In: The Transnational Circuitry of US History*, edited by Andrew Preston and Doug Rossinow, 96-122. New York: Oxford University Press, 2017.

Tyrrell, Ian R. *Reforming the World: The Creation of America's Moral Empire*. Princeton, NJ: Princeton University Press, 2010.

Unger, Corinna R. 'The Decolonization of Development: Rural Development in India Before and After 1947'. In *Internationalism, Imperialism and the Formation of the Contemporary World*, edited by Miguel Bandeira Jerónimo and José Pedro Monteiro, 253-78. Cham: Palgrave Macmillan, 2017.

Unger, Corinna R. *Entwicklungspfade in Indien: Eine Internationale Geschichte, 1947-1980*. Göttingen: Wallstein Verlag, 2015.

Unger, Corinna R. *International Development: A Postwar History*. London: Bloomsbury, 2018.

Unger, Corinna R. 'Towards Global Equilibrium: American Foundations and Indian Modernization, 1950s to 1970s'. *Journal of Global History* 6, no. 1 (2011): 121-42.

Upton, Robert E. '"It Gives Us a Power and Strength Which We Do Not Possess": Martiality, Manliness, and India's Great War Enlistment Drive'. *Modern Asian Studies* 52, no. 6 (2018): 1977-2012.

Valdameri, Elena. *Indian Liberalism between Nation and Empire. The Political Life of Gopal Krishna Gokhale*. Abingdon: Routledge, 2022.

Valiani, Arafaat. *Militant Publics in India: Physical Culture and Violence in the Making of a Modern Polity*. New York: Palgrave Macmillan, 2011.

Valiani, Arafaat. 'Physical Training, Ethical Discipline, and Creative Violence: Zones of Self-Mastery in the Hindu Nationalist Movement'. *Cultural Anthropology* 25, no. 1 (2010): 73-99.

Valiani, Arafaat. 'Recuperating Indian Masculinity: Mohandas Gandhi, War and the Indian Diaspora in South Africa (1899-1914)'. *South Asian History and Culture* 5, no. 4 (2014): 505-20.

Valiotis, Chris. 'South Asia'. In *Routledge Companion to Sport History* edited by S. W. Pope and John Nauright, 571-85. Abingdon: Routledge, 2010.

Veer, Peter van der, ed. *Conversion to Modernities: The Globalization of Christianity*. London: Routledge, 1996.

Veer, Peter van der. *The Modern Spirit of Asia: The Spiritual and the Secular in India and China*. Princeton: Princeton University Press, 2014.

Vertinsky, Patricia. '"Building the Body Beautiful": The Women's League of Health and Beauty: Yoga and Female Agency in 1930s Britain'. *Rethinking History: The Journal of Theory and Practice* 16 (2012): 517-42.

Vertinsky, Patricia. 'Yoga Comes to American Physical Education: Josephine Rathbone and Corrective Physical Education'. *Journal of Sports History* 41, no. 2 (2014): 287-311.

Vertinsky, Patricia, and Aishwarya Ramachandran. 'Imperial Benevolence and Emancipatory Discourses: Harry Crowe Buck and Charles Harold Mc Cloy Take the "Y" to India and China in the Early Decades of the Twentieth Century'. In *Critical Reflections on Physical Culture on the Edges of Empire*, edited by F. J. Cleophas, 101-11. Cape Town: Sun Press, 2021.

Vertinsky, Patricia, and Aishwarya Ramachandran. 'The "Y" Goes to India: Springfield College, Muscular Missionaries, and the Transnational Circulation of Physical Culture Practices'. *Journal of Sport History* 46, no. 3 (2019): 363–79.

Vertinsky, Patricia, Aishwarya Ramachandran and Bo Wang. 'How about Some Muscle? Charles H. McCloy's Contributions to Physical Education in China between 1913 and 1926'. *The International Journal of the History of Sport* 36, no. 15–16 (2019): 1372–89.

Vidal, Denis. 'Max Müller and the Theosophists or the Other Half of Victorian Orientalism'. In *Orientalism and Anthropology: From Max Müller to Louis Dumont*, edited by Jackie Assayag, Roland Lardinois and Denis Vidal, 17–29. Pondicherry: Institut Français de Pondichéry, 1997.

Viswanath, Rupa. *The Pariah Problem: Caste, Religion and the Social in Modern India*. New York: Columbia University Press, 2014.

Viswanathan, Gauri. *Masks of Conquest: Literary Study and British Rule in India*. New York: Columbia University Press.

Wagner, Kim. *The Skull of Alum Bheg: The Life and Death of a Rebel of 1857*. New York: Oxford University Press, 2018.

Wagner, Peter. 'Introduction'. In *African, American and European Trajectories of Modernity: Past Oppression, Future Justice?*, edited by Peter Wagner, 1–18. Edinburgh: Edinburgh University Press, 2015.

Walburn, Samuel W. D. '"A Most Disgraceful, Sordid, Disreputable, Drunken Brawl": Paul Cadmus and the Politics of Queerness in the Early Twentieth Century'. *The Purdue Historian* 8, no. 1 (2017): 1–15.

Wald, Erica. 'Health, Discipline and Appropriate Behaviour: The Body of the Soldier and Space of the Cantonment'. *Modern Asian Studies* 46, no. 4 (2012): 815–56.

Wald, Erica. *Vice in the Barracks: Medicine, the Military and the Making of Colonial India, 1780–1868*. Basingstoke: Palgrave Macmillan, 2014.

Wallach, Bret. *Losing Asia: Modernization and the Culture of Development*. Baltimore, MD: Johns Hopkins University Press, 1996.

Waller, David. *The Perfect Man: The Muscular Life and Times of Eugen Sandow, Victorian Strongman*. London: Victorian Secrets, 2011.

Wang, Peter Chen-Main. 'Caring beyond National Borders: The YMCA and Chinese Labourers in World War I Europe'. *Church History* 178, no. 8 (2009): 327–49.

Washbrook, David. 'Avatars of Identity: The British Community in India'. In *Settlers and Expatriates: Britons over the Seas*, edited by Robert Bickers, 178–204. Oxford: Oxford University Press, 2010.

Washbrook, David. 'Forms of Citizenship in Pre-Modern South India'. *Citizenship Studies* 23, no. 3 (2019): 224–39.

Washbrook, David. 'Intimations of Modernity in South India'. *South Asian History and Culture* 1, no. 1 (2009): 125–48.

Washbrook, David. 'The Rhetoric of Democracy and Development in Late Colonial India'. In *Nationalism, Democracy and Development: State and Politics in India*, edited by Sugata Bose and Ayesha Jalal, 36–49. New Delhi: Oxford University Press, 1998.

Washbrook, David A. 'India, 1818–1860: The Two Faces of Colonialism'. In *The Oxford History of the British Empire. The Nineteenth Century*, edited by Andrew Porter, 395–421. Oxford: Oxford University Press, 1999.

Washbrook, David A. 'Problems of Global History'. In *Writing the History of the Global: Challenges for the 21st Century*, edited by Maxine Berg, 21–31. Oxford: Oxford University Press, 2013.

Watt, Carey A. 'Cultural Exchange, Appropriation and Physical Culture: Strongman Eugen Sandow in Colonial India, 1904–1905'. *The International Journal of the History of Sport* 33, no. 16 (2016): 1921–42.

Watt, Carey A. 'Philanthropy and Civilizing Missions in India c. 1820–1960: States, NGOs and Development'. In *Civilizing Missions in Colonial and Postcolonial South Asia: From Improvement to Development*, edited by Carey A. Watt and Michael Mann, 271–316. London: Anthem Press, 2011.

Watt, Carey A. 'Physical Culture and the Body in Colonial India, c. 1800–1947'. In *The Routledge Handbook of the History of Colonialism in South Asia*, edited by Harald Fischer-Tiné and Maria Framke, 345–58. Abingdon: Routledge, 2022.

Watt, Carey A. 'Physical Culture as "Natural Healing": Eugen Sandow's Campaign against the Vices of Civilization *c.* 1890–1920'. In *Global Anti-Vice Activism, 1890–1950: Fighting Drinks, Drugs, and "Immorality"*, edited by Jessica Pliley, Harald Fischer-Tiné and Robert Kramm-Masaoka, 74–99. Cambridge: Cambridge University Press, 2016.

Watt, Carey A. 'The Promise of "Character" and the Spectre of Sedition: The Boy Scout Movement and Colonial Consternation in India, 1908–1921'. *South Asia* 22, no. 2 (1999): 37–62.

Watt, Carey A. *Serving the Nation: Cultures of Service, Association and Citizenship in Colonial India*. New Delhi: Oxford University Press, 2005.

Weiss, Richard S. 'Religion and the Emergence of Print in Colonial India: Arumuga Navalar's Publishing Project'. *Indian Economic & Social History Review* 53, no. 4 (2016): 473–500.

Williams, Chad. *Torchbearers of Democracy: African American Soldiers in the World War I Era*. Chapel Hill: University of North Carolina Press, 2010.

Wilson, Jon E. 'Early Colonial India Beyond Empire'. *The Historical Journal* 50, no. 4 (2007): 951–70.

Windel, Aaron. *Cooperative Rule: Community Development in Britain's Late Empire*. Oakland: University of California Press, 2021.

Windover, Michael. 'Exchanging Looks: "Art Dekho" Movie Theatres in Bombay'. *Architectural History* 52 (2009): 208–10.

Winter, Thomas. *Making Men, Making Class: The YMCA and Workingmen, 1877–1920*. Chicago, IL: University of Chicago Press, 2002.

Wittrock, Björn. 'Modernity: One, None, or Many? European Origins and Modernity as a Global Condition'. *Daedalus* 129, no. 1 (2000): 31–60.

Wu, Jialin Christina. 'A Life of Make Believe: Being Boy Scouts and "Playing Indian" in British Malaya (1910–1942)'. *Gender & History* 26, no. 3 (2014): 589–619.

Xing, Jun. *Baptized in the Fire of Revolution: The American Social Gospel and the YMCA in China, 1919–1937*. Bethlehem, PA: Lehigh University Press, 1996.

Xu, Guoqui. 'Networking through the Y. The Role of the YMCA in China's Search for New National Identity and Internationalization'. In *Networking the International System: Global Histories of International Organizations*, edited by Madeleine Herren, 133–47. Cham: Springer, 2014.

Xu, Guoqi. *Olympic Dreams: China and Sports, 1895–2008*. Cambridge, MA: Harvard University Press, 2008.

Zahid, Masood Akhtar. 'Islamia Anjumans and Educational, Development: Perspectives on the 19th Century British Punjab'. *Pakistan Journal of History and Culture* 34, no. 2 (2013): 1–23.

Zahran, Geraldo, and Leonardo Ramos. 'From Hegemony to Soft Power: Implications of a Conceptual Change'. In Soft Power and US Foreign Policy: Theoretical, Historical and Contemporary Perspectives, edited by Inderjeet Paramar and Michael Cox, 12–31. London: Routledge, 2010.

Zald, Mayer N., and Patricia Denton. 'From Evangelism to General Services: The Transformation of the YMCA'. *Administrative Science Quarterly* 8, no. 2 (1963): 218–21.

Zanasi, Margherita. 'Exporting Development: The League of Nations and Republican China'. *Comparative Studies in Society and History* 49, no. 1 (2007).

Zastoupil, Lynn, and Martin Moir. 'Introduction'. In *The Great Indian Education Debate: Documents Relating to the Orientalist-Anglicist Controversy, 1781–1843*, edited by Lynn Zastoupil and Martin Moir, 1–72. Richmond, VA: Curzon, 1999.

Zavos, John. *The Emergence of Hindu Nationalism in India*. Delhi: Oxford University Press, 2000.

Zemon-Davies, Natalie. 'Foreword'. In *The Allure of the Archives*, edited by Arlette Farge, ix–xviii. New Haven, CT: Yale University Press, 2013.

Zhong, Yurou. 'Script Crisis and Literary Modernity in China, 1916–1958'. Unpublished PhD dissertation, Columbia University, 2014.

Zimmermann, Andrew. *Alabama in Africa: Booker T. Washington the German Empire and the Globalization of the New South*. Princeton, NJ: Princeton University Press, 2010.

Zook, Darren C. 'Developing the Rural Citizen: Southern India, 1900–47'. *South Asia: Journal of South Asian Studies* 23, no. 1 (2000): 65–86.

Zubovich, Gene. 'The Protestant Search for "the Universal Christian Community" between Decolonization and Communism'. *Religions* 8, no. 2 (2017): 1–12.

Zweininger-Bargielowska, Ina. *Managing the Body: Beauty, Health and Fitness in Britain, 1880–1939*. Oxford: Oxford University Press, 2010.

Index

abstinence 135
acculturation 13
adaptation 6, 12, 84–5, 166
Adivasi (*ādivāsī*) 170
administrators 3, 13, 15, 18, 19, 23, 25, 48, 65, 73, 82, 100–1, 118, 137, 141–2, 149, 160, 167
adolescence / adolescent 22, 24, 97, 109–13, 115–17, 124–7, 129, 131, 135, 169
Afghan frontier 72
Africa 7, 8, 27, 43–4, 52, 56, 61, 65, 68, 75, 96, 104, 131, 149, 160, 162
African Americans 34
agency (sense of control) 10, 18, 81, 101, 132, 136, 145, 216 n.169
agency (organization) 40, 47, 86, 90, 116
agricultural
  agricultural communities 17, 151
  agricultural cooperatives 143, 235 n.113
  agricultural expert / expertise 12, 139, 154, 169, 237 n.159
  agricultural Institute, Allahabad 142, 150
  agricultural production 18, 43
  agricultural reform 9, 140, 144, 157
  agricultural schools 143
agronomist 140, 142, 148, 151, 167
Ahmednagar 52
akhāṛās 83
Alabama 149, 157
Albinocracy 104
All India Radio 131
Allahabad 29, 37, 54, 116, 124, 142, 150
Allahabad Kumbh Mela 54
American
  American Deep South 149
  American imperialism 1, 207 n.7
  American liberal modernity 6, 36
  American Presbyterian Mission 142

American radio sitcom 34
American South 149
American Southwest 160
American values 10
Americanization 4, 9, 10
Amos 'n' Andy 34, 190 n.182
Amritsar Massacre 94
anatomy 87, 97
Andrews, C. F. 42
Anglo-American alliance 38
anthropometric measurements 124
anti-alcohol 151, 236 n.133
anti-American sentiment 10
anti-Christian sentiment 170
anti-vice agenda 26, 135
anticolonial nationalism 2, 4, 141, 155
Arabs 65
archival memory 8
archives 6–9, 169
area history/ studies 1, 2, 31
Ariakode 42, 192 n.222
Arizona 7, 156
Armistice 51–2, 74, 199 n.81
Army Department 7, 11, 13, 50, 51, 74–6, 165
army huts 52
Arya Kumar Sabha 3, 22
Arya Samaj 3, 22–3, 26, 41–2, 84
Arya Vir Dal 26
asceticism 101
Association Press 30, 32
associational culture 16, 23
athletic
  athletic crusade 104
  athletic man 47
Atya-Patya 106
audio material 7
Australia 9, 29, 56, 97, 157
Australian and New Zealand Army Corps (ANZAC) 56

Austria 52, 117
authoritarian rhetoric 152
autobiographical writings 9
Azariah, V. S. 9, 42, 55

bacterial infections 124
Baden-Powell 110
badmashes 123
badminton 57, 88, 125, 151, 152
baithaks 106
Balkan Wars 25
Banaras Hindu University 22
Bandung 157
Bangalore 8, 29, 37, 50–1, 68, 71, 94, 116, 131, 205 n.191
Bangla 170
Banurji, H. G. 119, 120, 224 n.102
barbershops 57
Baroda 93, 156, 158, 218 n.195, 218
barracks 47, 77
baseball 88, 91
basketball 86, 88, 91, 95, 125
Basra 59, 60, 65
Batavia 157
bazars 49
Beall, Harold Gething 113, 124
Beatty, Jerome 146, 153, 155, 229 n.10
beauty
  beauty (physical) 82, 84, 103
  beauty (physical), male 84
bees 150
Belgian Capuchins 142
Benares 54
Bengal 23, 51, 83–4, 92–3, 119, 127
Berkeley University, California 44
Besant, Annie 42
Bharatiya Jan Sangh 170
bhāratīya kuśti 105
Bible study classes 28
Bihar 50, 125, 142
billiard 36, 61, 71
bio-moral 53, 78, 87, 98
bioscope (*see also* moving picture shows) 59, 78, 131
Bishop Whitehead 42
Birmingham 7
blackface 34
bleaching 103, 217 n.186

bodily practices 152
  and regimes 85
body
  body builders 82
  body language 82
  body, care of 101
Boer War 110
Bolshevism / Bolshevist 44, 47
Bombay 16, 26–4, 28–9, 44, 52, 69, 83, 93, 99, 105, 116, 118, 123–4, 127–8, 137, 184 n.76, 185 n.89, 195 n.13
bourgeois 6, 23, 28, 36, 77
Bovril 59
boy
  boy problem 14, 110–13, 117–19, 220 n.17
Boy Scout
  Boy Scout Movement 110
  Boy Scout(s) 22, 87, 110–11, 117, 128, 151
  Boy Scout Associations 117
  Boy Scout Association of India 128
  Boy Scouts of America 87
boyhood 14, 109–11, 116–17, 122, 125, 136, 167, 217 n.179
Boyology 14, 109–13, 116–17, 119, 123, 125, 133, 135, 137, 166–7
boys' branches 109, 116, 118, 120–2, 125, 131, 135–7, 167, 170
Boys' Brigade 22, 111, 115, 119
Boys' Department 7, 11, 109–10, 113, 115
boys' work 7, 10, 14, 41, 109–10, 115–18, 120–2, 124, 133, 135–7, 167, 169
  Boys' Work Secretary 39, 112, 121, 123
  boys' worker 112–13, 121, 123–4, 128, 135–6
Brahmo Samaj 23
Brayne, Frank L. 142, 153
breeding farms 158
British colonial administrators 13, 101
British colonial state 1, 16, 17, 92, 135
British Empire 16, 32, 38, 43, 47, 51, 55, 72, 110
British Red Cross 52
Brown, Elwood 97
Buck, Harry Crowe 14, 83, 94–7, 100–3, 105–6, 113
Buck, Marie 95
Buddhism/Buddhist 22, 102, 105, 183 n.62

Buildings for Brotherhood
   (B4B) 171
Burma 6, 8, 12, 14, 22, 28, 30, 70, 75, 88,
   91–2, 102, 109, 113, 117, 125, 136,
   159, 163, 188 n.143, 212 n.79
Burning Chats 54
Burr, Lawrence 131–2, 136, 228 n.178
Butterfield, Kenyon L. 155

Calcutta 16, 23, 28–31, 33–4, 37, 47, 51,
   73, 83, 90–2, 101, 115–16, 118–25,
   131, 133–5, 137, 195 n.13, 205
   n.191, 224 n.102
Calcutta Rotary Club 43
Calicut 42, 116
California 44
Callan, Joseph C. 50, 56–7, 64–5, 72,
   198 n.77
callisthenics 82, 99
Cambridge 44
Cammack, Robert W. 92, 219 n.98
Camp Fire Girls of America 87
campesinos 149
camping 22, 109, 125–7, 137
Canada 26, 29, 49, 75, 85, 87, 95, 113, 117,
   131, 145, 171
Canadian Standard Efficiency Tests
   (CSET) 124, 225 n.125
canal networks 17
cantonments 50, 54
capitalist
   capitalist ideals 217 n.186
   capitalist societies 86
   capitalist world system 160
Capra, Frank 132
caregiving 11, 13, 47–8, 51–2, 75, 171
carpentry 150
Carter, E. C. 39, 51, 59, 68
caste
   caste (status / system) 57, 91, 102, 126,
      129, 136, 151, 196 n.38
   half caste 73, 204 n.185
   low-caste 113, 133
   outcaste (*see also* Dalit,
      untouchable) 55, 57
   upper / high-caste 24, 105, 114–15,
      201 n.114
censorship 19
Census 144

Ceylon 6, 8, 12, 14, 22, 28, 30, 39, 51, 59,
   75, 88, 91–2, 96, 103, 105, 107, 109,
   113, 117, 125, 136, 156–7, 159, 161,
   163, 166, 169, 178 n.67, 183 n.62,
   188 n.143
Ceylonese State Council 157
character building 22, 110–11, 113,
   115, 167
charity 23–5, 42, 74
Chatterjee, Bankim Chandra 25
Chicago 34, 102, 121, 131
Chief Khalsa Diwan 24
Childhood 2, 14, 110–11, 220 n.14
China 10, 30, 34, 36, 88, 90–1, 97, 123,
   156–7, 159, 177 n.55
Chinese (ethnicity) 115, 128, 202 n.137
Chinese (language) 156
Christian
   Christian academic institution 85
   Christian agrarianism 154
   Christian internationalism 4
   Christian internationalist agenda 3
   Christian lay organization 1, 3, 13, 16,
      85, 92, 99, 135, 140
   Christian missionaries 16, 19, 23–4, 48,
      62, 142, 162, 222 n.50, 229 n.5
   Christian mores / values 21, 155
   Christian orphanage 131
   Christian-Orientalist knowledge 31
Christianity
   Christianity, muscular 28, 36, 83, 166
   Christianity, practical 27, 39, 40, 139
   Christianity, Protestant 5, 154
Churchill, Winston 72
cigarettes 59
citizenship
   citizenship rights 20
   citizenship training 3, 11, 20, 45, 53,
      76–7, 90, 136, 167
   citizenship, constructive 20
   citizenship, imperial 20, 182 n.45,
      219 n.8
civic
   civic activism 20
   civic engagement 3
   civic responsibility 19
   civic sense 124
civil society 1, 2, 4, 5, 16, 19, 23–4, 34, 74,
   110, 137, 141, 162, 168

civilising rhetoric 17
Clarke University 113
class prejudice 166
co-operation 103, 145, 150
co-operative method 150
cocaine 120, 224 n.102, 224 n.103
Cochin 156, 233 n.58
cocks 150, 158
Coimbatore 145
collective spirit 103
Colombo 12, 28-9, 37, 90, 92, 103-4, 116
colonial
    colonial discourse 25, 107, 109
    colonial domination 5
    colonial empires 1
    colonial era 2, 14, 19
    colonial modernity 3, 26
    colonial rule 2, 15, 38, 69, 97, 139
    colonial state 1, 4, 13, 16-18, 20, 81, 92, 94, 113, 135, 140, 142, 152, 162, 168, 171
colonialism 1, 14-17, 141, 166, 230 n.17
Columbia University 90
combat trophies 73
commercialization 15
'communalization' 26
communication 61, 77-8, 165, 199 n.87
Communist propaganda 154, 159
Company state 18
competition (event) 42, 52, 57, 135
Perfect Physique Competition 103, 104
concentration camps 42
Congress (see also Indian National Congress) 20-1, 35, 62, 97, 99, 105, 107, 143, 170, 172
consumption 10, 16, 85
conversion (religious) 23, 36, 39, 41, 77, 90, 107, 120, 144, 154, 165, 170, 198 n.78
conversion (to modernity) 107, 144, 154
coolie 57-8, 78, 115
Cornell 72, 140, 144-7, 151, 160-1
corporeal self-empowerment 84
cosmopolitan 4, 36-7, 96, 106, 190 n.194
cottage industries 150
cotton 15, 44
court cases 153
cricket 57, 84, 88, 95, 125
crime 111

criminal (adjective) 113
criminal (noun) 72
Criminal Investigation Department (CID) 44
cross-breeding 150
cruising 121
cultural
    cultural alienation 114
    cultural arrogance 8, 32, 35, 67, 78
    cultural brokers 63
    cultural frontiersman 106
    cultural imperialism 9, 81
    cultural rapprochement 54, 69
    cultural self-assertion 83
    cultural sensitivity 23, 54
    cultural stereotypes 48
curricula/curricular 18, 92, 99
curry powder 59

Dalit (see also outcaste, untouchable) 23, 41, 57, 133, 144
dāna (donation) 24
dandas 106
Danish (nationality) 84, 96
Darling, Malcolm 142
Datta, S. K. 7, 38-9, 42, 44, 55, 198 n.77
Davison Fund 7, 158
Dayananda Anglo-Vedic (DAV) College 22
de-Orientalization 103
debating clubs 24, 135
debauchery 54
decolonization 4, 14, 30, 141, 170
Defence Department 171
degeneration 49, 113
'degenerating' effects 167
delinquency 111
democracy 5, 6, 39, 91, 96-7, 107, 110, 125, 133, 135, 145, 150, 153, 166, 212 n.84
democratic
    'democratic' microcosms 78
    democratic participation 77, 167, 169
    democratic principles 6
demonstration farms 142
denationalizing 22
Denmark 157
Department of Visual Instruction 33
'depressed classes' 24

desecration 72
development
    development experts 150, 156, 160, 163, 167, 229 n.6, 231 n.23, 231 n.26, 233 n.71
    development knowledge 12, 14, 139, 156-7, 161, 167
    development management 154
developmentalism 4, 143, 171
deviant 113
diabetes 101
diarchy 15
diet 102, 152
diplomacy 1
disenchantment 16
do-gooders 3, 25, 158
Doggett, Laurence 88, 113
Dogra 194 n.4
dramatic performances 151
drugs 102
drunkenness 49, 54
duty 49
dyeing 150

East Africa 52, 56, 61, 198 n.69
East-West dichotomies 114
ecological consequences 17
economy (rural) 140, 148
Eddy, George Sherwood 7, 38, 43-4, 62, 74, 100, 143, 150, 168
education
    education system 111
    educational authorities 32, 214 n.130
    educational institution 3, 16, 19, 20-2, 97, 113, 116, 182 n.53, 221 n.39
    educational plays 151
    educational policies 18, 127
    educational reforms 3, 19
    English education 21
    formal education 21, 114
    informal education 14, 22-3, 110, 118, 167, 219 n.6
Education and Extension Panel 158
egalitarianism 5, 104, 136, 166
Egypt 56, 96, 156, 159, 163, 238 n.171
Eigensinn 100-1, 107, 216 n.169
Elitism 38
Elmhirst, Leonhard 142
embodied knowledge 83

empowerment 44, 84, 90, 100, 136, 166
enemy aliens 52
English
    English education 21
    English-educated urban youth 143
    English-medium schools 21
    English speakers 19
English Church Missionary Society 142
entertainment 13, 19, 6, 42, 47, 51-2, 57, 59, 61-2, 66, 70, 75-8, 111, 131, 169
epistemic community 141, 156, 163, 231 n. 23
espionage 59
esprit de corps 30
eugenics 87
Eurasian 13, 28, 48-50, 73, 76, 128, 165, 187 n.121, 195 n.13, 218 n.1
evangelization 29, 90, 155
every-day habits 103
ex-servicemen 77
exercise (physical) 22, 83-4, 86, 93, 95, 97, 101-3, 105-8, 152-3
exiles 61
expatriates 43
Expeditionary From India 57
expert 7, 12, 14, 49, 55, 83, 87, 90, 92-3, 101-2, 104-6, 109-13, 123-4, 127, 135-7, 139-42, 146, 148-50, 154-8, 160, 162-3, 167-9, 229 n.6, 231 n.23, 231 n.26, 233 n.71, 237 n.159, 238 n.171
extension work 157, 234 n.91

fair play 103, 153
famine 17, 23
famine relief 24, 25, 179
Faridkot State 97
farming 18, 144
Farquhar, John Nicol 31-3, 68
Fehraltorf 37
film *(see also* Hollywood movies) 7, 13, 32, 36, 61-3, 66, 152, 158, 167, 201 n.119, 203 n.164, 228 n.178
fin de siècle 84
First World War 13, 16, 45, 47-8, 56, 74-5, 82, 92, 94, 107, 109, 128-9, 131, 136, 143, 154
Fiske, George Walter 112
fodder grasses 150

Folk Schools 157
food
  food crises 17, 142
  food production 142
  food security 17, 152
football 57, 84, 88, 90, 95, 123, 125, 129, 226 n.131
Ford Foundation 82, 139
foreign
  foreign aid 4, 141, 156
  foreign rule 15
  foreign work 29
France 12, 52, 56–8, 61, 63–5, 74, 76, 169
fraternity 128, 131, 171
Free World () 160–1
frontier (geography) 72–3, 144, 204 n.179
frontier (metaphorical) 70, 95, 106, 111
fundraising 28, 51, 131, 241 n.15

Gandhi, Indira 171
Gandhi, Mohandas K. (*see also* Mahatma) 25, 38, 41, 43–4, 81, 98, 140, 143, 149–51, 153, 192 n.230
garrison towns 15, 50, 52
gender norms 167
Geneva 2, 4, 7, 27, 29–30, 121, 168
geopolitical constellation 6
Gibson, Henry W. 112–13
Girl Guide 110, 151
Glasgow 111, 119
global
  global biography 2
  global civil society 2, 4
  global development 167
  global history of sports 2, 81
  global modernization process 1
  global moment 84
  global-microhistory 169
globalization 15, 82
going native 69
go-between 54, 156
Gokhale, Gopal Krishna 24–5
Goorkha / Gurkha 74, 119, 194 n.4, 205 n.187
Gould, Helen Miller 134
Government Agricultural Farm 150
Government of India 7, 19, 51, 56, 59, 76, 92–3, 98, 127

graduate 7, 19, 29, 44, 53, 72–3, 88, 90, 92, 95–8, 103, 107, 109, 113, 124, 127, 143, 145, 156, 160, 166, 221 n.32
gramophone 13, 32, 61–2, 70–1, 78, 201 n.119
Gray, (Dr.) John Henry 83–4, 90–7, 99–102, 105, 113, 123–4, 212 n.79
Great Depression 30, 117
Great War 7, 25, 38, 44, 47–8, 51, 55, 61, 67, 74–6, 78, 127, 135, 142, 145, 165, 169, 199 n.88
Greek sculptures 103
Green Revolution 150, 158, 235 n.100
Greenwich 144
group solidarity 103
Gujarati 156
Gulick, Luther Halsey 85–8, 91, 112, 124, 210 n.42, 210 n.49, 212 n.84, 220 n.24, 225 n.124
gym / gymnasium 36, 83, 85, 89, 90, 95, 97, 103, 105, 121, 123, 125
gymnastics 92–3, 125

habit formation 167
Hall, G. Stanley 112–13, 115
Harte, A. C. 32, 37
Hartford 59
Hatch, Duane Spencer 7, 12, 14, 72, 73, 78, 140–2, 144–63, 167–9, 204 n.169, 229 n.10, 233 n.71, 234 n.91, 234 n.97, 235 n.99, 237 n.149, 238 n.171, 239 n.174
Hatch, Emily Gilchriest 145–7, 151, 153–4, 159, 171, 233 n.71
headquarters 4, 27–8, 34–7, 42, 51–2, 55, 59, 74–5, 85, 88, 115, 154
health
  health problems 91
Healthland 152
Healy, Warren D. 102
hegemony 10, 108, 139
Heinrichs, Waldo Huntley 7, 33, 73, 128–9, 200 n.106
hens 150
hierarchies 5, 17, 62, 67–8, 77, 102, 166, 169
Higginbottom, Sam 144, 155
high school 21, 87, 94, 97, 101–2, 113–16, 119–20, 125, 127, 134, 137, 221 n.39

Hilton, W. B. 115
Hindi 21, 33, 56, 114, 170, 189 n.159, 204 n.175, 215 n.152, 227 n.168
Hindoo Tract Preaching Society 35
Hindu Mahasabha (HMS) 26, 170
Hindu
  Hindu-Muslim riots 26
  Hindu reform 22–3, 182 n.52
  Hindu revivalists 3
Hinduism 16, 91, 101–2, 105, 120, 133
  bourgeois Hinduism 23, 184 n.73
  Brahmanical Hinduism 31, 41
Hindustani Seva Dal 26
Hindutva 170
Hobbs, Harry 47
hockey 57, 95, 97, 125
Hollywood movies (see also film) 36, 82, 132
Holyoke 85
home gardening projects 157
homosexuality/same-sex relationships 121
hoodlums 123
hook-worm 101
hooligan 111
Hopi 160
hospitals 24, 52, 57, 59
hostel 37, 44, 57, 95, 115
human material 99
humanitarianism 23, 25, 48, 185 n.91
husbandry 18, 142, 147
Hututu 106
Hyderabad 99, 124, 158
hygiene
  hygiene regime 42
  hygiene and sanitation 90–1, 97, 107
  hygiene, personal 97, 101
  hygiene, personal and sex 63, 84
  hygiene, sex/sexual 63–4, 84, 97
  hygiene, social 27, 87, 132

idleness 165
illiteracy 33, 61
immigrant communities 27
immoral
  immoral practices 121
  immoral relations 79
imperial
  Imperial Agricultural Research Institute 142

imperial citizenship 20, 182 n.45, 219 n.8
Imperial Durbars 17, 180 n.14
imperial government 13, 29, 45, 49–50, 77, 95, 165
imperial race science 124
imperial scholar 18
imperial self-image 17
imperial states 166
imperial world order 2, 104
improvement 5, 17, 18, 22, 50, 65, 87, 103, 107, 114, 142, 146, 150, 152, 154–5, 235 n. 110
impurity 120, 133
Indian National Congress (INC) (*see also* Congress) 21, 38, 41, 84, 98–9, 105, 114
Indian wrestling (see also *pahalvānī* and *kuśtī*) 218 n.193
indigenous
  indigenous reformers/reformism 4, 13
  indigenous support 17
  indigenous voices 170
individuality 6
'Indo-Saracenic' style 36
Indologists 31
Indonesia 159
industrial work scheme 105
industrialization 27
infantry 57, 169, 194 n.4
infrastructure 20, 166
intemperance 69
Inter-American Institute of Agricultural Sciences 159
intercultural contact 15
Intergovernmental Conference of Far-Eastern Countries on Rural Hygiene 157
international civil society organizations 1
International YMCA Training School 85
interracial sex 69
Iowa 74
irrigation 17
Islam 16, 25, 41, 1051 200 n.108
Ivy League 59

Jain Young Men's Association 22
Jainism 105
Japan 6, 10, 75, 82, 84, 177 n.56

Jazz 82
Jesudas 148
jiu-jitsu 82, 84
journals 7, 19, 36, 52, 59, 114, 134, 156
Jubbulpore 116, 205 n.191
judo 84
juvenile delinquent 131

Kabaddi 106
Kaiser-i-Hind medal 95
Kandivli 99
Kashmir 33
Kathakali 146
Kentucky 49
Khalsa College, Amritsar 22, 97, 183 n.60, 215 n.144
Khan, Sayyid Ahmad 22
Khasi 58
Kher, B. G. 99
Khilafat Campaign 41
Kho-Kho 106
Kingdom of Christ 27
Knapp, Seaman A. 149
knowledge
　agricultural knowledge 142
　colonial knowledge 72, 145
　development knowledge 12, 14, 139, 156–7, 161, 167
　indigenous knowledge 162
　knowledge formation 146
　local knowledge 146, 167, 233 n. 71
　pidgin knowledge 141, 167
　scientific knowledge 141, 154
　transnational knowledge circulation 166
Korea 10, 156
kuśti (*see also* Indian wrestling and *pahalvānī*) 83

laboratories 141, 161
labour recruitment / management 17
Lahore 3, 22, 28–9, 33–4, 43, 59, 65, 68, 74, 114, 116, 128–30
Lala Lajpat Rai 84, 114, 170, 209 n.34
Landour 30
language 19, 29, 30, 36, 47, 54, 58, 62–4, 69, 70, 77–8, 82, 96, 100, 121, 146, 151, 153, 156, 162, 170, 188 n.148, 233 n.58
Lannowe, Matthew 128

Latin America 13, 81, 159, 163
latrines 132, 151
leadership-training 87
League of Nations 163, 229
League of Nations Health Organization (LNHO) 157
leisure practices 62
libertarian 5
liberty 6
library 6, 7, 8, 36–7, 71, 89, 134, 151
Libya 25
licentiousness 49
linguistic
　linguistic regions 4
　linguistic skills 146
literacy
　literacy rate 19, 66
　literacy campaigns 33, 202 n.137
Literature Department 32
livestock 149–50
living standards 158
loans 143
locomotive workshops 50
logistical power 17
Lombardy 150
London 2, 4, 26
Lord Hardinge 51
Lord Willingdon 156
low Europeans (*see also* marginal whites, white subalterns) 49
loyalty 45, 59, 103, 170–1, 212 n.84
ludic diffusion 81

MacFadden, Bernarr 84
McClelland, Dalton F. 52, 137
McCloy, Charles H. 97
McConaughy, David 29–30, 35, 37
macro
　macro-perspectives 2
　macro-processes 9
Madhya Pradesh 170
Madras College of Physical Education (MCPE) 14, 75, 83, 94–9, 103, 106–7, 123, 169–70
Madras Missionaries' Conference 29
Madras University 99
magazine 7, 19, 61, 82, 134, 160–1
magic lantern slides / slideshow 7, 62, 78
Maharaja of Gwalior 36

Mahatma (*see also* Gandhi, Mohandas K.) 43, 143, 149, 234 n.97
Mahsuds 72–3, 204 n.179
Maine, Henry Sumner 18
Malabar 41, 233 n.58
Malaviya, M. M. 41
Malayalam 28, 30, 146, 156, 170, 233 n.58
malnutrition 101, 152
man-making mission 125
Mandarin (language) 151
manhood 14, 21, 42, 52, 83, 100, 143
Manuel 148
Mappila Rebellion 41
Mappilas/Moplahs 41
marginal whites (*see also* low Europeans, white subalterns) 194 n.8
marketing 157
Marseille 56–7, 63
Martandam 145–6, 148–59, 162–3, 171, 230 n.11, 233 n.58, 238 n.172, 239 n.182
Martandam Rural Demonstration Centre (MRDC) 7, 8, 140, 144, 147
martial arts 83–4, 127
martial race theory 74, 194 n.4
masculine
 masculine comradeship 77
masculinity 13, 54, 70, 77–8, 82–3, 103–4, 111, 166–7
 masculinity, 'civilised' 13
mass
 mass callisthenics 99
 mass campaign 62, 97
 mass performance 17
 mass protests 21
Massachusetts 7, 28, 85–7, 112–13, 169
Massey, Vincent 95
masturbation 101
Maymyo 50
medialization 165
mediator 54, 61–3
 mediatory role 61
medical missions 25
medico-moral policing 70
Meerut Conspiracy Case 44
Meiji 84
melā 32, 189 n.159
memoirs 72, 146

mental traits 103
merchant communities 23
Mesopotamia 12, 52, 56, 58–61, 63–5, 68, 72, 76–7, 144–5, 169, 198 n.69, 200 n.95, 200 n.110
messianisme démocratique 110
métissage 64
metropole 2, 16, 34, 36, 110
Mexico 59, 158–9, 239 n.195
MGM 158–9
Michel, F. J. 49–50
micro
 micro-credit / microcredits 143, 150
 micro-(hi)story 162
 micro perspective 2
 micro-social 17
middle class
 middle-class bachelors 85
 middle-class reformers 24
 middle-class professionals 16
Middle East 52, 56, 62
militant bodies 128
military recruitment 15
Miller, A. L. 74
millhands 105
minority 17, 28, 113, 115
miscegenation 64, 69
missionary
 missionary history 1
 missionary interventions 1
 missionary practice 146
mixed-race 57, 128, 166, 195 n.13
moderate wing 20
modern
 modern physical practices 82
 modern South Asian history 1, 173 n.3
modernism
 high modernism 139, 149, 229 n.3
 low modernism 149
modernity 1, 3–6, 9, 15–16, 18–20, 23, 26–7, 34, 36, 45, 76, 82–3, 86, 100, 104, 107–8, 114, 125, 146, 154, 165–9, 217 n.186
 modernity, American liberal 6, 36
 modernity, colonial 3, 26
 modernity, conversion to
modernization 1–5, 13, 15–20, 78, 107, 141–3, 146, 165–6, 168–9, 174 n.9

modernizing
  modernizing interventions 16
  modernizing mission 5, 12, 15–16, 26, 78, 142, 165
modes of production 10
Mojave tribes 160
Montagu-Chelmsford Reforms 15
Monthlies 30
Montreal 115
Moonje, B. S. 41
Moore, W. H. 67
moral restraint 64
Mosul 59
motives 50, 77, 118, 121–2
motor cars/boats 60
Mott, John R. 31, 47, 59, 117
movable type 19
moving picture shows (*see also* bioscope) 62
muhalla 132
Muhammadan Anglo-Oriental College, Aligarh 21
mule cars 60
Müller, Jørg Peter 84
Munro, Donald 93
Murree 128–30
muscular Christianity 28, 36, 83, 166
music 61, 146
Mysore 155, 158

Nagas 57
Nagercoil 145
Nagpur University 93
nation-building 3, 11, 103, 137
National Army Secretary (YMCA) 75
national perspectives 2, 24
National Physical Director 91
National Social Conference 24
nationalist 1, 3–4, 10, 13, 15, 18, 20–1, 24–5, 38, 40–4, 82–4, 99, 100, 105, 107, 114–15, 120–1, 125, 136–7, 140–4, 152–3, 168, 170, 174 n.9
Native Americans 160
natives 22, 28–9, 32–3, 36, 72, 83, 87, 89, 94, 118, 136, 146, 154, 161, 167
nature and needs 95
Navajo tribes 160
Navy, Army and Air Force Institute (NAAFI) 74

Nehru, Jawaharlal 159, 170–1, 238 n.172
Nehruvian
  Nehruvian developmentalism 171
  Nehruvian India 131, 228 n.195
  Nehruvian state 137
neo-imperial 162
Nepali 59, 62, 78, 169
nephritis 101
New Delhi 8
New Haven 7
New Jersey 150
new sanitary system 151
New York 4, 33–4, 37, 39, 47, 50, 72, 74, 85, 88, 117, 122, 134, 148, 154, 171
New Zealand 56, 97
newspapers 8, 19, 34, 59, 61, 69, 114, 131, 134
Niebuhr, Roland 43
night school 131
Niyogi Report 170
Nobel Peace Prize 47
Noehren, Arthur G. 83, 92, 102, 105–6, 124, 217 n.179, 225 n.116
non-Christian religions 31
non-governmental organization (NGO) 26
non-state
  non-state actors 20, 23, 26, 166
  non-state social service activities 131
non-violence 81
non-western societies 5
norms 13, 20, 28, 107, 139, 166–8, 206 n.1
North America 1, 3–4, 8, 10–11, 13–14, 16, 20, 27–30, 32–3, 38–9, 42–3, 45, 19, 56, 74, 81–3, 85, 88, 90, 94, 100, 102–4, 108–9, 111–12, 114, 118, 120–3, 128, 133, 135, 139, 144, 166–9, 211 n.71, 241 n.15
North India 21, 23, 65, 67, 152
North-West Frontier Province (NWFP) 72–3, 144
Nouvelle Calédonie 157
nurses 52
nutrition 151, 157
nutrition laboratory 157

obedience to authority 103
Omaha 131, 227 n.173
opium 15
Oriental superstitions 91

Orientalism
  academic Orientalism 31
  somatic Orientalism 100–1, 124, 166
  spiritual Orientalism 31
Orissa 125
orphanage 23–4, 131
orthodox Hindu 22
otherness 102
outdoor games 22, 95
outdoor leisure programmes 111
outreach 24, 48, 135
Ouwerkerk, Louise 155, 238 n.162
overcrowding 21
Oxford 116–17
Oxford University Press 156

pacifist 59, 68, 168, 200 n.108
paedophilic propensities 121
pahalvānī (see also Indian wrestling and *kuśti)* 83, 105
Pakistan 6, 109, 188
Pal, Bipin Chandra 21
Palestine 56, 198 n.69
Pallavaram 125
Pan-American Union 159
pan-Islamic conspiracy 25
Panchama (*see also* Pariah) 142
paramilitary 111, 127, 136,
parents 59, 120–1, 128, 133, 136–7, 167
Pariah (*see also* Panchama) 142
Paris 2, 27, 57
parūpkār (benevolence) 24
Pas-de-Calais 57
paternalism 149, 153, 158, 170
Paterson, C. S. 115, 119, 121, 125
Pathans 74, 194 n.4
patriotic
  patriotic history writing 19
  patriotic service 44, 97
patriotism 21, 83, 120, 170
Paul, K. T. 14, 38–9, 42, 55, 68, 93, 145, 147–8, 150, 166–7, 170, 191 n.210, 200 n.106, 236 n.125
peasant 17–18, 33, 140–1, 143–4, 149, 152–5, 162, 169
pedagogical reform 154
Peterson, Harold H. 34
Philadelphia 29, 35, 115

philanthropic
  philanthropic activities 15, 47, 77
  philanthropic campaign 13, 48
  philanthropic schemes 3, 23, 166
philanthropy 20, 23–4, 48–9, 67, 74, 145, 166, 171
the Philippines 97, 104, 152, 157
philosophy 25, 87, 102, 111, 210 n.49
photographs 7, 82
physical
  physical culture 2, 7, 81–5, 88, 90–1, 105–7, 122, 123, 125, 127, 167, 209 n.27
  physical directors 86–7, 92–3, 97, 101, 103, 105, 107, 113, 123–4, 166
  physical ministry 14, 90, 107, 166
  physical regeneration 95
  physical sessions 90
Physical Department 11, 83, 87, 91, 166
physiological psychology 87
physiology 87, 97
pidginization 12, 108
pioneers 27, 90, 94, 100, 141, 153–5, 171, 229 n.7
Platonic elite 25
play
  play and pleasure 86
playful/playfulness 82. 86, 95, 107, 166
Playground Extension Committee 87
plebeian agrarian Muslim community 41
poetry 85
Point IV speech 141
political
  political autonomy 25, 121
  political empowerment 90
  political leverage 20
  political liberation 146
  political mobilization 16
politics 5, 19, 28–9, 45, 68, 92, 100, 102, 110–11, 141, 149, 175 n.20
Poona 25, 50, 116, 170
Popley, Herbert A. 42
popular culture 10, 31
porters 57
posed photographs 82
post-independence 4
post-Second World War 140, 141, 149, 163
post-war 45, 52, 54, 74, 76

postcolonial
    postcolonial government 11, 137
    postcolonial nation 171
    postcolonial nation states 11
    postcolonial societies 110, 167
    postcolonial state 127, 171
poultry co-operatives 152
POWs (prisoners of war) 52, 59, 75
Powell, Baden H. 18
Prarthana Samaj, Bombay 23
Prasad, Rajendra 137, 170
prayer meetings 28
press reports 41, 111
prestige 18, 26, 47, 69, 92, 104, 121, 154
preventive medicine 102
primary schools 21
primitive 70, 112, 126, 133, 149
princely states 12, 15, 24, 32, 93, 143, 158, 213
Princeton 60
print capitalism 19
professional village workers 156
Progressive Era 9, 86
propaganda 8, 32–3, 44, 56, 59, 62, 69, 154, 158–9, 161, 163
proselytization 26, 50, 77–8, 91, 155, 167
Protestant
    Protestant Christianity 5, 154
    Protestant internationalism 2, 11
    Protestant pedagogic project 162
provincial government 7, 76, 92, 98–9, 105, 107
psychology 87, 106, 153
public
    public philanthropy 145
    public playgrounds 124
    public-private partnership 50, 123
    public relations 8
    public sphere 19
    public spirit 3, 132–3
    public swimming pools 92
publishing houses 19
pucca sahib 72–3, 204 n.172
Pudokottai 158
punch-ups 153
Pune 25, 83
Punjab 15, 17, 23, 65, 74, 128, 130, 142
Punjabi (ethnicity) 34, 57, 97, 169
Punjabi (language) 34, 56, 65
purity 49, 50, 67, 114, 150, 155

Quebec City 158

race
    racial harmony 54
    racial improvement 87
    racial prejudice 35, 72, 104, 136
    racial stereotypes 34, 124, 190 n.182
    racial vitality 101
    racialized (colonial) discourse 107, 166
racism 43, 54, 70, 78, 204 n.168
racist prejudice 8
radio 34, 131, 167
Rai, Lala Lajpat 84–5, 114, 170, 209 n.34, 209 n.35
railway bookstalls 32
Railway colony 50
Railway Department 49
Railway Institute, Jamalpur 50
railway workers 13, 49, 118, 165
Raj 13, 16–18, 20, 135, 165
Rajput 194 n.4
Ramakrishna Mission 23, 42
Ranade, M. G. 24
Rangoon 12, 29, 102, 115–16, 118, 120, 128–9, 131
rape 41
Rashtriya Swayamsevak Sangh (RSS) 26, 170
rationalization 5
Rauschenbusch, Walter 27
Reader's Digest 158, 229 n.10
reading audience 19
rebellion 17, 41, 127, 191 n.214
recreation 50
recreational practices 118
recruitment
    labour recruitment 17, 121
    military recruitment 15, 201 n.118
Red Cross 25, 52, 131
Red Triangle 53, 198 n.78
reformers 3, 13, 20, 24–5, 40, 65, 81, 113–14, 125, 142–3, 153
refugee 41–2, 56
religion 1, 4–5, 21, 23–5, 27, 29, 31, 48, 54–5, 69, 74, 85, 167, 196 n.38
religious
    religious belief systems 16
    religious message 27
    religious neutrality 21

religious revivalism 19
religious service 168
religious tolerance 54
repression
  repressive machinery 152
reservations 22, 121
revolutionary 2, 44, 81, 127–8
Rio Grande 149
riots 26, 41
rituals 17, 122
Robinson, Edgar M. 39
Rockefeller Foundation 139, 158
Roman sculptures 103
Roosevelt, Theodore (Teddy) 111, 114
Rouen 57–8
Royapettah 95
rule of difference 6
(the) ruled 17, 28, 119
rulers 14, 17–18, 28, 68, 82, 100, 106, 119–20, 142, 145
rural
  rural decay 142
  rural development expert 7, 163, 231 n.26, 233 n.71
  rural economies 141
  rural hinterland 15
  rural populations 140
  rural reconstruction 7, 14, 18, 39, 42, 139–46, 148–9, 152–3, 155–8, 161, 163, 167, 171, 229 n.7, 229 n.9
  rural sociology 144
Rural Demonstration Centre 140, 144–5, 158
Rural Department 11
Russo-Japanese War 84

Saidapet 95, 97, 99, 103, 106–7
St. John Ambulance 52, 129
Salt March 43
saṃnyāsin (renouncer) 24
Sanatan Dharma Sabha 23
Sandow, Eugen 82, 84, 209 n.27, 209 n.28
sanitation 15, 65, 67, 90–1, 94, 97, 107, 143, 158, 235 n.119
Sanskrit 31, 85
Sanskritists 31
Saunders, K. J. 44
savagery 112, 127
scalps 162

Schaetti, Henry 37, 191 n.199
school
  school boys 93, 115–16, 120, 169
  school for democracy 96
  school, night
  schools, agricultural 143
  schools, English-medium 21
  schools, primary 21
Scott, Adam 75
Scottish Free Church 28, 142
scout work 33, 128
scouting 22, 109, 117, 125–30, 136, 155
sculpture 103
seaport 15, 52
secular 1, 5, 11, 13, 24, 26–8, 34, 39, 41, 78, 99, 109, 134, 139–41, 154, 165, 167–8, 177 n.55, 182 n.53, 218 n.1
secularization 16, 27
Secunderabad 124
Second World War 45, 75–6
sedition 44
seeds 150, 158
segregation 50, 57, 128, 136
self
  self-assertion 69, 83
  self-defence 106
  self-fashioning 16, 20, 25
  self-help 25, 127, 148–9, 154
sepoys 48, 61, 64–7, 71, 77–9, 197 n.65
Servants of India Society 24–6, 41–2
servicemen 13, 62, 64–6, 74–5, 77, 93, 166, 169
sevā (service) 23–4
sex
  same-sex relationships 121
  sex/sexual hygiene 63–4, 84, 97
  sex scandal 8, 121
  sexual abuse 121
  sexual transgression 8, 64
  sexually harassed 121
  sexually transmitted diseases 69
shellac records 33, 61
Shimla 29
Shivaji 124
Siam 96
Sikh Golden Temple, Amritsar 54
Sikhism 16, 23, 105
Sikhs 22, 74, 194 n.4, 205 n.187
Sindhi 156

Singh, Harbail 97, 215 n.144
Singh Sabhas 23
Sino-Indian War 171
Sioux City 74
sipāhī (see also soldiers and sepoys) 61, 194 n.4
skulls 72
Slack, Frank V. 125
sobriety 144
sociability 86
social
 social castes 151
 social Darwinist theories 112
 social discipline 132
 social engineering 1, 3, 11–3, 15, 86, 155, 166, 168, 171
 social oppression 5
 social reform 12, 16, 45, 140, 165, 174 n.9
 social responsibility 24, 2–7, 127, 132
 social service 23–6, 38, 41–2, 45, 109, 131, 133, 153, 184 n.76, 185 n.88
 social work schemes 1
 socialization programme 150
Social Reform Party 35
socio-economic 154
sociological concepts 5
soft power 1, 4, 10–11, 13, 168, 178 n.62
solar topee 72
soldiers (see also sepoys, sipāhī) 12, 47, 50–1, 53–7, 61, 64–5, 67–8, 70, 74–9, 165, 167, 194 n.4, 198 n.72, 204 n.168
Somme 57
Somerville, A. N. 28
Souri, D. R. D. 156
South Africa 44
South Asian Muslim societies 25
soya bean 157
Spanish influenza pandemic 101
spirit 23, 25, 30, 32, 49, 56–7, 103, 111–12, 120, 132–3, 142, 158
spiritual
 spiritual leadership 88
 spiritual orientalism 31
 spirituality 16
sport
 sport facilities 28
 sport and fitness programmes 22

sportizing missions 81
sports professionalism 87
Spratt, Philipp 44
Springfield, MA 53, 85, 89–90, 92, 107, 112–13
Springfield College 7, 37, 40, 85–9, 92–4, 105, 109, 123–4, 126–7, 129, 134, 212 n.84, 213 n.98, 221 n.32, 223 n.90, 225 n.124
Sri Lanka 6, 30
Sriniketan 142
Star-Spangled Banner 128
state
 state authority 17
 state education 18
 state intervention 18, 74, 76
statistics 33, 165
Stead, W. T. 10
Storey, John W. 113
Strong, Tracy 121, 126
strongman 82, 84
structural
 structural asymmetries 154
 structural racism 70
 structural transformation 5, 15
student missionaries 29
Student Volunteer Movement (SVM) 28
students 19, 38–9, 54, 59, 65, 85–7, 92–3, 95–7, 99, 101–2, 105, 107, 113–14, 124–5, 134, 137, 156
subaltern studies 8
subalterns
 civilising subalterns 166
 Indian and Nepali subalterns 78
 South Asian subalterns 77
 white subalterns (see also low Europeans, marginal whites) 49, 77, 118
subsidiary cottage vocations 150
śuddhi (purification) 41
sugarcane 15
Sustainable agriculture 167
svadeśi 99, 215 n.152
Swadeshi movement 21, 24, 120
Swami Dayananda Saraswati 23
Swami Kuvalayananda 105–6
Swami Vivekananda 23, 25
Swamidoss, Daniel 14, 39–40, 128, 191 n.210
swearing 135

Swedish Drill 92
Switzerland 6, 27
syphilis 102
Syracuse University 145

Tagore, Rabindranath 140, 142
Tahiti 157
Taisho 84
tamāśā ghar (house of spectacles) 79
tamāśāvāle (showmen) 79
Tamil 28, 30, 33, 146, 148-9, 170, 233 n.58
teachers 19, 65, 85, 92, 99, 199 n.87
team sports 84, 86, 97, 107, 125
technology 10, 34, 62, 70, 160, 201 n.119
technological innovations 5
technological project 5
temperance 50, 69, 114, 135, 151-2, 222 n.50, 236 n.133
Tennessee 149
Tepoztlan 158
tertiary educational institution 19
textile factories 105
The Englishman 43-4
The Inquirer 30
The Statesman 47
The Young Men of India 40, 88
Theosophical Society 31, 35
Theosophist 42
toddy tappers 169
'Tommies' 48, 54
track-meets 57
traditionalization 17
training equipment 84
transliterations 65
transmission of sport and physical education 13
transnational
    transnational approach 2, 6
    transnational entanglements 169
    transnational knowledge circulation 166
    transnational trends 14, 109
transregional 4, 13, 185 n.91
Travancore 93, 140, 145-6, 148, 151, 153, 156, 162, 233 n.58
travelogue 88
travels 4
trends 4, 14, 109-10, 116
triangle (YMCA symbol) 27, 53, 56, 146, 198 n.78

tribal languages 58
Trivandrum 145, 154-5, 187 n.122
troops 13, 44, 47-8, 51-9, 61-3, 65-70, 72, 74-8, 119, 128-9, 198 n.69, 203 n.159
'tropical' countries 157
Tropical Hygiene and Sanitation 97
Tropp, Jacob 161
Truman 141
Tucson 7, 160
Turk 68
Turnen 82
Tuskegee Institute, Alabama 157
tutelage 97
tycoon 35, 115

underclasses 27
UNESCO 156, 159, 167
uniforms 111, 152
Union Jack 128
United Kingdom 6-7, 50, 74-5
United Nation's Food and Agricultural Organization (FAO) 158, 160, 240 n.199
United States 4, 6, 12, 14, 26, 29-32, 34, 36, 43, 51, 59, 72, 75, 78, 82, 85, 87-8, 90, 94, 104, 110-11, 113, 117, 119, 121-3, 131, 136, 144-5, 149, 151, 156, 160, 167, 171, 175 n.14, 187 n.106, 209 n.35, 235 n.118, 232 n.48
Universal Union of YMCAs 27
universalism 109
universities 19, 22, 31-2, 59, 65, 84, 92, 94, 97, 114, 141
university degree 25
untouchable (*see also* Dalit, outcaste) 144
untouchable uplift 23, 25, 41
*updeśak*s (missionaries) 41
urban
    urban centres 15, 26
    urban 'educated' middle classes 19
    urban elites 115
    urban modernity 167
    urban slums 33
    urban vice 85
    urban youth 3, 143
urban-rural divide 15
urbanization 27

Urdu 33, 56, 65–6, 134, 194 n.4, 204 n.175
Urkatastrophe 56
US
  US Air Force 129
  US Bureau of Indian Affairs 160
  US Colonial Educational
    Department 157
  US Congress 43
  US foreign policy 1
  US postmaster general 115
  US presidents 38
  US State Department 139, 159

Varkey, C. J. 99
vegetarian 102
Velayudan, C. K. 156
venereal disease 69, 102
ventilation 21
Vernacular Press Act 19
vernacular printing presses 19
vernacular public spheres 19
veteran 7, 44, 94, 110
vice 49, 66, 69, 85, 111, 165
Viceroy 51, 93, 95, 156–7
village
  village development 3, 18, 72, 140,
    142–4, 146, 150, 154, 156–7, 162–3,
    167, 169
  village uplift 18, 140–1, 144, 150,
    155, 158
violence 44, 54, 56, 180 n.12, 206 n.1
visual media 10, 32, 45, 158
visual (source) material 7
volleyball 57, 86, 95, 125, 151, 153
voluntarism 95, 107, 154, 166
voluntary workers 168
VUL (broadcasting station) 34
Vyayam 7, 97
vyayāmśālās (gymasiums) 83

Walter, Howard 59, 68, 168, 200 n.108
Wanamaker, John 35, 115, 190 n.187
war
  war emergency work 75, 117
  war hospitals 52
  war-maps 61
  war work 7, 26, 45, 47–8, 51–2, 55–6,
    59, 62–3, 68, 72, 77, 198 n.69

Washington, Booker T. 65, 149
Waziristan 72
weaving 150
Weber, Frank 127
welfare
  public welfare 24
  social welfare 171
  welfare 74–5
  welfare centres 75
  welfare programme 13, 132, 136
  welfare schemes 76, 165
  welfare work 11, 47, 131, 171
Wellsburg 121
Western education 18, 21, 114
Western educational institutions 16
Western missionaries 3, 25, 118, 170
Western paternalism 170
Westernness 14, 82
Westernization 19
wheat 15, 152
White Leghorn chickens 150, 152
white workers 27
Whitehorn, R. D. 67
whiteness 104, 145, 188 n.129, 217 n.186
Wilcox, Ella Wheeler 69, 203
women specialist in Physical education 95
women's work 23
workout devices 84
World Conference of Y.M.C.A. Workers
    among Boys 116–17
World YWCA 27
worldviews 22, 45, 168

Y orientalism 31
Y secretaries 3, 30–2, 39, 42, 55, 57–8, 61,
    69–70, 76, 93, 102, 104, 110, 119,
    122, 133, 154, 168
Yale University 7, 65
Yapp, A. K. 70, 72
YMCA army centres 50–2
YMCA Scout troop 128
YMCA world conference 27
YMCA World Organization 27
yoga 83, 105–6, 206 n.5
yoga *āsanas* 106
Yokohama 31
Young Men's Arya Association 22
Young Men's Buddhist Association 22

Young Men's Muslim Association 22
Young Men's Parsee Association 22
Young Men's Sikh Associations 22
Young Women's Christian Association
    (YWCA) 7, 10, 27, 52, 218 n.1

youth
    youth organizations 22, 36, 105, 110–11
    youth work 22, 110, 131, 167

Zurich 37